IDEAS OF ASCENSION AND TRANSLATION

IDEAS OF ASCENSION AND TRANSLATION

A STUDY OF THE LITERARY AND CULTURAL MYTHOLOGICAL TRADITION OF THE WEST

Peter Sorensen

Academica Press, LLC
Bethesda

Library of Congress Cataloging-in-Publication Data

Sorensen, Peter J.
 Ideas of ascension and translation : a study of the literary and cultural mythological tradition of the West / by Peter J. Sorensen.
    p. cm.
Includes bibliographical references (p.   ) and index.
 ISBN 1-930901-48-8
 1. Translation to heaven. 2. Jesus Christ—Ascension. 3. Smith, Joseph, 1805-1844. I. Title.

BL465.S67 2004
204'.2—dc22   2003017659

British Cataloguing data are available

Copyright 2004 by Peter Sorensen

All rights reserved. Printed in the United States of America. No part of this book may be used or reproduced in any manner whatsoever without written permission except in the case of brief quotations embodied in critical articles and reviews.

Editorial Inquiries:
Academica Press, LLC
7831 Woodmont Avenue, #381
Bethesda, MD 20814
Website: www.academicapress.com
To order: (202) 337-6811

Contents

Acknowledgments	vii
Chapter 1: Introduction	1
Chapter 2: The Ancient Texts: Sacred and Quasi-Sacred	11
Chapter 3: Translation as Theology: Orthodox Christianity's Neglected Ascension–Translation Narrative	47
Chapter 4: Translation Narratives in Literature	91
Chapter 5: (Cult)ural Metaphor	153
Chapter 6: Ascension in the New World	209
Chapter 7: Conclusion	245
Bibliography	249
Index	257

Acknowledgments

I wish to thank my many student assistants over the years (and I hope I haven't left anyone out): Jesse Brossard, Patricia Carrington, Jennifer Pappas, and one unofficial assistant, Jennifer Sorensen. My thanks goes to Nathan Walton for designing and typesetting the book. I am grateful to the students in the editing classes at Brigham Young University for checking the sources and proofreading the galleys, particularly Joseph Miller, Michelle Preisendorf, and Amy Reynolds. I appreciate Linda Hunter Adams and her editorial assistance. I thank the Brigham Young University English Department for its generous release-time support for its faculty, as well as for its stipends for research materials. Thanks to my favorite Romanticists, John Ehrstine of Washington State University and Gordon K. Thomas of BYU. And though it will surprise them, I thank Paul Brians and Thomas Faulkner of Washington State University, the former for allowing me to teach the humanities course in mythology, the latter for introducing me to the tradition of epic criticism.

Even in his nineties he is too busy reading and writing to care or even notice, but I thank Hugh W. Nibley of Brigham Young University, the father of Mormon scholarship and the best-read human I've ever met, for being my most consistent inspiration since I was a college freshman—he is the one man who made a virtue of sticking his nose where it didn't belong.

I had better thank Joseph Smith, the founder of Mormonism, for being the most noble and delightful hero since Hector, and who might have been translated had he not been betrayed by his friends and slain to satisfy the bloodlust of his enemies.

Last and dearest of all, my wife Elaine, my best friend: you breathe life into my shell of a body.

Introduction

I have chosen to write this interdisciplinary treatise on the unusual features of certain literary and other cultural items that are connected with the very ancient idea of "translation," including the motif of ascension, a phenomenon complete with its own premises, literary and narratological conceits, but one that has been overlooked as an influence on Western culture and religious thought. My specific purpose here is to examine how other people (mostly in other ages) have shaped the idea of translation to meet their own cultural or even aesthetic needs; thus I am unconcerned in this study whether the examples and commentary are "true" in any absolute sense (though some of them may be), but only with their relative accuracy as reflections of various cultural and possibly artistic conceits.

Definition: "Translation" as used in this study refers to the ascension and immortalizing of a mortal individual before death can occur or have any effect, and to the individual's subsequent actions within the world from which he/she was delivered, as well as the conscious or unconscious choices or processes that attend such an event. Joseph Campbell places these types of events under the general category of *apotheosis* but seems uninterested in distinguishing the various forms of divine encounter except as they can be understood in Freudian psychological terms, such as atonement with the father. In Campbell's theories of the heroic, apotheosis is merely a stage in the ongoing sequence of departure–initiation–return,[1] but in my version, the return is a task for the hero, after he is already admitted to the divine family. Thus, for example, in the ascension and translation of Elijah, the "return" is established in his appearing from time to time on earth to bring messages from Yahweh to humankind, or to "prepare the way" for the appearance of Yahweh, as the Israelite prophet Malachi predicted. The only way the return can be the end of the journey is if the hero begins his existence with the gods, abandons heaven, then returns later on, as with the gnostic redeemer, the gnostic Pistis-Sophia, or the errant young man in the gnostic *Hymn of the Pearl*.

Those who are translated do not die, or at least the moment of death between mortality and immortality is so instantaneous as to render death insignificant, and not remotely fearful; this sort of event occurs (or nearly occurs) in heroic tales as old as the quest of Gilgamesh (to whom the goddess decreed that death was the common lot of all humanity) and as recent as the philosophical transcendence of the New Age guru Annalee Skarin (whose death only recently put to rest her absolute conviction that she was a translated being). Those who are translated may commune with the gods on an extended and intimate basis, and they dwell in comfort and beauty, partaking of heavenly light; they often have specific titles or duties that distinguish them as gods or immortals.

The attraction for readers and listeners has always been that somehow, in some magnificent way, certain mortal beings manage to sidestep the demands of decaying nature, to defy the one law people regard as universal: everyone must die. The meritorious attainment of immortality by at least an elite few encourages the reader or hearer of such tales to believe that, like Beowulf of old, if one tries his absolute best, there is a slim but tangible chance he will overturn the decree of fate.

The fear of death and decay is ancient, even primordial, because when people die, they not only stay dead, but get less permanent as time goes by, a problem of which those who practiced mummification were most cognizant and with which they were morbidly (pun unavoidable) concerned. The few catatonics who only appeared dead, then suddenly awakened, may have been the source (as in Poe's tales) of the morbid fear that the dead may not stay dead, but such events are unlikely to be the source of ascension–translation narratives, because their subjects are still mortal and do not ascend in any sense. Coming back to life in any form would be hailed as a good thing only if no corruption of the body had occurred. Among many, if not most ancient cultures, even if the "soul" or spirit survived death, death was still discussed in very negative terms. The Hebrew *sheol*, for example, is a dark cave where one might exist after death but where there is no light, no movement (work) or hope for anything; in terms of desirability, the Greek Hades is not much different from *sheol*. And touching a corpse or even touching an embalmer or his equipment (in ancient Egypt) could defile a priestess or princess, priest or prince.

Even though translation was mythically possible anciently, the granting of immortality was not always done democratically, but more often capriciously; heavenly rewards in an afterlife seem limited horribly to a very privileged few, leaving most ordinary people very desperate indeed. If we can accept the premise that for most people death is terrifying, not something one leaps toward bravely, we will understand the great "absent presence" in ancient culture that the ascension–translation myth fills.*

Many ancient tribes out of despair devised darkly stoic or wildly hedonistic systems to play out the allotted life span. These systems acknowledge implicitly that the gods' gifts and punishments for nearly all ancient people were to take place in this life only. It must be admitted, then, that for many, in ancient times as well as today, death is a genuine relief from what has turned out to be a disappointing earthly life—yet that is not a ringing endorsement of death, but the escape route from disease, feebleness, and sorrow. Even allowing for the benefits of death for a weary mortal, though, I can't think of anyone who wants to die if life is reasonably interesting and healthful, and I can't think of many people who would rather have allowed loved ones to die tragic or pathetic deaths if a really clever and delightful means were found to circumvent the rigors (pun intended) of death.

The features of ascension–translation, that cleverest, most delightful of circumventions, are roughly these (allowing for individual variants within individual accounts):

---

* In *The Hero with a Thousand Faces*, Joseph Campbell notes of the hero, "Needless to say, the hero would be no hero if death held for him any terror; the first condition is reconciliation with the grave."[2] He follows this declaration with a Jewish legend of Abraham's ascension and translation, in which Abraham's servants, on seeing the personification of Death, immediately fall dead in terror, thus demonstrating that ordinary people fear death, and only the most heroic can face it down.

1. The gods discover an exceptional creature, exceptionally clever or righteous, or of exceptional ancestry.
2. The candidate is invited to look briefly into heaven, or may steal or force the way in to look.
3. She is sent back to this world with a task, mission, or quest.
4. He is informed he must pack up and prepare to go to heaven permanently.
5. She bids farewell to her associates and ascends through various means out of their sight.
6. He is enthroned in glory in the heavens but is seen from time to time on earth helping those in need; he is ranked higher than the angels and is "god" of sorts to this world.*[3]

With these basic criteria we will be able to follow more easily the motif's appearance in various fragments and mutations throughout Western cultural and literary history.

Other Definitions: I hope to aid the reader in following my discussion by laying some ground rules, since I am not a trained folklorist. The words *translation, assumption,* and *dormition* will be used interchangeably, while the word *ascension* will be used only to refer to that phenomenon. *Transcendence* is a semantic bridge between *ascension* and *translation* but does not always imply physical translation. I hope to use consistently William Bascom's very practical definitions for myth (prose narratives thought truthful by the narrator and his audience, usually set in the remote past), *legends* (regarded as true, as with myth, but less remote and more this-worldly), and *folktales* (narratives not attached by place or time that are ahistorical, but are often didactic or entertaining).[4] These categories of narrative I will try to keep separate from the overtly literary versions of such narratives, whether poems, dramas, short stories, or other genres. I hope that using terminology from folklore will not be confused with popular terminology which denigrates or celebrates stories as absolutely false or true. The term *pseudepigraphic* (a text that proposes as its author a mythic character that may or may not have authored the text) is also to be seen as a neutral term, neither to denigrate nor celebrate the text. So also *myth*, which in popular consciousness inherently condemns a narrative as false or evil. Other definitions I will address as they appear in the text.

---

* My list of steps is based on my own research.

Social Context for This Discussion: Even after this fairly clear-cut definition of translation, many of my readers will inquire why a separate study is needed for the idea of translation when so many theological, literary, and folklore studies have dealt with everything from death and departed spirits to the nature of supernature. The key here is to remember that for translation the premises on which the motif is built are very different from those attending, say, survival of the spirit beyond the grave or physical resurrection from the dead. First, implicit in the idea of translation is that the common lot of most mortals is not eternal life with the gods, but rather mortality, after which a return to dust, a complete dissolution of body and spirit. Thus, translation occurs, when it occurs, in sharp contrast to the prevailing experience of death, which in most contexts, such as in dramatic tragedy, is overwhelmingly dismal. I go so far as to assert that the survival of the "spirit" or "soul" is only occasionally relevant to our discussion, since escaping death in the first place is the main benefit of translation. The translation of any being is obviously a theological and textual exception, despite striking examples to the contrary, to the general Judeo-Christian ethic and often occurs, I contend, somewhat in defiance of, for example, ethical paradigms such as atonement for sins, reliance on grace, and surrender of the self. Indeed the premise of translation is that its acquisition is assuredly meritorious, that is, proceeding from one's own cleverness, ancestry, or moral rectitude. I needn't add here that the overwhelming majority of published opinions on immortality concern the state of the soul after death, or whether the soul survives after death; to that group may be added those who defend or denigrate the idea of physical resurrection or reincarnation—mostly philosophers and theologians. My concern is exclusively the effect of the motifs of ascension and translation on narrative strategies. We will have occasion to refer back to the premises I have listed and their implications for modern Christianity, but we must first look at the ancient settings for such narratives.

My research has occasionally led me to scholarly discussions of "ascension texts" (The Ascension of Moses, Isaiah, or the like), but most scholars perceive ascension as being only coincidentally connected to translation, and not an essential prelude to it. My contention is that some ascension texts are in fact stunted narratives of translation. The word *assumption* as used in Catholicism treats ascension and translation as essentially one event, ending in the quasi-deification of, for example, the Virgin Mary. The best discussion of ascension texts is without doubt

Edward T. Jones's "A Comparative Study of Ascension Motifs in World Religions." As a devout Mormon, I find Jones's attitudes towards the ascension narratives of other cultures refreshing:

> When one interprets the religious experiences of a religious tradition other than one's own, one must be extremely careful not to let his own attitudes interfere or corrupt.... But more than sympathy and understanding are necessary. When dealing with religious experience one must be willing to admit that such experience is actually a possibility; otherwise one's personal bias regarding that experience will cloud the interpretation of it.[5]

I will use the same approach as he, even when discussing "pagan" myth in defunct civilizations—thus to me, Sumerian beliefs should be accorded the same dignity as, say, Christian, Muslim, or Jewish narratives in our day. This approach I find considerably more respectful (and honest) than the thinly veiled invective of such books as Randel Helms's *Gospel Fictions*,[6] which, although often clever and insightful (Helms's Greek is a strong point in his favor), does great harm with its insensitivity.

For what sort of audience were such ascension narratives written anciently? I suggest the audience would sometimes be surprisingly pragmatic, even cynical, and firmly grounded in the grim reality of this world (such as the dour Sumerians), but also willing to embrace a miraculous event if its details are similar to other accounts with which the audience is familiar—that is, the audience will be willing to suspend disbelief in the secret hope that some such experience might happen in fact to someone in distress. Thus (as I will point out later) the reader of Nathaniel Hawthorne's "The Gray Champion" is excited by and approves of the sudden appearance of the old man, who with godly power withstands the might of a royal army, because it fits a tradition in which translated beings come back to keep their hands in the work that occupied them while on Earth (as distinguished from angelic creatures, who normally aren't portrayed as having existed on Earth in any form and thus have no personal interest in such human affairs). Returning to my example, Hawthorne's account is complete enough in its detail and its high seriousness to make the reader feel (that is, believe emotionally if not intellectually) that such an event could occur again for the benefit of the reader's society had they any pressing need for the help. After the terror of 11 September 2001, the desire for a new crop of heroes to protect the innocent and helpless gave us the New York police, firefighters, and even the lame-duck mayor—not to mention a planeload of heroes who died diverting a jet from its terrorist target. (Note that in Hawthorne's story, the rescue the gray champion performs is for a large community, not for an individual, as might be recounted in, for example, "guardian angel" narratives.) In regard to the reader of such a narrative, it is most important to note that the reader normally is not reading with the hope of being translated herself, as though the narrative were a key of some sort that could trigger translation; rather it is enough for her that she has read or heard of someone who *was* translated. That reality offers the reader the comfort that as long as she knows a few who have been thus delivered from death, it is not as fearsome, and there is some ultimate hope of some sort for all humanity. The best evidence of this reaction to a text is the *parathanatic* or near-death experience. People are enormously cheered and uplifted by the many popular books, often written by doctors or like professionals, containing accounts of those pronounced technically dead, yet who come back to life, bearing similar tales about hovering above one's own body, then moving through a long tunnel, seeing a light at the tunnel's end, meeting with a glorified person who radiates love and acceptance, and finally returning, with mixed feelings to a decidedly second-rate mortal existence. (The best of these books, Dr. Raymond Moody's *Life after Life*, has left an indelible mark on society.)[7]

From a psychological viewpoint, the idea of translation is partly a youthful view; that is, it is associated with the youthful conviction that one cannot die. This is one reason Gilgamesh makes such a good candidate for eternal life, avoiding death altogether. He has not reached the age, even as king, where death seems a reasonable option. This idea of translation is not much different from the absolute conviction of many reckless teenagers (yes, I was one) in America who, behind the wheel of a car, on a sled, hanging from a rope over a cliff, or other dangerous position, feel they are invincible, incapable of suffering injury, let alone death. Their conviction grows mostly out of their positive experiences with growing up; their physical skills and attributes seem more and more refined and masterful, elegant, even godly, as they move toward adulthood, and in most cases, they are right about that; they simply don't realize there are other possibilities. (I suspect young people living in urban war zones of street gangs are much more inclined to see how mortal they really are—middle-class white teens are, relative to teens in the ghetto, very much immortal.)

This youthful denial of death in fact happened to the poet William Wordsworth, who, in the reflective poem "Nutting," understands only as an adult the destructive crime the little boy has committed in tearing a branch from a beautiful tree. Thus, among those who are translated, this class of youthful, ignorantly confident beings is represented, translated because of their wit, cleverness, and bravado rather than for any such reflection, purgation, or self-annihilation as, for example, William Blake's mythological characters undergo.

But the psychology of translation also allows for a class of beings for whom human life is flawed, fragmented, and broken—a mere shadow of what it was in a golden or paradisiacal age. In this group it is only through the ascetic, contemplative life can one hope to attain the restitution, or restoration of the perfect human, implicit in the idea of translation; righteousness, even moral perfection, seems essential. Into this category of translation we must place the priestly group of candidates, such as Enoch or Elijah, whose personal righteousness or perfection is the hallmark of their service toward God.

Overview of This Study: In this study I will first not only treat selected ancient texts, especially those connected with the Bible, but also *Gilgamesh* (the Babylonian epic poem), and extracanonical works that expand or modify the materials in the Bible that concern translation, such as pseudepigraphic works from various eras. From these we may with fair success examine not only the essential features of the translation–ascension narrative (as well as to distinguish it from items that resemble such narratives in only superficial ways) but also discern the types and needs of audience for this sort of material. Once again, I will work from the premise that for its original audience, each document was deemed an expression of historical truth on the one hand, absolute truth on the other (especially concerning humanity's relationship to God or the gods).

I will not refer more than occasionally to Asian cultures, since I am unqualified to speak to the doctrine's manifestations in those complex societies. I am also not a rigorous student of Muslim lore, so my references there will also be few. But this admission does in no way imply that such ascension and translation narratives are not to be found in these cultures. Jones's article provides a striking example of the ascension of Muhammad, to which I will refer in another chapter in connection with the Spanish epic of the Cid.[8] An ascension with concurrent translation is part of the mythology of India, in the case of Tukaram, who some two hundred years ago ascended in a chariot of fire.[9] Such narratives of ascension at least can be found in the Vedas and in Brahman lore; even Buddhist lore contains such narratives.[10]

Following this section on the more recondite narratives, I will demonstrate the crucial and difficult theological issues presented to Christianity in trying to preserve and/or absorb the idea of ascension and translation, with specific reference to interpreting the meaning of Jesus' three roles as Suffering Servant, sacrificial victim, and translated hero. I hope to show the narrative challenges of trying to reconcile these very different views of Jesus, views that while not mutually exclusive nevertheless are designed to appeal to different audiences and were recorded for different purposes. Since this topic is particularly sensitive to Christians, I must again remind the reader that I am not attempting to deconstruct the harmony of the Gospels; my religious devotion bars me from such an approach, but the consideration of the heroic Christ has been, I believe unfortunately, neglected in the ongoing discussion of what is heroic. I might add that I am also dealing with Jewish and Muslim mythology, and I am just as concerned with not violating the sensibilities of those who hold their own mythology sacred, as I am with holding Christian narrative sacred.

The largest part of this monograph treats the appearance of ascension and translation motifs in literature subsequent to their appearance in sacred texts in ancient times. Here we will discover how these motifs have metamorphosed, evolved, or otherwise changed over time to adapt to the needs and desires of particular writers and audiences. We will see not only variations on the theme but genuine antitypes, some of which appear in the nineteenth century during the time of the gothic novel and the revival of dualistic heresies; we will note as well the imaginative power such motifs conjure in the mind of a true artist.

The last section will deal with some step-children of the original motifs of ascension and translation, beginning with the very orthodox Virgin Mary, followed by a discussion of Mary Magdalene, and then proceeding to the manifestation of the images in the relatively recent (nineteenth-century) chronicles of the founder of Mormonism, Joseph Smith. Last of all we take a unique opportunity to examine a colorful character who died only recently, and who for a time attracted attention as the newest and most significant advocate and example of the incarnation of heterodox religious ideals since the days of Joanna Southcott: the energetic yet mystical Annalee Skarin. This last section should bring us to our own day, giving us a workable though not exhaustive list of examples of the ideas of ascension and translation.

1. Joseph Campbell, *The Hero with a Thousand Faces*, 2d ed., Bollingen Series (Princeton, NJ: Princeton University Press, 1968).

2. Ibid., 256.

3. See also George Widengreen, in *Muhammed, the Apostle of God and His Ascension* (Uppsala: Universitets Arsskrift, 1955), 92, as quoted in Edward T. Jones, "A Comparative Study of Ascension Motifs in World Religions," in *Deity and Death* (vol. 2 in the Religious Studies Monograph Series), ed. Spencer J. Palmer (Provo, UT: Religious Studies Center of Brigham Young University, 1978), 95–96.

4. William Bascom, "The Forms of Folklore: Prose Narratives." *Journal of American Folklore* 78 (January/March 1965): 4–5, 79–105.

5. Jones, 93–94.

6. Randel Helms, *Gospel Fictions* (Amherst, NY: Prometheus, 1988).

7. Raymond Moody, *Life after Life: The Investigation of a Phenomenon—Survival of Bodily Death*, intro. by Elisabeth Kübler-Ross (Harrisburg, PA: Stackpole Books, 1976).

8. Jones, 87–88.

9. Ibid., 89.

10. Ibid., 90–91.

The Ancient Texts: Sacred and Quasi-Sacred

My first area of concern is to treat the original, most ancient myth narratives concerning ascension–translation. My list here is extremely narrow and limited, yet it properly shows the evolution of narrative style and purpose, and even the earliest concerns with style and purpose, in which even very ancient cultures excelled.

Gilgamesh

When Gilgamesh, the famous leader mentioned in the Sumerian king-lists, seeks the secret of immortality, the goddess Siduri reminds him, "You will never find that life for which you are looking. When the gods created man they allotted to him death, but life they retained in their own keeping."[1] Metamorphosis, as Ovid envisioned it, is mentioned when Gilgamesh, in a tirade against Ishtar, accuses the goddess of turning spurned lovers into wolves or blind moles. In this same speech, Gilgamesh reveals that the gods do have the power to change mortal humans into other sorts of beings, a sort of echo of the substantial change from mortal to immortal. Later, Utnapishtim, a Babylonian character much like the Semitic Noah, tests Gilgamesh to see if he is worthy of everlasting life, by requiring that he stay awake six days and seven nights. Gilgamesh fails this test miserably, as is proven by seven loaves of bread, one for each day the hero slept.[2] As a "consolation" prize, our hero is told of a plant in the deep water that bestows eternal youth, though not immortality. Gilgamesh finds this plant, but a snake steals it (thus allowing the snake to shed its old skin). Thus Gilgamesh's grief over his fate and over that of his slain companion Enkidu haunts him till his dying day.

Although there are myriad commentaries on the *Gilgamesh* fragment, which contains portions clearly older than the Babylonian Empire, I will not be reviewing in detail the entire text nor the scholarly bibliography it has engendered, but wish rather to focus on one aspect of the text: the avoidance of death and the bid for eternal life. Several things are important about this text. First, parts of the story go back even to preliterate times in Mesopotamia; it is extremely old and therefore an ideal beginning place for the development of the idea of translation. Second, it is impossible to mistake the story for anything like the journey of the disembodied spirit, since the civilizations of this area (as opposed, for instance, to some aspects of Egyptian belief) did not hold out much hope for an afterlife. Not only that, but the gods of the pantheon of this story seem violently opposed to granting humankind anything like eternal life. Thus, the story of Gilgamesh is a heroic epic about being human. Third, in the characters of Enkidu, Gilgamesh, and Utnapishtim, we find illustrated the very stages I contend make up the ascension and translation narrative.

Let us first consider Gilgamesh himself. He is a young king, but fears growing old and dying—an immature view perhaps for some, but for others a real enough human response. However, Gilgamesh possesses two of the three qualities the candidate might require: he is two-thirds divine, and he is heroic and clever enough to attract the gods' attention. The quality Gilgamesh obviously lacks is uprightness, or purity and piety, the desire to serve the gods faithfully. Many critics doubtless conclude that Gilgamesh's failure to achieve his goal teaches us two great philosophical lessons: (1) acceptance of humankind's fixed mortality and destiny and (2) the maturing of the young king who now can sympathize and empathize with the fate of his companion Enkidu as well as show concern enough for his subjects that he would wish to bring them eternal youth. I find that in some ways such a critical approach tells us more about the pessimism of the late twentieth century than it does about Gilgamesh. In fact, there are three sets of binary oppositions in the text (or more, depending on how one approaches the problem) that, albeit far from making all humans immortal, nevertheless show the potential for the gods' laws to bend or for exceptions to laws to be made in certain cases. The presence of one member of a binary set presupposes the existence of its opposite (the old literary idea of "absent presence"). Thus, for example, Enkidu is the "true contrary" (William Blake's term) of Gilgamesh; the binary here is not simply between wild nature and civilization, although that is important. It is also the confrontation between those who have the chance to be translated and those who simply cannot have it under any circumstances. Based on my formula for qualification, Enkidu because of his heroism may qualify to be translated, and he is certainly a likable fellow. But in his heroism, for all its godly virtues ("There was virtue in him of the god of war, of Ninurta himself"; "he is like an immortal from heaven"[3]), he is categorically different from Gilgamesh: the gods' enmity toward Enkidu is obvious and is represented in several ways. Enkidu is synonymous with nature and is the very "natural man" so common in eighteenth- and nineteenth-century fiction. As such, he is a creature of water and clay, entirely bound by the cycle of nature, and he must die just as all nature does. He is not descended of the gods because his birth is not from the womb of the goddess. The gods' enmity is obvious in his seduction by the harlot. Before that time he was one with the animals and clearly not self-aware. Afterwards he becomes self-aware and the animals despise him. He is an outcast from his "tribe," if you will, doomed to follow the cycle of nature but cruelly estranged even from it because he now *knows* he will die and can contemplate it and suffer from it. In the forest journey that follows, Enkidu is constantly grieved and fretful as never before, as the two heroes battle monsters. And Gilgamesh doesn't help matters by reminding Enkidu constantly of human mortality: "Here in the city man dies oppressed at heart, man perishes with despair in his heart."[4]

Thus when after the heroic slaying of the Bull of Heaven the gods declare that one of the two heroes must die—surprise! Enkidu is so fated, dying of sickness rather than dying heroically. The cards seem stacked against Enkidu in a way they do not for Gilgamesh, despite his awareness of his own mortality. For as the descendant of the gods and humans, he is heroic in partially the same sense as the great god Enlil, also called a hero.

Gilgamesh is celebrated in later myth as a judge of the underworld, and because he is two parts god and one part man, his situation is not unlike that of Achilles,[5] so the potential for his ascending and being translated seems clear enough: he has the genealogy and the heroism required. In his despair over the death of Enkidu and over the stark reality of his own unavoidable death, he vows to seek eternal life—not through the path of death, but by finding Utnapishtim, who "has entered the assembly of the gods."[6] On encountering Gilgamesh as he approaches the wall of heaven, the scorpion men remark a difference in the appearance of Gilgamesh; he is "flesh of the gods," another indication that Gilgamesh is of another nature entirely from Enkidu. Yet, in his turn, Gilgamesh can see nothing at all unusual about the features of Utnapishtim, whom he meets later, suggesting that to see the gods as they see each other, the gods must prepare the candidate through some ritual—one of the precise purposes of ascension in the Old Testament.

When Gilgamesh reaches the "garden of the gods," he notices immediately that the garden is made of precious stones, not the fruitful garden of Genesis. Medieval Judaism has preserved this image in the Sepher Ha-Yashir, where Aaron's rod is of sapphire, plucked from paradise. Implicit in this imagery of precious stones is the rejection of the life cycle of fertility and decay, and the embracing of eternal, unchanging stone (coal is "translated" into diamond, matchless for its hardness and beauty). Then, during the narrative of the flood given Gilgamesh by Utnapishtim, it is revealed that the relentless striving for goodness and faithfulness before the gods is what made Enlil offer Utnapishtim—and his *wife*, it should be remembered—eternal life.

It is this very last test that Gilgamesh fails, the test of "righteousness" (or the nearest Sumerian equivalent), and this despite the gods' obvious affection for Gilgamesh and even (perhaps grudgingly) for the luckless Enkidu, and despite their clear heroism. The horrid test involves watchfulness, without sleeping, for six days and seven nights. As a test of righteousness or uprightness, it has its counterpart in Jesus' command to the apostles to "watch" and wait while he prayed in the garden setting of Gethsemane. Just as the apostles, Gilgamesh fails to stay awake, and so loses his chance to be translated. In clear imitation of that gift, however, Gilgamesh is offered "a secret thing, . . . a mystery of the gods," a plant whose name means "The Old Men Are Young Again."[7] Sadly, however, Gilgamesh loses even this hope as it is cruelly snatched from him by a water serpent.

The "moral" of this epic poem, then, is not "All men must die and only the gods live eternally," as one might conclude (nobody needs a poem to tell her she is mortal and will die!), but rather "With enough righteousness, heroism, and bloodline, one can lay claim to translation," as did Utnapishtim and his wife. In the case of Gilgamesh, however, without the requisite personal integrity or spiritual strength, translation is hopeless.

Isaiah Template

Ascension narratives are a subgenre in Jewish lore that includes both Old Testament and extracanonical, pseudepigraphic narratives. They are part myth, for they reach back to remote times; part legend, for the characters involved are often historical; part literature because examples of such texts proliferate in roughly the two hundred years B.C.E. A good illustration of the difficulty in classifying such narratives can be seen in the ancient Martyrdom and Ascension of Isaiah.[8] To begin with, it "is a composite work which falls very obviously into two parts," of which the older is the martyrdom. The martyrdom is a Jewish legend; the ascension or visionary section is Christian.[9] Thus the scribe or author has combined two tales into one, the result being a clearly literary product, whose authorship spans as much as a six-hundred-year period. Indeed, the two portions circulated independently.[10] The work is legendary, since Isaiah was a historical figure who played a part in the ongoing recorded history of Israel, a history that becomes more and more accurate as time goes on and civilization evolves. Yet the ascension motif draws on the myth of the ascending hero, which is as remote as Sumerian civilization, with its list of godlike kings.

There is no question that Isaiah dies in the tale, for "Beliar . . . sawed Isaiah in half with a wood saw" (5:1). So the ascension narrative, not being able to follow smoothly on the heels of such a violent and decisive martyrdom, is cleverly set during the reign of the good king Hezekiah rather than during that of wicked king Manasseh. The ascension narrative is thus a literary flashback, being spatially situated after Isaiah's martyrdom. I shall offer more examples of authorial resourcefulness in finding ways to preserve the tradition of the hero being translated, thus cheating death, but the Isaiah example establishes the necessity of preserving the idea of conjoined ascension and translation. Isaiah's ascension includes roughly the same vision of the seven heavens as the pseudepigraphic Enoch material (examined next). However, the ascension here is recorded by a Christian, who must infuse both portions of the narrative with Christian symbolism that will further substantiate that Isaiah, of all the Old Testament prophets, knew of Christ's mission most completely. At the same time, however, Isaiah cannot be translated gloriously to heaven, for his being so deified would outshine the ascension of Christ (described in chapter three of this book) and would seem to circumvent the necessity of Christ's atonement. (Being a character in the Old Testament seems to doom potential heroes, such as Isaiah, to questionable status under the new covenant.) Thus, although Isaiah does have approximately the same ascension experience as Enoch, the narrator uses the strategy of Isaiah's body remaining in the palace while "his mind was taken up from him" (6:10), which dovetails figuratively with his later martyrdom, during which while being sawed (presumably laid out horizontally), "he did not cry out, or weep, but his mouth spoke with the Holy Spirit until he was sawed in two" (5:14). This "mental ascension" is also more congruent with the vision of Isaiah in the Old Testament (chapter six) in which Isaiah sees Yahweh's throne; what is interesting, of course, is that in order for Isaiah to endure the vision, one of the fiery seraphim must "cleanse" Isaiah's tongue with a hot coal from the altar of God—which event orients Isaiah *physically* and *spatially* within *Yahweh's* heavenly palace! Thus I would assert that this ascension text suffers from the "anxiety of influence" (critic Harold Bloom's term) in which any text must be balanced between tradition and innovation in literary and cultural history. This difficulty with tradition and innovation is primarily a literary issue but can affect mythology and legend as well, since none of these narrative strategies exists in a cultural vacuum.

Importance of Scribal Glossing, Authorial Prooftexting

The activity of thus editing and glossing ancient texts, recombining them with other literary, mythic, legendary, and folk elements, has a very ancient precedent indeed. Joseph Smith, the charismatic founder of Mormonism (to be treated at length in chapter five), was aware of glossing in ancient times, and he engaged in glossing the revelations he received from God. At one point, Smith, himself glossing the Hebrew of the opening verse of Genesis (Smith had some slight knowledge of Hebrew by the last year of his life), declares with his delightful but harmless satire, "When the inspired man wrote it [*berosheit*—in the beginning], he did not put the *baith* there. An old Jew without any authority added the word: he thought it too bad to begin to talk about the head [*rosh*]!"[11] Smith didn't abhor glossing itself, but felt he had more authority to gloss (and more inspiration) than the original scribe.

Often Smith used the word "translate" when what he was doing with texts was more precisely *glossing*, however inspired.* At times, glossing involves wholesale appropriation of portions of other scripture—for example, the minor prophets in the Old Testament, who quote each other; Jesus' repeated glossing of Isaiah; or even the Book of Mormon's† character Nephi appropriating, then glossing, whole chapters of Isaiah, or another character, named Mormon, who, in a passionate Bloomian fit of belatedness, overlays much of the book with Christian glosses and commentary. The gnostics, such as the ancient writers and compilers of the Nag Hammadi codices, glossed the opening chapters of Genesis to prove that Yahweh was a demiurge, a hypostatic materialist creator, thus completely inverting the orthodox gloss.

Such glossing and editing is most interesting because it seems to be entirely within the province of holy men or priests to perform. Rabbinical commentaries in the Talmud are well known, as are the even more mystical commentaries in the Zohar. Indeed, the entire cabalistic tradition is founded on the scribal or priestly right to gloss and edit scripture. Even glossing of philosophical treatises was

---

* The best example of Joseph Smith's glosses is found in his "inspired version" of parts of the King James Bible; he dismissed the Song of Solomon (or Song of Songs) as not being "inspired scripture." I have concluded that what he rejected was the desperate attempt by English-speaking scribes and editors to "gloss" the text of the poem. Smith was correct in his criticism. The love poem is inspired, very beautiful, and highly praised by no less than the ancient and influential Rabbi Aqiba—but the gloss is naive at best. How are we to take seriously the gloss "The love of Christ and his church, the church's love unto Christ" or "the church's graces, and love to Christ" when the text reads, "I sat down under his shadow with great delight, and his fruit was sweet to my taste" (2:3) "Thy two breasts are like two young roes that are twins" (7:3), or even more sexually explicit, 5:1–6? Smith, as a Mormon elder and high priest, preferred his own very estimable gloss on his own scripture—the early (1833) Book of Commandments, glossing Song of Songs 6:10, "Who as she that looketh forth as the morning, fair as the moon, clear as the sun, and terrible as an army with banners?" Smith added the part of the passage beginning with "fair" to what became section five of the Doctrine and Covenants, the canonized edition of the earlier book, inverting for some reason the words "fair" and "clear." He repeats the inversion in a later revelation from the same work (105:31); finally, in 109:73, the passage appears as it is in the Song of Songs. It is interesting that Smith preserves the general symbolism of the church as a host (army), or as the bride of Yahweh, which echoes the Anglican phrase "Church Militant," but wisely refuses the *reductio ad absurdum* of the orthodox gloss.

† Smith's pseudepigraphic history of the fate of an ancient Israelite tribe. Mormons regard it as scripture, accurate history, and authored by ancient scribes; the book exists now in the tens of millions of copies in most of the major languages of the world.

common; for example, Chaucer drew on the glosses Jean de Meun provided for *De Consolatione Philosophiae*; furthermore, Latin glosses on Boethius's work, as well as lengthy Latin commentaries, were also available to Chaucer and others. Such an important treatise as this of Boethius was glossed simply because the priests and scribes felt they had the right to do so, since they were also preserving the work itself. Thus, the glosses and commentaries of Remigius of Auxerre, William of Conches, and William of Aragon on Boethius end up affecting Boethian elements of, for example, Chaucer's Monk's and Knight's tales, and *Troilus and Criseyde*, or De Meun's *Roman de la Rose*.[12]

I have concluded, for example, that the most serious sin Chaucer's Wife of Bath (Alisoun) commits is neither lechery nor greed, though she is guilty of both. Rather, it is her lengthy gloss of the scriptures, a scribal or priestly duty, that condemns her (at least from the point of view of medieval Catholic priests). If she had merely glossed (though it is undeniably Chaucer behind it all!) as did Margery Kempe,* and to a lesser extent Julian of Norwich, she would have committed a venial sin. But Alisoun does a satirical gloss on the New Testament, interpreting Jesus' words as a justification for her bad behavior:

> ... with barly-breed, Mark telle kan,
> Oure Lord Jhesu refresshed many a man.
> In swich estaat as God hath cleped us
> I wol Persevere; ...
> In wyfhod I wol use myn instrument
> As frely as my Makere hath it sent.[13]

Her profanation of scripture is clearly Chaucer's satirical portrait of the clerical abuses of glossing, which only reinforces the fact that glossing was a priestly or monastic duty in Christianity. It is certainly not simply a late Catholic invention, as the commentaries on the scriptures by Flavius Josephus, Philo of Alexandria, and Clement of Alexandria, attest.

---

* Margery Kempe is a historical reality; but the Wife of Bath comes across as more "real" than Kempe or even Julian of Norwich, showing that a cunning narrator can make a saint's life so real that we believe in him regardless of his historicity.

Enoch–Metatron

This brings us to our next point of reference: The most significant Old Testament ascension is that of Enoch, who has somehow attracted considerably more attention than he ought, if one follows only the brief account of him in the Old Testament (Gen. 5:18–24). But the huge extracanonical collection of Enoch texts cannot be ignored. Behind these texts stands an *urtext* of the oldest Enoch, one whose life and eventual translation are very complex indeed. Genesis, especially the chapters preceding the tales of Abraham, contains extremely abridged and rarified versions of much older and longer tales. Thus, I suggest that the original Enoch character, on which the scribes drew for their ascension texts, is far older than 200 B.C.E. Sumerian tales of creation, often preserved in Babylonian texts, are clearly older than the earliest available texts of Genesis, and those tales contain immeasurably more information than their counterparts in Genesis. For example, the council of the gods, before the deluge, is completely ignored in the Bible, but the Sumerian accounts record in detail the heavenly debate.

Much of the Enoch material resembles the Sumerian or Babylonian material more than it resembles the material in the Bible, the latter referring to the translation of Enoch only elliptically. As I stated above, most of the extracanonical Enoch material is traditionally dated no further back in time than about two centuries B.C.E. Some accounts of Enoch were clearly written in the Middle Ages in Europe, altogether too late, so the specialists would argue, to be worth considering as "historical" in any sense. My point here is not to argue the historicity of Enoch or of his translation, but rather to point out that the tradition and oral narratives of Enoch's translation are extremely old, older than the Bible texts, and that the survival of the fuller account of Enoch's life and ascension has been continuous and extensive since the time of the story's ultimate origin. The Bible account of Enoch, then, is extremely clipped (most likely for the literary effect the author of J had in mind) and is not the best source for the Enoch tale. The importance of this continuity will become clear as I proceed.

Among the many Enoch texts dealing with his pious life, his ascension, and his translation are long passages in the medieval Book of Jasher (Sepher Ha-Yashir), the Ethiopian Enoch (translated in 1821 by Richard Laurence), the Slavonic Enoch, and the Joseph Smith Enoch, included in Smith's pseudepigraphic Book of Moses.*[14]

What features do these documents share? First, they always cite his descent from the most noble stock—even the Bible preserves Enoch's genealogy. Second, they acknowledge the rigid purity of Enoch's life and studies, as well as his absolute allegiance to God:† Third, they all mention his battle, in various forms,

---

* This account is extremely late, dating from roughly 1830, and is the work of Joseph Smith, the Mormon prophet, whose amazing insights into Enoch's position in cabalistic lore cannot be explained (this according to Jewish critic Harold Bloom)—since no Enoch texts were available to Smith. In his account of Enoch's preaching and trials, Smith captures with uncanny sophistication some of the most basic themes in the Enoch texts of every earlier age. The Enoch account is found within the pseudepigraphic Book of Moses, itself found in a volume of extracanonical narratives entitled The Pearl of Great Price. Smith's Enoch account followed fast on the heels of the publication of Smith's best-known work, The Book of Mormon.

† God's anger was increasing in those days against the sons of men, to destroy them . . . for their evil doings. . . . And Enoch . . . served the Lord, and despised the evil ways of men. (Book of Jasher 2:30, 3:1)

There was a wise man, . . . and the Lord conceived love for him . . . that he should . . . be an eye-witness . . . of God Almighty. (Secrets of Enoch 1:1)

And the soul of Enoch was wrapped up in the instruction of the Lord, in knowledge and understanding. (Book of Jasher 3:2)

Enoch . . . a righteous man . . . saw a holy vision. . . . [He] heard all things and understood. (Ethiopian Enoch 1:1–2)

I came out from the land of Cainan . . . a land of righteousness to this day. (Book of Moses 6:41)

God's purposes for Enoch are also remarkably consistent in the various Enoch accounts: he is a preacher of repentance to an extremely wicked and dangerous group, sometimes identified with the *nefilim* (fallen *b'nai elohim*, also called "Watchers"), sometimes with giants (the children of the fallen angels), and sometimes with evil kings and warriors:

I beheld the land of Sharon . . . Omner, . . . Heni, . . . Shem, . . . Haner, . . . and . . . Hanannihah, and all the inhabitants thereof;

And the Lord said unto me: Go to this people, and say unto them—Repent lest I come out and smite them with a curse, and they die. (Book of Moses 7:9–10).

Turn not from God before the face of the vain, who made not Heaven and earth, for these shall perish and those who worship them. (Secrets of Enoch 2)

Go tell the Watchers of heaven, who have deserted the lofty sky . . . that on the earth they shall never obtain peace and remission of sin. (Ethiopian Book of Enoch 12:5–7)

with evil. These sorts of details seem to be part of the *fabula*, or connected logical events of the Enoch tales.

Yet in spite of fulfilling the criteria I discussed in connection with the *Gilgamesh* epic, these elements do not distinguish Enoch from any of the great religious figures of the Old Testament that end up dying rather than being caught up to heaven. Thus the survival of the narrative details of Enoch's ascension and final translation is the great mystery. Even when the texts offer an account of those events, certain keys are missing. These constitute what I believe to be the great textual mysteries of ascension and translation, and even knowing where to look for such interpretive keys is part of the mystery. Within those narrative keys lies the blurred or elliptic vehicle or means of translation that creates the dramatic tension of the many texts in which it occurs, and this baiting of the reader further excites her consciousness of the narrative mystery.

The apocryphal and pseudepigraphic accounts of Enoch's ascension and translation reveal this tension quite starkly. The gap in the texts—the failure of the writers to receive the *gnosis* or divine knowledge of how such things work and how one prepares oneself for them—is thus responsible more than anything else for the preservation of the idea of the ascension and translation of Enoch. All the texts are failed visions in this regard, because it is abundantly clear that the authors have no idea how one qualifies to become translated or even how to ascend to heaven to converse with God and the angels.

There is in fact an implicit despair and hopelessness connected with knowing or believing that Enoch ascended and was translated and realizing with far greater certainty that we lack the keys to repeat the event and will without any doubt die. I find the most pathetic example in Enoch's son Methuselah, who, according to the Book of Jasher, "acted uprightly in the sight of God, as his father Enoch had taught him." The text implies that Methuselah was every whit as righteous as his father, for "he did not turn from the good way either to the right or to the left" (4:3). Yet after living 960 years (969 in the Old Testament), Methuselah died. Genesis in the Old Testament is mute concerning the pathos of death and the possibility of hope for life; the Book of Jasher contains a gloss that anticipates that very question (who shall live or die among the righteous): "The Lord willed them to die, so as not to behold the evil that God would bring upon their brothers and relatives, as he had so declared to do" (5:21). This sort of medieval gloss attempting to reconcile the harshness of the

Genesis text is to be expected, but it fails to account for Enoch's being allowed to live in heaven and avoid death entirely. One thing such a gloss *does* do, however, is point out that translation, as the binary opposite of mortal death, is by implication a state which requires its recipients to "behold the evil" that those who die are spared. Thus we should, in translation accounts, expect to find some evidence (even if through negation) that the delightful "paradise" of Utnapishtim and his wife is only one aspect of life for the being so translated; another facet may require considerable suffering, labor, and diligence. To see the translated being as just as busy and concerned as he was in mortal life with the needs and troubles of others is a surprising turn but fits well with the idea that the translated being continues to work for God (the gods) as a messenger or minister of justice. Indeed, that the translated being continues his labor in this regard is evidence that being translated, "caught up into heaven," makes him more than an angel—actually divine, a god in some minor sense just as Psyche, the goddess praised by Keats as the latest member of the pantheon, is a minor goddess. The translated being becomes a member of what Blake scholar Foster Damon would call "the divine family."

Thus it is that the *Gilgamesh* tale is essential for our appreciating and recognizing the ironies and the drama of translation in later accounts, as well as the qualities the gods require of the person so honored: noble genealogy, heroism, and uprightness before the gods. Concerning the first quality, it is safe to say that only select people within a bloodline qualify; more names get included as time goes on, but the accretion is partly a rationalistic gloss, partly hyperbole, and partly an attempt to reveal the gnosis of who gets translated, why, and how.

The best indication that the translation to heaven proper is consciously left out of many narratives, or is buried, removed, or altered, is found in the numerous ascension accounts, many biblical and others extracanonical. In such accounts prophets, patriarchs, and other Old Testament figures are allowed a tour of heaven but are required to return to earth to live out an ordinary existence. Jacob, for example, sees the stairway to heaven in a dream-vision (Gen. 28:12), soon after which he wrestles with an angel (Gen. 32:24–32). Isaiah has an encounter with God very much like Enoch's (Isa. 6). Ezekiel's vision of God is spectacular and vivid and seems to transport Ezekiel to other worlds and other places (Ezek. 1). Yet the Old Testament avers that these patriarchs and prophets died. The pseudepigraphic Joseph Smith revision of Genesis contains a delightful digression on the merits of Melchizedek:

... Melchizedek ... was ordained an high priest after the order of the covenant which God made with Enoch ... after the order of the Son of God ... neither by father nor mother; neither by beginning of days nor end of years ... and ... delivered ... unto as many as believed on his name ... that every one ... ordained after this order [shall] stand in the presence of God. ... And men having this faith, coming up unto this order of God, were translated and taken up into heaven. ... And his people wrought righteousness, and obtained heaven. (Gen. 14:25–40, Joseph Smith Translation)*

This passage incorporates material also found in the Epistle to the Hebrews, and makes explicit that which is only implied in Hebrews 7:1–3, though this New Testament passage shows how we may make a natural intuitive leap from seeing Enoch as a unique translated being to seeing Melchizedek in the same position:

For this Melchisedec, king of Salem ... [was] King of righteousness ... and King of peace; Without father, without mother, without descent, having neither beginning of days, nor end of life; but made like unto the Son of God; abideth a priest continually.

I cannot emphasize enough the importance of the passages in Hebrews and in Joseph Smith's Genesis revision; Smith's tale of Melchizedek shows us the key narrative event of the vision of God, a pattern that may be used in other examples. The passage in Hebrews shows us as well that there was a tradition about Melchizedek involving his being made a heavenly being and that the ascension motif is preserved right along with it. Suddenly, references within and outside of the Bible start to fall into place. It is no wonder that the Babylonian Noah, Utnapishtim (*and* his wife), are

---

* Smith recast several parts of the Bible, with his most stunning alterations in Genesis, in an "inspired" version of the KJV, whose major alterations are offered the reader in the notes and appendices of the Oxford–LDS joint edition of the KJV (Salt Lake City: The Church of Jesus Christ of Latter-day Saints, 1982). In Smith's revised Genesis, for instance, is a remarkable narrative on Melchizedek. Though this written material cannot be demonstrated scientifically to be a product of ancient Israel any more than it can be shown to be the invention of Joseph Smith, the idea of translation in nineteenth-century consciousness most interests me, not finding scientific proof that Smith's Enoch text is of ancient date. It is noteworthy, however, that in my hearing a noted Enoch expert from Edinburgh acknowledged, in a discussion with BYU Professor Hugh Nibley, that Smith's Enoch account is genuine pseudepigrapha; that is, its claims to antiquity are as valid as those of the other Enoch texts, which finally surfaced, curiously enough, after the time of Joseph Smith. Laurence's translation of the Ethiopian Enoch (1821) was of course as yet unavailable to Smith in 1830–1831.

the chosen ones to greet and instruct the wayward but grieving Gilgamesh. It is not that a mistake was made or that mythologies became confused, but rather that ascension and translation seem to be a persistent option for a certain body of holy (that is "set apart") people. Hebrews 11:33–34 suggests that the great power inherent in the priest–king Melchizedek is connected with the Christian ideal of faith (specifically in Christ):

> ... through faith [these prophets] subdued kingdoms, wrought righteousness, obtained promises, stopped the mouths of lions, quenched the violence of fire, escaped the edge of the sword ... [and] turned to flight the armies of the aliens.

Here it cannot be so much a question of knowing exactly what the process is as it is an acknowledgment that there is a process and we apparently can't know it. Just as the New Testament is unable to describe to us exactly how the resurrection of Christ occurred, that is, the process or event of resurrection, so also there is no substantial narrative to show us how translation is possible, how it works.

While our task is to explain the various ellipses in the Enoch texts, it is also to show why all the other worthies of the Old Testament, such as Abraham, Isaiah, and Moses, were *not* translated as part of their narrative. It should already be clear in this study that the lacunas or elliptical portions of so many of the ancient narratives of ascension and translation mislead readers into erroneous conclusions; after all, that is why so few students of mythology have addressed the problem. For example, in a passage previously cited, Joseph Smith provided the missing portion of the elliptical narrative of Melchizedek through a brilliant recombining of elements of the Epistle to the Hebrews and of elements of the cabalistic Enoch tales (to which of course Smith had no access). Thus, the Bible's recorded death (or simply the abandoning of the narrative) for Old Testament figures is likely either a desperate attempt to fill a hole in the narrative (it is safe and logical simply to record that someone died, but much harder to record that God took them bodily to heaven!), or it is a very literary attempt by a scribe or other writer to restrain the text for the sake of realism or perhaps to highlight those few translation narratives that occur from remotest history.* It should thus surprise nobody that apocryphal

---

* Harold Bloom, providing commentary for the sensational The Book of J, found himself able to reconstruct the personality and tastes of the author of J, who, Bloom asserted with astounding ease,

ascension texts exist for Moses, or that Moses, who was metaphorically "buried by the hand of the Lord" was, in an alternative reading, actually translated. Joseph Smith in his account of Moses' call to labor does not scruple to offer the reader an ascension text, with visions of heaven and an apocalyptic account of Israel's fate. In such cases it would be safe to conclude that if all three criteria are met—genealogy, heroism, and righteousness—*and* an ascension text exists, the theory of narrative pattern would allow for a translation text as either a predicted yet absent part of the *fabula*, or as an actual rhetorical artifact, whether discovered and translated or not yet discovered. Thus, ideally, where (as in Genesis) there is an ascension text for Jacob, the stage is set as well for his translation, for he has the proper genealogy, heroic temperament, and loyalty to Yahweh. Though Jacob's fear of his brother Esau's revenge may seem anti-heroic, even cowardly, Yahweh sees Jacob as courageous. Jacob's wrestling with God (or with his angel) is the occasion of his receiving a "new name": Israel. This honorific name-title implies that Jacob (whose name, Yakov, means "usurper") has, through his tenacity, even cunning, earned a place with God.

Enoch's heroism lies in his fearless delivery of God's message to the *nefilim* (the Watchers) after Enoch returns from his initial ascension to God's throne. The medieval Jasher and the Slavonic Enoch do not focus on this aspect of Enoch's calling, preferring to emphasize Enoch's personal righteousness and seclusion in preparation for his permanent separation from humankind through translation. But both the Ethiopian Enoch and the Joseph Smith Enoch preserve Enoch's confrontation with the wicked. In the Ethiopian Enoch, Enoch is given great power over the Watchers, the fallen angels; Enoch writes that the "Mighty One . . . has . . . created and given to me the power of reproving the Watchers" (14:2). The most terrifying portion of Enoch's curse follows: "Judgment has been passed upon you: your request will not be granted you. From this time forward, never shall you ascend into heaven" (14:3–4). The Joseph Smith Enoch gives a vivid portrayal of Enoch's heroic confrontation with the Watchers:

---

was a woman, and likely a member of Solomon's court![15] While such ideas are impossible to verify, his "creative fiction," as he called it, was meant to show us an author with a *literary* more than a doctrinal or theological agenda—not to mention a bit of a proto-feminist agenda (when one considers how many colorful and assertive females there are in Genesis—Eve, Sarah, Hagar, and Rachel, among others).

... and he spake the word of the Lord, and the earth trembled, and the mountains fled, even according to his commands; and the rivers of water were turned out of their course; and the roar of the lions was heard out of the wilderness; and all nations feared greatly, so powerful was the word of Enoch, and so great was the power of the language which God had given him.

There also came up a land out of the depth of the sea, and so great was the fear of the enemies of the people of God, that they fled and stood afar off and went upon the land which came up out of the depth of the sea.

And the giants of the land, also, stood afar off; and there went forth a curse upon all people that fought against God. (Book of Moses 7:13–15)

Smith's version confirms my observations about the rhetorical vacuum created when, in a text where one might expect a translation, the event is rhetorically subverted by ellipsis, alternative events (such as death), or weak retelling of the event. Though Smith describes Enoch's ascension in some detail, and even mentions the founding of an entire city which is translated with him,* yet he ends his Enoch narrative with the deceptively simple biblical gloss, "And Enoch and all his people walked with God, and he dwelt in the midst of Zion; and it came to pass that Zion was not, for God received it up into his own bosom; and from thence went forth the saying, ZION IS FLED" (Book of Moses 7:69). In other places, Smith expounds at length on Enoch's translation, and so it is most revealing that he mutes these events in this single instance. Thus I contend that a simple ascension narrative may easily be, in terms of the *fabula*, a stunted translation narrative.

Another aspect of Enoch's translation that we must not skirt is his ultimate destiny once he is translated. In the Jewish cabalistic lore he becomes Metatron, who, as Harold Bloom notes, is sometimes called the "lesser Yahweh."[16] It is only natural that the monotheism of even the cabalah would prevent even one so great as Enoch from becoming, in any sense, a god; it is enough that he becomes an archangel with powers to judge the wicked beings, both celestial and terrestrial, that play foul in the age of the mortal holy man Enoch. Yet the narratives describing Enoch's celestial character cannot be ignored: they are the equal of the superlatives later used to declare Christ's deification. Enoch is "put ... into the garments

---

* This represents a very typical cabalistic conflation of two characters, Enoch the son of Cain, and Enoch the son of Jared. The medieval Jasher performs the same rhetorical act, but in reverse, by taking the obviously poetic phrase "a man to my wounding, and a young man to my hurt" and interpreting it as referring to two people that Lamech killed.

of [God's] glory" (Secrets of Enoch 22:8). He must warn his children against worshiping him: "Do not say: 'Our father is standing before God, and is praying for our sins'" (Secrets of Enoch 53:1). The Book of Jasher notes that the kings of the earth "feared to approach [Enoch] on account of the Godlike awe that was seated upon his countenance; therefore no man could look at him, fearing he might be punished and die" (3:20). If we look back at the prototypes for such an event, however, we will have to conclude that the narrative implies *deification*, not merely a changed nature. For example, it is typical, even in the Bible and not merely in the *Gilgamesh* epic, to distinguish other creatures from the gods in terms of what they are or are *not*. When the Elohim declare(s)* "Behold, the man is become as one of us, to know good and evil" (Gen. 3:22), he is ironically stating that man has in fact not become even remotely a deity—his resemblance is superficial. The tree of life denied Adam and Eve (3:22–23), though a real enough loss for them, is also a satirical poke at all humanity, for whom the tree is not only lost, but forever undiscoverable—that is, as the *Gilgamesh* epic contends, mortality is the common lot of all humanity. The reminder to Adam is stated in a nasty play on words (3:19); he and Eve are made of "dust" and will become dust again. Adam's name is a constant reminder that he is mere dust: *Adam* is cognate with *Edom* and refers to the red clay of the earth—especially that used by potters.

We may justly conclude from this discussion that the Enoch literature is the survival of a very old tale, doubtless dating to ancient Sumer, that confirms that humans may occasionally cheat death. The conditions are stringent and involve a harrowing ascension to be "reviewed" by the gods. The final result, however, is nothing short of the acceptance of the candidate into the pantheon or family of gods, after which the new member becomes a god of sorts to the mortals he left behind. The tale's survival is both a scourge and a balm, for it shows that some

---

* I am at a complete loss as to how to address the Elohim of Genesis, whose plural name denotes "majesty"; the masculine plural -*im* came to have such a meaning when monotheistic scribes, bent on "correcting" the reading without violating the text, gave the suffix an allegorical or philosophical meaning to replace its literal meaning. The literal meaning of "gods" would fit the pantheon of the *Gilgamesh* epic or any number of Sumerian or Babylonian tales, and the specific "Lord God" (*elohim adonai*) of later chapters in Genesis clearly is the single god in the pantheon, Enlil, who is willing to take up humankind's benefaction when all the other gods wish humanity destroyed. He comes out resembling very much the goodhearted Prometheus of Greek myth.

may be saved because of extraordinary effort, but most creatures will never measure up to the heroics of their translated counterparts.

Jacob's Ladder

The phrase "stairway to heaven" is almost a cliché, having been appropriated by rock groups and writers of New Age literature. It has been portrayed over and over in art from ancient times in Judeo-Christian culture. Solomon's legendary temple had a spiral stairway ascending to the holy of holies, where the high priest was literally in the presence of God. (Yahweh appeared as a pillar of cloud or fire above the mercy seat where the gold cherubim of the Ark of the Covenant came together or touched their wings.) Among the Pend d'Oreille tribe of native Americans is the legend of the "mad wolf," who, jealous of the moon, climbs up Devil's Tower to attack the lunar inhabitants,[17] this corresponding to the ziggurat Nimrod builds (the tower of Babel) so that he can ascend to the heavens and kill Yahweh in his sky palace. For the Freemason, the ascension by steps represents the acquisition of the liberal sciences and arts, geometry being most revered. Echoes of the ascension of Jacob occur in every imaginable circumstance, for the metaphor of ascent and of the means to accomplish it (a ladder or stair) somehow touches our sense of heroism to the core. The existence of "insurmountable odds" demands that one overcome them, transcend them, and even Beowulf believes that if one is heroic enough, he may be able to subvert fate. The metaphor of ascent as heroic conquest is ubiquitous. (Consider Mount Everest, for example; the climber's cliché is, One climbs it because it is there!) Armed with such a metaphor, and perhaps with the old maxim "Nothing ventured, nothing gained," we may now consider the heroic retelling of the Old Testament patriarch Jacob's near miss at translation—as strange a tale as one can find in literary history.

In Jacob's stairway to heaven, the narrator of Genesis has preserved elements essential to the hero's ascension—but they are fragmented and out of order. To demonstrate how the narrative of Jacob becomes fragmented, as well as how an ascension–translation narrative falters, I will separate two passages unnaturally conjoined: Genesis 28:10–15 and 16–22; and join two more maladroitly separated: Genesis 32:1–2 and 32:24–32. Before we consider these passages, something must be said of Jacob's quality as a candidate for such divine favor.

His name, a typical Old Testament pun describing the character of its owner, means "usurper" (*yakov*). Because his name is changed to Israel, or "He wrestled with God," and because he is the father of the twelve tribal patriarchs over the Israelites, well-meaning readers see him as worthy because of his righteousness or because Yahweh, in his righteousness, willed it so; certainly, after the change of name, Jacob becomes the sort of person befitting the new name. But that he was in any sense "righteous" simply cannot be. All we have is the narrative, and like Samson, who judged the Danites and the Philistines, Jacob is unscrupulous and self-centered; he is as clever as Samson was strong. God loves Jacob for the same reason Zeus loves Odysseus; he is cunning—irrepressibly so! Any milder epithet than "usurper" will not do for this incorrigible trickster:

1. Rebekah is delivered of twins—we forget that. Esau (who is covered with red hair at birth—a version of Enkidu) is a cunning hunter, that is, skillful; but elliptically, such words apply to Rebekah and Jacob's efforts to deceive Isaac. Jacob appears to have been a shepherd, for he completed some very astute animal husbandry for Laban; but clearly, at the dinner table Isaac loves the wild game more than mutton stew. Isaac prefers Esau's cunning (as noted earlier, Edom, is the same as Adam, red like the potter's vessel)*—with Esau being the older brother, and therefore, the chosen heir. The fact that Esau seems flippant about his birthright is mediated by his starving when he encounters the soup, which Jacob has cooked up. Jacob, a great bargainer, immediately sizes up the potential of this meeting. Abraham bargains with Yahweh to save Sodom, while Jacob bargains with a hungry man for his birthright, which, as Esau observes, can do him little good if he is dead.

Perhaps no more powerful drama exists in the Old Testament, with the exceptions of young Isaac's near-sacrifice by his father or of David's loss of Absalom, than in the pathos of Esau's voice as he realizes that Jacob has stolen not only his birthright, but also his father's great blessing. Though Rebekah must share the blame for the deception, Jacob clearly acts to further the conspiracy by suggesting to his mother that he would be recognized and cursed because of his smooth skin if he attempted to take his brother's place. And it is likely that his deception barely

---

* Bloom pictures God as creating Adam by shaping his body, with his hands, making him a vessel into which God infuses or into which he fills or pours the breath of life (Commentary, The Book of J).[18]

passes muster, for he cannot imitate his brother's voice. Later in his life, Jacob fears Esau's wrath, with the guiltiness befitting the usurping heel-clinger.* Thus Jacob, as youngest son, has some precedent for his behavior, but it is nonetheless not righteous behavior: it is merely clever.

As mentioned earlier, in a remarkable bit of trickery, Jacob pays Laban back for withholding Rachel back to offer Jacob the older sister, Leah. Here we see Rachel, the younger daughter, preferred over the elder. Jacob must bide his time (fourteen years of servitude), but, as they say, revenge is a dish best served cold. In a business decision that would do credit to a Wall Street broker, Jacob's cunning surpasses Laban's, for Jacob enriches himself through selective breeding of the herds. Shakespeare's Jewish lender Shylock, who, as Harold Bloom points out in *The Anxiety of Influence*,[19] is a not-much-improved version of a character from Christopher Marlowe, finds the tale valid enough to justify what seems to be unjust usury:

> When Jacob graz'd his uncle Laban's sheep—
> This Jacob from our holy Abram was
> (As his wise mother wrought in his behalf)
> . . . .
> When Laban and himself were compremis'd
> . . . .
> The skillful shepherd pill'd me certain wands
> And in the doing of the deed of kind,
> . . . .

---

* One of the greatest ironies in the Old Testament is that the birthright should be with the eldest son (patrilineal), but in many significant cases, the younger son receives the birthright and blessing. Cain is held in infamy, Abel is beloved, and after him Seth; Isaac is prized over Ishmael; Joseph is preferred before Reuben, Simeon, and Levi, because he is the eldest son of Rachel, though born after the first three; in blessing Judah, Israel gives him the scepter, but to Joseph goes an equally grand inheritance; and Benjamin (the ancestor of King Saul, ben-yamin, whose name is euphemistic and means "son of the right side") was more prized by his father after Joseph, his elder brother, was betrayed by his brothers; and in a most bizarre example, Israel gives the blessing and birthright to Joseph's youngest son, Ephraim, and when Joseph attempts to reposition the old man's hands, Israel stubbornly insists on choosing the younger son. The prophet Nathan chooses Jesse's youngest son, David, over his seven brothers. The exception also occurs in Joseph Smith's pseudepigraphic Book of Mormon, in which a younger brother, Nephi, is chosen to rule over his brothers. Two firstborns in the Bible who do retain the birthright are Moses and Jesus, whose births were surrounded by extraordinary events.

[Fell] parti-color'd lambs and those were Jacob's.
This was a way to thrive, and he was blest;
And thrift is blessing, if men steal it not. (1.3.71–90)

However bad Shakespeare's portrait of Jews, Shylock's comparison is apt: if we assert that Jacob is rewarded for trickery, both Judaism and Christianity suffer a moral dilemma. Shylock rationalizes pernicious usury, glossing Jacob in self-defense. Antonio cannot condemn Shylock without condemning Jacob, descendent of Abraham, and thus without casting doubt on God's motives for rewarding a usurper. It is simply not possible to say Jacob was rewarded for righteousness, for his behavior is manifestly unrighteous, and it implies somehow that Yahweh is somehow perverse.

There is another approach to this ethical dilemma: remove righteousness and ethics from the mix. The story of Jacob's cunning is essential only to the narrative of the stairway to heaven. For example, we could grant that God disapproves of Jacob's behavior but loves Jacob for Abraham's or Isaac's sake (not an uncommon pattern); or, just as likely, Jehovah regards Jacob as a diamond in the rough—not unlike Samuel's recognition of the inner man in David's stripling body, or Merlin's comment about Uther Pendragon in John Boorman's *Excalibur*: "'It's easy to love folly in a child.'" Like David, Jacob must be tested to determine if he can be a man and rise above juvenile sibling rivalry. One can also argue that in tribal religion (the Israelite nation consists of twelve *tribes*), absolute laws of right and wrong, such as "virtue is its own reward" have no place; rather a system of kapu or tabu governs the tribe. "Taboo," as opposed to absolute morality, would state, "On Wednesday you may steal from your neighbor, but on Thursday, you may not, and if you do, we will cut off your right leg." Kapu or tabu simply means "forbidden"; it applies no ultimate abstract value to stealing or not stealing.

The encounter with the gods (the *b'nai elohim*, the angels or sons of God) is in fact that test, for Jacob has the chance, if found worthy, to receive a hero's welcome into the divine family. Here, then, is my reconstruction of the narrative of Jacob's near miss with immortality:

And Jacob went out from Beer-sheba, and went toward Haran.
And he lighted upon a certain place, and tarried there all night, because the sun was set; and he took of the stones of that place, and put them for his pillows, and lay down in that place to sleep.

And he dreamed, [but was in vision] and behold a ladder set up on the earth, and the top of it reached to heaven: and behold the angels of God ascending and descending on it. (Gen. 28:10–12)

. . . the angels of God met him.
And when Jacob saw them, he said, This is God's host: and he called the name of that place Mahanaim. (Gen. 32:1–2)

And Jacob . . . [held onto one of them and] wrestled [with this one who appeared to be a man] with him until the breaking of the day.
And when he [who appeared to be a man] saw that he prevailed not against [Jacob], he touched the hollow of [Jacob's] thigh; and the hollow of Jacob's thigh was out of joint as he wrestled with [the man].
And [this other being] said, Let me go, for the day breaketh. And [Jacob] said, I will not let thee go, except thou bless me.
And [this manlike being] said unto him, What is thy name? And [Jacob] said, Jacob.
And [the manlike being] said, Thy name shall be called no more Jacob, but Israel: for as a prince hast thou power with God and with men, and hast prevailed.
And Jacob asked him, and said, Tell me, I pray thee, thy name. And he said, Wherefore is it that thou dost ask after my name? . . . (Gen. 32:24–29)

And, behold, [it was] the Lord [who] stood [before Jacob], and said, I am the Lord God of Abraham thy father, and the God of Isaac: the land whereon thou liest, to thee will I give it, and to thy seed;
And thy seed shall be as the dust of the earth, and thou shalt spread abroad to the west, and to the east, and to the north, and to the south: and in thee and in thy seed shall all the families of the earth be blessed.
And, behold, I am with thee, and will keep thee in all places whither thou goest, and will bring thee again into this land; for I will not leave thee, until I have done that which I have spoken to thee of.
And Jacob awaked out of his sleep, and he said, Surely the Lord is in this place; and I knew it not.
And he was afraid, and said, How dreadful is this place! this is none other but the house of God, and this is the gate of heaven.
And Jacob rose up early in the morning, and took the stone that he had put for his pillows, and set it up for a pillar, and poured oil upon the top of it [to sanctify it as God's holy monument].

And he called the name of that place [where God revealed himself] Beth-el [God's house], [to mark it as a monument of his covenant and testament of the God of his fathers, so that all in the city might see it and wonder!] but the name of that city was called Luz at the first. (Gen. 28:13–19)

... [But] Jacob called the name of the place Peniel: for I have seen God face to face, and my life is preserved. (Gen. 32:30)

And Jacob vowed a vow, saying, If God will be with me, and will keep me in this way that I go, and will give me bread [food] to eat, and raiment to put on,
So that I come again to my father's house in peace; then shall the Lord be my God:
And this stone, which I have set for a pillar, shall be God's house [read temple, palace]: and of all that thou shalt give me I will surely give the tenth to thee [the tithe for the keeping of the temple priest]. (Gen. 28:20–22)

And as he passed over Penuel the sun rose upon him, and he halted upon his thigh.
Therefore the children of Israel eat not of the sinew which shrank, which is upon the hollow of the thigh, unto this day: because he [God] touched the hollow of Jacob's thigh in the sinew that shrank. (Gen. 32:31–32)

We should not be surprised that after such an experience, Jacob (now Israel) reconciles with the brother he had wronged; his humility and penitence are all the more real after he is made lame. God has to "cheat" to win the wrestling match. There is a lot more going on than this, of course. Jacob's attempt to wrestle the being he thought was at best one of the host of heaven is not accidental. Jacob has every intention to climb the stairway, fearlessly ascending to God's throne. If Genesis 28 is "correct" that God stands above the ladder, clearly in his own celestial element, the wrestling match would then be the last test. Calling the place the "house of God" suggests his having been in God's palace. One might add that seeing the face of God should have destroyed him, whether he had a vision or a real wrestling match. When the sun rises, the man who saw the face of God can look at the sun and be certain which of the two is the true god (Abraham in the medieval Sepher Ha-Yashir arrives at the same conclusion through similar observation). God's blessing is entirely earthly, but symbolically it represents the greatness and richness of God's own palace and lands. Jacob is content with these, for both he and God know that if God hadn't insisted that Jacob remain on earth (Jacob's dislocated hip representing the lot of a man who is loved by God but doomed to live out his days on Earth), Jacob might have become part of the divine family (and of course, Israelites, whose ancestor Jacob is, recognize that their nation is always in God's presence, in his temple, or as the allegorical bride of Yahweh).

The parallels between this reconstruction of the narrative and other such tales of failed translation should be obvious. The wrestling match, as a ritual test for the hero, is found in Herakles' besting a wrestler who cannot be defeated if his feet touch ground; Herakles embraces him, lifting his whole frame off the ground, then strangles him one-handed. Beowulf, in a vexed passage about his encounter with Grendel in the mead hall, grips him strongly, tearing off the enemy's arm entirely. Challenging God or openly attacking him is found in the *Iliad*, when Diomedes attacks both Ares and his sister Aphrodite. God's using an "unfair" advantage is found all through classical mythology and forms the basis for Milton's Satan reasoning that the only reason God succeeded in defeating him was that God was more powerful, not that his cause was just.

The purpose of this reconstruction is not to ignore the narrative as the J writer constructed it, but to show that the elements of the ascension and translation are easily transposed into other narratives, in effect disguising them. Jacob's story is a failed translation—there is no other explanation for the wrestling match. In Esau we see preserved the "earthy" character of Enkidu, created with no divine element in him. In Jacob we see Gilgamesh, the self-indulgent king who is humbled by the gods into accepting kingship and mortality as his destiny, bearing both with dignity and wisdom. That the heroic elements of the *Gilgamesh* tale should be found in the Old Testament shows their durability, but also suggests that the early Hebrew (*hapiru*?) perception of God was utterly and completely anthropomorphic. It was left to philosophers, theologians, and glossing scribes to abstract from that vivid portrait a God indivisible to whom nothing earthly or mortal could be compared, making him not distant, necessarily, but indescribable in any earthly manner.

Elijah

With the Elijah narrative, we are able to examine several additional or variant aspects of ascension and translation. The first of these is a binary opposition, in which the Old Testament writer consciously chooses narrative over prophetic discourse. What are called the "major prophets" of the Old Testament are books of warning, teaching, and prophecy by a group of men (*ne'vi'im*) whose own lives are outlined only sketchily, leaving much to inference—a giant lacuna of sorts. In the case of Elijah, however, no Bible book bears his name, even pseudepigraphically. Did Elijah write no book? Perhaps, perhaps not, but such a book seems unimportant to those compiling the Old Testament canon in pre-Christian times. Editorially speaking, the scribes have given themselves the choice of Elijah the man and Elijah the book—the first a narrative construct, the second contemplative and philosophical (no matter how electric the rhetoric of such a book of prophecy).

Another important innovation of the Elijah narrative is its unmistakable claiming of Elijah as Israel's own "god." The ultimate result of this coloring of the tale is that Elijah looms over every orthodox Jewish act or speech in our own time. He is the missing but anticipated guest at every Passover meal; his absence, rather than being the binary opposite of his presence, is rather a presence of a different sort; it is the sign of Elijah's translation, for it is certain proof that after the search for his body, Elijah could not be found. Like the witness of the empty tomb in the New Testament, Elijah's absence from the table defies logical explanation; if he had merely died, no place would be set for him. If he were only a mortal prophet, no matter how holy, no absence could have existed, no vacuum that another might try to fill (for example, John the Baptist or Jesus as the returning Elijah). The myth of Elijah's return could not have taken on narrative validity and shape had he not departed with equal narrative power and physicality—a man who never returns to the dust in the first place has no trouble returning fully and physically distinct.

With Elijah's ascension and translation, however, is his "gospel," his teaching, acts, and priestly legacy. We are forced to reckon with an increasingly precise formula, based on his life, for Elijah's candidacy for translation. It should be clear that as translation narratives move forward in time and become closer to us, their narrative detail (not necessarily the *fabula* itself) will become far more richly detailed and complex, as though the cumulative narrative adventure of every candidate for ascension and translation is placed on the shoulders of each succeeding candidate as a sort of "mantle." I use the mantle metaphor deliberately, since, in the fashion of a metaphor from a Marlowe tragedy, the metaphor of the mantle becomes literalized* in this narrative of translation.

Yet another feature added to the Elijah narrative of translation is scribal or authorial anxiety: the closer the narrative event is to the present time of its recording, the greater the implications of the narrative for that author or scribe. That is, what is remote never terrifies, but what is contemporary produces incendiary reaction, critical anxiety, and a vain attempt at distancing. To illustrate, one might use the example of, say, a Catholic or Baptist university, at which one new faculty member discovers a scientific or religious truth utterly at odds with the policies or founding creeds of the universities or their parent churches. The faculty member bravely, but with considerable naivete, offers an article on the subject in a national journal, assuming that in the cause of truth, people's feelings, traditions, and potential reactions are entirely irrelevant. The university regents start to get pressure from millionaire alumni, whose faith and traditions are being challenged by this rebel faculty member. Meanwhile, the local pastors are taking up petitions to censure the faculty member and the university for wasting church monies on so-called "progressive" research. To the faculty member's everlasting surprise, he is suddenly no longer a candidate for tenure, and the university does everything in its power to disguise the fact that such a scandalous character was ever on campus in the first place.

While the translation of Enoch, even though found in the Old Testament, is not remotely threatening to orthodox religious tradition, Elijah, being a central figure of both orthodox Judaism and orthodox Christianity, and appearing in a part of the Bible recognized as the first serious historical chronicle (i.e., traceable chronologically through contemporary events), is in fact threatening to the point of being terrifying. For example, when the adoration of Elijah became a cult among the Israelites, and that not long after the fact of Elijah's narrative, it became common among the scholarly Israelites to state that Elijah did not ascend to heaven and was not translated.[20] What is the fear inherent in such a renouncement? Simply, the

---

* I must give credit to one of my mentors, Louise Schleiner, who drew our attention, if memory serves me, to this idea, but acknowledged that Harry Levin, the noted Renaissance scholar, first suggested the idea.

idea of translation is so attractive to people that they will instantly embrace such a notion to the exclusion of other narratives about Jehovah's relationship with his chosen people—notably the fact that Jehovah doesn't offer any such option to ordinary people. Mortality and death are the *rule*, not the exception. It was not an option merely to delete wholesale the Elijah story, because Elijah is also symbolic of Israel's unified faith in Yahweh and of the rejection of pagan religion.

The sudden departure of Elijah, as mentioned earlier, also created the narrative field for his sudden return. Jews consistently identified Elijah with the Messiah or with his precursor, the one prophesied by Malachi to come "before . . . the great and terrible day of the Lord" (Mal. 3:23). Alarmed at the potential for political upheaval attending such a revolutionary return, Jewish scribes and leaders, especially during the Roman occupation of Israel in early Christian times, might wish to demythologize Elijah, and so they did.[21]

Christians as well as Jews had a love–hate relationship with Elijah. He is identified at times either with Jesus or with John the Baptist (Matt. 11:10; Mark 9:11). Because he could raise the dead and death had no power over him, Elijah was said to be the angel that presided over the resurrection of the dead. Elijah's anticipated appearance and hoped for deliverance of Israel from bondage, together with the announcement of the Messiah, was a key narrative and mythological event of the Passover season. Thus a key element of a successful narrative of Christ's life was to subsume under the banner of the Acts of Christ all those acts ascribed in the Bible to Elijah. Christ's death and resurrection at Passover time, his feeding of the five thousand, his miracles on the water, and his transfiguration all enfold or comprehend Elijah's acts, as well as those of Moses, rendering them as mere antetypes of Christ rather than narrative rivals; leaving Elijah and Jesus as old-covenant vs. new-covenant hero would have been a contradiction far too stressful for most first-generation Christians (mostly Jewish converts and God-fearers) to endure.

The Elijah figure is troubling enough that medieval Jewish mystics made him an "angel who dwelt only temporarily on earth as a human being, before again ascending to heaven";[22] he is allowed in such mythology to keep his body of flesh so he can return to earth as needed to aid humankind—a typical activity of translated beings in all the mythology. His body is thus not born of "dust," but is made from the tree of life itself. Such mystical exegesis (or more precisely *eiso*gesis) helps to solve one of the narrative problems of Elijah's life as the Bible relates it:

he is a "Tishbite," but beyond that appears to have no genealogy, neither root nor branch (a situation recalling the status of Melchizedek in the allusions in the New Testament Epistle to the Hebrews). It is perhaps because of his mysterious origins, or perhaps it is a cause for the mystery itself, that Elijah is given his name, which means "My God is Yahweh," which certainly connotes Elijah's marvelous relationship with Yahweh as well as serving as a play on words for his life's mission, which was to make Yahweh the uncontested sole deity of Israel. Ironically, this very monotheistic narrative sets the stage for an embarrassing conflict of influence between Yahweh and Elijah in future commentary and apocryphal narrative, such that Elijah's anticipated return during the Passover season and his anticipated role as forerunner to the Messiah ends up obscuring Yahweh's *narrative* importance (if not religious importance) in the Seder feast and its surrounding traditions. (It might be added, as well, that Moses, whom I earlier mentioned as a likely object of a now-discarded translation narrative, also overshadows the events of Passover in general and of the Seder Feast in particular.)

Probably the most disturbing narrative elements (at least for later scribes and interpreters of the OT in general) of Elijah's life story as related in the Old Testament are these, for which I offer in each case a suggestion of the narrative plight each example creates: First, Elijah can open or close the heavens "according to *my* word" (1 Kings 17:1, emphasis mine), putting him on the same level as Tammuz or Ba'al, or even Yahweh, all of whom are thunder and rain gods in early Canaanite and Babylonian narrative. Second, although Yahweh clearly feeds Elijah and sends him to the widow woman, Elijah plays the role of the visiting god as found in Greek and even Hebrew narratives in order to test the obedience of a household to the universal law of the guest–host relationship (1 Kings 17:11–17).* Third, Elijah himself, not only Yahweh, proves more powerful than Ba'al because

---

* Consider, for example, Yahweh's test of Abraham's and Lot's hospitality and of the destruction of Sodom for its inhuman abuse of guests within its walls. In Greek myth, the infamous behavior of Tantalus toward the gods who visited his palace serves as the negative exemplum, Demeter at the well of Eleusis as the positive (although later events betrayed that initial trust and goodness). The New Testament resonates with the narrative of the gods visiting homes. Jesus, of course, mentions constantly the importance of treating guests as though they were Jesus himself, an angel, or even God; he also promises to sup with (and of course bless the house of) all who open their doors to him. Jesus has his special lessons to teach on the subject of kindness to strangers, best illustrated by the Good Samaritan parable.

at will he can call down fire from heaven and open the windows of heaven, where neither Ba'al nor his prophets can do either. While it must be acknowledged that Elijah makes no claim for himself—the people fall down and acknowledge that "Yahweh is the [only, or most powerful] God, Yahweh is the [only] God"—nevertheless, Elijah has already raised the widow's son from the dead, an act attributable to a god of both the "quick and the dead." Last, when Elijah is about to be taken up to heaven, he says to Elisha, who, among others of the prophets, has followed him to Jordan, "Ask what *I* shall do for thee" (2 Kings 2:9, emphasis mine). Elisha's response puts Elijah in much the same position as Enoch and Moses, whom Yahweh makes lesser "gods" to the people; in Moses' case, he becomes Aaron's god, and Aaron his prophet to the people. Elisha asks for a double portion of *Elijah's* spirit to dwell with him, a gift enclosed in the folds of the mantle Elisha catches as Elijah ascends. Elisha's cry at his ascent, "My father, my father, the chariot of Israel, and the horsemen thereof" (2 Kings 2:12), makes Elijah a godlike patriarch much like Enoch. It is thus that the "spirit of Elijah doth rest on Elisha" (2 Kings 2:15), and not only does Elisha end up reenacting the miracles of Elijah, but we can assume, despite the narrative, that Elisha is either meant to be caught up at some point as Elijah was, or that Elisha represents the earthly presence of the translated Elijah, the "true contrary" of Elijah, as Blake might have called Elisha.

John the "Beloved"

> Peter seeing him [the disciple Jesus loved] saith to Jesus, Lord, and what shall this man do?
> Jesus saith unto him, If I will that he tarry till I come, what is that to thee? follow thou me.
> Then went this saying abroad among the brethren, that that disciple should not die; yet Jesus said not unto him, He shall not die; but, If I will that he tarry till I come, what is that to thee? (John 21:21–23)

This extremely odd, enigmatic passage has hints of pathos, of envy, indeed of several very human emotions. It also contains a striking if oblique reference to translation and has more and more narrative impact with the passing of time. The last sections of John's Gospel deal with the post-resurrection activities of Jesus and his mortal apostles, material often referred to as the forty-day ministry and marked in the orthodox Christian liturgical calendar by the space between Easter Sunday and Ascension Day. There is in this scene between Peter and Jesus an implicit acknowledgment of the unusual gift of never seeing death—translation in the heroic tradition of Enoch and Elijah. The way the narrative is pieced together here, Peter's question follows Jesus' very certain prophecy that God has no such deliverance in store for Peter, who in verse 19 of this chapter seems doomed to be crucified, much as his Master; and while Jesus' exhortation to "Follow me" is as insistent in Peter's case as it is in other Christians' cases, there is a dark tone in it, for Peter will be led, according to Jesus, "whither thou wouldest not" (21:18).

Peter's envy and disappointment at his lot are understandable, when Jesus, turning to his "Beloved Disciple,"* proposes that John "tarry" in the flesh till Jesus comes again. Peter's lot recalls dimly the pathos surrounding the death of Enkidu and the loss by Gilgamesh of the plant of eternal youth; the juxtaposition of Peter's predicted crucifixion and the Beloved Disciple's "tarrying" purposefully implies that Peter's fate is inferior, the reward of a disciple who, however goodhearted, simply has not passed the key tests of absolute worthiness—perhaps the main reason so many minor incidents in the Gospels center on Peter's impetuousness, his unwillingness to submit totally to Jesus' will in spiritual matters, his forsaking of the Master at key times.

The odd disclaimer following this exchange between Peter and Jesus points out a much larger issue, which will be touched on at greater length in chapter three of this book: "Yet Jesus said not unto him, He shall not die." An epistle meant to comfort early Christian converts attempts to subvert its own narrative out of charity for fellow Christians, many of whom struggled in those days (as they still do) to meet even the minimum requirements of discipleship, for the way the narrative is cast initially, Peter, "chiefest" of the apostles, is held unworthy of translation. Only the Beloved Disciple, tied ineffably to his Master through some spiritual umbilical cord, merits ascension. Clearly desiring to minimize the difference between ordinary church members and those worthy of ascension and translation, the writer, much in the fashion of later Catholic commentators on the saints' ascensions, insists that a death of some sort is inevitable, even for those blessed to be "caught up."

---

* The mysterious "Beloved Disciple" is assumed to be John because of tradition and certain internal textual evidence, but the fact is that several people have been proposed as objects of Jesus' special favor, among them Lazarus of Bethany, whom Jesus raises, earlier in this Gospel, from the dead.

The *didache* here is emphatic: for the overwhelming majority of even the most faithful Christians, death is the final act, the final step of life. The beauty and courage of one's death must be the best measure of the well-lived Christian life. That the hope of ascension and translation was still dangled as a bright jewel for the truly faithful is evident in the preservation of the *logion* attributed to Jesus, "Some standing here . . . shall not taste of death, till they see the Son of man coming in his kingdom" (Matt. 16:28, also preserved in Mark and Luke). This phrase's proper context is not anticipation of Armageddon, nor is it a reference to the resurrection from the dead. Rather it is a prologue (in all three Synoptic Gospels) to Jesus' "ascension" and "translation" at the Mount of Transfiguration, to which, it is noteworthy, only Peter, James, and John [the Beloved Disciple?] were witness. Jesus' triumphant *return* as the ascending hero involves what fundamentalist but charismatic Christians colorfully call the "rapture," the catching up of the righteous Christians, and their subsequent and immediate translation, as the outcome of their vigilance in awaiting Christ's speedy return. To be precise, we must recognize that the incident at the end of John's Gospel is the culminating "judgment" scene in which Jesus appoints his disciples either to death or to ascension. The significance of this scene for Christian doctrines of the resurrection shall be treated in the next chapter.

The effect of such a scene as depicted at the end of John upon later religious narrative is surprisingly profound, given that the scene is heterodox and actually, as I will demonstrate in chapter three, a threat of sorts to the whole orthodox notion of Jesus' blood atonement as the unique event toward which all generations supposedly gazed—future generations in retrospect and previous generations in anticipation. I believe that the translation narratives must influence our perceptions of the function or purpose of atonement and resurrection. To offer but one instance of the survival of heterodox translation narrative, I wish to mention several characters from Mormon narrative (the influential religious narratives with which I am most familiar) that clearly partake of the fiery spirit of the Elijah narrative though cast nonetheless in a Johanine narrative backdrop. The first of these is a recasting of the "Beloved Disciple's" (precisely identified as John by Joseph Smith's narrative commentary) scene with Peter and Jesus as a secret or hidden "parchment" in which John supplied the pieces to what Smith was convinced were narrative *lacunae* in John's Gospel narrative. To accomplish this feat, the Smith narrative puts in John's mouth words whose meaning cannot be misconstrued as merely figurative, thus promoting the closure and even the totalizing that the original New Testament narrative stubbornly resists: John, in direct answer to Jesus' question about his desires, pleads, "Lord, give unto me power over death, that I may live and bring souls unto thee" (Doctrine and Covenants 7:2).*[23] Lest John's desire seem self-serving, thus perhaps disqualifying him from receiving such a gift, Smith's narrative expands Jesus' remonstrance of Peter: ". . . he desired of me that he might bring souls unto me, but thou desiredst that thou mightest speedily come unto me in my kingdom"; so while Peter's desire was good, "my beloved has desired . . . a greater work," and Jesus "will make him a flaming fire and a ministering angel . . ." (7:4–7). The last item is, of course, consistent with the apocryphal Elijah and Enoch narratives, in which the translated being is made to be utterly Other—a separate creation, at once resembling humans, angels, and God himself. What is utterly astounding about Smith's narrative, however, is not the dramatic conflation of the Elijah and Johanine narratives, but the additional *didache* on translation as a "greater work" than ordinary Christian service, a sublime desire to serve that implies—and this is very difficult to argue around because it is expressed with nineteenth-century frontier clarity—that blood atonement, death, and resurrection are for ordinary people, but to a certain class of people, John included, God has given the exact same power that Jesus alone ostensibly brought and achieved through atonement and resurrection: "power over death" (D&C 7:2). Smith's narrative reveals its author's unmatched ability to take a text (that found in John 21 of the New Testament) and *re-vision* an overlooked detail of a narrative into a text with terrifying narrative potential—the ability to force any reader who accepts the revised text to perform a *strong misreading* (Bloom's term for inspired misprision) on the entire orthodox canon. That sort of narrative activity, which both deconstructs and reconstructs written traditions is what really occasioned medieval and even early Christian book burning, and the destruction of Cathar civilization: the fear that one text, attractively packaged and creatively produced, might cause an entire orthodox superstructure to

---

* The Doctrine and Covenants of The Church of Jesus Christ of Latter-day Saints, a book of revelations given to Joseph Smith and other founding church leaders, outlines principles of church government, doctrines of the faith, Mormon cosmology, including angelology, and forms of church sacraments, including several items no longer officially sanctioned by the church. It is cited by section number and verse, its versification following the style of the King James Bible.

collapse (Hitler's *Mein Kampf* or Mao's infamous little red book produced an extreme effect: one must *destroy* all written tradition that would expose or deconstruct the newer reactionary work). In itself the reinterpretation of the past could account for the odd ways in which ascension–translation narrative, becoming a "key" to the past, evolved and survived even to the present day.

Joseph Smith's narratives do not abandon this "restoration" of the Johanine narrative of the "Beloved Disciple's" translation. While the narrative previously mentioned was recorded by Smith and a colleague in 1829, the famous Book of Mormon,*[24] published in 1830, contains other expansions of this narrative—all these, by the way, previous to the publication of Smith's challenging Enoch narrative (late 1830, 1831), mentioned in the Enoch section of this chapter. John's Gospel narratives and the Apocalypse or Revelation at the end of the New Testament (which has often been thought by even educated Christians to have been written by the author of the Gospel of John) are mentioned prominently early in the Book of Mormon (in 1 Nephi 14, for example). I mention them in passing because of Nephi's narrative declaration that John's secret writings "are sealed up to come forth in their purity . . . in the . . . due time of the Lord" (1 Nephi 14:26), a clear narrative anticipation of the additional narrative from the hidden parchment recorded as Doctrine and Covenants 7, and typical of Smith's consistently amazing ability to create and maintain complex chronology even in diverse narratives.

But the most exciting contribution of the Book of Mormon to our discussion of the function and survival of translation narrative is in the events surrounding the ascension–translation of several beings now part of a complex Mormon allusive narrative expression: "The Three Nephites." Their tale, as preserved in the Book of Mormon and expanded in the collective narrative social consciousness of modern Mormons (as urban folklore), is an amazing, conscious example of the absolute human need to preserve translation narrative, despite its remoteness and seeming irrelevance to the lives of the people trying hardest to preserve it.

---

* The Book of Mormon is similar in format to that of the King James Version: books (titled), chapters, and verses. In pseudepigraphic form, it creates an additional Israelite mythology concerning a wealthy merchant family, among other pilgrims, who leave the Old World to seek a promised land in the New. The action at points extends from thousands of years B.C.E. to some five hundred years C.E.

In the Book of Mormon, Smith's narrative preserves a special "testament"* of Christ, which most Mormons take to mean another "witness" of Jesus' divinity, but which, I believe, also carries the traditional Early Modern English denotation of "covenant," referring to a special land-covenant Yahweh, and later the resurrected Christ, established with the pilgrim cultures of the Book of Mormon, most notably a group called the Nephites. In what for critic Harold Bloom is the most (perhaps the *only* for him) significant narrative event in the Book of Mormon, Jesus, resurrected and in complete control, visits the New World pilgrims, instructing them in essentially the same fashion as one finds in the carefully collected and constructed logia of the Synoptic Gospels of the New Testament. Toward the end of this "descent of the gods"† Jesus chooses twelve special disciples, after the pattern of the Old World apostles,‡ to carry on his work among the Book of Mormon peoples. Nine of these disciples collectively respond as Peter did in the narrative version of John 21 in Smith's Doctrine and Covenants, with an extra codicil that the nine disciples will live till they are seventy-two (a multiple of *nine*), then "speedily" die and enter "thy kingdom" (3 Nephi 28:2–3). The three remaining disciples are stated explicitly to desire "the thing which John my beloved, . . . desired of me." The narrative tenaciously reaffirms the ancient conviction that one is "more blessed"

---

* The full subtitle recently added to the Book of Mormon is "Another Testament of Christ."

† I am using that phrase in all seriousness, for, mythologically speaking, the ancient pattern of the descent of the gods, preserved dramatically in the literal *deus ex machina* of ancient theater, is wonderfully preserved in Smith's narrative and has much of the flavor of the Sumerian myths of the gods descending to visit their temples with power and glory, occasioning great feasts and the entreaty for divine favors which could be granted on the spot. In drama, the touching scene of the gods' descent at the end of, for example, Euripides' *Hippolytus* illustrates the benificent gods' restoration of order to a tragic scene (which tragedy the gods also helped create). The descent of the gods is simply the reversal of the ascent and translation of the heroic figure, except that the descending gods generally grant blessings only for this life, except for a select few. In Smith's narrative this pattern, still recognizable, is heavily overlaid with Christian exegesis on the resurrection of all the dead, but as I will note elsewhere, resurrection is the rule which proves the exception—that only a scant few avoid death entirely.

‡ With remarkable insight, Smith seemed to realize that the original twelve apostles were the twelve princes or judges over the twelve tribes of Israel in Jesus' proto-restoration of Israel with himself as king, just as the "seventy others" (Luke 10:1) Jesus later appointed were to become a new Sanhedrin; the Nephite twelve disciples (Mormon 3:19) judge only the Israelites of the New World.

(28:7, that is, "happier," as the word is used here) not to die at all, even if by dying one can enter Christ's kingdom more quickly. Jesus ends up touching *the nine disciples who will die*, an unexpected twist to the narrative, but an interesting one, suggesting that, as we saw in the case of Gilgamesh, humans are generally *appointed to die*, for that is the lot the gods have dealt them.

Mormons, at least up until recently, in general had a genuine fixation on the idea of translated beings; now, however, only fringe groups maintain any real interest in the topic. This fixation includes the delightful tradition that not only the Three Nephites, but also John the Beloved, keep interfering for good in the progress of the Mormon church.* Thus even in the mid-1990s in the relatively urbanized sophistication of the Wasatch Front mountain chain in Utah, an almost irresistible urge to keep alive the ancient narratives of ascension and translation still affects a portion of the population, including, apparently, people with significant amounts of education.† The most remarkable thing about such survivals is that they seem necessary even if a culture already has a mythology that accounts for human existence and humanity's ultimate, cosmic destiny.

---

* A good example of the canonization in folk consciousness of translation narratives is preserved in R. Clayton Brough's *The Doctrine of Translated Beings*.[25] In spite of a zeal for objectivity in choosing stories with "possible validity," Brough includes a remarkable collection (roughly a third of his book) of folktales and superimpositions of Mormon folk readings on established texts that in every case bears the marks of Smith's own very ingenious retellings of translation narratives. Among the folk narratives, some of which have non-Mormon counterparts in folklore taxonomies, are misprisions of a nineteenth-century history, rewritten as an appearance of the Three Nephites, an apocryphal account of angelic assistance in the 1948 Israeli war, rewritten as military aid from John the Beloved and the Three Nephites, and Mormon retellings of Indian mystic visions, reshaped with translated Mormon narrative figures taking the place of tribal spirits—all of this, of course, recorded by a white man in a reminiscence published in a Mormon magazine. The original Mormon narrator of this last example, G. W. Hill, leaves the identification of the visionary visitors openended, but Brough attempts closure by placing the account in his book so that more people will reach his conclusion that the vision was of the "Three Nephites."

† Brough, mentioned in the previous note, has an M.S. in geography, with considerable experience in meteorology. His interest in Mormon translation narratives, while undoubtedly devout from his viewpoint, nevertheless troubles him, for in several places in the slim volume he defends his work as being firsthand, objective, and not on the fringe of discussion, which defense seems superfluous unless one fears that readers will raise objections to the topic or its treatment. As later chapters of my treatise will continue to demonstrate, such fears are real enough, for the ideas of ascension and translation test the liminality of orthodox religious truth as well as the liminal boundaries of socially acceptable behavior in even an ostensibly "free" nation such as the United States.

1. *The Epic of Gilgamesh*, trans. N. K. Sanders (New York: Penguin, 1972), 102.

2. Ibid., 114–15.

3. Ibid., 63.

4. Ibid., 72.

5. Ibid., 21.

6. Ibid., 97.

7. Ibid., 116.

8. I am using M. A. Knibb's introduction and translation found in James H. Charlesworth, ed., *The Old Testament Pseudepigrapha* (Garden City, NY: Doubleday, 1985), 2:143–76.

9. Ibid., 2:143.

10. Ibid., 2:147.

11. Joseph Fielding Smith, comp. and ed., *Teachings of the Prophet Joseph Smith* (Salt Lake City: Deseret Book, 1969), 348.

12. See Alistair Minnis, "Aspects of the Medieval French and English Traditions of the *De Consolatione Philosophiae*," in Margaret Gibson, ed., *Boethius: His Life, Thought, and Influence* (Oxford: Blackwell, 1981).

13. "Fragment 3 (group d): 'The Wife of Bath's Prologue,'" in *The Complete Works of Geoffrey Chaucer* (Boston: Houghton Mifflin, 1933), 145–50.

14. Book of Moses, Pearl of Great Price (Salt Lake City: The Church of Jesus Chrsit of Latter-day Saint, 1982).

15. Harold Bloom, Commentary, The Book of J, trans. David Rosenberg (New York: Grove Weidenfeld, 1990).

16. Harold Bloom, *The American Religion* (New York: Simon and Schuster), 92.

17. In the appendix of *The Library: Apollodorus*, trans. James George Frazer, LOEB Classics (Cambridge, MS.: Harvard University Press, 1921), vol. 2.

18. Bloom, Commentary, The Book of J, 175.

19. Harold Bloom, *The Anxiety of Influence* (New York: Oxford University Press, 1973).

20. *Encyclopedia Judaica*, s.v. "Elijah."

21. Ibid., esp. subentry "In the Aggadah."

22. Ibid., esp. subentry "In Mysticism."

23. The Doctrine and Covenants of The Church of Jesus Christ of Latter-day Saints (Salt Lake City: The Church of Jesus Christ of Latter-day Saints, 1981).

24. The Book of Mormon (Salt Lake City: The Church of Jesus Christ of Latter-day Saints, 1981).

25. R. Clayton Brough, *They Who Tarry: The Doctrine of Translated Beings* (Bountiful, UT: Horizon, 1976).

3

Translation as Theology: Orthodox Christianity's Neglected Ascension–Translation Narrative

In this chapter, I wish to treat what I believe is a key ascension–translation narrative which, in combination with certain Hellenistic narratives, connects ancient ascension–translation narrative with that preserved in Western literary tradition in the Common Era; that narrative centers on Jesus. This narrative is "disguised," as it were, by an overlay of other narrative interests for other audiences, and those layers must be removed before one can find the heroic narrative that is, in its own special way, profoundly influential today. What I have discovered will no doubt seem heretical to some, though heresy is not intended. I am in fact following the critical path Harold Bloom has called the "criticism of religion." It may be distinguished from ordinary theology in that it claims the detachment and critical objectivity to analyze theology itself without participating as such in theology.

The dissimilarities in Gospel accounts of Jesus, which tend to obscure the heroic dimension of his life, may be explained in part by the audience being addressed in the narratives. The Gospel of Matthew contains a clearly Jewish focus and seems intent on convincing an educated class of people that Jesus was king of the Jews. Mark is the most clearly biographical and seems devoted to an early Christian audience. Luke has a non-Jewish audience, one that needs more explanation and context to follow the narrative. John is clearly directed at an audience with a knowledge of the esoteric, of the mystic elements of all religions—its audience is profoundly philosophical and theological—but addresses a contemplative rather than an analytical audience. The metaphors all these Gospels employ to describe the meaning of Jesus' presence on the earth are narrative approximations and, within the limitations of human discourse, give us a hopeful narrative and a sense of completeness. Concerning those approximations, I have found a heroic narrative of ascension and translation, in addition to at least two other narrative paradigms: Jesus as Suffering Servant and Jesus as sacrificial victim. That these three versions of Jesus may seem in conflict at times does not bother devout Christians in the least, since, if Jesus was who he claimed to be, such reconciliations are not required. But for my purposes here, I will describe the three as discretely as possible, though some overlap is inevitable.

The only significant treatment of Christ as hero is folklorist Alan Dundes's "The Hero Pattern and the Life of Jesus,"[1] which notes that even Lord Raglan failed to discuss Jesus in his well-known work on the hero.[2] On Jesus as the marred servant, I will employ volume 2 of S. R. Driver and Adolf Neubauer's voluminous *The Fifty-Third Chapter of Isaiah according to the Jewish Interpreters*,[3] which contains numerous references to the Suffering Servant as the Messiah, while other passages suggest he is not, concluding that the servant is in fact the Israelite nation. On Jesus as sacrificial victim, I chose René Girard's remarkable *Job: The Victim of His People*,[4] which shows the discrete and unique qualities of the truly innocent victim of violence.

The Heroic Jesus

Dundes's article is significant for a number of reasons, only a few of which are really relevant to my own discussion. First is Dundes's declaration,

> The fact that a hero's biography conforms to the Indo-European hero pattern does not necessarily mean that the hero never existed. It suggests rather that the folk repeatedly insist upon making their versions of the lives of heroes follow the lines of a specific series of incidents. Accordingly, if the life of Jesus conforms in any way with the standard hero pattern, this proves nothing one way or the other with respect to the historicity of Jesus.[5]

I feel an obligation to stress that in considering Jesus as hero, I am not attempting to modify the historical Jesus, but rather to show how different narratives achieve different ends. In fact, using criteria set forth by Otto Rank and Lord Raglan, Dundes lists the following heroic elements of the New Testament of Jesus:

(1) virgin mother, . . . (4) unusual conception, (5) hero reputed to be son of god, (6) attempt to kill hero, (7) hero spirited away [flight into Egypt], (8) reared by foster parents [Joseph], (9) no details of childhood, (10) goes to future kingdom, . . . (13) becomes "king" [cf. The mock title of king of the Jews: INRI], (14) "reigns" uneventfully for a time, (15) prescribes laws, (16) loses favor with some of his "subjects" (e.g., Judas), (17) driven from throne and city, (18) meets with mysterious death, (19) at the top of a hill, . . . (21) body is not buried, and (22) he has a holy sepulcher.*[6]

The chief drawback to Dundes's treatment of Jesus is, ironically, its precision in adhering to the folkloristic standard of myth as "ultimate origins." The theogyny of Jesus as hypostasis, as member of a divine family, turns Dundes's argument all too easily away from the ritual models of Lord Raglan and toward the Freudian model of repressed desire and of sexual icons as expressions of Jesus' relationship with his mother (typified, for example, in the nursing Madonna). But his list justifies my consideration of Jesus as a heroic candidate for ascension and translation.

To begin this section on Jesus as hero, I wish to use a key narrative from the New Testament that will set in bold relief the essential heroic ascension–translation narrative of Jesus. The event, called the Transfiguration of Jesus, is the first part of an interrupted narrative of the heroic ascension–translation of the prophet, priest, and king—a human being who, because of his righteousness, is accorded the same gifts as Elijah and Enoch.

> And after six days Jesus taketh Peter, James, and John his brother, and bringeth them up into an high mountain apart,
> And was transfigured before them: and his face did shine as the sun, and his raiment was white as the light.
> And, behold, there appeared unto them Moses and Elias talking with him. . . . and behold a voice out of the cloud . . . , This is my beloved Son. . . .
> And as they came down from the mountain, Jesus charged them, saying, Tell the vision to no man. . . . (Matt. 17:1–9)

To recognize this as a fragmented translation narrative, one must understand the Early Modern English sense of "transfigured." It does not merely denote that Jesus' face went through a change (which the narrative specifically mentions) but

---

* Dundes adds that Jesus scores higher in points of comparison than many accepted heroes of ancient times.

connotes that the one so changed has been exalted or glorified (a sense of the word preserved in some dictionary definitions). Caroline Walker Bynum points out that by the 1300s "the body Jesus displayed at the Transfiguration was . . . his normal body, manifesting the beatific vision he constantly possessed."[7] This "vision" is the revelation of the incarnation of *Logos* as Jesus, but I find the phrase "normal body" very instructive, for it presupposes that Jesus as mortal hero must be transfigured as part of ascension and translation. The ascension of the high mountain to be thus transfigured foreshadows that divine ascension and permanent translation expected for the hero (Joseph Campbell's "ultimate boon," in which, in many heroic tales, "the hero must trick them of their treasure,"[8] but which, in Jesus, is the reward of perfect obedience, righteousness, and love).

Thus, I propose that the narrative is but a foreshadowing of Jesus' final ascent; Matthew as narrator performs a poetic "swerve" (to borrow Bloom's terminology in *The Anxiety of Influence*) to avoid the heroic implications of such foreshadowing, by "sidetracking" the reader into an apostolic debate over Elijah's place in Christ's kingdom, not an irrelevant topic, but one that is either tangential to the vision or filling a considerable lacuna in the narrative. Mark's more ascetic rendition of the same event sidetracks it into an apostolic debate over resurrection. While Mark's swerve equivocates by avoiding closure to the event, it does, quite by accident, raise the real problem of the narrative event: given that only great heroes are translated, to what does rising from the dead refer? (Mark 9:10).

The appearance of Moses and Elias (whose names are Greek transliterations of Moshe and Elijah) raises several significant issues in regard to translation narrative. What Jesus really says to these beings and they to him is not preserved in the narrative, suggesting a genuine "otherness" to the vision, a divine language in which the apostles and other New Testament narrators cannot or dare not (because of its sanctity as a *mysterion*) communicate. The pseudo-debate of Jesus and his *three* disciples is clearly a narrative substitute for the missing text of the three translated beings' conversation. This raises a second issue, one that demonstrates my thesis of the elliptical or fragmented narrative of the biblical heroes who logically should be translated, but whom the extant narratives do not allow to be. The presence of Moses represents Matthew's supplying of an alternative reading of the end of Moses' life, concerning which Deuteronomy makes the equivocal statement, "And [the Lord] buried him in a valley in the land of Moab, over against Beth-peor: but no man knoweth of his sepulchre unto this day" (Deut. 34:6). Moses and Elijah, in the ancient Israelite consciousness, are true Israelite heroes, so the absence of Enoch in the vision is possibly understandable, though for many Christians, Enoch and Melchizedek were ideal antetypes of Jesus.* Moses is the idealized angel (messenger) of God; Elijah is very much a hero in the Mosaic image, battling wicked kings and performing incomparable miracles—even raising the dead.

So, to return to Matthew's narrative of the Transfiguration, a clear narrative purpose associates Jesus with Moses and Elijah. Jesus' roles as lawgiver (reinterpreting the Torah) and prophet, as well as miracle worker, are parts of Matthew's purpose. But in addition, Matthew is creating a hero who, through comparison with other translated heroes, deserves himself to be translated. How this role contrasts and compares with Christ as "only begotten son," Suffering Servant, and bloody sacrifice will be seen. As Robert Graves and Joshua Podro daringly but convincingly show, the essence of Christ's claim to be the Messiah, or anointed deliverer of Israel, saving Israel from Rome even as Moses saved it from Egypt and as Elijah from Ahab's perversions, was that he qualified as Israel's prophet, priest, and king.†9 Matthew's Gospel is, therefore, partly a justification for kingship, including even genealogies, grouped numeralogically to proclaim the letters of King David's name;‡ not to mention the exclusive narrative of the visit of the "Great Ones," the wise men from the east, bringing kingly gifts and paying homage to the child king; and the triumphal entry into Jerusalem, imitating Solomon's

---

* Refer back to chapter two, the section on Enoch; Jude's epistle apparently quotes from the Ethiopian Enoch as a prophecy of Christ's millennial return and reign, and of the "perfect" man who "walked" with God.

† See Robert Graves and Joshua Podro, *The Nazarene Gospel Restored*, whose widely vilified thesis (fleshed out in novel form in Graves's *King Jesus*) is presented with creativity and brilliance, often involving the ostensibly unforgivable act of tearing Gospel narratives from their traditional settings and giving them new but equally plausible contexts. Popularizers, such as Hugh Schonfield in *The Passover Plot*, did much the same thing, with less success, but with no fewer recriminations from the devout.[10]

‡ The genealogy in Matthew includes three groups of fourteen generations each; David's name in Hebrew has three letters, whose numerical equivalents, a 4, a 6, and another 4, which add up to fourteen. The only people who could possibly be influenced by such a bizarre, mystical argument,

riding on a colt, with throngs hailing Jesus as "son of David." In addition, Jesus is the new Moses: Christ's insistent recasting of Mosaic law, found throughout the Synoptic Gospels, is designed to prove him more than the equal of the great lawgiver—for example, his "violations" of the Sabbath, his forgiveness of the woman taken in adultery, his insistence that all sin is forgivable save that against the Holy Ghost.* Yet another area in which Jesus fulfilled the criteria for the heroic man who is finally translated is his miracles. A survey of Jesus' miracles shows in many cases an overt narrative attempt to re-create or even outdo the miracles of Moses and Elijah: Elijah raises a widow's son from the dead, and so does Jesus. Elijah gives the widow woman flour and oil, Jesus creates wine from water. Elijah brings the famine, Jesus prophesies the destruction of the temple. Moses brings manna, Jesus creates bread and fishes. Moses crosses the Red Sea dry-shod, Jesus walks on the water. Moses sends plagues of sickness, Jesus heals those hopelessly ill.

The triumphal entry of Jesus into Jerusalem is of course the re-creation of Solomon's entry into Jerusalem, riding on the colt, with the crowd hailing him as the successor to David's throne. But it is much more than that, and the priest-Sadducees knew it. With his twelve princes and seventy judges, Jesus was planning to dismantle completely the puppet regime of the Romans, and in its place erect a political structure that would directly affront and confront Roman authority in Israel and elsewhere.†[11]

---

would be Jewish priests, scribes or Sanhedrin members specifically loyal to the restoration of the true line of King David to the throne. Jesus' entire relationship with the Jewish leadership in Jerusalem had to rest on this premise of his rightful kingship, as Graves and Prodo perceived. It alone accounts for the Sadducees' and priests' sudden plotting against Jesus, who of course entered Jerusalem in the fashion of Solomon, on a humble donkey, but whose "twelve" princes—the apostles—and "Sanhedrin"—his seventy others—laid the groundwork for his appearance in Jerusalem (Schonfield's point about sending disciples secretly to fetch the donkey from a contact man, using the code "The Master hath need of him" to obtain the beast).

* The poet William Blake made quite a point of how many of the Ten Commandments Jesus violated, but overreached considerably by attempting to prove Jesus had broken all of them, hardly likely for a Jewish rabbi (Jesus was a rabbi, it is clear, from his unjunction to call no man "master"; clearly many called him Rabbi as a name-title).

† These political elements I gleaned from John A. Tvedtnes's remarkable *The Church of the Old Testament*. Tvedtnes insists that Jesus' church is the successor to the ancient order of Israel: twelve

But Jesus' heroism extends beyond the boundaries of the Gospels or of the religion founded upon his teachings. Jesus also reminds us here, in binary opposition, of the return of the ill-fated Gilgamesh, empty-handed, to his royal city, his hopes of eternal life for himself and eternal youth for his people dashed beyond recovery; Jesus is the Gilgamesh-that-wasn't, the triumphant king who, as a translated being, would lead his people into an era of unprecedented peace and prosperity, for through his influence, his subjects would "live to the age of a tree," and he himself would reign for a thousand years.*

The heroic end of this version of Jesus *must* be translation; nothing else suits his accomplishments as a mortal. Indeed, the certainty that while on Earth Jesus was altogether mortal is one thing the Synoptic Gospels all agree on and defend. Jesus hungers and thirsts, he sweats, he feels pain, he cries, he works at a trade (if we can accept the implicit narrative of a son following his father's trade). He *can* be killed, but he *won't* be, for cheating death is the reward of the exceptionally righteous, courageous, or cunning hero, be he an Utnapishtim, a "Beloved Disciple," or Jesus. The final seal of Jesus' heroism is that Rome will fall, bested by a Jewish patriot, for, like Herakles of old, Jesus the Messiah-King is protected by Israel's God.† Furthermore, Mary's miraculous conception reveals that Jesus, like so many heroes, has divine parentage and thus has just claims to press his suit for glory.

---

tribal chieftains and seventy tribal elders as judges. My political conclusions from this are partly my own, partly those of Graves and Podro, and to a slight degree those of Hugh Schonfield.

* Rev. 20:4: The honored martyrs are raised from the dead to reign with Jesus a thousand years; Isaiah 65:22: ". . . as the days of a tree are the days of my people," suggesting long, vigorous life, if not necessarily immortality for the king's subjects, consistent with the myth of the hero's mortal friends, who received *earthly* blessings and curses from the gods. That Jesus understood and accepted the Pharisees' view of the function of resurrection is clear, when John 5:28–29 records Jesus saying, "Marvel not at this: . . . all that are in the graves shall hear his voice, and shall come forth; they that have done good, unto the resurrection of life; and they that have done evil, unto the resurrection of damnation."

† Satan, of course, is the author of that idea, for in the narrative of Jesus' forty-day fast, Satan reminds him that God will make certain the hero will receive no injury, no matter what folly he commits. (Satan alludes to a text not in the Bible: "It is written, 'He shall give his angels charge concerning thee: and in their hands they shall bear thee up, lest at any time thou dash thy foot against a stone.'" It is one of the supreme ironies of this scene that it is Satan himself who supplies us with an important but utterly unknown holy scripture, even a prophecy and sign of Jesus as the Son of God.

Thus, at least from a narrative standpoint, the true heroic end to Christ's life is not to be found in the Crucifixion, but in the Transfiguration, which prefigures the later ascension and translation of Christ—events that follow a forty-day special ministry,* as recorded in Acts:

> When they therefore were come together, they asked of him, saying, Lord, wilt thou at this time restore again the kingdom of Israel?
> And he said unto them, It is not for you to know the times or the seasons, which the Father hath put in his own power. . . .
> And when he had spoken these things, while they beheld, he was taken up; and a cloud received him out of their sight.
> And while they looked stedfastly toward heaven as he went up, behold, two men stood by them in white apparel;
> Which also said, Ye men of Galilee, why stand ye gazing up into heaven? this same Jesus, which is taken up from you into heaven, shall so come in like manner as ye have seen him go into heaven. (1:6–11)

The significance of this scene has been overlooked, because it has been set in the context of the Crucifixion and Resurrection, which give it entirely an otherworld tone; furthermore, the fact that Jesus did not "come in like manner" from heaven in the succeeding two thousand years† has forced a weak misreading of the narrative to refer to some distant apocalypse rather than to what all the disciples

---

* Discussed brilliantly by Professor Hugh W. Nibley, his simple yet alarming thesis is that there is overwhelming evidence, from earliest times, of a narrative in which Jesus teaches the higher mystery (*mysterion*) of exaltation, offering key words, rites, accounts of the original hypostasis of the *b'nai elohim* and the ultimate destiny of the true initiates.[12] The gnostics make pretense of possessing the complete forty-day narrative, and Christian apologists, including Clement of Alexandria, assure us there was a *secret* Gospel of Mark, available only to select Christians (Morton Smith's astounding discovery).

† However, he has returned, much as Elijah, from time to time, to reveal his purposes to those visionaries who are graced to endure his presence. The "absence" of Christ has given rise in Catholicism to a poetic "swerve" (as critic Harold Bloom calls it) involving the appearance of the Virgin Mary, who consistently advises true believers that Jesus will return: thus Bernadette, Catherine Laboure, Theresa, and other visionaries have *strongly misread* (again Bloom) the Transfiguration and ascension. On the other hand, the account of Joseph Smith, the Mormon visionary, brings Jesus back "in like manner" in 1820, 1832, and 1836, a visionary confrontation with the precursor that establishes Mormonism as the "last dispensation" (divine period of time) of the earth's history and the Mormon church as the kingdom of God on Earth.

obviously anticipated in this and a dozen other narrative passages: that Jesus would return during their lifetimes to restore the kingdom of Israel.

In order to see this ascension narrative in its proper context, we must reorient ourselves, find a new prospect or vantage point. For example, the idea that the gospel ("good news") would be preached among all nations to the ends of the earth cannot be understood originally to refer to the roster of the United Nations, for Jesus was not speaking to the U.N. General Assembly, but to a very small assembly of Jews who accepted his Messianic cause—"the uttermost part of the earth" (Acts 1:8) being basically the ends of the Roman Empire, which, one has to admit, covered an awful lot of the known world, but which fell short of being the entire world.*

The allegorizing of the preaching through *time*, not merely to the ends of the earth, occurs because the "end times," anticipated in the first generations of Christians, after the sack of Jerusalem and the Roman persecution of Christians, were not followed by the return of the ascended hero. The kingdom of the ascension narrative of Jesus is neither the spiritual giant of the Universal Church nor the spiritual kingdom of heaven, but simply the messengers of the hero-king Jesus warning every nation in which Jews might reside that the end is coming for the wicked Empire and that the Elijah-like Messiah (who is Jesus) will come down from heaven in his chariot with his angels (recall the power and position of Metatron–Enoch) to restore David's heir to his proper throne, to make the city of Jerusalem once again the city of Solomon, the city of the gold temple that was the envy and terror of Egypt. Saul's journey to Damascus is in essence an Elijah-like return appearance of the heroic Messiah, who wishes Saul to be his apostle (or "one who is sent") instead of the hitman for the high priest at Jerusalem.

Modern readers have every reason to universalize the Gospel narratives, for what the reader reads out of the sacred text is as important as what the narrator intends. The serpent in the Garden is literal, the comparison to Satan symbolic or

---

* Actually the narrative scope is so minuscule here that the text has Jesus offer for examples of "uttermost part" the far-flung regions of Samaria and Judea! Many Bible students make similar errors about the confusion of tongues at the Tower of Babel—assuming that languages like French and German were the immediate result of Yahweh's anger at the Ziggurat of Babel, when of course such languages are relatively young. Akkadian and Proto-Indo-European would be better candidates for the original confusion of tongues.

allegorical. Yet a frequent misreading that Satan is the literal presence in Eden and that the serpent is symbolic or allegorical does not violate the text; it merely allows the reader the same privilege the narrator allows himself. As Bloom points out again and again in *The Anxiety of Influence,* all poetic texts are misread, but the strong poet finds critical space for his strong misprision by dethroning the kingly poet or precursor through a six-stage confrontation. In the ascension–translation text above, for example, Graves and Podro reenvision the texts (based on textual comparisons and recombinations) in this manner:

> Now, the disciples were amazed to see Jesus of so shining a countenance, for he had fasted three weeks at tidings of John's death.... Then said they unto Jesus: "Surely thou fastest beyond reason. Thou wilt do thyself hurt." He answered and said: "It is written that Moses fasted forty days on Sinai, and afterward his face shone, so that he veiled it because of its brightness; likewise did Elijah fast forty days on Horeb. Yet each came thence to do great works."*13

This is an interesting restructuring of this aspect of the narrative, though it attempts to demythologize what is, in folkloristics, already legendary by definition. But it also fails to account for the translation motif that is logically a part of Jesus' role as messianic hero or deliverer. For the same authors, the ascension motif, which, as we have seen, follows rather than precedes chronologically Jesus' translation, also demands revision:

> Peter saith again: "Didst thou not foretell that many of us which are now here shall never taste of death, but enter alive into the Kingdom of Heaven?..." And he said...: "... I go away and am with you but a little while..." ... And he led them forth as far towards Bethany as is a sabbath day's journey, and there he lifted up his hands and blessed them, saying: "Peace remain with you." Then they saw him no more, for a cloud received him out of their sight as he went up into the mountain of Olives unto the house of Simeon son of Cleophas.†14

---

*I ought to add that such fasts are far from impossible if one drinks water; Jesus' fast in the wilderness must have allowed water, since Satan could hardly tempt a thirsty man with bread. My own brother witnessed fasts in Goa, India, lasting several weeks, but water was excluded from the prohibitions.

† I have severely clipped the critics' reconstruction to emphasize only those points germane to my book's focus.

Graves and Podro adopt a variant of the worn-out "swoon" theory of Jesus' "survival" after crucifixion. They also contend that Jesus, rejected by his disciples as a failed king and messiah, wanders forlorn and bereft of companions, appearing only occasionally for fear of reprisals from disaffected followers. But more importantly, these critics merely humanize or literalize the metaphors of ascension and translation, much as the Elizabethan playwright Christopher Marlowe did with metaphors for his conquering hero Tamburlaine. Ironically, Graves and Podo's misprision makes the ascension and translation more historical and realistic because they try to take away its supernatural aura. Thus on one level they perform a weak misreading on Jesus' ascension and translation.

Most remarkably overlooked by students of religion is a scriptural allusion to the heroic ascension–translation of Jesus cast into the midst of the Resurrection narrative; it is found in John 20:16–17, when Jesus reveals himself to Mary Magdalene before any other witness:

> Jesus saith unto her, Mary. She turned herself, and saith unto him, Rabboni; which is to say, Master. [Implicit in the text: Mary rushes to embrace Jesus.]
> Jesus saith unto her, Touch me not; for I am not yet ascended to my Father: but go to my brethren, and say unto them, I ascend unto my Father, and your Father; and to my God, and your God.

In the section following this scene, Jesus *does* return, a translated being who appears in the middle of a roomful of disciples who have closed the doors out of fear, and eight days later, he even allows Thomas to touch him. Jesus retains the wounds of the crucifixion, yet they are not bleeding sores, but scars, used to identify him as the same Jesus who in fact died. Between his encounter with Mary, who cannot touch him, and that with Thomas, who can touch him, his body has been purged of blood, indeed of all its earthly humours,* which are the life of the *nephesh*, or mortal living soul, so that the body is no longer ritually unclean. He now enters rooms with closed doors, but he is not a wandering ghost (Luke 24 is

---

* I refer to the four *humours* of Renaissance medicine, which represent the four classical elements (air, fire, earth, water): blood, yellow bile, black bile, and phlegm. The classical gods and Milton's angels are separate creations, containing within them the fifth element, ether (or ichor), which replaces mortal blood in the ascending hero. Ever equal to the old Greek–Jewish–Christian angelology, avid students of Mormon doctrine believe that God and gods (the exalted heroes of Mormonism, who are either translated or resurrected) have spirit matter flowing through their veins.

clear on that point) and not a revived cadaver, but a tactile being who is recognized by the emblems of his death. The resurrection itself, in John's narrative, is actually incidental to the ascension, which must take place so that Jesus may join the divine family. John's narrative, however, telescopes this ascension and translation into a lacuna or ellipsis, for the ascension, as important a text as it is, must give way to the powerful account of the suffering in Gethsemane, the eyewitness testimony of the Crucifixion (whose narrative details, by the way, directly confront the "swoon" narrative), and the Resurrection, in which Jesus, though assuredly dead, leaves both an empty tomb and a bewildered, weeping woman as the evidence of his resurrection. I might suggest here that Jesus' refusal to be touched initially stems from an Israelite fear of ritual contamination—possibly from touching Jesus, but just as likely by Mary's contaminating *him*; but Mary's recognition of him, and Jesus' argument that he must first ascend to his father, belong more precisely to the *heroic* narrative of ascension and translation than they do to the idea of return from the dead.

My point in mentioning these scenes of Jesus' heroic ascent is that they demonstrate that there is more than one narrative Christ in the New Testament: one whose heroic acts culminate in his ascension and translation (along with a few associates; see chapter two), one who is scourged for the sake of the sins of Israel, and one who is overcome by the world, is conquered by death, and is retained in his followers' hearts only in the hope of eternal life *after* death.

Now of course it will be objected that the resurrection of Christ constitutes his conquest over death, that this is itself heroic, and that the physical resurrection is the pattern for ultimate human salvation. But it is an important feature of Jesus' burial that the body has no time to decay or to be embalmed (the spikenard saved against that day becoming essentially an unusable rhetorical artifact), but here I am not concerned with what Christ actually did or did not do (and again, my own religious devotion is that Jesus did in fact conquer death). Rather, I am showing what contrasting narrative accounts tend to do. The tension in these three accounts (Suffering Servant, sacrificial victim, and hero) is at the heart of some major theological rifts in Christendom, and while this is not the place to pronounce judgment on the truth of one or more of the accounts, the theological rifts the narratives create will likely continue as long as the several narratives are totalized into one biographical narrative of Christ.* The endless attempts by theologians of all Christian credos to "harmonize" the Gospels are in themselves proof that the narratives are difficult for even the well-educated person to integrate. Thus the items I group together as belonging to the "heroic" myth of Christ may be pulled—some will think *yanked*—from their original settings in the Gospels.

What, one immediately demands, is the occasion for the other narratives? Who is the other Jesus, the protagonist of a tragic drama of an Osiris, abandoned by the gods, who must die in order to live; or, like Naaman of old, is blemished with scourging or leprous sores? Why would other narratives intervene, co-exist, or be superimposed on the heroic narrative of the translated Christ? The answer seems inescapable: the hero died, completely undoing the (apparent) integrity of the first narrative. Clearly, the first narrative, of the translated and ascended hero, is the older of the two narratives, for it is *anticipatory*, predicting, based on what Jesus apparently did and said, and on the outcome of his ascension and translation (which, by the way, demonstrates that Jesus' disciples were contemplating recording or preserving his history much earlier than scholars normally propose—in fact, even as it was unfolding). This of course raises troubling problems, if one grants the heroic narrative as I have constructed it. How could such a narrative survive, given that the historical person Jesus certainly died, and as a result of crucifixion, not old age?

Of course, devout Christians may refuse to see the heroic narrative as distinguishable from the other parts of the Gospel narratives, but I must emphasize that what the *narratives* do is not the same as what *Jesus* necessarily did. I am merely trying to account for three essentially discrete narratives of what Christ *apparently* did with his life. Only the death of Jesus would demand a narrative which ends properly with Christ's death (and to a lesser degree with the resurrection narrative), a narrative that is *retrospective*, rather than the *anticipatory* narrative of the heroic Christ.

---

*These sorts of rifts are possible only among devout Christians. The most harmful form they take is in myriad attempts to "harmonize" the Gospels. The urge to make the story of Jesus smooth and reasonable is the Western thing to do, but I have always felt that such efforts destroy the narrative more than they help it. Of course, committed, "detached" scholarship has gone to the opposite extreme, fragmenting the Gospels so completely that almost nothing remains of Jesus' sayings, let alone his actions.

Jesus as Victim

We must begin by acknowledging that even the best Christian exegetes can only approximate how Jesus did what he did; no matter how one describes the ordeal, one is confronted by a host of inexact but hopeful metaphors. This is the great mystery (not *mysterion*) of Christianity; its solution is the greatest quest of devout Christian thinkers. The magnificent "showings" of the anchorite Julian of Norwich come as close as visions can conceivably come to sharing with us the *gnosis* (divine knowledge or revelation) of how Jesus achieved what the narratives *attempt to show* he achieved.

But words fail us. If we say "achieved," we suggest an award for an athletic event, a business venture, or an acting performance. The word is entirely this-worldly; it is goal-oriented; and so with all the metaphors. Jesus is the "re-purchaser" or "redeemer," buying us out of hock with coined pain. He is the "good Samaritan," the wretched, outcast enemy of Israel who alone is willing to care for the everyman, beaten and left for dead on the road to Jericho, binding his wounds, anointing him, giving him a cloak, taking him to the hotel to recover, paying his way (while the priest, approved of God, passes by the hapless victim of robbery). Jesus is our "advocate," arguing in our defense for mercy at the bar of God, while the prosecuting attorney (*Satan*, the accuser in *Job*) presses his suit for justice to the line, righteousness to the plummet. Jesus is the "best friend," the old war buddy who is willing to take a bullet in battle to shield a fellow soldier from death. He is the "deliverer," rescuing his maiden congregation from the usurping devil. He is the "mediator," settling a dispute between two intractable parties: God and sinners. He makes atonement (at-one-ment), reconciling the rebellious children with their loving but estranged father. He is the "scapegoat" of Yom Kippur (the day of atonement) who, having had the sins of Israel laid upon his head by the high priest, is carried out to the wilderness to perish; and he is also the goat, the burnt offering to atone for Israel's collective sins. The dominating metaphor, however, is Christ as victim, ritual sacrifice, and tragic protagonist—the Lamb of God.

René Girard has spelled out for us, in no uncertain terms, the terrifying implications of accepting the model of the lamb slain. In *Job: The Victim of His People*, a deceptively slender volume, Girard paints contrasting pictures of Job's God (the God of victims) and the God of Job's accusers (the God of the persecutors). Girard is convinced that these are not merely two faces of the same God, but rather a false God, made in the image of mimetic human violence, vs. a true God, who refuses to participate in violent retribution, one who appears weak or impotent, but who can walk no other path because reciprocal violence is a ceaseless, escalating terror that takes away moral agency, replacing it with an enforced righteousness that is truly perverse and Satanic.

Reminding us that "like all the Greek gods, Zeus is a god of vengeance and violence," Girard insists that the true God must be categorically different, for "if Job's cause were to triumph through violence (just for once, the innocent . . . avenged and the wicked punished), how would it differ from the justice of Eliphaz or Elihu" (Job's so-called friends who equate misfortune with the just punishment of God)?[15] What this means, as far as the metaphors for Jesus' mission on Earth are concerned, is that the sacrificial victim is absolutely *unwilling* to turn and rend those who wish to slit his throat and drain his blood onto the stones of the altar. The image of the *Lamb* of God is, for all its good qualities, an insufficient metaphor to describe what the victim must undergo. A lamb is young, innocent, incapable of fighting off the high priest (chief sacrificer) who will spill its blood. This is the chief weakness of the medieval mystery play *Abraham and Isaac* (Brome); Isaac is a spindly, sweet ragamuffin of a little boy, hardly able to "consent" to his own sacrifice. The story in Genesis more likely concerns the test of Isaac, not Abraham, for, as the apocryphal Abraham texts suggest, Abraham at one time was on the point of being sacrificed by his father, Terah. This noncanonical narrative explains Abraham's willingness to surrender all things to God (leaving Ur, his family, his Sumerian religion, his inheritance, and his personal safety for the life of a desert chieftain abiding in tents). As important as that alternate tradition is, it is also important to realize that Isaac is not some ruddy youth with rosy cheeks and hairless face, but rather an adult undergoing the supreme test of allegiance to God; he could overpower his old father, could run and decide upon retribution against a father whose desert deity demands human sacrifice (the ultimate sign of mimetic violence). It is extremely important that it is *not* a lamb caught in the thicket, to be offered in place of Isaac, whose father's hand is stayed by the angel of God; rather, it is a *ram* (Gen. 22:13), a horned male adult that could lower its head and take aim at poor Abraham's midsection had it not been caught in the branches.

The whole point here is that Israel's God does not demand the sacrifice of innocent children to satisfy the disorder, imbalance, or injustice in the cosmos. Thus Jesus *chooses* not to turn and rend those who deliver him to the murderers; he is a conscious, aware adult who could rebel, exchange blows, cross swords with his enemies. Girard insists that any other construct of the God of victims is unworthy of the Jesus of the New Covenant. It is indeed the Romans and the Sadducees who slay Jesus. This is not his weakness, but a pattern he offers us of a God who will die for a good cause, but will never murder for a good cause: "Jesus enjoins men to imitate him and seek the glory that comes from God, instead of that which comes from men. He shows them that mimetic rivalries can lead only to murders and death."[16]

Yet Girard cannot escape the heroic Jesus, which narrative runs in and out of the victim narrative. One cannot simply ignore that Jesus makes a scourge of rope, becoming the scourge of God or the sword in God's right hand, executing righteous judgment during his mortality, and cleansing the temple (the fulfillment of the Baptist's promise that the Messiah will thoroughly purge the threshing floor). Jesus is capable of genuine righteous indignation; the scourge was meant to whip the moneychangers as the wages of their sins against the helpless, poverty-stricken suppliants who were shortchanged when buying unblemished animals for the burnt offerings (which creatures had their throats slit, their blood drained out, and their bodies burnt to make a "sweet savour" to rise up to the heavens and into God's nostrils). It does no good at all to assume that Jesus made a scourge of ropes simply to overturn the moneychangers' tables—no, he clearly meant to clear out the rabble, "a den of thieves," from the outer courts of the temple precinct.

In terms of the narrative, moreover, Jesus as sacrificial victim is not to be confused with the Jesus who is resurrected. The tragic death loses its significance if the offering is not altogether permanent and final. *Tragedy*, literally the "goat song," is that mournful ode the chorus offers as the goat is led forth to the sacrifice. Jesus is a tragic protagonist but is utterly sinless (in the sense that he lives the Mosaic law to perfection, never dropping so much as a jot—Hebrew *yoth*, the tiniest of consonants, shaped like a single closing quotation mark). For example, once Macduff slays Macbeth, we know Macbeth will not rise from the dead two or three days later. Though Lear regrets his folly, neither will he come back to life. Jesus, paying for the folly of all mortals, must remain dead to satisfy the demands Paul confronts us with in Romans 6.23: "The wages of sin is death."

The resurrected Jesus is altogether heroic, for he *conquers* death. But orthodox Christianity notes that Jesus, during those three days (really closer to two) between his death and resurrection, descends into Hades (the Greek underworld, as opposed to the dark pit of the Hebrew *sheol*), a story preserved in the vivid medieval "harrowing of hell." It is thus tempting to see this *descensus* as heroic rather than tragic, for, of course, the same journey is made by Orpheus, Aeneas, Odysseus, Perseus, and other heroes. His descent will torment the demons, the *nefilim* or "fallen" archons or Watchers of the Ethiopian Enoch text, and then he will rescue the shades unjustly held captive in Tartarus, establishing or at least legitimizing Paradise, the place of rest for the ancient worthies, such as the Trojan prince Hector or father Abraham. His descent and re-ascension to the outer sphere of our mundane, sublunary sphere provides the mirror image, the binary opposition of Lucifer's attempt to mount to the heavens to unseat God, only to be cast out of heaven, brought low to the dust, shaking the nations. And indeed, for the overwhelming majority of Christians, Paradise and Tartarus are the Judgment Day—they are heaven and hell. The survival of the spirit after death, despite orthodox doctrines of the physical resurrection, is the source of hope for "eternal life" with God. Thus, for example, though the Mormon *credo* or *Articles of Faith* argues for physical resurrection, for Mormons celestial resurrection is connected to exaltation—humans joining the divine family as kings and priests, the essence of ascension and translation. However, the hope of salvation in cultural terms is a separate construct that assures all people of a life after death, a Paradise for the good and well-intentioned and innocent, and a Tartarus for the benighted, the sinner, and the demoniac.

Thus Mormons have far more in common with Catholics in the cultural perceptions of their churches' theologies, than with Protestants, with whom they are often still classified. It is noteworthy that both Catholics and Mormons practice proxy salvation for the dead: Mormons perform baptisms, ordinations, lustrations, even marriages for the dead, through proxy services in their temples, with the goal of offering the dead what they were denied in life, for whatever reasons, to give them light and peace in Paradise instead of darkness and misery in Tartarus (the Mormons call it the "spirit prison"), while Catholics offer masses for the dead, votive candles for the saints' intercession for their loved ones' eventual release from the rigors of spiritual purgation, and last rites (extreme unction) and confession to the dying, as well as burial in consecrated ground for all excepting suicides (self-slaughter, the only unforgivable mortal sin). Jesus is heroic in his descent into the underworld, but only his death as tragic protagonist allows such an extension of his heroics into what is essentially the cult of the dead, with Paradise being only the newer part of the neighborhood for heroes and poets whose only choice of abode before that time was the Tartarus of watery shades, with Hades–Pluto as king and god. Even after Paradise (the Garden of Eden for dead Christians) evolves, Jesus cannot remain *there* as ruler, for his truly heroic agenda of ascension and translation stares at us from the first chapter of Acts and from the Mount of Transfiguration.

Jesus is of course not a Macbeth or a Lear; he is, in the words of John's Gospel, "the true vine," suggesting the mythology of planting and harvesting, of the life cycle; and death, the wages of sin, is a corrective to the false vine, Tammuz–Dionysius. Jesus is not self-interested, at least not as a sacrificial or tragic victim. Though theologically a late development, the idea that Jesus is really a human manifestation of Yahweh's presence in the world is part of this tragic model, in which God must *lower* himself, not raise himself, in order to be a human being.* That is, Gilgamesh is a man gazing upward toward his heavenly origins, but Jesus as the Word, the *logos* or *d'bir*, is a manifestation of the Great All, placed upon the Earth, Yahweh's footstool. The gods are Other; humans cannot be gods—that is the ancient Sumerian rule that governs Western theology for thousands of years, and the hard lesson Gilgamesh, the first failed translated being, must accept.

Jesus is meant to come to Earth with but one purpose in mind: to offer himself as a human sacrifice as the ultimate statement of his mortal but unblemished nature. His expiation begins as soon as his status as an infant is changed from Blake's innocent "little lamb" to the lamb to be slaughtered: "Behold the Lamb of God," says the Baptist early in Christ's ministry (John 1:36). Jesus is marked for death even as

---

* Joseph Smith's Book of Mormon depicts a vision in which a young initiate into the mysteries, named Nephi, is asked by his angelic guide, "Knowest thou the condescension of God?" to which Nephi, whose perceptions of Yahweh are vague, answers only that he knows that God "loveth his children." Later the angel allows Nephi to see the baby Jesus, whose "condescension" into mortality lies some 600 years in the future (1 Nephi 11:16–22).

he is circumcised the eighth day after his birth; to his mother, Simeon the prophet predicts, "Yea, a sword shall pierce through thy own soul also" (Luke 2:35). He is hounded by his own prophecies of his destruction, by strange antetypes in Jonah and the rejected prophets, and by the death of the Baptist and the storm of controversy that surrounds his ministry—as well as unmistakable death threats from the priests and Sadducees.*

Christ, the victim of his people, is concerned with matters of philosophy and the human predicament completely at odds with the heroic narratives—even in such characters as Enoch and Elijah, though their narratives dwell at length on bizarre cosmology and visionary experience. Christ in this portrait is consistent with the great tragic protagonists—Oedipus, Lear, and others—who teach not deliverance from suffering but offer formulae for enduring suffering, with death as the ultimate deliverer. The Beatitudes, whose beginning word "blessed" means "happy," are meant to be intensely ironic, for the conditions mentioned, such as poverty, mourning over the death of loved ones, hunger and thirst, persecution, passivity in the face of violence, and wrongful prosecution,† are precisely those which the Messiah, as envisioned by ancient students of Isaiah, was sent to alleviate. The miracles, campaign-like foreshadowings of how life would be under Jesus as king, remain only figurative, of course, because Jesus never became king of Israel; the fact of his death is what undoes a literal reading of the Beatitudes or other such teachings, and that same death forces a rereading of the literal narrative to establish workable figurative interpretations. Thus Augustine's attempts at

---

* John records that after Jesus raised Lazarus from the dead: "Then from that day forth they [the priests and clearly the Sadducees, though the text mentions priests and *Pharisees*, showing a bizarre, later narrative convolution scholars have debated for years] took counsel together for to put him to death. Jesus therefore walked no more openly among the Jews . . ." (John 11:53–54).

† Phrases are clearly added to the Beatitudes to soften their impact, such as poor *in spirit*, hunger and thirst *after righteousness*, and persecuted *for righteousness' sake*; in such additions we find evidence of one narrative voice intruding on another, correcting and interpolating the heroic voice of one who promises *real* food to a cosmic abstraction of spiritual food. The miracle of loaves and fishes is thus evidence of the distinct heroic translation narrative, while the attempt common among theologians to read the feeding of the five thousand as a symbolic or allegorical narrative statement is consistent with the contrary narrative, in which Jesus offers the Samaritan woman not real water from the well, but "living" water—heavenly, spiritual light, with Christ himself as the spiritual "bread of life."

allegorizing the scriptures come less from the low regard in which he held biblical diction or rhetoric than from a need to reknit narrative binary oppositions at the figurative or allegorical level.

The Crucifixion of Christ is inherently tragic, despite the alternative narrative of the Resurrection. Christ's path to Calvary is appropriately called the *via dolorosa*, the Way of Sorrows, because it marks the end of the hopeful times and the beginning of real sorrows. Nothing is more ironic to this ending of the life of Christ than his declaration, at the beginning of his ministry, "Take my yoke upon you . . . for my yoke is easy, and my burden is light" (Matt. 11:29–30), for in fact he had to take their yokes upon himself and, following the sacrificial narrative, those yokes were indescribably heavy.

Despite the prophecies and symbolism, it is clear from the second narrative that Jesus neither wanted nor expected to die, especially as a humiliated pawn of the Romans; he was in hiding from the time of Lazarus's resuscitation to the moment of his crucifixion, arranging for meetings through third parties, cautioning even disciples not to tell anyone of his actions. That he might suffer is not antithetical to the heroic model, for that is consistent with the challenges facing the hero, but the suffering cannot be shirked, but must be approached fearlessly, recklessly, as the medieval poem declared of its heroic thane, Jesus:

> Then the young Hero stripped himself . . . strong and stouthearted. He climbed on the high gallows, bold in the sight of many, when he would free mankind.[17]

The meek, fearful Jesus of Gethsemane, who begs God to let another take the cup, is no Theseus, taking the land route to Athens in the hope of more exciting and heroic challenges. More likely, this is a very anti-heroic God, forced by his mission to partake of sufferings and death intrinsically repugnant and horrifying to someone inherently unable to be harmed, much less killed—he will do what no god has ever done (except for the uncontrollable Dionysius, whose life and teachings were a constant threat to the Olympians, and whose death and return mark the dying vine, then the new leaves in spring): experience death as *mortals* experience it. One could even picture Zeus taking a fall at some distant point, but Death?* Even Prometheus,

---

*I grant that Osiris dies (murdered, really), but his death and return are clearly tied to the ebb and flow of the Nile, yet another fertility symbol.

though captive and tortured, could not die. So the very earth and heavens would shake as the natural cosmic order was violated—a God would suffer natural death.

That the death was a political event is undeniable; Jesus was a threat to the puppet regime in Israel, and ultimately a threat to Rome itself, for although Jesus came from an unimportant if pugnacious Roman possession, Rome would not soon forget the power of a mere slave—Spartacus—to challenge the might of even the Roman legions. That Jesus expected opposition to his bid for kingship is clear; that he would be betrayed into the hands of Israel's greatest enemy, Rome, he likely did not anticipate—at least so it appears from the narratives, in which Jesus either has nothing to say or allegorizes his entire Messianic mission into a sort of Essenic battle of Darkness and Light.* In fact, the Romans never even enter the narrative except in the most tangential way, and Jesus actually seems to tolerate the Roman authority in his famous "render unto Caesar" speech and in the healing of the centurion's servant. Bible critics have long contended that the New Testament writers, in order to curry favor with Roman authority, purposefully subverted history so the blame for the Crucifixion could be directed entirely against the Jews, but of course this sort of fiddling with the original source narratives would have occurred long after the fall of Jerusalem, when Christians, now mostly Gentiles rather than Jews or God-fearers, wished to divorce themselves from the Jewish origins of Jesus and the Christian religion.† But the shifting of blame for all

---

* Although in historical fact it is unlikely that anyone heard what Jesus said at his trial, since the disciples, except for the clandestine Nicodemus and Joseph of Arimathæa, were doubtless not important enough to be allowed to attend. Jesus' Israelite followers have always been considered to be the *ame ha-aretz*, the earthy people, many descendants of Babylonian transplants, who anciently were forced to settle in Galilee.

† My most recent realization in this regard came when I noticed, one Easter Sunday, the positively perverse ritual of having *ham* at Easter; my guess is that replacing the Israelite custom of lamb with the meat most repugnant to Jewish sensibilities must be a very ancient act, dating at least to the Middle Ages, perhaps earlier even than the Dark Ages. Pope John Paul II has recognized formally what Shakespeare had already exposed in *The Merchant of Venice*, that Catholics were willing to mistreat Jews even if it meant gross hypocrisy and even transgression on their part, in order to distance Jews from fellowship; the pope recently acknowledged the Jewish origins of both Jesus and Christianity, even crossing the Tiber to be the first pope to visit a Jewish synagogue in Rome that had been there when St. Peter was preaching in Rome. (See Carl Bernstein and Marco Politi, *His Holiness: John Paul II and the Hidden History of Our Time* [New York: Doubleday], 1996.)

of Jesus' troubles from the Saduccees, undoubtedly the real culprits in the original narrative, to the Pharisees, who, from all available evidence, were Jesus' only important support in Jerusalem,* suggests further the disillusionment that must have attended the apostles' and even Jesus' realization that not only did the Saduccees† not want him to be king, but were ready to betray a Jewish brother to Israel's worst enemies. Not willing to admit the *prima facie* rejection of Jesus as Messiah, the Gospel narrative shifts, alters, and allegorizes the whole event to soften the genuine historical and narrative reality that Jesus was completely rejected as candidate for King and Messiah.

The next narrative hurdle is the actual death of Jesus. All the Gospels, but most specifically John, are at pains to describe completely and precisely the exact circumstances of the death of Jesus. Why? For one thing, it is imperative that Jesus be known to have died in order for his resurrection to have any meaning or singularity at all. But what is odd is not that everyone claims that Jesus was not resurrected, but rather that they claim *he never died in the first place*. Such accounts survive not only among the nonbelievers but also among the gnostics and are actually preserved, elliptically or through negation, in the Gospel accounts themselves—thus the incredible excess of the soldier's stabbing Jesus

---

* Consider that Nicodemus and Joseph of Arimathæa, the only two Jerusalem dignitaries preserved in Christian tradition in any favorable light, were Pharisees, both friends to Jesus. Pharisees also believed in the physical resurrection and in the purity of Israel's law and religion, of which they felt themselves the caretakers. The Pharisees held numerical superiority in voting in the Sanhedrin, which may explain why the trial of Jesus, reports of which were doubtless scanty, was thought orchestrated by Pharisees, when there is every reason to believe the Saduccees, with their Roman connections and allegience to the royal house of Herod and to the priesthood currently in power, had more motive, opportunity, and means (they were, as a rule, wealthier than the Pharisees) to orchestrate Jesus' betrayal.

† Graves and Podro, in *The Nazarene Gospel Restored*, are convinced Paul was working for the high priests and Sadducees in his quest to control the spread of the apostles' message—not to the Gentiles, but to congregations of Jews in other lands and cities, where the high priest's demands might command respect. Thus the troops that helped Paul on the road to Damascus were not Roman guards, as some might think, but members of the temple guard—all Jews attached directly to the authority of the high priest. Graves and Podro even go so far as to insist Paul's original name Saul was actually a Jewish transliteration of the Latin name Solon, thus undercutting Paul's claim that he was a Pharisee himself, sitting at the feet of the great Gamaliel.

through the side to make sure he was dead.* The point is not that the event didn't happen exactly that way, for it certainly could have, but why make a narrative issue of it? It works against the Old Testament prophecies, sending the Gospel narrative scurrying around the Old Testament in search of some comparable antetype. To mention the sword in the side when it is certain that the Romans had had generations of practice crucifying criminals (crucifixion is a form of *execution*, after all) seems ludicrous, unless the writer of the narrative fears some ugly rumor—something a lot worse than merely spiriting the body away (in fact, sword wounds are a poor preventative against grave robbing). Rather, the sword is an example of narrative *overkill*, something like one might find in a really bad Indian attack scene in a Cooper novel. Certainly Christianity as it survives today would have no reason to contend that Jesus did not die, yet besides the disciples (many of whom ran away) who witnessed the Crucifixion (again, we are speaking of the narrative event, not the historical event) are Mary, John, and others, including at least one Roman, who fears he has slain a god. Certainly no Jewish leader who despised Jesus in life would question his death or even fail to ascertain it, as John's record attests rather well, so we are left only with those who knew Jesus well but didn't witness, didn't expect, and afterwards didn't believe the reality of his death by crucifixion. The Gospel narratives that survive insist upon his death in part for the narrative foundation of the Resurrection, but given the fact that everyone in the entire empire knew what crucifixion was and did, the scene with the sword (and indeed other aspects of the death narrative) indicates that the scenes described were to convince certain followers of Jesus that in no way could he have survived death.

---

* I should add at this point that we see here the limits of metaphor. The lamb or the goat has its throat slit (consistent with Abraham's near-sacrifice of Isaac); its blood is drained into a bowl and is sprinkled on the altar or even the mercy seat of the ark. Jesus is not unblemished (scourging); he is sheared (his clothing is gambled away, imitating the chopping up of the burnt offering); he does not have his throat slit, but is stabbed in the side after death (of dubious symbolic value); he is not bound, as with an offering (but is nailed to the cross); he is not slain within the temple precincts upon the altar (the cross is simply an instrument of Roman torture, though Joseph, in a stirring legend, catches Jesus' blood in the bowl or "cup" of the Last Supper, thus imitating the priestly rite); and he is assuredly not burned after his death.

The "swoon" theory, that Jesus was out cold for a while but was revived later, has been justly belittled by devout Christian theologians, and Graves and Podro's efforts to "revive" the theory are pitiable, even silly. But what everyone ignores is that the ultimate narrative origin of such theories, which is as old as the narratives of Jesus' death and resurrection, has to be, not nonbelievers ridiculing resurrection, a doctrine valued only by the Pharisees,* but those who really wished Jesus had *not* died. Perhaps these were the disciples who, out of fear, abandoned Jesus in his extremity, then, shamefaced, came back to see if he were still alive and ready to be the Messiah—as good an explanation for Judas's actions as anything one might imagine. He thought Jesus was the Messiah, and realizing his horrible miscalculation, killed himself out of grief for betraying a friend and brother whom he assumed was deluded and had deceived others.

The utter fear and desolation of the disciples comes out strongly in the narrative. These emotions again serve a dual purpose: first, they make the idea of hallucination or mass hysteria concerning the resurrection of Jesus improbable because expectation and anticipation are gone altogether; furthermore, these dismal feelings, when contrasted with the utter joy, absolute conviction, and utter fearlessness of the early chapters of Acts, lay a narrative foundation that admits no "figurative" or philosophical change in the apostles' outlook, and liberal theologians look ridiculous when they suggest that a bunch of lower-class locals such as Peter, Andrew, James, and John could come to any kind of abstract, philosophical inner light about Jesus' ethics apart from a genuine witness that Jesus was truly resurrected.

Now while I personally am devout on the point of Jesus' divinity and resurrection, I do not mean to imply here that the second narrative makes only one rhetorical outcome possible. Indeed, a second context for the fear and disappointment after Jesus' death centers on the disciples' utter shock that Jesus *could* die or that their religious cause could be in any danger of fragmentation.

---

* The reason its value is confined to the Pharisees is that resurrection as preached in that era had nothing to do with living forever in the flesh, but only with being raised up so one could be judged for the sins of the flesh while in the flesh. Jesus' resurrection is consistent with the raising up of the great martyrs who reign with the Messiah for a thousands years, a distinctly earthly paradise designed to re-create the garden Adam was forced to vacate—a thousand years being an appropriate reign for the second Adam, for the original lived nearly that long, but a modest reign indeed when compared to that of Gilgamesh, as recorded in the Sumerian king lists.

We read in John 19:38 that Joseph of Arimathaea makes burial arrangements "secretly for fear of the Jews." Mary Magdalene sees no other explanation of the body's disappearance from the tomb than that some parties "have taken away my Lord, and I know not where they have laid him" (John 20:13), an indication of how rushed and secretive the burial was. The disciples hide after Jesus' death, with "the doors . . . shut where the disciples were assembled for fear of the Jews" (John 20:19). Thomas, whose name is preserved as the Doubter, must be certain it is the same Jesus who died, ironically checking for the marks of the stabbing and the crucifixion, not simply to prove the Resurrection occurred, but to be certain it was Jesus who truly died and was crucified. Peter is shaken so terribly by fear that three times he denies knowing Jesus (a narrative device to prove Peter's fear and rejection were not accidental [John 18:17–27]). Judas of course commits suicide, despondent that Jesus did not assert his power before the Sanhedrin. When the women bring spices to anoint the body, they "fle[e] from the sepulchre" when they find the empty tomb, "for they trembled and were amazed: neither said they any thing to any man; for they were afraid" (Mark 16:8). The fearful disciples, who "mourned and wept," refuse to believe Mary Magdalene when she declares Jesus risen (Mark 16:10–11). In fact, no disciple believes the witnesses, whoever they are, about the Resurrection. The most incredible statement is at the end of Matthew: even when Jesus appeared to the disciples at a mountain (the place of ascension, if we accept the harmony of the Gospels on this point) and the disciples worshipped him, "some doubted" (28:17). In fact, in the well-known tale of the two disciples on the road to Emmæus, they are unable to recognize Jesus at all till he breaks bread with them. What do these things suggest, beyond their devout but nonetheless nagging inconsistency concerning Jesus' physical reality as a resurrected being?

I would like to propose that these experiences are the fragments of the tale of the *death* of the heroic Jesus of the first Gospel narrative. It takes only a little effort to see the doubt, the disbelief, and the confusion not as narrative threads of the Resurrection, but of unwillingness to believe that Jesus had really died. The inability to recognize Jesus is the fate of those in hiding during the Crucifixion and the subsequent daring but risky burial. The refusal to believe the women's account—the same three women who witness the Crucifixion, by the way (Mother Mary, Mary the sister of Martha, and Salome)—is, speaking only of the narrative thread, the account of Jesus' horrible death, explaining Thomas's eerie statement that he will not believe anything happened until he can feel the marks in Jesus' hands and thrust his hand in the side of the body. Here was a man so attached to the invincibility of the Messiah (a being destined to ascend and be translated, the king who, as the second Gilgamesh, attains what is denied the Sumerian hero) that he refused to believe Jesus could even be *taken captive*, let alone be *killed*. This key event, the death of Jesus, coupled with his rejection as king by the Jerusalem political establishment, was the horrid fragmenting of a heroic narrative which should have ended (and actually does end narratologically) with Jesus' ascension to heaven, with his having been made king of Israel and having bravely endured trials and suffering before bursting his own bonds and undoing his enemies' plans. He would be gone for but a single generation, so many alive at his departure would see him return to wreak vengeance on the Romans and restore the dignity of the throne of David, as well as to give Israel and the God-fearing Gentiles an Edenic life denied them through the fall of Adam (and of Enkidu and Gilgamesh). All this heroic vision is undone by the death of Jesus.

Jesus as Suffering Servant

Between the heroic and tragic narratives of Jesus is a third narrative, not a pastiche of the other two, but a separate and distinct narrative. It is actually bittersweet, not rising as high as ascension and translation, but not sinking as low as ritual sacrifice. Jesus is said to be the Suffering Servant of Isaiah 52–53; (I have purposely removed the elements that are either heroic or tragic):

> Behold, my servant shall deal prudently, he shall be exalted and extolled, and be very high.
> As many were astonied at thee; his visage was so marred more than any man, and his form more than the sons of men:
> ... the kings shall shut their mouths at him. ...
> ... he hath no form nor comeliness; ... no beauty that we should desire him.
> He is despised and rejected of men; a man of sorrows, and acquainted with grief : ...
> Surely he hath borne our griefs, and carried our sorrows: yet we did esteem him stricken, smitten of God, and afflicted.
> But he was wounded for our transgressions, he was bruised for our iniquities: the chastisement of our peace was upon him; and with his stripes we are healed.

... and the Lord hath laid on him the iniquity of us all.

He was oppressed, and he was afflicted, yet he opened not his mouth: he is brought as a lamb to the slaughter, and as a sheep before her shearers is dumb, so he openeth not his mouth.

He was taken from prison and from judgment: and who shall declare his generation? ...

Yet is pleased the Lord to bruise him; ... thou shalt make his soul [*nephesh*—the physical body?] an offering for sin, he shall see his seed, he shall prolong his days, and the pleasure of the Lord shall prosper in the hand.

He shall see of the travail of his soul, and shall be satisfied: by his knowledge shall my righteous servant justify many; ...

Therefore will I divide him a portion with the great, and he shall divide the spoil with the strong. ...

To purposely blot out the references to the servant's death may seem like unconscionable prooftexting, but bear with me for a moment. The servant is consistently tied to the Messiah, but the dominant argument is that the Suffering Servant is merely a personification of Israel; and it is by no means a universal judgment that the servant must be as well the Messiah. The one thing on which all the rabbis are agreed is that this is a mortal being, not a god, and that he has a long reign, but is altogether human, and if we divorce the servant from the Messiah, we also lose the motif of ascension–translation, which a midrash on the servant declares is exalted above Moses, Abraham, and the angels. The servant, no longer one with the Messiah, becomes a separate icon and will die just as any other of the fortunate humans who die of natural causes.

Another narrative strategy the rabbis use is to personify both the northern kingdom (Israel—Joseph and the ten tribes) and the southern kingdom (Judah, Levi, some of Benjamin) as Messiah ben Joseph and Messiah ben David, I assume on the strength of their nations' collective "anointing" as God's chosen people. But one can also argue that two messiahs were to be anticipated, gathering Israel and reestablishing the greatness of David's and Solomon's glorious reigns, one dying as innocent victim and sufferer, the other inheriting the progeny, glory, and long reign. Commenting on the complexity of the rabbinical readings, which often seem to be in part counter-arguments to the assertion that Jesus could be Messiah and/or Suffering Servant, the Rev. E. B. Pusey, the brilliant Oxford Hebraist and student of the midrashes, remarks:

Some Rabbinic Jews thought it was the righteous among them, or any just man; some, that it was Jeremiah, or Isaiah himself; some, Hezekiah; one, Job; some, the seed of David in exile and the Messiah, so that all the expressions of contempt refer to the seed of David in exile, and all the glorious things to the Messiah; some divided the sufferings and the glory, in like way, between the Messiah ben Joseph and the Messiah ben David."[18]

My purpose in dealing with the Suffering Servant is to demonstrate the likelihood that the heroic, messianic narrative ending in ascension–translation is discrete narratologically from either the tragic narrative or that of the Suffering Servant, showing the self-sufficiency in all of them. Indeed all three are myths of origin, but in the quotation above, I draw your attention to Job (mentioned by Eliezer the German).[19] Girard's treatise on Job is particularly important to illustrating a high-born Israelite who has fame, a long reign as a chieftain, a great progeny, yet is a mortal, whom God tests in an attempt to vindicate a righteous man before the onslaught of the "accuser," Satan. Job's body is covered with boils, then scarred from his scraping them with shards of pottery; his wealth and status, even his family, are dashed to pieces. His friends turn on him, and his wife pleads with him to "curse God and die"; yet, though he begs God for an explanation, Job neither reviles nor repudiates Jehovah, but rather cries out in distress for God to alleviate his affliction. The narrative ends with Job's days being lengthened, his wealth and family restored (a vexing point, since we like to think our children are irreplaceable!). We assume he dies of old age, leaving a grand earthly and literary legacy, but not only does he *not* ascend to heaven to be translated, but Yahweh chides him for his lack of divine knowledge ("Where were you when I was creating everything, when the stars sang, and the angels shouted? Well? Speak up, if you know so much!" [Job 38—my poetic license]). Job is actually the ideal model for the third narrative, one requiring neither harmonizing with other narratives nor disparagement because it is human-centered.

Neither ascension nor death are at the center of this narrative: Jesus is born naturally (Graves in *King Jesus* implies, gratuitously I think, that the rumors of Mary's indiscretion are valid), is the dutiful apprentice to his father's traditional craft of carpentry, but has the intuitive perception of his mother (who, in the apocryphal Gospels, is a ward of the temple before her marriage). Jesus is a quick study, and from his youth turns his attention toward study and contemplation. His lineage suggests his fitness as a legitimate heir to the throne occupied by Roman puppets (the Herodians), but he is dogged his whole life by those who fear his popularity and possible usurpation of the throne. He falls in love with a rich man's sister (Mary of Magdala, sister of Lazarus and Martha of Beth-ani), marries her at a ceremony in Cana (expected of any rabbi, heir, or stable, useful citizen of Israel), then gathers an embryo government about him, including twelve princes to govern the traditional lands and tribes of ancient Israel, then seventy others who will serve as judging elders, a Sanhedrin). He takes his case to the people, promising the deliverance from Rome and from poverty of body and spirit, if they will accept his cause. He has friends among the Pharisees (Nicodemus, Joseph of Arimathaea), a brother (James) who is a priest with temple connections, and the support of young zealots and friends (Lazarus, Simon Zealotes). His enemies are proximately the Sadducees, ultimately the Romans. He performs the miracles expected of a man destined to hold all three sacred offices (prophet, priest, and king). His triumphal entry to Jerusalem is overwhelmingly successful, for he takes symbolic stances as priest (cleansing the temple), prophet (announcing the fate of Israel if they reject him), and king (to which the Jews will assent). He becomes king, but Rome's hegemony will not abide Jesus' attempting to overthrow Roman occupation. For his failure to destroy Rome (an impossible dream, one must admit), he is publicly punished and humiliated either by Annas and the priests and the temple guard, or by the Roman soldiers under Pilate, or by both. He is scourged, crucified, but not killed, but makes sufficient atonement for his failure in that he remains on the throne, although a figurehead, scarred for life, but gaining the approbation of the temple priests for his willingness to be publicly humiliated and scourged, and the love and respect of the *'amay ha'aretz* (common Israelites, people of the earth, as styled by Harry Emerson Fosdick). And in his old age he establishes a bloodline and progeny to insure the "eternal" survival of David's throne, restoring a measure of Israel's lost glory. Perhaps, like Moses, Jesus, in old age, is "buried by the hand of God," leaving rumors of the miraculous in his wake.

It is easy to imagine I have been watching too much of *The Last Temptation of Christ*, or reading too much *King Jesus*, but my ideas here grow naturally (and predate my encounter with either of these productions) out of the human side of Jesus, the part of him we know and love—the man who took time for little children, the Good Shepherd or Samaritan. The ending to this narrative, which assumes Israel accepted Jesus as their king, obviously did not play out that way, but the narrative of Jesus as Suffering Servant would have ended this way, for the elliptical end of this narrative is anticipated in the *tendencies* of the other, more accessible parts of the narrative.

The Results of Imposition of the Resurrection

The last point to consider about the heroic and tragic narratives themselves is what I believe must be the final narrative addition to the story of Jesus, one that is neither the heroic nor the tragic narrative, but rather the *comedic* narrative (comedic in the sense of "happy ending," *not* in the sense of "humorous"). This is the Resurrection, a condition not possible in the ascension–translation narrative, for death itself is not part of the construct and is inappropriate, even antithetical to the tragic narrative. Yet the Resurrection is a unique attempt to resolve the real narrative problem of the anticipation created by the first narrative and undercut by the second. That is, a resurrection narrative is essential to reconcile the experiences of the disheartened heroicists and the believers in Christ as incarnate deity. In the first case, the suffering of Christ should not have resulted in violent death, for that was not requisite even for the "Suffering Servant," and in order to be the Messiah, Christ must defeat his enemies, become king, and ascend and be translated. In the latter case, only resuscitation of the god is sufficient to demonstrate the divinity of the creature who has died, for divinity is essential for any sacrificial lamb whose sacrifice is to save *all humanity*. If, on the other hand, Jesus is simply offering, as Girard suggests, an example for us to emulate or imitate, it is not clear to me that a god is essential to that end.

The necessity of a physical resurrection should be clear from a narrative viewpoint; the narrative must be consistent with all the narratives of dying gods, for Jesus is just such a god (at least for devout Christians).* Readers expect Jesus to be restored just as Dionysius, and the narrator in John is aware of that when he has Jesus declare himself a greater god than Dionysius: "I am the true vine, and my Father is the husbandman" (John 15:1). Following this declaration Jesus spends fully eight verses to expound the idea of himself as the vine, the disciples as the

---

* I do not wish to imply here that Jehovah's Witnesses, to name but one group, are not Christians because they may not find Jesus co-equal with God; that is a form of demonizing I hope to avoid.

branches, the works they do as the fruit, and God as the husbandman. In addition, the New Testament, but especially the Gospel of John, contains grape, vine, and wine imagery, as well as bread imagery, which calls to mind Demeter, the other dying and resurrecting fertility god. The last supper is a mystery rite for a god, and Jesus' first miracle was to turn water to excellent wine (which C. S. Lewis, in *Miracles*, insisted was a shortcut of natural processes, not an undermining of Mother Nature!).[20] Jesus suffered persecution, much as Dionysius, and the parting of his garment is a symbol of the tearing apart of Dionysius by his enemies (preserved also in the breaking of bread). The Holy Ghost, the center of life and power in the Gospel of John, is a Christian version of the spirit of inspiration from Dionysius, which gave us the great tragic dramas associated with the festival of Dionysius. Such gods, who die on the vine, must be restored to the same or better condition as when alive.

The idea that Jesus was resurrected is thus at the heart of embracing him as a god, for it is the absolute proof that he was in fact a god, and not just a heroic man whose mission went awry. The Resurrection narrative is, however, best preserved in Mark and has its greatest impact in its original form, *sans* ecstatic visions and additional visitations:

> And when the sabbath was past, Mary Magdalene, and Mary the mother of James, and Salome, had bought sweet spices, that they might come and anoint him.
> And very early in the morning the first day of the week, they came unto the sepulchre at the rising of the sun.
> And they said among themselves, Who shall roll us away the stone from the door of the sepulchre?
> And when they looked, they saw that the stone was rolled away: for it was very great.
> And entering into the sepulchre, they saw a young man sitting on the right side, clothed in a long white garment; and they were affrighted.
> And he saith unto them, Be not affrighted: Ye seek Jesus of Nazareth, which was crucified: he is risen; he is not here: behold the place where they laid him.
> But go your way, tell his disciples and Peter that he goeth before you into Galilee: there shall ye see him, as he said unto you.
> And they went out quickly, and fled from the sepulchre; for they trembled and were amazed: neither said they any thing to any man; for they were afraid.
> (Mark 16:1–8)

Students of the New Testament will notice that I left off the last section of this chapter from Mark, which catalogues, in summary form, the various appearances of Jesus. I am convinced this is a later addition to Mark, and that the original narrative ends at verse. The power of Mark's narrative is its internal consistency and its absolute grounding in the real world. The "angel" (messenger) inside the tomb is much more likely an Essene than an angel, into which ethereal form, unfortunately, other Gospel narratives transform him. Jesus is gone from the tomb, leaving the eloquent testimony of the empty tomb and throwing the argument into the court of the cynics and nonbelievers. The text shows surprised and fearful women who, without planning, fail to consider the task awaiting them to remove the stone rolled in front of the cave and run from the site as soon as the man in white leaves his message. The reader must somehow account for the empty tomb, the witness of the Essene, and the shock of the women to counteract the powerful narrative effect of this restrained telling of the Resurrection.

From the narrative models presented, it is essential that Jesus retain his physical body forever, so that he may fulfill the other conditions of his calling as Messiah, thus anticipating the needs of the heroicists as well as the "tragedists," so trying to imagine Jesus as anything but physically and permanently resurrected damages the comedic or happy ending. Thus, even if, like Dionysius, he is born on earth, the son of an immortal god and a mortal mother, nevertheless, Jesus is admitted to heaven as a god.

Yet I did acknowledge earlier that part of this hope of the hopeless rests on being able to accept rather than harmonize the three conflicting narratives of the life of Jesus to allow him to be resurrected and to draw all humanity to him even as he rises triumphantly into the clouds. Is this not somehow, in spite of everything, the fulfillment of a heroic antetype of some sort, in which Jesus is only momentarily defeated and heroically vanquishes his foes, including death, at the end? There are strong reasons for considering this resurrection narrative to be part of a heroic myth, but one supplied retrospectively, after the fact of Jesus' death.

The first clever component of this narrative is the heroic descent into hell, which cannot fit into the ascension–translation and presents problems even for the tragic death narrative. Students of epic poetry are aware of this component, found in *Gilgamesh* when the hero attempts to cross the great river and descend below the mountain in search of Utnapishtim; but it shows up in greater depth and detail in Aeneas's and Odysseus's searches for special knowledge from hell. Most interesting about the descent, even in the case of Orpheus, Herakles, Perseus, and others, is that a hero *must* make the trip without dying; in fact, one can visit hell once, but not twice, without dying to get there (pun intended). Occasionally the descent involves a poor soul held prisoner in hell—someone like Persephone, but just as often the descent involves a search for knowledge, as Dante knew when imitating Virgil's hero in the descent of the pilgrim into the Inferno. The clever device of Christ's descent into hell *after* his death should give us pause, for such a descent may also belong with the myth of a living, human hero, not a dead god; clearly the Gospel writers and readers of Jesus' day hoped that all good people would pick up on the mythical allusion while ignoring the physical fact that Jesus died. The idea of sending the conquering, heroic Messiah into *sheol* to punish the departed wicked is also extremely clever but again represents a narrative device that allows Jesus to finish his role of deliverer by delivering departed souls from sin and death. The medieval *Harrowing of Hell*, mentioned earlier, builds precisely on this continued heroic tradition preserved so well in *The Dream of the Rood*. In fact, Jesus outdoes even Prometheus and Zeus, for, after having cast the Watchers or *nefilim* into the abyss (the Hebrew version of an old Babylonian myth), Jesus goes to preach to them to fetch them back out of that same abyss (see 1 Peter 3:18–20).

The raising of Jesus from the dead is essential to the heroic narrative and is a psychological balm to heal us from the shock of the narration of Christ's death. The raising of the rest of us from the dead seems unnecessary to the heroic narrative, except in the Pharisaic sense of being judged "in the flesh." Mere immortality of the spirit, or even the body, as the Pharisees and the Greek philosophers understood, was of no value or comfort whatsoever if existence was to be the "same dull round," as William Blake would call it, of suffering and abuse. The question is never whether there is life after death, or even whether there is a resurrection, but rather whether there is any transcendent happiness or joy in these states of being that will somehow make continued existence preferable to total annihilation.

The mortalists, often called monists, reject the existence of a spirit apart from the *nephesh* or body because they assume that the resurrection is supposed to be a great reward following the sleep of death. That idea cannot be demonstrated from the narrative, which supports only the ideas that Jesus must conquer death itself in order to remain true to the ascension–translation narrative and that life after death must be considerably better than mere annihilation in order to justify its replacement of death as the release from the pains of mortality. The narrative suggests, quite surprisingly, that the chances of being damned in the spirit (the harrowing of hell) or in the body (Pharisaical idea of resurrection) are quite great. But once again we find ourselves in the theological dilemma of how best to live one's life to merit blessedness in the life to come: does one conquer or reject the world, rejoice in life and drink it "to the lees" as Tennyson's Ulysses, or run around in dust and ashes, as Ninevah, waiting for the day of doom?

Yet a third element of the heroic aspects of Jesus' resurrection is in the condition of his body after the Resurrection. First, although the body has received only preliminary preservation, there is not a problem, because Jesus is actually dead for only a day and a half.* So his resurrection is of a man who descended into the pit of Hades, but did so not as a permanent, dead resident, but only as a visitor who would be returning above ground very soon indeed. This idea of a heroic descent by a *living man* is, I am convinced, why New Testament narratives preserved the marks of death upon his body: to prove at once that he died and at the same time that his death doesn't count as a true death, because at his return he retained the wounds he received at the crucifixion! For it is in fact essential to the heroic ascension–translation narrative that Christ truly *cheat* death. Such narrative reasoning accounts for Peter's well-reasoned discourse in Acts 2, built around Psalm 16:8–11, that Jesus, rather than David of old, is the hero whose dead body *never saw corruption* and was not left in the *sheol* of the grave. That Jesus did in fact cheat death, that his death doesn't really count as a death,† and that like the heroic Isaac of old he is "delivered" from death is the clear intent of an unusual

---

* Remember that he is hurriedly removed from the cross and buried because the Sabbath is about to start—at six p.m. Friday evening (Mark 14:42), and by the time the women come "very early in the morning" to anoint his body (Mark 16:1–2), Jesus is long gone.

† Christian exegesis here is astonishing, insisting that crucifixion and death are essential to the Suffering Servant motif, when they are not. It is essential only to the tragic or Dionysian vision of Christ—the vegetative deity. It is fascinating to me how the Medieval Brome mystery play of *Abraham and Isaac* preserves the foreshadowing of Christ's *death*, but not his *suffering*, much as does the Genesis A ms. of *The Sacrifice of Isaac*, in which *wudu baer sunu* can mean either "The Son bore the wood" or "The wood bore the Son,"—again foreshadowing Christ's *crucifixion* but *not* his actual blood atonement, which occurs symbolically in his intense sanguine-like sweating and agony in Gethsemane.[16]

subnarrative in Luke (24:36–43) in which Jesus must prove he is a mortal being just as they are and that his death doesn't "count" in the heroic balance. Jesus is just as alive as any other hero, and please pass the broiled fish and honeycomb, thank you.

Even in the existence of three different Christs, one a very heroic man,* there is brief mention in the pseudepigrapha of a Messiah ben-Joseph, a hero from the tribe of Ephraim, who fills some of the same roles assigned to the Messiah of Judah. With more than one messiah to choose from, as it were, it should not be surprising that conflicting Messiah narratives would occur in the New Testament, though both the ascension–translation narrative and the dying–resurrecting god narrative have elements that transcend and predate the messianic tradition: one a plucky human doing his best to be an example to others and the other a forsaken deity. The conflicting Messiah narratives are not a problem for me or for other believing Christians, since our faith allows us to reconcile the incongruities of the being called Jesus and to assign his life and works to a sphere of eternal contemplation without absolute understanding and certainly without the need for scientific objectivity. The real theological dilemma is that the two narratives, the one heroic and the other tragic, have produced two very different and irreconcilable ways of qualifying one as a Christian. This binary opposition of how to be Christian is the source of more hatred and evil than any other binary within the whole scheme of ascension–translation in cultural and literary history.

The two forms are basically these: following the heroic tradition of the translation narrative, one is obliged to embrace the philosophy of the *imitation of Christ*, an idea prominent during most of Christian history and built on Old Testament models of retribution and reward. "Imitation" here refers to a Latin term, *imitatio*, which states that one becomes like Christ by imitating his behavior, and one tests her goodness by using the "mirror" of a given lifestyle, whether one is a queen or magistrate, and seeing the ideal person in the mirror, or a poor imitation, so one can

---

* The idea of multiple Messiahs is not unfamiliar to me. First, there is the account in Isaiah of the so-called "Suffering Servant" (chapters 52 and 53), who dies as a sacrificial lamb dies, for the sins of the people. It is unclear from the text how this human sacrifice was to function Messianically, though he is set in the Messianic context of the latter Isaiah. But it is clear from the text that this figure, whoever he is, will have eternal satisfaction only in the survival of his posterity and in the eventual destruction of the wicked. He seems to be a type of the righteous Israelite who bears the injustice of this world in spite of and possibly because of his innate purity and goodness— a condition not unlike the sacrificial lamb's.

gauge how far she has come and how far she has to go. Such imitation is clearly designed for superior people of good family, good education, and genuine sophistication, so one would never see in the renaissance a "mirror of all Christian day laborers and hod carriers." It is the mode of salvation for the lucky few—entirely in keeping with the heroic tradition of translation, and supported with a particular *strong misreading** of the Bible.

The other philosophy stems from the idea of Jesus as atoning or bloody sacrifice and is built on the premise that nothing a mortal being can do could ever lift him out of the abyss of death and eternal suffering for sin; only God has the power to save, and all humankind must rely on the "merits" of Christ, that is, upon his blood atonement, for salvation from sin and death. Confession of Christ, conviction of one's inherent worthlessness, and abject humility are essential ingredients in this vision of Christian redemption, supported equally as well as the heroic vision from strong misreading of the Bible. The merits of this second argument are beautifully illustrated in a delightful Hawthone short story entitled "The Celestial Railroad." In the story a group of people have bought tickets for a new railroad designed to take people easily and safely to heaven. As the trip progresses, those aboard have the chance to look at Bunyanesque pilgrims walking wearily on stony paths off to the side of the train and to disparage such old-fashioned conveyances to heaven. At last the train stops at a station that opens on a quay, and the train's passengers board a ferry boat for the last leg of the journey to heaven, which they can see in the distance. Unfortunately, the group realizes too late that the city of God is receding from their view, that the ferryman is actually Charon, and that the formerly light-hearted group is actually on its way to hell.

By implication of course, Hawthorne is rejecting the nineteenth-century fashionable doctrine of transcendentalism,† which in our day is the fashionable New Age religion. The story presents the suffering of life's woes as the only path to

---

* A term coined by critic Harold Bloom to describe his theory that every text is misread by everyone, since the text is but the rhetorical artifact of an original artistic vision that is gone forever; the quest of the reader is thus to misread *strongly*, or creatively, rather than weakly, or *pedantically*.

† I can't take credit for this observation. More than one Hawthorne scholar has remarked on the author's loathing of the spectral extremes of both the upbeat transcendentalism of his day and the unbending Puritanism of yesteryear.

sanctification and redemption. One does not attempt to improve on life's suffering or circumvent the necessity of Christ's blood atonement; rather one must, through abject humility and self-denial, reject any of the world's comforts in order to merit comfort after death. Of course, the "celestial railroad" is not the way of the hero, either. But the narrative of translation–ascension has for its premise that the hero must seek out adventure, danger, and success and that he alone is responsible for his ultimate fate. Indeed heroic righteousness is *tested* righteousness, not the righteousness of avoidance or passivity. Just as the pilgrims on foot are not the central characters of Hawthorne's story, so followers of the suffering Christ seek self-annihilation, at least to this world. To be heroic demands the kind of relationship with God that would simply not permit blood atonement to be central to the narrative.

Of course, it can be argued that even Enoch and Moses appear to be lowly creatures when God first notices them and that they become heroic only by degrees. Yet in a way that very increase in heroism is antithetical to the spirit of the Suffering Servant. Moses and Enoch begin as awkward speakers, but eventually rise to greatness, even in their speech; yet of the Suffering Servant we read that even at his trial he was speechless, not opening his mouth.

But while Satan can make Job's life a hell on earth, he is *not* allowed to kill the venerable elder. Job, however, is never promised eternal life. In fact, just as Gilgamesh, Job is told that death is the allotment of humanity and that only the gods are eternal. Job is clearly disturbed by his ongoing suffering, but when he finally confronts Yahweh—the response is unsatisfying for the reader searching for *gnosis*.

Since the last part of the tale is devoted to showing how magnificent God is, compared to ordinary people, the point of the book clearly is that most people, even righteous ones, ought not to expect too much from life. Though the book of Job has marvelous literary elements, dialogues of great depth and beauty, and very powerful poetic phrasing, as a frame tale it has all the marks of the *Gilgamesh* philosophy and likely is one of the oldest things in the Bible, I would guess of Sumerian origin. But from Job's story we can agree, I think, that even the Old Testament is adamant that only a very lucky few will ascend and be translated; and that suffering is a ritual test of obedience for heroes having little inherent meaning if death is its only outcome. Job clearly does not qualify as an Utnapishtim but is magnificent enough in his possessions and dignity to belong to the same class of people as Gilgamesh himself.

In the modern world that sort of person is a realist, sometimes an existentialist, and occasionally a social Christian. But the heroic and tragic models presented in Jesus have the effect of forcing ordinary people into two different camps, depending on which story touches them most deeply. In the heroic ascension–translation narrative, the Christian is absolutely right, has God completely on her side, and is destined to overcome all problems and march toward the rapture with a smile and a militant hymn running through her head. Such people try to convert the world, as do Mormons, Adventists, Jehovah's Witnesses, and others. They also convert with the sword, as in the Moorish wars against Christian Spain, the Crusades to deliver Jerusalem from the Saracens, the Catholic troops that slaughtered the "heretic" village of Albi, and, in a recent example, Bin Laden's definition of *Jihad* as "bloodbath" rather than "spiritual struggle." Such heroes win the right to live with Jesus in heaven because their narratives demonstrate valor; examples are found in the chivalric codes—the acquisition of virtues that make Lancelot invincible in battle, that decide the winner between the wicked Templars and the brave, young Saxon knight, Sir Wilfred of Ivanhoe, and that assure David's victory over Goliath, and Gideon's vastly outnumbered Israelites' victory over the Midianites. Along the way there is feasting—the banquet of Odin, the banquet of Allah, the ambrosia and nectar of the gods; and there is even romantic love, for Lancelot's reward for his virtue is to capture the heart of the queen he serves, just as surely as Agamemnon deserves Cassandra, and Odysseus deserves to go home to Penelope. It is all a never-ending garden of rewards for those brave enough to face great risks.

Into the second category, the tragic version of Jesus, go all the Jews who endured the Holocaust without overt resistance, Mahatma Ghandi, Martin Luther King, and other advocates of passive resistance. These are they who rely entirely on the next life for any sort of peace and reward. Into this class as well go those tormented by ill health and poverty, insanity, and the violence of the wicked, and those who cannot hope to conquer in this life, but for whom any sort of next life, including complete oblivion, is a step up, for whom death is the great equalizer and deliverer. Actually, when it comes right down to it, for many of these people death could be a friend, one to welcome with open arms. Well might many of the downtrodden feel that there is no need for eternal life because nothing that life has shown these people is worth having eternally.

This latter group ironically includes many Christians, who believe that the world is entirely hopeless and meaningless without Jesus' atonement and saving grace, for all the evidence is that humans are a depraved lot, and even the best of them come far short of the heroic righteousness, courage, or strength characterizing an Enoch, Elijah, or Herakles. Into this bedraggled group we must fit the gnostics, who, finding no meaning in blood sacrifice, yet aware of the importance of the heroic model, make Jesus into a gnostic redeemer who comes into the midst of this fallen, miserable world just long enough to leave with his key disciples the *gnosis*, a secret word of power that will awaken the divine spark within people and allow them to redeem themselves through a rediscovered personal relationship with God the Father. Jesus as gnostic Redeemer can not only re-ascend as soon as he completes his mission (as in the gnostic *Hymn of the Pearl*), but in some gnostic systems he can even bypass the crucifixion entirely by placing a clone double on the cross while the real Jesus, the eternal god-spirit, looks down benignly from above the cross.

Consider the difference such basic premises about the narrative of Christ's life can make on one entire belief system. One who believes in the translation–ascension myth of Christ believes Utopia is possible in this life, that if enough of us change individually, on the one hand, or collectively through legislation, on the other hand, we can of our own selves introduce paradise into the world we now live in. The result of such beliefs will come as a genuine shock to some, but it is clear that in this sort of thought pattern one may group both liberal progressives and conservative capitalists!—provided that members of these groups claim to be devout Christians. The imitation of the Christ model—partly heroic, partly tragic—asserts that through righteous and heroic acts, one can achieve a millennial state of plenty, a state of health, strength, happiness, and light. The Utopia offered by liberal progressives has as its basic premise the heroism and inherent goodness of civil government, a heroic figure which, in the United States, at least, is invincible and eternal—there will always be a president and Senate, even if individual faces change. Through taxation, and sometimes through overspending, a country and its politicians offer cures to all the ills that plague humanity—war, violence, poverty, sickness, hunger, and ignorance. The belief—again built on a heroic premise that comes from the *strong misreading* of the New Testament—is that if one spends enough money and is only aware enough of everything that can go wrong, it is possible to anticipate and eradicate the problems before they occur. The political debate of the election year 1996 focuses on the year 2000, then 2004, as the date for the new "millennium" of jobs and prosperity, giving the winner of the election four years to prepare us for that momentous, very religious turn of the great astrological arc. No student of the Bible will fail to hear echoes of Revelation in the target dates the candidates are setting before us, and that *we* will achieve the restoration of paradise, for we are the gods, the heroes.

The conservative capitalist scheme evolves from the same heroic premise, but instead of government being the hero, the businessman, the entrepreneur, and the corporate executive will lead the people to victory and millennial splendor. If the middle class can make enough money, goes the argument, the economy will improve to the point that everyone can be fed, be employed, be healthy, and be happy. It is, after all, the private sector that must prosper if the government is to run smoothly, if the arts are to survive, if the quality of life is to improve generally. With this prosperity from sound business practice goes a utilitarian frugality that cuts waste, corruption, excess, and exploitation—making business more powerful, cutting the government's size, and making those who are middle class or better the heroes of the new millennium, with efficient, well-run hospitals and art museums, car factories and computer-chip businesses. It is a model that, like the progressive government model, says that, in spite of other teachings of the New Testament, humanity was meant to rule the world, and that it is possible, through imitating Christ's greatest heroic virtues, that we will, on our own, become Christs and receive things denied even to him during his earth life. Either model could lead to the sort of expansionist philosophy that allowed England to dictate policy in India and allowed American enterprise in Vietnam. Devout Christians were no doubt involved, even at high levels, in both situations, neither of which was destined to bring about any kind of perfect millennial order. Though it might hurt the sensibilities of some of my liberal friends, the spirit of Franklin Roosevelt is alive and well—in Bill Gates. Both men descend from a Paul Bunyanesque American model that really has its roots in the ascension–translation model of Jesus.

What sort of people fit the other model, then? Well, not many of them are Republicans, it is true, but they don't make particularly good Democrats, either (and I *don't* mean followers of Ross Perot). Their whole agenda is anti-heroic; their victories are victories of the soul, of the abstract reality, of the other world. Such figures can occasionally be rich or powerful people, but they tend not to be unless someone re-creates them, narratologically speaking, in such a form. They are tragic figures themselves, as often as not, for they tend easily to be abused by the world. They categorically refuse to use the system, for their power comes from an inner force. They tend to be intensely, ecstatically religious, but their efforts are often more toward alleviation of personal grief of the moment than merely a cosmic "perking up" of the people, and they offer no clear-cut program for anything except some extremely difficult philosophical concepts such as forgiveness, passive resistance, endurance, the dignity of suffering, intuition, and meditation—in short, nothing that would put food on the table. People will of course disagree with my choices for this category, for they read the narratives of these lives differently, whether the figures are historical or merely fictional. The literary examples seem to shout out at me: Hester Prynne, the prime American example of how to turn shame to dignity, to live life out without any hope of success in the next world; Shakespeare's Lear, the greatest literary example of all of someone whose inner and outer self can be undone entirely without his desiring or anticipating it, and whose only redemption is the blessed relief of death, since as a pagan he has no hope of a Christian heaven; Billy Budd, Melville's hapless Adamic sailor, based on a real sailor who miraculously did not shake even minutely, let alone convulsively, at his hanging, as he was supposed to do—his only crime is to share a ship with the worst villain since Iago: Claggart, who induces the ignorant lad to commit murder; Mersault, Camus's *etranger*, whose failure to cry at his mother's funeral absurdly shows up as evidence against him in his trial for shooting an Arab; Candide, Voltaire's ironic observer of life around him in which he becomes involved by accident, but from which he learns that cultivating one's own garden is likely the least harmful thing a human can do.

The historical examples are just as clear: Martin Luther King, who saw visions of what was surely part of another existence, with people of all races voluntarily holding hands; St. Bernadette, promised happiness by the Lady of her visions only in the next life, with only suffering and rejection in this life; Ghandi, whose goals were nothing short of the transformation of the very soul of India, but who suffered immensely until the day he was assassinated; those recovering from alcoholism, drug addiction, violent or abusive behavior, or those with terminal illnesses—AIDS, cancers, blood diseases, defective organs—all of whom must learn to accept that there is no cure and that the purpose of life now is to learn how to cope with or endure the hand one is dealt.*[21]

The classic confrontation between the two models is the heroic type who demands that the tragic type lose weight and that then all her problems will be solved. She has chosen instead, because of her psychic needs, to accept her body *as it is* (a key form of therapy in cases of bulimia and anorexia), not as some ideal model dictates. Or one can see it in a family in which the father is an indefatigable go-getter; the mother acutely, clinically depressed. The father can't understand why his wife doesn't just "take hold of herself" and be happy. The wife considers getting dressed in the morning a major accomplishment, given her condition. The two models of orthodox Christianity are bound to conflict if this family is devoutly Christian, especially if fundamentalism is present. The transcendent model is convincing: if you have enough faith you *can* be healed; no problem is too great for God to fix. And he would not give any commandment, such as the beatific "blessed," meaning "happy," for which he would not provide the means to obey it. Such a view implicitly rejects suicide (the very name, "self-slaughter," has bad connotations), and euthanasia and abortion are for many outrageous surrenders to beatable foes—the challenges of life to be fought and opposed, even conquered, but not "endured" or "accepted." The tragic model—the one the classical drama critics are always raving about—tells the protagonist in life's drama that since you can't escape defeat, your only goal is to behave nobly to the last, to carry your burden with dignity, to suffer with silent courage.

Notice that none of the three narrative paradigms is without aesthetic power; neither is less celebrated than the other. All three can be trivialized in art as well as in life (such as calling the failure of some literary work to sell a "tragedy," as some of my artsy friends like to do), but in their grandest forms they are both

---

* Elisabeth Kübler-Ross, whose interviews with and studies of some five hundred terminal cancer patients resulted in the landmark book *On Death and Dying*, has shown that it is an essential survival process of the human psyche that teaches those with terminal illness to go through the now-classic "five stages of dying," including anger, denial, bargaining, mourning, and ending in calm acceptance. This theory works as well for the bereaved and for those wrestling with other irreversible conditions in life.

intensely human, representing the best humans can do when they have power to win, and when they are power*less* to win. Yet all three models, though mutually exclusive,* have been combined in the New Testament narratives, making it next to impossible for Christians to find agreement on the correct path to follow to become "Christlike," or at least a true "Christian."

The odd thing about the New Testament narratives, with all their contradictions, is that the whole of their narratives is considerably greater than the sum of their parts. People are forever and profoundly changed by the Jesus of the Gospels, though some think of him as Jeffrey Hunter and others as Robert Powell.[†] Perhaps that is the essence of accepting the trinity: Jesus, however illogical it may seem, is the high priest performing the sacrifice, he is the sacrificial victim, and he (his spirit) is the fire that consumes the slain lamb. And maybe it is just as well that we have more than one face of Jesus to examine. The downtrodden need their model every bit as much as the successful folks need to imitate theirs.

---

* By "mutually exclusive" I simply mean that Odysseus can either die like Hector or arrive home safely and rescue the family back at Ithaca—those are the choices; he can't do both. The amazing thing about the Jesus narratives is that Jesus actually *does* do both!

† Hunter was the angry young Jesus of *King of Kings*, Powell the reflective, suffering tragedian of Zephirelli's *Jesus of Nazareth*. My own leanings artistically and in nearly every other way are heavily toward the Powell portrayal, but a lot of people I know like their film savior to stand six-two, have rippling muscles, flash blue eyes, and speak like James Earl Jones.

1. Alan Dundes, "The Hero Pattern and the Life of Jesus, in *In Quest of the Hero* (Princeton, NJ: Princeton University Press, 1990), 179–203.

2. FitzRoy Richard Somerset Raglan (Lord Raglan), *The Hero: A Study in Tradition, Myth, and Drama* (Westport, CT: Greenwood Press, 1975).

3. S. R. Driver and Adolf Neubauer, eds. and trans., *The Fifty-Third Chapter of Isaiah according to the Jewish Interpreters* (translations), 2 vols., Library of Biblical Studies (1876–77; reprint, New York: Ktav, 1969).

4. René Girard, *Job: The Victim of His People*, trans. Yvonne Freccero (Stanford, CA: Stanford University Press, 1987).

5. Dundes, 190.

6. Ibid., 191.

7. Caroline Walker Bynum, in *Fragmentation and Redemption: Essays on Gender and the Human Body in Medieval Religion* (New York: Zone Books, 1992), 231.

8. Joseph Campbell, *The Hero with a Thousand Faces*, 2d ed., Bollingen Series (Princeton, NJ: Princeton University Press, 1968), 182.

9. Robert Graves and Joshua Podro, *The Nazarene Gospel Restored* (London: Cassell, 1953); Robert Graves, *King Jesus* (London: Cassell, 1946).

10. Hugh Schonfield, *The Passover Plot* (New York: Bernard Guis Associates, 1965).

11. John A. Tvedtnes, *The Church of the Old Testament* (Salt Lake City: Deseret Book, 1980).

12. Hugh W. Nibley, "Evangilium Quadraginta Dierum," *Vigilae Christianae* 20 (1966): 1–24.

13. Graves and Podro, 927.

14. Ibid., 997–1000.

15. Girard, 146.

16. Ibid., 156.

17. *The Dream of the Rood, The Norton Anthology of English Literature*, 5th ed. (New York: Norton, 1986), 1:23.

18. E. B. Pusey, Introduction to the English Translation, *The Fifty-Third Chapter of Isaiah*, lxi–lxii.

19. Ibid., lxi, note m, and cited by Sh'muel David Luzzatto, 415.

20. C. S. Lewis, *Miracles* (New York: Macmillan, 1947).

21. Elisabeth Kübler-Ross, *On Death and Dying* (New York: Macmillan, 1969).

4 Translation Narratives in Literature

Herakles

I have chosen Herakles (Hercules) as a representative figure from "pagan" tradition that shows the continuing survival and importance of the idea of ascension and translation in literary history. The Greek pantheon have always been fit subjects for literature—especially the epic narrative or the stage drama, and they find their way, for instance, into Milton's portrayal of angels and demons in *Paradise Lost*. The angels have ichor in their veins and may be wounded though not killed, as Book Six of Milton's epic informs us in re-creating the War in Heaven,[1] and Book Three creatively suggests translated beings and elemental spirits could be located on the moon (459–62), that is, in a position on the border between the Ptolemaic superlunar, ethereal powers and the sublunar, elemental forces. Herakles is of interest in this study because he is one of only a very few characters, all descendants of the gods, allowed to ascend to Olympus and join the Greek pantheon. He is not a priest and is not a particularly good person—his clear counterpart in Israelite legend is Samson—yet he ascends, even when Samson and Gilgamesh do not. What happened between the writing of *Gilgamesh* (and even of Bible heroes) to allow such a character to join the gods?

Before I can address that question I need to deal with the "death" of Herakles. Euripides[2] ends the hero's narrative, as students of mythology will remember, by placing Herakles on a funeral pyre, where he is consumed by a magnificent rush of flame. As Edith Hamilton writes, "Hercules was seen no more on earth. He was taken to heaven, where he was reconciled to Hera and married her daughter Hebe."[3] At first glance, the death of the hero precludes his being considered in this study. Yet Euripides' poetic rendering of Herakles' funeral pyre is revealing for a number of reasons and actually reinforces the assertion that Herakles is part of the same heroic mythology as Gilgamesh.* First is his divine parentage. Zeus (the old goat) is his father (as he is all too often). A subnarrative is implicit in that statement, for Herakles was thought to be merely the son of his earthly father, Amphitryon, and of Alcmena, though his grandfather was said to be the son of the heroic Perseus. The illegitimacy here is a recurring myth motif, in which an illegitimate birth is explained by a visit from a god—against which attack a woman is of course helpless. The god complicates matters by disguising himself, in this particular case as Alcmena's husband. (It is Flavius Josephus who tells the ribald story of a woman who is promised by her pagan priest a tryst with a god, provided she enters the temple at midnight, unseen in the shadows. Then of course the priest himself seduces her, she all the while assuming a god has done it. Josephus's wry comment is that everyone in Rome knew the truth of the matter except the woman in question.) This makes Herakles of divine parentage by 50 percent, a figure notably higher than that of some heroes and likely entitling him to a fair, evenhanded debate among the gods as to his ultimate fate.†

Herakles is willing to test his mettle against the Olympians. At one point, when Herakles violated the oracle at Delphi, he would have willingly gone head to head

---

* Edith Hamilton notes that Apollodorus, Euripides, Pindar, and Theocritus are all more complete and helpful than Ovid, which, she tells us, is normally far more detailed than the others; she is of course right on all counts and is invaluable as always; I prefer Hamilton to Bullfinch or Robert Graves.

† This is the real significance of the accusations of illegitimacy against Mary in the New Testament narrative; it has less to do with Joseph's being swindled out of a "virgin" bride (remember that Isaiah's prophecy refers to a "young maiden," not a "virgin" as we think of it) than it does to establish that Jesus had the right as a 50 percent divine mortal to ascend and be translated! The obviously deliberate supplying of "narrative-enhancing" genealogies in the New Testament (see chapter 3) is interesting here, for Matthew's (remember the magic numbers of this genealogy) has to do only with kingship, while Luke's clever genealogy creates a rhetorical trap for the reader revolving around the word "son" or "descendant of." One works his way back to the son of Seth, who was the son of Adam, who was the son of God, and arrives at Jesus' divinity. The KJV preserves this play

with Apollo had not Zeus intervened, calming all injured parties. It goes without saying that because he was the product of one of Zeus's affairs with mortal women, Herakles was the lifelong object of Hera's anger and spite. And it is clear that the Olympians could not have defeated the giants without the help of Herakles.[4]

He passes all the ritual and other tests for ascension, including the descent into hell. The twelve (in some accounts, thirteen) labors of Hercules are remembered in popular lore; furthermore, Herakles qualifies as a deliverer and savior, a benefactor of both humans and gods: he rescued Thebes from the Minyans, he became the means of rescuing Prometheus from his torment, and in his twelfth labor, he descended to the underworld to bring back Cerberus, the hound of hell. The Christian image of Christ's "conquering" death becomes a *literalized* metaphor in the tales of Herakles, who wrestled Death himself over the life of a friend's wife. (It is doubtful Herakles could have gone to Hades twice without being forced to remain, so he wrestles Death by the woman's tomb, a convenient narrative device suggesting that the twelfth labor of Herakles, with its required descent to the underworld, was already a well-known myth even in the days of the Greek tragedians.)

Thus, Herakles' "death" is only a narrative device. The pyre, whether a funeral pyre or a sacrificial pyre, had a very logical, practical quality to it. Anyone could see that as the offering burned, the flames and smoke ascended to the heavens. In Greek myth, as in the Old Testament, the gods smell the smoke of the burning (the KJV calls it a "sweet savour"), proving that the essential offering has ascended to heaven, leaving behind only mortal dross. Herakles clearly could not ascend if he merely died, for death leads inexorably to the underworld—Hades. Thus fire,

---

on words, but the argument is weakened horribly by the distance between Jesus and Adam. Thus the virgin birth from a heavenly father is more to prove Jesus the equal of the *heroes* of all ages than to prove he actually is God incarnate. This misreading of Jesus' role to say that he was the absolute incarnation of deity itself is inherently impossible from a narrative viewpoint. The narratology of the Gospels simply doesn't support such a thing. We must wait a century for Hellenistic mysticism to create the tri-une deity of orthodox Christianity. Not surprisingly, the Greeks give us Jesus' form as the incarnation of deity (with some real help from Paul's radical version of Christianity): Jesus=LOGOS and becomes mystically equated with the Hebrew *d'vir*, or "word," but specifically denoting Yahweh using the "speaker" or *d'vir* of the Ark of the Covenant; *ergo*, Jesus=Yahweh. Thus my argument in the third chapter that Jesus is also a god means that he is so in the same sense as Dionysius.

as with Elijah's chariot of fire, becomes in reality a metaphor for the process of transformation—translation—to heaven. This of course is the meaning of the Old Testament phrase "the refiner's fire": all that is dross is burned away, allowing what is pure gold to be preserved.* I will have occasion to refer back to this point in the next chapter, in connection with St. Joan.

Thus Herakles, who has suffered greatly because of the torments of a magic coat, much as a "Suffering Servant" suffering for his *own* errors, overcomes some of the obstacles that keep Gilgamesh from being translated: (1) he is the son of the chief deity and is 50 percent divine, (2) he is invincible to the point that he can literally conquer Death (and at times, like Odysseus or Diomedes, set the gods at defiance—they like a certain amount of pluck, though not *too* much!) (3) he is a great benefactor of both men and gods, making him an extremely fine choice for translation. It is hardly surprising that of Greek myths in general, those surrounding Herakles are among the best remembered, with Herakles himself being the most popular of all gods and heroes, with the possible exception of Odysseus. In the same way Keats's Grecian urn becomes immortal as a celebratory ode, so Herakles becomes immortal in popular consciousness, remaining forever young, forever triumphant. It is not surprising to recall that both Enoch and Elijah are among the best-remembered Old Testament figures, preserved in thousands of years of tradition and popular lore, despite the fact that Enoch receives only a few lines of narrative in Genesis, and of Elijah's words, none remain, if there were any written words to begin with. Their immortality likewise is reflected in the narratological immortality of scriptural exegesis and mystical lore.

One last aspect of the translation–ascension of Herakles needs to be mentioned in the context of its resemblance to biblical narratives of translation: its similarities to and differences from the biblical narrative of the Hebrew counterpart of

---

* In fact, the idea of a "glorious" or fiery image of the resurrected Christ works only if one borrows the refiner's fire image and superimposes it on the narrative of the physical resurrection, which by itself leaves the *nephesh* with the marks (sometimes called "blows," as in hammer blows) of death and the capacity for earthly functions, such as eating fish or bread. Thus the "glorious" aspect of Jesus' resurrection, which really occurs only after his ascension (remember the foreshadowing of the Transfiguration), is subconsciously superimposed by the narratee on Jesus at the very moment of his resurrection, a superimposition impossible to support from the Gospel narratives themselves (keeping in mind that the real ascension occurs in Acts).

Herakles—Samson. From a theological viewpoint, Samson is a major embarrassment. That he "judges" (that is, exercises retribution) in Israel is beyond doubt; he is the classic "scourge of God" who is *ritually* pure enough to be Yahweh's tool for punishing the Philistines, the redoubtable tribe that produced the giant Goliath. Why is Samson's end tragic, when Herakles is honored by the Olympians?*

The Book of Judges produces some remarkable heroes, among them Gideon, whose bravery against the Midianites is remembered in the battle cry, "The sword of the Lord and of Gideon," a phrase suggesting that Gideon is the sword or scourge in the hand of God. Gideon is from the dimly lit but still colorful heroic age in Hebrew myth; Gideon compares favorably with the likes of Diomedes or Hector. The age of heroes effectively ends in Hebrew myth with David, a slayer of giants who becomes a transition figure as Israel's successor to King Saul and who consolidates monarchic and economic power in Jerusalem. David in fact is a later, very righteous and single-minded version of Samson, using his sling and stones to kill lions and bears before he faces, without armor, Goliath of Gath.

Samson thus is in the same position in mythic development as Herakles—a mythology whose hypostasis runs from the age of gods to that of demigods, to that of heroes, to that of kings. The movement of mythology through the "ages" is even preserved in the Sumerian king-lists, in which monarchy by gods, then by demigods, then finally by men is reflected in the decreasingly fantastic figures documenting the length of their reigns.† Thus, as we see Zeus–Herakles–Oedipus in the developing Greek mythological narrative, we see Yahweh–Enoch–David in the Hebrew narrative.‡

Yet Samson, who takes a Nazarite vow, is destroyed when he pushes down the pillars of the Philistine temple, while Herakles, the poets inform us, is received into

---

* I conclude that Samson is a tragic rather than heroic character based not merely on his death but on the judgment of John Milton, whose blank verse closet tragedy *Samson Agonistes* is an attempt philosophically to redeem Samson through a formal recognition before the protagonist's death. As drama the piece has real problems, leading me to believe that Milton "staged" the drama as an artistic device for presenting characters' inner thoughts aloud.

† Gilgamesh is part of that list, which includes at its beginning, reigns extending over hundreds of thousands of years and reigns closer to ordinary life spans at its end.

‡ No student of mythology would fail to notice the fantastic life spans of Adam or Methuselah, decreasing slowly through Abraham and Moses till, at the time of David, life spans are normal.

the presence of the gods. It is not enough to argue that Israel had no conception of an afterlife and so Samson's "eternal reward" goes unmentioned. No, for Hades was not that great a deal in the Greek heroic age, either. And besides, the point is that the person translated actually "cheats" death, so that discussing the idea of a life after death is irrelevant to this narrative problem. If we note that Herakles has a better lineage than Samson, we would be correct, except that in the Hebrew tale Samson's birth is accomplished through God's direct intervention and at the expense of the natural course of things.* So while we cannot say that God visited Manoah's wife in the fashion of a pagan deity, the miracle of the birth is important evidence.

Narratologically speaking, this has to do with the narrator's being forced, as his narrative moves closer in time to his own day, to deal with such realities as recent memory, accurate genealogies, and written records of wars, financial transactions, and treaties. As a rule, the closer the event being narrated is to one's own time, the more precise and detailed the accounts. This explains the fact that in the Old Testament, Kings, Chronicles, and Samuel have a huge amount of detail and cover relatively less time than, say, Genesis, which covers a lot of time but is comparatively short on detail. Clearly the writer of Chronicles is much closer to the events he chronicles than the writer of Genesis. Such realities of the act of narration explain why scholars have reached the conclusion (abhorrent to devout Christians and Jews) that Moses didn't write the first five books of the Bible, that such books as Genesis started out as oral tradition, its myths being recorded, with wonderful literary power, centuries after the fact. An interesting sidelight here is that Genesis is, contrary to what I have just stated, a very stark and compressed version of myths preserved in far greater detail in the Sumerian originals (for example, the debate of the gods over whether Earth should be destroyed by flood, which debate is at best an ellipsis in the Bible—Yahweh merely exclaiming what "we" will do. By the way, the "we" here is not a "royal we" as later monotheistic scribes would have it. It is the last reminder of the *elohim* or pantheon of gods implied in Genesis 1 and preserved in Sumerian and later Greek myth). The issue for narratologists would be, then, whether the abridgment of the Genesis material is deliberate—sort of an ascetic's way of trimming the excessive material off the older version (a position very attractive to devout believers, who would call such a deliberate recension "inspired" editing)—or whether Genesis is but a dimly remembered oral account of lost Sumerian myth that has finally been written down. His other theories aside, Zecharia Sitchin is right on target in *The Wars of Gods and Men* when he insists Abraham was a Sumerian prince and that Ur was a Sumerian city.[5]

* Judges 13:2–3: "And there was a certain man of Zorah, . . . whose name was Manoah; and his wife was barren, and bare not. And the angel of the Lord . . . said unto her, Behold now, thou art barren, and bearest not: but thou shalt conceive, and bear a son." The angel is clearly one of the ancient Hebrew pantheon, for Manoah later asks the angel's name in order to make thank offerings to it, and the angel responds that the name is "secret" (13:18). And, as if to confirm my own suppositions about the function of the fire in which, as I contend, Herakles ascends to heaven and

I mentioned ritual purity in connection with Samson, for ordinary measures of goodness seem practically irrelevant in this discussion; yet ritual purity itself is put to shame by Samson's behavior. Like Herakles, Samson is a "roistering blade," full of practical jokes and ready to fight at the drop of a hat. He consorts with the enemy, marries outside his clan, gambles using riddles as objects for stakes. If his goal is to deliver Israel from the Philistines, his effort is as unsubtle as it can be. And Samson violates his own ritual vows when drinking, so that cutting his hair in defiance of the Nazarite vow would seem superfluous, if God were to reject him for violating his vows. Yet Herakles does not hesitate to violate things sacred to the gods—at one point stealing the tripod from the oracle at Delphi when his questions went unanswered.

So if ritual impurity is not the occasion for the tragic ending to Samson's life, what is? It is very revealing that Samson, possibly because he didn't get nearly the polished narrative treatment available to Herakles through the Greek tragic poets, seems seldom to feel any remorse for his actions. There is much to be said for Herakles' remorse when he accidentally kills someone, and perhaps that is the deciding quality endearing him to the gods. There is something intensely beautiful about Herakles' self-denigration, contrasting as it does with the inexhaustible self-esteem that allows him to deem himself the gods' equal. One is reminded in Herakles' great remorse and self-punishment of the humility exercised by the glorious Trojan king Priam in begging his son's body from Achilles. Such literary moments as these allow us to love even the most wretched creatures—such as the nun in *The Song of Bernadette* who refuses to believe the girl's vision and is unspeakably cold and cruel to the girl until God gives her a sign, when she realizes the magnitude of her sin of pride and devotes the rest of her life to helping the now-stricken Bernadette in any way she can. That remorse is certainly what Milton tries to infuse into his dramatic Samson (*Agonistes*), so that, unlike the account in Judges, Milton's Samson is motivated by something greater than selfish vengeance when he destroys the Philistines' temple: "Happen what may, of me expect to hear / Nothing

---

is translated, the narrative of Samson declares that when Manoah offered up his burnt offering, "the flame went up toward heaven from off the altar, [and] the angel of the Lord ascended in the flame of the altar" (13:20). Invariably, after such experiences with "angels" of God, the visitants are certain they "shall surely die, because we have seen God" (13:22). It would be hard to find an image connecting the two myths more convincingly.

dishonorable, impure, unworthy / Our God, our Law, my nation, or myself" (*Samson Agonistes*, 1423–25).

It may seem odd that such an inherently human quality as remorse should please the gods so greatly, but from a narrative standpoint, in order to guarantee a literary character any literary "immortality," the character must touch our hearts. While it is true that evil makes a fitter subject for literature than good, because the former has more dramatic qualities, it is nevertheless true, as Percy Bysshe Shelley maintained about Milton's Satan, that it is the noble qualities in the evil character that we embrace and long for, not the base qualities that we must shamefacedly acknowledge as part of our own character. The Herakles that ascends to heaven is a human who transcends his humanity; the Samson who is literally buried remains below, for his proud, self-centered spirit does not aspire to transcending this world, but merely to making it a miserable place for everyone, including himself!

The Problem of Oedipus: Did He Ascend, and Was He Transmuted?

Outside of the Sumerian *Gilgamesh* epic and perhaps certain Chinese myths, the oldest myths of ascension belong to Egypt, in the falcon-flight of the pharaohs toward the sun (Ra or Re) to join with the divine family. The ascension of the pharaoh was actually a complicated rite, performed by human priests after the pharaoh's death. Oddly enough, this ancient myth and the rite through which the ascension is realized are keys to solving a great literary mystery: was the Oedipus of Sophocles' last play, *Oedipus at Colonus*, transmuted, then taken up to Olympus to be with the pantheon of Greek deities?

Oedipus at Colonus is clearly the most esoteric and mystical of Sophocles' three Theban tragedies. (*Oedipus Tyrannus* and *Antigone*, the other two, are still very popular, anthologized I believe because they are inherently more accessible to students than the mysterious *Oedipus Coloneus*.) As you will recall, this last play tells of the wanderings of Oedipus, guided in his blindness by his most loyal child, courageous Antigone, who later confronts King Creon over the burial rites (and rights) for her brother Polyneices. Oedipus and Antigone come to the forest of the Eumenides, to a rock Oedipus has envisioned as proof of a fit place to rest in safety. The Eumenides, formerly the fierce, implacable Furies that hounded and tortured the guilty for their sins, were ever after changed into benevolent protectors of all needing succor when Orestes was willing to admit sins and accept punishment for the acts really orchestrated by Apollo: This principle of repenting for another's sins was an astounding breakthrough in a culture whose dramas and epics so often demanded only justice, requital, and reciprocal violence (for example, the escalating verbal violence between Teiresias and Oedipus, or between Creon and Haimon). The theory of reciprocal violence, explained by the passionate René Girard in *Violence and the Sacred*,[6] suggests that the pattern cannot be broken unless one chooses categorically not to join in the battle at all. That is the main issue of *Oedipus Coloneus*: has Oedipus truly changed, refusing to be a party to more violence and thus winning the gods' favor, or does he continue to joust verbally with prophets, kings, and family?

Oedipus encounters several people in the forest: Creon, brother to Iocasta; Polyneices, brother–son; and Theseus, ruler of Athens, as well as a chorus of townspeople investigating the news of a stranger in their midst. His conversations with them should reveal his intentions. The purification rites mentioned early (*OC* 466–67) in the drama suggest that Oedipus wishes to be initiated into the higher mysteries of Demeter: among the stipulations for making atonement is that the last of the three bowls to be used in the lustration contain water and honey but not wine (*OC* 481). The rites are apparently effective, for later in the play Theseus is promised that if he never discloses the location of Oedipus's death, his city will be forever blessed (*OC* 1518–34). This obligation of silence is the clearest clue that these rites are initiatory to the higher mysteries. Theseus is very kind and friendly toward both Oedipus and Antigone, observing the rites of hospitality toward the two strangers. His willingness to suspend any judgment against Oedipus shows Theseus in a very favorable light, contrasting sharply with the dark motives of both Creon and Polyneices in the play, who seek out Oedipus only to gain his support and the good omen of his presence in the camp of either Polyneices or the entrenched Creon (and Etiocles). Yet if Oedipus comes to the forest only to die, what mystery is so great surrounding his death that Oedipus and the gods forbid Theseus to mark even the *location* of his death?

There are two possibilities: (1) Oedipus, like Elijah of the Old Testament, is to be caught up to heaven in a manner so magnificent that only his catechumen (Theseus, in the role of Elisha) is permitted to witness the event; or (2) Oedipus is to be slain ritually by the gods, a priest, or perhaps even by Theseus as the final act of atonement—with the outside possibility that Oedipus has failed to atone and must therefore be slain violently as the sign of his failure to extricate himself from the vicious cycle of violence that has hounded his family line for generations (Cadmus, Actaeon, Laius).

There is little doubt that Oedipus still harbors some of his old hatred, mostly because he was banished from his homeland by his own sons (*OC* 600). But Creon is a direct and more immediate threat to the blind king's security, for he declares his intention to take Antigone and Ismene captive; only the direct intervention of the good-hearted Theseus prevents Creon from such infamy. (Creon, in *Antigone,* takes Oedipus's place, re-creating the exact confrontation with Teiresias that occurs in *Oedpus Tyrannus*!)

Using the formula that I offered in the introductory chapter of this book, we can estimate fairly quickly whether or not Oedipus has any direct claim on ascension and translation. He is the great grandchild of Harmonia, the child of the brother-sister union of Ares and Aphrodite (notice the unfettered inbreeding of brothers and sisters in Olympus; Zeus and Hera are also so joined). Thus Oedipus has no strong suit genealogically. He cannot be accounted righteous, since, like the Old Testament character Jonah, he runs from a divine oracle, thinking (as did Jonah with regard to Yahweh) that regional Theban deities have no power in another region. He is heroic, much as is Theseus, for Oedipus delivers Thebes from the Sphinx but does so by solving a riddle; it seems not to occur to Oedipus that the oracle from which he ran so desperately could also be talking in riddles, so that patience and wisdom could eventually crack the code. And, of course, Oedipus's heroism is limited by the Sphinx's committing suicide—a strange end indeed for a monster— and by Oedipus's killing an old stranger at a crossroads while in a foreign land. Thus Oedipus is only selectively clever, where Diomedes is unflinchingly heroic and Odysseus consistently quick witted. Therefore it comes down to analysis of this last Sophoclean play to discern whether he ascends or not, ritual atonement or purity and initiation into the higher mysteries being the only conceivable means to do so.

It is interesting that there is one culture, consistently connected to antique Greece, whose kings ascend, through ritual initiation and preparation, to the heavens to become gods, members of the divine, immortal family: Egypt. In his enlightening contribution to the work of two generations of Egyptologists,

Whitney M. Davis notes the following key feature in the pyramid texts of the pharaoh's mortuary ritual:

> In some fashion, the purification of the corpse was transformed into the cleansing of the soul or life-essence. This process was most likely analogous to the awakening of the ka in the transmission of the life-essence from body to "soul" at the moment of death. The transformation was, of course, a prerequisite for any existence in the afterworld.[7]

What is remarkable for my current study is the unmistakable desire to avoid the *appearance* of death. The transition of life-essence to the *ka* is an attempt to get around the obvious: Pharaoh is the living god and must not *seem* dead, for the mere appearance of death is as strong an indictment against the ascending hero as, for example, the mere *appearance* of evil in the righteous person's bid for exaltation based on a life perfectly lived. To bolster the pharaoh's claim on the afterlife, and to reassure, in this world, that the people have not been deceived or misled, the ascending monarch is "able to use his own powers to *demand* a place in the hereafter, always successfully, for [quoting a pyramid text] 'you demand that you ascend to the sky and you *shall* ascend.'"[8] Such braggadocio goes so far as to make the pharaoh's ascension the result of bullying the divine pantheon! The monarch is held to be "supreme mortal—and the power that he possesses as killer of the gods and as one able to threaten the divine host is perhaps [a means of connecting earthly power] to celestial manifestation."[9] This odd behavior is manifest in Oedipus in any number of ways, but mostly in his belligerence toward the gods, even Apollo, god of truth and light (and reflected in Creon's assumption of the Theban throne, from which "catbird seat" he is able to force Antigone to choose between obeying her king or honoring the gods through proper burial of her slain brother Polyneices).

Yet why connect Oedipus to Egyptian ascension myth at all? Of what value is such a comparison? It suffices to say that connecting Greece to Egypt any earlier than a few centuries before the common era has been oddly resisted by classicists, partly because Egyptology, like the even more remote Sumerology, demands a lifetime commitment to itself alone. This is true despite such obvious connections as the story in Plato's *Timaeus* and *Critias* of Solon's discussions with the Egyptian priests in 900 B.C.E. concerning the ancient tale of the destruction of Atlantis. With all the garish paint chipped off ancient Greek statues of Zeus, Athena, or Apollo, such sculpture suggests a sophisticated, three-dimensional realism and restrained aesthetic that makes even early Greek art look worlds removed from its Egyptian models—yet once the garish paint-by-numbers research restores the paint to the ascetic white statues, they are as decadent-looking as any middle or late dynastic *kitsch* in Egyptian art or sculpture. The Greeks improve upon Egyptian columns in terms of decoration, but if the pillars are garishly painted, illustrating scenes of Greek life not unlike that depicted on Egyptian columns, the Greek "aesthetic" again dissolves.

There are further connections between Greece and Egypt: the Sphinx is a Greek name for a clearly Egyptian invention; Ozymandias is early on a Greek transliteration for Rameses II; the Boetian Thebes has a sister city in Egypt also dubbed Thebes by the Greeks; and Heliopolis is a cult city in Egypt for the same deity revered by the Greeks. And, last of all, there is a bold book that proposed a real pharaoh behind the character of Oedipus: Immanuel Velikovsky's *Oedipus and Akhnaton*.[10] To my knowledge this book has been ignored almost without exception by both classicists and Egyptologists, presumably because relatively few could judge the merits of both parts of the argument. Reviews were tentative and guarded; the book was listed in the selected bibliography of the 1970 Norton Critical Edition of *Oedipus Tyrannus*. Only one student of ancient culture found Velikovsky's interpretation of the name Oedipus the most plausible.[11] Velikovsky, a brilliant student of ancient Mediterranean languages and literatures, as well as a founding member of Hebrew University and a European-trained M.D. with a specialty in Freudian psychiatry, proposed, based on a revised chronology of certain events in Egyptian history, that because of similarities already mentioned above, and others, the story of Oedipus likely had its origins in the Egyptian reign of the so-called "heretic pharaoh," Akhnaton (or Akhenaton). Showing that Akhenaton likely gained both his reverence for nature and life as well as his and his immediate family's libidinous incest from his early upbringing in exile among the Mittanians, Velikovsky noted that certain familial aberrant physiological characteristics, such as swollen lower limbs, portrayed on murals, were actually medical conditions growing out of inbreeding, not merely stylized art from the period. From that condition, Velikovsky deduced that Oedipus's name could mean "swollen lower leg" as likely as it could mean "swollen foot." Such discoveries of course undermined the accepted wisdom of Egyptologists concerning Akhenaton's single-minded monotheism, albeit for a sun god called Aton (thus the theomorphic name Akhen-*Aton*). Akhenaton was in some circles held to be a forerunner of Moses and Jewish monotheism, which, if Velikovsky's views were correct, would assure one that the perverse, narcissistic, and altogether disgusting religious practices of Akhenaton, which isolated him from the people, from the priests of the traditional, stable polytheistic religion, and from any sort of sane diplomacy with foreign powers or normalcy in civil matters, could not remotely have led Moses to the highly sophisticated moral codes and understanding of God characterized by the Torah and the Israelite allegiance to the unseen God Yahweh.

The importance then of this Egyptian connection, for the question of ascension in *Oedipus Coloneus* is, was Akhenaton initiated and prepared in the way the pyramid texts demanded, or was he denied the possibility of ascension? First, was his corpse honored, the key to survival of the *ka*? Second, were proper rites observed to guarantee Akhenaton's falcon-flight toward the sun—could he demand the right to dwell with the divine family? Was he granted the *illusory death* essential for righteous, kingly, or heroic ascent?

The oath binding Theseus not to disclose the location of Oedipus's final encounter with the gods or his death and burial is connected to Egypt by the most fragile of skeins—and a tangled one, at that. The controversy surrounding the ultimate fate of Akhenaton and his beautiful bride, Nephertiti, bears a striking similarity to the Oedipus tale. A very recent article in *National Geographic*, "Pharaohs of the Sun,"[12] shows that the mystery surrounding this heretic pharaoh has not abated, but that recovering the last details of his life is as hard as ever. That Akhenaton (spelled a half dozen different ways, with the *Geographic* article favoring Akhenat*en*) is forced out of Thebes in Egypt is certain, and he heads for a "new capital . . . 180 miles to the north on the eastern bank of the Nile," where he builds a temple complex called Akhetaten, meaning "horizon of Aten."[13] The area, now an archeological site called Tel Amarna, once contained a city of some 20,000 residents.[14] The replacement of Amen by Aton reflects the wilderness encounter Oedipus experiences with the Eumenides, who previously were the Furies. The political disarray in the Thebes of the Oedipus myth reflects the civil strife in Egyptian Thebes, and Rick Gore's up-to-date *Geographic* article shows a concerted effort by the priests of Amun-Re to eradicate any evidence that Akhenaton and Nefertiti ever existed. "Nefertiti's cartouche was chiseled from [every stone] as Akhenaten's was elsewhere."[15] Granted that his tomb is now known, it was certainly off limits after the priesthood took back control of traditional religion in ancient Egypt: "Soon the names of Akhenaten and his god were eradicated and their temples torn down. Amarna was gradually abandoned." The powerful Horemheb "followed Aye to the throne and ruled for 27 years, obliterating every record of Nefertiti and Akhenaten that he could."[16]

The point here is clear, I think: Oedipus dies and does not ascend. Theseus's oath is the remembrance of the old Egyptian religion's attempt to prevent the heresy of Oedipus–Akhenaton from infecting any new generation. It is worth noting that Creon, Iocasta, Antigone, Etiocles, Polyneices, and Oedipus die under clouds of suspicion, ill will, violence, and mystery. The ever-astounding poet–engraver William Blake (1757–1827) connects his Oedipus character Tiriel to the same combined Egyptian–Boetian myth that Velikovsky uncovered generations later.* However speculative this view is, it is the only one that clearly shows us a solution to the age-old problem of interpreting the final moments of Oedipus in Sophocles' last Theban tragedy.

The Metamorphoses: A Variation on the Theme

Ovid's best-known (and likely his best) work is the collection of myths titled the *Metamorphoses*, or "transformations," some two hundred tales ending in a physical transformation. For example, in the story of Pygmalion, a beautiful statue fashioned by a good-hearted sculptor comes to life to reward his devotion to the gods and to art; the myth in its turn became the inspiration for (or at least the mythic precedent for) George Bernard Shaw's play by the same name. There is no doubt

---

* Blake's first drawing, to accompany the ultimately unengraved dramatic poem *Tiriel*, pictures this clearly Oedipal character (blind, at war with his children, forced to leave his own palace and reign after the death of his wife, Myratana) about to curse his sons. The chief son, the crown prince, is named Heuxos (a variant of *Hyksos*, the Egyptian–Aryan or Semitic shepherd-kings of Egypt), and he and his brothers stand in front of three Greek pillars, while in the background there is an Egyptian pyramid, showing Blake's awareness that there is an Egyptian Thebes and that the Sphinx, whose riddle Oedipus solves, is assuredly the Egyptian Sphinx as well. Later, Blake's protagonist Tiriel does "battle" with his brother Ijim, who is pictured in the poem's accompanying drawings as a lionlike creature who tests Tiriel at the entrance to Ijim's forest and whom Tiriel tames and forces into his service. (Ijim's name comes from *Isaiah* in the Old Testament; Ijim is a satyr, as averred by both Northrop Frye and Harold Bloom, well-known literary critics and specialists on Blake.)

that Ovid, of all the Latin poets, had the greatest influence on English literary tradition, if not all continental tradition. Ovid's tale of the judgment of Midas provided the ass's ears for Shakespeare's character Bottom; the Romeo and Juliet tale, though proximately based on a French poem, is ultimately the story of Pyramus and Thisbe (which also is parodied in *A Midsummer Night's Dream*).

Yet as concerns the myths of ascension–translation, Ovid must be styled a "variation on the theme," first, because many characters in the tales die tragically and second, only some of these deaths can be called failed ascension narratives. One tale that *can* be so designated is that of Phaethon.* He, like Gilgamesh, is partly divine; Phaethon indeed is the son of the Sun but has a mortal mother. He is vulnerable, however, for when he "entered the palace" and "turned toward the face [of] his father . . . he could not bear that radiance." The young man seeks a boon from his divine father, who swears by the Styx to grant it. His father is shocked when the young man asks to drive his father's sun-chariot across the heavens. Much as the gods' reaction to Gilgamesh's heroics, Phoebus declares, "Your lot is mortal, but what you ask is beyond the lot of mortals." Indeed, not even Jove himself, but only Phoebus, can control the chariot. The test would surely fix the lot of Phaethon: death for any ordinary mortal, but ascension and translation for anyone who could succeed. The warnings of the father do no good, and the god is bound by his oath (the classic tragic plot of the rash vow). The young man is off to a good start at the gates of Aurora, but in midflight, he loses the divine touch on the reins:

> It did not take the horses long to know it,
> To run away, beyond control; the driver,
> In panic, does not know in which direction
> To turn the reins, does not know where the road is,
> And even if he knew, he could do nothing
> With those wild plunging animals.[17]

The devastation on the earth and in the heavens is unimaginable: the constellations are out of control, and the Mediterranean is the scene of mass destruction

---

* I am using Rolphe Humphries's translation of the *Metamorphoses*; the Phaethon myth is one of the better developed of Ovid's tales. The original tale existed at one time in a play by Euripides, but the myth itself is a Babylonian sun myth that may hearken back as far as the Sumerian panetheon, whose sun god, Shamash, challenges the heroic Gilgamesh.

of cities, forests, and mountains. Jove finally hurls a thunderbolt to end the young man's journey as he completely loses control of his chariot. Curiously, he is buried after his death but is not the object of metamorphosis: rather, his family, who mourn him inconsolably, are changed variously into trees or swans.

Phaethon, though mortal, clearly could have succeeded, had the myth occurred for that purpose—to exalt a fortunate hero. Yet Phaethon joins Gilgamesh, Alexander the Great, and many other heroic figures who gamble for divinity but lose the bet. What sort of human could succeed when Phaethon, semidivine, could not?

The hapless Phaethon is counterbalanced by a marvelous though brief reference in Ovid (also in Livy) to the "transfiguration" of Romulus, the legendary founder of Rome. Mars comes before Jove, reminding the chief of the gods of a former promise made for which Mars now seeks the fulfillment: "There will be one whom Mars / Shall bear to the blue Heaven." Mars swooped down under the cover of Jovian clouds and thunders "as Ilia's son was giving judgment. . . . He caught him up from earth, his mortal body / Dissolved into thin air, as a leaden bullet . . . and now a new and fairer form is given him, / Worthy of the high gods' couches." That such a metamorphosis is in fact a "transfiguration" should clearly establish that this is not anything approaching a "death." He is in fact a god, receiving the new name "Quirinus." An added detail in Ovid's account that touches on our framing of the ancient narratives of translation is that the new god's former queen consort, Hersilia, is also invited to ascend to the home of the gods, where Romulus "changed her body, / Her former name, and called her Hora, goddess . . . ."

The last selection in the *Metamorphoses* also provides an affirmation of heroic ascension, and, while not explaining the origin or purpose for the most ancient tale of Phaethon, Ovid's last selection nevertheless does explain the inclusion of Phaethon among Ovid's vast assortment of tales: I refer to the deification of Caesar. Ovid's logic comes very close to Catholic logic in deifying the Virgin Mary as the "godbearer." Ovid says of Augustus and Julius Caesar, "We cannot think him mortal, our Augustus. Therefore our Julius must be made a god to justify his son." Julius Caesar is thus made "immortal through his son" (read *descendent*, for Augustus was Julius Caesar's grandnephew). Catholic exegetes have at times sidestepped this important connection between Jesus and his mother, following Thomas

Aquinas's argument that Mary had to be completely human in order for Jesus to be truly human as well as, through his divine father, truly god. There is every reason to believe that the deification of both Mary and Jesus, at least in the Jewish "Christian" congregations in Rome, was a reaction to Ovid's popular narrative of the deification of Augustus, just as the Ethiopian Jewish Christian designation of Mary as Queen of Heaven responded to the narratives of the cult of Isis. It is no accident that Ovid runs into precisely the same narrative complication that plagued the chroniclers of the heroic ascent and translation of Jesus and Mary: Julius Caesar was murdered, and the whole world knew of his death. His deification must occur then *in spite of* his death. The text relates that

> Venus, all unseen, came to the temple,
> Raised from the body of Caesar the fleeting spirit,
> Not to be lost in air, but borne aloft
> To the bright stars of Heaven. As she bore it,
> She felt it burn, released it from her bosom,
> And saw it rise, beyond the moon, a comet
> Rising, not falling, leaving the long fire
> Behind its wake, and gleaming as a star.

What should be noted here is the absolute necessity of metamorphosis; the mere survival of the shade of Julius Caesar is insufficient for deification. He must become a heavenly body (recall the funeral pyre of Herakles, and the ascending angel in Gideon's altar fire) much as Jupiter or Mars. While the Ptolemaic universe allows for the ascension of the disembodied spirit, there is a world of difference between the ascension of the spirit (a reward for faithfulness to Catholicism or, in an earlier time, to Rome itself, by ordinary people) and admission to the divine family. It is thus no surprise that Ovid promises his fellow Romans that Augustus, like Julius Caesar before him, "shall leave the world he rules, ascend to Heaven, / And there, beyond our presence, hear our prayers!" Ovid does not anticipate that same sort of glory for himself but merely hopes that he will exist in some form after his death and that his poetry will immortalize him (the metaphoric translation or metamorphosis from mortal poet to immortal text). The parallel here with Mary as divine intercessor hardly needs elaboration. The fact of his historical death presents the same plot complication for the ascension–translation of Caesar as it does for the ascension–translation of the heroic Messiah, Jesus.

Ovid himself clearly hoped to benefit from the deification of Caesar. To immortalize Caesar in his text is in itself a metamorphosis. At the same time Ovid himself is metamorphosed into an immortal:

> The better part, immortal, will be borne
> Above the stars; my name will be remembered
> Wherever Roman power rules conquered lands,
> I shall be read, and through all centuries,
> If prophecies of bards are ever truthful,
> I shall be living, always.

His prophecy was fulfilled spectacularly, for it is Ovid's writings that have been "translated" (pun intended) and have endured: "It will endure, I trust, . . . beyond Time's hunger." The motives behind the narrative are certainly political and self-aggrandizing. But precisely such clever tactics have impressed the gods in many an ascension or translation narrative.

Some Comments on *The Dream of the Rood*

Until this book was well under way, I could not think of anything in Anglo-Saxon poetry to connect to the motifs I am examining. But there are, in fact, a number of "dream poems" containing ascending characters, though the images are occasionally hard to spot. That Anglo-Saxon religious poetry had a literary function as well should be quite clear. For example, in the poet Cynewulf's treatment of Christ's ascension in *Christ II*, from the *Exeter Book*, he follows Gregory's homily for Ascension Day[18] and includes spiritual "key words" given by Christ to the apostles immediately preceding his ascension. The ascension is a type or sign to turn human gaze upward—a sort of spiritual ascension. Oliver Grosz reminds us that the ascension is the final leap, after the "six leaps" in Cynewulf's poem, and adds, "The whole idea of the leap, then, becomes metaphorical for the sudden change from one level of existence (or thought) to another without rational explanations, but rather in mystery."[19] Furthermore, Christ's leap to heaven is the proper conclusion to the *descensus*[20] that occurs in the medieval *Harrowing of Hell*. The connection of Christ's ascension to other examples of ascension–translation was covered in chapter three. But in connection with Cynewulf, Peter Clemoes sees that event as "a supreme manifestation of [Christ's] sovereignty," and he sees contained in Cynewulf's account "the elements of heroic literary tradition as linguistic resources for image-making,"[21] which is to say, Cynewulf finds narrative (literary) strategies to complete the heroic elements of Christ's ascension.

A more familiar Anglo-Saxon poem, *The Dream of the Rood* contains some of these elements of the ascension myth. Students and at times scholars find this poem particularly troubling because of the tenuous connection between the heroic thane Jesus and the rood's role as Suffering Servant. But it is precisely the poem's narrative strategy of separating the motif of ascending hero from that of Suffering Servant that interests me.

To begin with, there are *two* crosses in the narrative, the gold-adorned, transmuted cross (wood alchemically changed to gold and jewels), which is ascending (*on lyft laedan*) and glorified (*beama beorhtost*). The angels assemble around it (much as in Cynewulf's account), its beams recalling the supporting joists of the mead-hall ceiling, the earthly equivalent of heaven's mead hall or temple. This is the glorified cross of the cathedral, of the king's chapel, adorned and placed high above the worshipers.

The pilgrim contrasts this heroic cross with the cross representing the marred servant—the two images alternating, seemingly beyond the control of the visionary poet. When the cross begins to speak, it suffers the marring of black nails (*deorcum naeylum*, an astonishing awareness of the crude iron that symbolizes Roman rule in Daniel's vision of the giant statue) and is blood-soaked from arrow wounds with arrows; its ascension and redemption are of a different order from Christ's, yet the heroic pattern is confirmed. The old cross, beaten and weary, is raised up and covered in gold, to become an ensign not unlike Moses' brazen serpent, healing those who look up toward it.

The narrative strategy the poet chooses (for clearly, as in chapter three, these are parts of separate narratives) in order to make the two crosses one is to give the cross a voice, letting it speak in the first person (*ic*), thus forcing the two narratives together—a strategy not unlike that of the scribe John in Revelation, whose glorious Christ connects himself explicitly to the mortal Jesus of Nazareth. By the time *Rood* is recorded, of course, the narrative of Christ's mortal role of Suffering Servant, combined with his role of sacrificial victim, and of ascending hero, had been fixed in the Latin Bible and in the Anglo-Saxon translations.

What is remarkable about the description of Christ, as everyone knows, is his warrior's attitude. He undresses, as if he were ready to challenge Breca to a swimming contest, then ascends (the root is *stigan*, which can mean "ascend" or, given Cynewulf's account, "leaps") onto his own cross (with a warrior's sense of honor), grabs hold of it (*clyppan*, whence our paper "clip"), and struggles on the cross as the victorious Lord, with sin representing something akin to a dragon or a demon-seed such as Grendel or his mother. In the poem as a whole, Christ is relatively unmarked; the cross doesn't kill him, but his body shines as though he were still wearing his armor. He gets a hero's burial and is transformed into the iconographic ascending hero while the cross gets wounded and battered. Naked and wounded, it is the cross that is wrapped in gold leaf to hide its shame. Its reward is to be the new sign of Christian allegiance, the bright cross (*beacna selest*, best of beacons). Christ, as ascending hero, sits down to a hero's feast in the heavenly mead hall. The innovation of the poem, its razor-thin passage through the oppressing traps of orthodox Gospel narratives, is remarkable and makes it one of the best Anglo-Saxon treatments of the ascension pattern.

The Ascent of Chaucer's *Troilus*

Troilus is the embodiment of a pagan-Christian synthesis of ascension and translation myth. Boccaccio is the source of the tale itself, but it is Chaucer who turns it into a grand romantic epic, containing a love tragedy—but with an utterly comedic postscript. There is certainly no doubt that Oedipus is slain, for as Book Five of *Troilus and Criseyde* declares, "And whan that he was slayn in this manere, / His lighte goost ful blisfully is went . . ." (5.1807–8). Yet Troilus, instead of joining Hector, Patroclus, and Teiresias in Hades (the underworld), is elevated "up to the holughnesse of the eighthe spere" (1809). According to John W. Conlee, this surprising turn of metaphysical events has left Chaucer critics in a quandary, for on the one hand, Troilus is a pagan, unworthy of such an ascension, and on the other hand, one cannot ignore the Christian cosmology that makes the eighth sphere so holy—its closeness to God's throne.* Conlee reminds us that such ascents were granted mostly to heroes or heads of state and adds that such figures

---

* Even the text is debated, with some texts yielding "seventh" rather than "eighth" sphere.[22] Conlee's argument is by far the best—the solution is in ascension myth from ancient sources.

were divine creatures to begin with, descending through the planetary spheres till they arrived on the earth as mortals; thus when such beings "die" they merely ascend back from whence they came, being "divested ... successively of each of the attributes of the planets so that [their essential being] was once again purified when it reached the holiness of the eighth sphere."[23] In this case, death is not an event as much as a process of divesting the hero of the decadent trappings of mortality. What remains is not a shade, but an essence (ether, ichor?), like Milton's angels, and could still be wounded but never could be slain.

From the perspective of Chaucer's narrative strategy, I find additional echoes of the motif of the ascending hero. Chaucer has redeemed the Troilus myth from its original source in Boccaccio, and the hero ascends partly because Chaucer has lifted him to the status of an epic romance hero. Troilus, hardly more than a footnote in the ancient past, is exalted through the epic power of romantic love. Much as metaphors in scripture (according to medieval thought) were designed to lead one to higher truth through earthly images,[24] Chaucer's hero is the earthly, pagan conceit from which the true Christian could propose a higher sort of Christian romantic hero (perhaps something on the order of Spenser's Redcrosse Knight). Here Chaucer anticipates Ficino and the Italian Neoplatonists whose views influenced the romantic formula that physical love (eros) can be the means of transcendence to heavenly love (agape).* Troilus is the tragic-heroic embodiment of medieval courtly love, but his ascension may be said to distantly reflect a parallel Christian myth of the ascent of the soul. The issue of transcendence in *Troilus and Criseyde*, then, is not whether Troilus has the right to be where he is, not even remotely how his location integrates with Christian theology, but only that the gods (or the poet-narrator) have some heroic justification for the ascension. Theology is a red herring here; too much is assumed from the word *holughnesse*, which is not used exclusively as a Christian state of being.

---

* In asserting this, I take my leave of Conlee, who is more inclined to see Troilus's ascension as a marriage of Christian and pagan traditions that incorporate the numerological properties of the number eight. On the Neoplatonism of love, M. Schumacher notes, "[For Ficino, the human soul is] the image of the God-head, a part of the great chain of existence coming forth from God and leading back to the same source, giving us at the same time a view of the attributes of God of his relations to the world."[25]

The word, like the Latin *sanctus*, means "a condition of being set apart," so that the idea of holiness is as relevant to pagan as to Christian theology. As Morton Bloomfield has suggested, Chaucer invites his readers to join him in prayer for Troilus, who, as a pagan, cannot achieve the Christian heaven. Such an invitation is an act of Christian benevolence,[26] not a theological strategy. To sum up my argument, then, Troilus ascends because of the greatness of his love. His distancing from earth allows him a measure of godly perspective, as most Chaucer critics would allow, but the reward of immortality for the great lover is an innovation only Chaucer could envision.

A final note: Chaucer's Troilus may be said to be translated much as Ovid's heroes are: to become a constellation in the starry eighth sphere. The ascending hero may also be in the ascendant, placed in a superior position in relation to other constellations, due to the phenomenon of precession, known anciently, that occurs because of the earth's slight "wobble."[27] Chaucer may have been subtly implying that a change in cultural values was occurring in which the absolutely Christ-centered mind-set of medieval thought would give way to a human-centered renaissance of Hellenism.*

Paradise Regained

In John Milton's brief epic one finds abundant evidence for the heroic model of Christ that culminates in ascension and translation, the same model proposed in chapter three of this book and contrasted with the model of the sacrificial lamb. In fact, William Blake's comment on Milton's theology is ironically appropriate in this context: "Milton was of the Devil's party without knowing it." Blake had reference to Milton's rebel political spirit which infuses his poetry and prose with a heterodox or even heretical sense. Thus Milton may be aware of the dynamic but contradictory models he creates in his own poetry. He gives Jesus a heroic desire for (righteous) glory when as a youth he visits the temple and both hears and speaks to "the Teachers of our Law":

---

* Man becomes the "measure of all things." Jesse M. Gellrich as much as says that Chaucer attempted to escape the influence of the Middle Ages (the example used is *The House of Fame*). Chaucer breaks with the tradition that demands one language, one text. Yet he still resolves conflict using the medieval notion of faith rather than true Renaissance skepticism (169–72).

>   . . . this not all
> To which my Spirit aspir'd, victorious deed
> Flam'd in my heart, heroic acts, one while
> To rescue Israel from the Roman yoke,
> Then to subdue and quell o'er all the earth
> Brute violence and proud Tyrannic pow'r,
> Till truth were freed, and equity restor'd. (1.214–20)[28]

His own mother is partly responsible for instilling in him such heroic sentiments; she counsels him, "By matchless Deeds express thy matchless Sire" (1.233). At this point she reveals to him his divine parentage, much as young Phaethon learns it, empowering him.

When Jesus disappears into the wilderness, the apostles, newly called after Jesus' baptism but before his wilderness ordeal, express wonder at his sudden disappearance after the grand witness of his calling by John the Baptist. Their doubts clearly and consciously evoke the doubts the apostles endure after the Crucifixion, which has the effect of correlating the wilderness temptation as a redemptive act and the Crucifixion and the Resurrection. Their first conjecture is that Jesus has been "for a time caught up to God, as once Moses was in the Mount" (2.14–15), a clearly heroic ascension; an allusion quickly follows to Elijah, "the great Thisbite who on fiery wheels / Rode up to Heaven, yet once again to come" (2.16–17). They comfort themselves feebly with the notion that since Elijah would come again, so also would Jesus. Milton goes so far with this subplot as to allow Jesus' new disciples, much as Elijah's disciples, to seek him in all the nearby towns.

Paradise Regained asserts and never falters in the proposition that the wilderness temptation is for Milton the proper historic and mythic analog to the fall of Adam, resulting in the heroic return of the "second Adam" to paradise. That Christ does not, indeed cannot, die in this ordeal, but triumphs wholly and completely, is the irreducible premise of the entire poem. The Atonement, the Crucifixion, and the Resurrection put away Sin and Death, the incestuous products of the Satan of *Paradise Lost*, but Satan himself, the prime mover of hell and the chief protagonist of the first books of *Paradise Lost*, is defeated here in the Judean desert in a meeting of champions dueling with verbal weapons in the heroic tradition of the meeting of Patroclus and Hector in the *Iliad*. Milton's argument, at the end of Book Four of *Paradise Regained*, sums up what exactly Jesus accomplished in this encounter:

>   . . . by vanquishing
> Temptation, [Jesus hath] regain'd lost Paradise,
> And frustrated the conquest fraudulent:
> He [Satan] never more henceforth will dare set foot
> In Paradise to tempt; his snares are broke:
> For though that seat of earthly bliss be fail'd,
> A fairer Paradise is founded now . . . (4.607–13)

What emerges in these lines is that Jesus as hero–Messiah must win a personal battle to assure his ability to win the later battles with sin and death, much as David must defeat Goliath in single combat to qualify him to rule all Israel and subdue all the nations occupying Canaan. Lest anyone assume that the paradise mentioned above refers to humanity's life after death, one must keep in mind that Milton was a mortalist, not believing in a life after death but only in the physical resurrection. Paradise is meant to depict the millennial reign of the Messiah, where Satan, bound for a thousand years according to Revelation, will be unable to tempt or try humankind.

But the effect, despite Milton's ultimate intentions, is to create of Jesus another Metatron or Elijah, one whose defeat of Satan in single combat precedes and foreshadows his ascension–translation as a meritorious hero. Perhaps Milton died before he could write *Paradise Regained II: The Battle against Sin and Death*, or perhaps he felt disinclined when the four Gospels, especially John's, cover the Atonement, the Crucifixion, and the Resurrection with such tragic grandeur; but in any case, *Paradise Regained* is remarkable literary proof of the viability of the model of Christ as conquering hero, ascended and translated.

There is support for this view of Jesus in Milton's prose writings, specifically in *De Doctrina Christiana*, a manuscript work neither translated nor published until 1825.[29] Milton declares, "Before the law, this [glorification of Christ] was typified by the translation of Enoch (Gen. 5:24), as it was under the law by that of Elijah" (2 Kings 2:11).[30] Milton, in a fashion typical of the entire treatise, cites scripture after scripture establishing the typology of glorification, beginning with the prophecy attributed to Enoch in Jude verses 14, 15, which in fact is preserved in the Ethiopian Enoch, which had been published in translation only in 1821. Milton is insistent that certain of those caught up to heaven are more meritorious than others: "It appears that all the saints will not attain to an equal state of glory";

Milton mentions 1 Corinthians 15:41–42 in support: "There is one glory of the sun, and another glory of the moon, and another glory of the stars; for one star differeth from another star in glory: so also is the resurrection of the dead." Milton's heroic vision of Jesus is predicated on the notion of a man, a mortal human, who heroically fulfills God's will and thus merits an exalted station: "That Christ was very man is evident from his having a body." How this mortal nature of Christ is reconciled with his divine nature, or specifically with the divine office of mediator which he holds, Milton simply concludes, "It is too profound a mystery, in my judgment at least, to warrant any positive assertion respecting it."[31] In light of these statements, I believe that Milton is arguing for the meritorious glory of the mortal Jesus as something acquired at his resurrection, but not something which he already possessed before he came to mortality. Milton consistently preaches the doctrine of the imitation of Christ: "Men hereafter may discern / From what consummate virtue I have chose / This perfect man, by *merit* call'd my Son, / To *earn* salvation for the sons of men" (*Pardise Regained* 1.164–67).[32] In fact, Milton considers the role of mediator to consist of the clearly meritorious offices of prophet, priest, and king.[33] It goes without saying that during his own lifetime, Jesus did not receive his kingship, and his priestly office went hand in hand with his role as sacrificial victim, although he clearly held the prophetic office, but only for those people who chose to follow him.

Although Milton clearly rejects the Catholic doctrine of supererogation, "whereby more is done than the law prescribes, insomuch that some of the saints . . . have been enabled to purchase eternal life not only for themselves, but for others"; nevertheless, it must be acknowledged that Jesus, as Milton portrays him, heroically achieves just that end and that mortals are to imitate this heroic pattern is tacitly acknowledged further on: "Those counsels of the gospel . . . which the Papists affirm to be . . . supererogation, are not in reality . . . of a higher nature than [precepts], . . . but are . . . given, not to all mankind, but to certain individuals, for special reasons and under special circumstances." Furthermore, despite Milton's protestations of "the vanity of human merits,"[34] we have already seen that Milton embraced the Pauline doctrine of varying degrees of glory (or heavenly reward). Though it is ostensibly far from Milton's purpose (indeed, he implies in several places, as C. S. Lewis has noted, that Satan's great evil was a form of hubris in which, like Phaethon, he saw himself the equal of his Creator);

nevertheless, Milton clearly admires the heroic qualities of Christ and of great Christians. As Shelley's *Prometheus Unbound* makes clear, it is not Satan's heroic qualities that condemn him; rather it is Satan's pride (coupled with the vengeful nature of Milton's unfortunate portrayal of God) that condemns him. It is undeniably heroic of the premortal existent Jesus of *Paradise Lost* to stand between God's wrath and helpless, fallen humanity—heroic because of the inherent danger of defying the gods, and noble because, unlike Satan, Jesus is not self-interested:

> Behold me, then: me for him, life for life,
> I offer; on me let thine anger fall;
> Account me man: I for his sake will leave
> Thy bosom, and this glory next to thee
> Freely put off, and for him lastly die
> Well pleased; on me let Death wreak all his rage;
> Under his gloomy power I shall not long
> Lie vanquished. (3.236–43)

This wonderful image of being "down for the count" but heroically struggling to one's feet, ultimately to vanquish the foe, is precisely the same heroic device Satan uses earlier in *Paradise Lost* to pick himself off the mat in dark Chaos, where he has been cast. Milton's narrative and theological risk in pleading Satan's heroic cause in Book 1 and Book 2, saving Jesus' dramatic scene for Book 3, is not merely a study in ironic parallels, for compared to Milton's God, a distant being whose purposes a third of the host of heaven took for tyranny, Milton's Satan is Promethean, as true a benefactor to humans (at least outwardly) as Prometheus was in defying Jupiter's wrath.

Acknowledging as he does Enoch's and Elijah's "special reasons and special circumstances," which resulted in their ascension and translation, purely as types, in anticipation of Christ's heroic ascension and translation, Milton places certain people in a special, heroic category that defies his own pronouncements on the absolute dependence of humans on the "merits"[35] of God through Christ.

Pope's Ascent of the Lock: The Variation Resumed

The heir to Ovid's literary riches concerning metamorphosis is not Shakespeare, however much Shakespeare was influenced by Ovid. Alexander Pope's *The Rape of the Lock* is the purest literary heir of the transcendence inherent in the

Metamorphoses. I assert this, all the while knowing that there is nothing new in seeing echoes of Ovid in this marvelous mock-epic. Furthermore, the story's mild social satire does not militate against its employing the metaphysics of classical myth. On what basis, then, is Belinda's lock taken to heaven? Perhaps one ought to ask, why the lock of hair and not Belinda herself? The last lines of the poem sharply contrast Belinda's own fate with that of her prized lock:

> When, after millions slain, yourself shall die:
> When those fair suns shall set, as set they must,
> And all those tresses shall be laid in dust,
> This Lock the Muse shall consecrate to fame,
> And 'midst the stars inscribe Belinda's name. (5.145–50)

The lock is exalted rather than Belinda because of the nature of the poem. Critics such as William Frost have pointed to the heroic elements of the poem in relation to the *Iliad*, specifically to Pope's own brilliant translation of it. The heroic epic is not being parodied, as such; rather, the indecorous behavior of all the parties in this mock-heroic are petty and microcosmic versions of the larger-than-life heroes of classical mythology. There is at least one tacit admission in the Horatian wit of *Rape*, and that is the paucity of fit heroic subjects. It is remarkable that in the age when classical literature was most admired, its chief figures, immersed in the anxiety of influence, could not find fit heroic material for an original epic. They stood in the shadows of the tormented but brilliant Tasso, the mighty Milton, and the brilliant Cervantes and had no end of admiration for the great national heroes of the past: El Cid, Roland, and Redcrosse Knight. But Pope despaired of producing such a heroic epic, preferring the philosophical epic of the planned *Moral Epistles*. Pope's translations of Homer are unsurpassed, but lesser poets who made the attempt traditionally failed (Cowley's *Davidias* comes to mind). Milton's Samson is of heroic stature, but Milton cannot compete with the powerful action of the King James rendition of Judges, and the characters of his dramatic poem are reduced to philosophizing, Job-like, to fulfill the daunting requirements of a two-thousand-year-old legacy of prescriptive epic criticism. Dryden's *Absalom and Achitophel* pales in comparison to the dramatic Old Testament narrative on which it is based; in fact, this political *epylion* requires so much literary compromise in order to account for various characters to conform to their real-life counterparts that its heroic qualities (designed to vindicate Charles II) fall easy prey to the vices of most political allegory, with the exception of Achitophel's brilliant sophistry, as reminiscent as it is of Milton's heroic Satan. Concerning the morass of epic criticism and the state of poetic genius in eighteenth-century literature, Voltaire threw up his hands at Le Bossu's strictures on the epic subject, intimating that the only thing worse than reading Le Bossu's prescriptions would be to read any epic based on such rules!

If Belinda's lock is truly translated (and the narrative allows only the supposition of the metamorphosis), it is a stunning witness to the loss of the heroic in eighteenth-century society. Lord Byron's "pedestrian muse" was brutally though comically honest when he admits, "I want [meaning both "lack" and "desire"] a hero." But Byron does not want the cheap heroes "cloying the gazettes with cant"; his solution is an anti-hero, Don Juan.[36] Though Byron deconstructs the epic genre itself, his poetic lack/desire is a genuine angst over the lack of transcendent heroes. It is precisely his generation of poets, including Wordsworth, Blake, and Shelley who reinvent the genre and offer the first artists-as-heroes. It is not unreasonable to argue the death, at least in Europe, of the ascending, transfigured hero, dating from the death of Milton.

Yet the idea of ascension–translation is certainly not dead; it merely metamorphoses through the literary experiments of British and American poets and novelists.

Gnosis vs. Blood Atonement in Blake

William Blake, an engraver, artist, and poet of remarkable vision, has been canonized only in the twentieth century. In his own lifetime (1757–1827), he was largely ignored. His efforts to preserve ascension–translation myth take the curious turn of a very ancient, little known (in Blake's day) form of Christian gnosticism.[37] His personal mythology combined gnostic redemption (and its less antinomian counterpart in Neoplatonism) and the ascension–translation of Christ and all his true disciples. Blake placed his understanding of gnostic redemption, ascension, and translation in the literary context of his "visionary forms dramatic" and perpetual forgiveness of sins.

Gnosticism in general and Christian gnosticism in particular grew in part out of the perceived discrepancy between God's perceptions of time and our own temporality, a concept explored at some length in Melville's *Pierre* in the chapter on horologicals and chronometrics but perfected in Melville's most ingenious creation, Bartleby, whose entire existence, like God's, seems entirely out of sync with that of the real world. The discrepancy is this: we mark earthly time through changes—changes in the sun's position in the skies, changes in the seasons, and changes in ourselves and our surroundings—including the death of everything from leaves on trees to great civilizations to languages to ourselves. God, however, represents what is unchanging, immutable, timeless, and unmoved by the physical universe. To God, then, the fact that Israel waited many years for redemption from a cruel pharaoh becomes almost an irrelevancy, since from his divine perspective, all mortal existence is illusory. But gnosticism's rejection of material time and space can be found in a far older tradition of the hope of a privileged few to escape death itself, the ultimate marker of material existence. The essence of the ascension and translation of the exceptionally courageous, righteous, or clever human is a transition from mutability to immutability, from being acted upon to being that which only acts upon others. Why this is so must be obvious: to be acted upon is to be victimized, to be changed by one's surroundings, and thus to be temporalized and mortalized. Therefore ascension and translation are the logical mythical precursors of gnosticism, whether in its Greek, Jewish, Christian, Mandean, or Manichaean varieties.

This discrepancy between what is temporal and what is eternal creates a *dualism* (a hallmark of gnosticism, Neoplatonism, and mystery cults), in which temporal things become illusions to the minds of eternal beings in the same way eternal points of reference elude mortal or temporal minds. The idea of *gnosis* (a Greek word for divine knowledge), then, is to reveal (as in revelation) divine understanding to mortal beings, so that finite minds can perceive the infinite. Such cosmic understanding has a "down side," of course: a disdain for and rejection of the material world.

The early Christian gnostics loved the idea of Jesus' being a redeemer sent by God, in fact containing within him a hypostatic emanation from the All (one of many gnostic terms for the unknowable god of gods). Indeed, the opening verses of John's Gospel in the New Testament are the purest sort of gnostic revelation. While the incarnation of Jesus as the Word (*logos*) fits the benign role of the *demiurgos* (the artificer or creator of material existence) found in Neoplatonism rather than gnosticism, nevertheless, the gnostics saw Jesus as a gnostic redeemer. To make him their redeemer, however, certain things about the historical Jesus had to be ignored or reinterpreted: (1) his birth was heralded in the Gospels as a great event, when gnostics believed that being born into mortality was a sort of imprisonment, and (2) Jesus died, creating the kind of tragic victim the gnostics associated with the worst aspects of mortal delusion. Birth, as we all know, is the initial event leading to death, and human history attests that after every birth a death is inevitable; no death would be possible without a birth. That Jesus would partake of such a cycle of temporality doesn't fit well, in gnostic estimation, with God's rescuing humanity from the evils of material creation. Rather, God seems in the Gospels to condescend, getting trapped horribly the way any ordinary mortal might. Orthodox apologists pointed out, of course, that God's love allowed him to jump into the abyss of mortality, so that people could relate to God better. From a gnostic perspective, however, just the opposite should happen: God might be trapped in this world in some form, yes, but not because he wished to relate to us. Rather, he came to raise us to his level and seemed to get trapped in the attempt. (This scenario shifts a lot in gnosticism, but I think this represents the gnostic pattern accurately.)

Jesus' death is an even bigger obstacle than his being imprisoned in flesh to begin with. If God descended in order to raise us to his level, of what possible good was the death of Jesus? In terms of temporality, death would be, from the viewpoint of the eternal mind, the ultimate illusion, something to ignore or see beyond, possibly to transcend, but certainly not anything in which to participate actively. To the gnostic, the whole idea of physical resurrection would be ridiculous, an antic sideshow, if the real purpose of sending the gnostic redeemer was to save us by giving us *divine* perspective.

It is for this reason that gnostic methodology became a cultural text for early followers of Christ. Indeed, I think it is becoming increasingly clear that gnostic forms of Christianity, including early gnostic Gospels (in particular the Gospel of Thomas), were alternative forms of Christianity from the movement's beginning and that what we now consider orthodoxy was just one of several approaches to Christianity.* When Jesus died, the Messianic movement—doubtless led by James the Priest and other Jews—had to be sublimated into other modes of discourse, notably the possibility Jesus didn't really die on the cross (a story later ascribed to Jesus' "enemies"),†

---

* This view is held by Elaine Pagels, in *The Gnostic Gospels*,[38] who found the same sort of demonizing going on among gnostics against the orthodox, ecclesiastic view of Christianity as was done by such orthodox figures as Iranaeus and Hippolytus against the gnostics.

† Again, Pagels, this time in *The Origin of Satan*,[39] shows that demonizing one's rivals was the ideal means of keeping one's own theological approach in the ascendant.

with a final ascension, translation, and "return" in the near future of the man whose body disappeared from the tomb. Yet another group embraced the Adonis–Tammuz–Dionysius myth of the god who descends in order to suffer blood atonement and to teach us how to die with dignity. Another group blended the two previous perceptions into the difficult mix of (apparent) tragedy and triumph currently found in the New Testament. But still another group was so taken aback by Jesus' death that it abstracted the entire incident, relegating the Crucifixion to the category of illusion. One gnostic account goes so far as to depict the true Jesus standing invisibly above his cross laughing while a clone hangs on the tree of shame. In all the gnostic accounts Jesus accomplishes his mission not through blood atonement but through the offering of gnosis, divine revelation, to all who are prepared to hear the message. The Resurrection is a symbolic act for the more sedate ancient gnostics, but for more wild-eyed gnostics it was an affront to one's sense of the divine.*

---

* At this point it is important to talk about the most curious aspect of the assertion that Jesus was literally raised from the dead, then ascended with that body, just as even the dead will rise at the last day. As mentioned earlier (chapter three), the only purpose the Pharisees saw in resurrection was that God could then judge people's works "in the flesh," perhaps allowing the dead to live again during the reign of the Messiah. All Christendom traditionally embraces the Resurrection narrative in the New Testament as at least an important symbol, but curiously, even those professing vehement faith in the Resurrection can't seem to find a place for it in their daily and long-range theological views. It is traditionally brought up at burial services, but the idea that when we die we all go to heaven immediately (or to hell if we are evil) cannot be erased from our cultural memory. Dante's vision of heaven, hell, and purgatory is likely the culprit, for its images have filtered down to all Westerners through Catholicism, the single greatest creator and preserver of culture before the Renaissance. Baptists, despite profession of a strong belief in resurrection, are as much at a loss as Catholics to keep the life after death idea with its entirely noncorporeal judgments from supplanting the idea of a judgment after resurrection. Seventh Day Adventists have solved the irritating problem by being monists, specifically mortalists, so that thinking about a spirit world after this life becomes merely the result of demonic temptation, not of a genuinely alternative Christianity. Jehovah's Witnesses have become mortalists for the same reason; they conclude (logically enough) that death isn't much of a punishment for sin if everyone is just going to go on living after death and that resurrection is pretty much a useless reward if the spirit world is as delightful as the parathanetics tell us. Mormons have been overcome in recent years with the idea of life after death, blurring their own theological stances on resurrection by reuniting separated families as soon as someone new dies (i.e., a beloved family member awaits the departed on the spirit world side of the "veil"). In fact, Jesus' "paradise" has evolved theologically into an after-death Garden of Eden where people are completely, blissfully fulfilled. (In fact, Dr. Raymond Moody, author of *A Life After Life*, culled many near-death experiences from Mormons.)[40]

In gnosticism, the message itself, brought by the gnostic angel or redeemer, is the means of transcendence, ascension, and translation to any soul that can receive it and embrace it. The difference in the gnostic version (a result of the influence of Greek philosophy, Jewish exegesis, and mystical rites) is that the whole thing happens inside your head. The illusion the rest of the world sees when gazing at a gnostic adept is of a rather nonproductive mystic very self-absorbed and completely unamenable to earthly authority of any kind—including Christian bishops and priests, which is why the orthodox church ended up warring against gnostic "infiltration" in the ranks.

Gnosticism is at once the most democratic and elitist transcendence imaginable, for though only those who are "prepared" are able to receive the revelation, anyone who fully comprehends the message will be no different from God himself. Every gnostic is a successful version of Gilgamesh, eternal life beginning the moment the secret "word of truth" or "word of power" is revealed. It represents the absolute rejection of temporality, a rejection in which one simply walks away from this world—not merely runs away from it in fear or desire, as did Gilgamesh. This gnostic perception is remarkably heroic, yet Buddhistic in the extreme, for the loss of fear and desire in this world is the beginning of *true individuality*, not of nihilism. Thus the gnostics were at once *dualistic* and *monistic*, for though temporal existence created duality, when the smoke clears away it is discovered that in fact there is only one real reality and that the invisible, timeless world of God is thus more concrete than anything in this material world which the gnostics rejected so emphatically. And blood atonement, in the gnostic reading of culture, cannot confer this divine knowledge of who we really are any more than a sacrificial lamb could teach the Sermon on the Mount.

I credit William Blake with being the first and possibly the only literary figure to read the "book" of Jesus in such diverse ways and to make coherent sense and system out of his readings, resulting in the Blakean "Bible of Hell," or the major and minor poetic prophecies that make up the bulk of Blake's engraved works. I will use passages from several of Blake's engraved works to show Blake's clear understanding of the "heroic" Jesus, the evil of blood atonement, and the rejection of death and the embracing of translation (or transfiguration) and ascension as means of salvation for all who accept the gnostic awakening or call from the gnostic redeemer of Blake's myth.

In Blake's *The Marriage of Heaven and Hell*, a satirical romp through Swedenborgian thought, the poet clearly rejects the entire theological system set up to justify or rationalize the fact that all of us will eventually fall apart and die: "Now is the dominion of Edom, & the return of Adam into Paradise,"[41] with Blake himself as the new Adam, redeemed from the Fall and allowed to reenter the garden of the immortals. (Blake was consistently and intensely visionary his entire life, having seen, at age three, God's face through his bedroom window.) Blake's contemporaries were to receive generally what Milton envisioned for Jesus in *Paradise Regained*: Jesus, the Second Adam, defeats Satan and enters the Garden of Eden. It goes without saying that Blake's generation will not have to experience death and will thus not sleep in death until the morning of the resurrection. To make his statement clearer, Blake affirms that the body and spirit are bound together inextricably, making the doctrine of life after death a sham: "All Bibles or sacred codes. Have been the causes of the following Errors. 1. That Man has two real existing principles Viz: a Body & a Soul. . . . But the following [is] true 1. Man has no Body distinct from his Soul for that calld Body is a portion of Soul discernd by the five Senses" (*Marriage* 4). Because Blake anticipated the Millennial reign of Christ in his lifetime, the heroic congregations of the truly faithful of Blake's generation would not taste death, but would be caught up to heaven to dwell in eternal flames or else to rest in the garden of delights. Like Jehovah, "he who dwells in flaming fire" is the Mosaic icon of the bush that burns continually but is never consumed—that is, never overcome by the four alchemical elements, for which fire is the symbol.*

Blake knew from his angelic messengers "that the world will be consumed in fire at the end of six thousand years" (14), and he knew that he, an Elijah figure, was the forerunner of the new age. He also knew that "the whole creation will be consumed, and appear infinite and holy whereas it now appears finite & corrupt" (14), and he reemphasized that the fire burns away only the "apparently" finite, much as acid on copper plates touches only the parts that Blake, the engraver, has chosen to remove, and "displaying the infinite which was hid." The process cannot result in death, but only in transfiguration. Translation, as well as its fiery furnace,

---

* Blake clearly embraced the theory of the four alchemical elements: earth, air, fire, and water, each assigned to a cardinal compass point and representing the four *zoas* or beasts of Ezekiel's vision.

the refiner's fire, is analogous to Ezekiel's wheels and Elijah's chariot of fire. One of the angels who teaches Blake this infernal revelation is "consumed and arose as Elijah" (24).

The most fiery character in Blakean myth is Orc, also called Fuzon, who, as the icon of revolution, will burn but never be consumed, for, as Blake reasoned, his fire and upheaval usher in the Millennial reign of Christ, who for Blake is eternally alive. When the French Revolution turned ugly, Blake had to revise this vision considerably, for he realized that he had anticipated the return of Christ far too soon, not unlike the Thessalonians, whom Paul warned not to be deceived, for the tribulation of those days would be much longer before Jesus returned as king. But in his early prophetic works, Blake saw himself as an Orc figure, revealing the Man of Sin before the terrible day of the Lord. Orc, not unlike the mythical Phaethon, rises in the east like the sun's chariot, "spurning the clouds written with curses, stamps the stony law to dust, loosing the eternal horses from the dens of night, crying, Empire is no more! And now the lion & wolf shall cease" (25).

Blake of course recognized that resurrection was necessary for all who had died: "The bones of death, the cov'ring clay, the sinews shrunk & dry'd. / Reviving shake, inspiring move, breathing! / Awakening! Spring like redeemed captives when their bonds & bars are burst" (*America: A Prophecy* 6.3–4). But to an elect few who are chosen to live at Christ's return, death has no meaning. And it is essential to realize that the ascension–translation of someone like Blake is not the result of Christ's blood atonement, which has no meaning for those who are chosen to be taken to heaven, their imperfections "burned away"; more correctly, they have received special signs and tokens that permit them to bypass what is for the rest of us an inevitable end.

The fear of self-annihilation is strong in Blake's mythology, but the goal of Blake's prophetic works is to convince the reader that the dissolution is apparent, not real. The cloud, a speaking character in Blake's *The Book of Thel*, declares this to the distraught daughter of the fiery angels who dwells in the paradisiacal "Vales of Har": "Fearest thou because I vanish and am seen no more[,] / Nothing remains; O maid I tell thee, when I pass away, / It is to tenfold life, to love, to peace, and raptures holy" (3.9–11). The process is recast in a longer poem of Blake's, *Milton*, in which a gnostic redemption occurs, one of enlightenment, rejection of the material world, and ultimate transfiguration: "I come in self-annihilation & the grandeur of Inspiration . . . To take off [the cosmic human's] filthy garments, & clothe him with Imagination (41.2–6); "The Negation must be destroyd to redeem the Contraries . . . To Cleanse the Face of my Spirit by Self-examination" (40.33–37).

As the narrator of *Milton*, Blake completes the first half of the mystery initiation—ascension—but returns to his "mortal state" (42.26) after the vision closes, and finds himself fallen and "outstretched upon the path" next to his wife, Catherine, his "sweet Shadow of Delight" (42.25–28). Though Blake is not translated or taken to heaven permanently, the text of his poem *is*, becoming Christ's red robe of judgment, "written within & without in woven letters: & the Writing / Is the divine Revelation in the Litteral expression . . . the Woof of Six Thousand Years" (42.13–15). His text has leapt off the page and become a living garment.

Wordsworth as Transcendent High Priest

Another dualistic type of ascension–translation can be found in the poetry of William Wordsworth. That Wordsworth would have a dualistic or gnostic strain in his poetry might seem surprising, but I believe it is evident in the pastoral poem *Michael* and in the "Intimations Ode.*"*[42] But I am concerned here with transcendence as an offshoot of ascension–translation myth, so I am not at this point arguing primarily about gnostic systems; nevertheless, I suspect that Wordsworth's notions of transcendence correspond very well to gnostic perceptions.

Wordsworth and Blake may have been the first poets to "democratize" the ideas of ascension and translation (transcendence), which, in terms of historical narratives, could occur only with holy people, heroes, or kings. Indeed, Thomas De Quincey, in *The Confessions of an English Opium Eater*, mentions that King Charles II should properly have been translated (the popular term in this era was "evanesced") rather than dying, as he did do. Wordsworth accomplished this feat of making ascension–translation available to ordinary people (who nonetheless needed exceptional sensibilities) first by celebrating the common person in his poetry, second by making the artist a hero, and third by turning the remote God of Deism into a loving, omnipresent father figure.

The celebration of common humanity pervades Wordsworth's famed poetic experiment, the *Lyrical Ballads* (1798);[43] in the preface to its second edition

(1800) he describes his attempt to capture "incidents and situations from common life," employing "language really used by men." In the poem "Resolution and Independence" Wordsworth—using his godlike poetic powers to create as well as elevate—exalts, translates, and evanesces the lowliest creature imaginable, an old man "bent double" whose profession is to gather leeches—one of nature's most repulsive creations—to sell to physicians. Wordsworth is caught off guard, however, when the leech-gatherer's words turn out to be "a lofty utterance, . . . above the reach of ordinary men" (lines 94–96). Here is the humblest human being transcending language and mortality, ascended and "translated" into Wordsworth's poetic text. The chance encounter with the leech-gatherer was, in fact, based on an actual event. Wordsworth is able to elevate commoners as well—beggars, rustic guides, shepherds—transcendent beings as "heroic" as the leech-gatherer.

Wordsworth also celebrates the artist as the type of hero deserving ascension and translation. For example, he anoints himself High Priest and Prophet of Nature in his philosophical narrative *The Prelude*:

> . . . To the open fields I told
> A prophecy: poetic numbers came
> Spontaneously to clothe in priestly robe
> A renovated spirit single out,
> Such hope was mine, for holy services. (Book First, 50–54)

Another of his roles is as guide. Like a heavenly messenger, a Metatron, he raises a warning voice to any who would violate nature. For example, he advises his sister Dorothy, "Then, dearest Maiden, move along these shades / In gentleness of heart; with gentle hand / Touch—for there is a spirit in the woods" ("Nutting," 54–56). In fact, the lengthy poem *The Prelude* is all about the philosophical "ascension" and "translation" that allow Wordsworth, by the poem's end, to declare confidently that his mind has grown sufficiently for him to begin a poetic career. Evidence for his figurative ascension can be found in Book Fourteenth, symbolized in the ascent up Mount Snowdon, the highest mountain in England or Wales. A "trusty guide" sponsors Wordsworth's ascent, much as the poet Virgil leads Dante into and back out of hell. The light of the moon is hidden by mist on the mountain, the ascent taking place at night; but when the poet reaches the summit, the moon (the Romantic poets' favorite source of light) "hung naked in a firmament / Of azure without cloud," its light falling "like a flash" (39–41).

Typologically speaking, the ascent is toward a "majestic intellect" (God himself) who greets Wordsworth as a new member of the divine family, one of "Transcendent power," "ideal form," and "more than mortal privilege" (70–77).

This transcendent joining of the mortal poet with an immortal but quite human God is the realization of Wordsworth's longing, from his youth, to be translated as were Enoch and Elijah. In the Fenwick Note, a bit of autobiographical commentary written to a friend and often preceding editions of Wordsworth's most famous poem, The "Intimations Ode," the poet admits, "I used to brood over the stories of Enoch and Elijah, and almost to persuade myself that, whatever might become of others, I should be translated, in something of the same way, to heaven." What follows in the ode is a representation of our descent from heaven, "trailing clouds of glory . . . / From God, who is our home" (5.7–8). Our task in this life, then, is to reunite ourselves with God through the transcendent powers of nature itself. Wordsworth himself, buried in the churchyard of St. Oswald's in Grasmere, obviously did not escape death; but his *heroic* subject, also himself, *did* escape death. Forever transcendent,* that is, ascended and translated, Wordsworth's literary persona, which grew alongside the poet from 1798—through many revisions—survived the poet's physical death.

It is beyond doubt that the poet's attempt to gain immortality through the survival of her or his published work is a very old poetic conceit—Shakespeare's sonnets make countless references to the survival of the sonnet despite the death of the poet himself or of the poetic object (the "fair friend" or the "dark lady"). But the idea of transcendence implies both a metamorphosis *and* ascension. Thus George Herbert's poem "Easter Wings," with its verses printed in the form of wings, implies not only a transformation but a means of escaping the constant tug of materiality, where Shakespeare's sonnet is entirely sublunary ("my mistress when she walks treads on the ground").

---

* Though some scholars claiming to be poststructuralists insist that language cannot transcend itself, that meaning is a cultural construct that conditions all discourse, I must argue that some words, some meanings are transcendent, perhaps because the sign is godly to begin with. While there is no doubt that words are inadequate to capture such a "vision" (they are approximations) we cannot conclude there was no vision, or that only language and culture gave shape to the vision. Ironically, poststructuralist arguments demand the reasonable use of language to convince their nonbelievers; visionaries don't rely upon reason, because they are outside the boundaries of reason to begin with.

The final element of Wordsworth's notions of transcendence is the "leveling" of the remote god of the Deists. The descent of the gods is an ancient motif and may in fact be the "true contrary" (as Blake would call it) of the ascension–translation of heroic mortals. The classical *deus ex machina* literally brought the gods on to the stage from above, so that in, say, Euripides' *Hippolytus*, Aphrodite and Artemis may descend rather conveniently at the end of the drama to restore order on earth. In fact, in most Western mythology the gods simply cannot leave earth and its people to their own devices, for division and evil on earth tend to pit the gods one against the other in the heavens. Of course, the more the Greek gods meddle, the worse everything tends to get on earth; Yahweh's interference seems to ameliorate his people's spiritual or physical condition in the Old Testament narrative, but even here there are instances in which the narrative seems unable or unwilling to justify Yahweh's punishments—for example, when people handle the Ark of the Covenant poorly, whether they are well-meaning or not. But the descent of the gods is as old as Genesis—with Yahweh or the *b'nai elohim* descending constantly either to bless or curse humanity (for example, walking in Eden in the cool of the day, then punishing Adam and Eve, or blessing Abraham, then cursing Sodom).

God's spirit inhabits the Lake District, the paradisiacal northwest corner of England. His incarnation is Michael, the subject of Wordsworth's pastoral tragedy of the same name, and is based upon an incident that took place in a neighboring community. Because of the sheep industry in this part of England, the many pastures support many shepherds. Wordsworth seeks the perfect shepherd to create a sympathetic portrait of the common human who is capable of reading all the winds, all the signs of nature. This incarnation of God is less threatening (more like the Jesus of the Gospels—a mortal who calls his Heavenly Father *abba*: "Daddy"), a shepherd who endures human suffering (the loss of his only son vs. the loss of his land, sheepfold and all). He is indeed the Neoplatonic *demiurgus*, the "artificer" whose monument to the worth of the common man is a slate rock sheepfold which Michael ("Who is like God?") and his young son Luke (Lucanus, Lucifer, light-bearer) build together. The young son must leave paradise and journey to the big city to make enough money to pay the old shepherd's encumbrance on his land (a debt of honor); like the prodigal son, Luke loses his moral compass and never returns to the vales. *Michael*, this long blank verse poem very much akin to to Milton's *Lycidas*, is the best evidence of Wordsworth's desire to make God accessible to ordinary people.

Keats: The Vale (Veil) of Soul-Making and the Platonic Ideal

In Keats's poetry, we encounter the ideas of ascension and translation in yet another romantic variation on the original. John Keats, whose Neoplatonic leanings are most evident in "Ode on a Grecian Urn," was nonetheless forcibly attached to this mortal world. Much like Wordsworth, Keats embraced the ideal of mutability, that is, the necessity and inevitability of change; at the same time, Keats longed for a perfected and idealized existence, represented for him in his poems, whose immortality Keats counted on, since his own life was to be cut short by consumption (tuberculosis). Translation is, then, the survival of the body of one's poetic work; one's soul becomes the immortal poem.

Ascension is the poetic ecstacy, the flight of the poetic mind or imagination, that precedes the transformation or transmutation of the poet's mortal body into its immortal form, the body of the poem—the sum total of whose poetic parts is still called the *corpus* or total output of the poet, author, or composer.

Keats's mixed feelings about earthly existence do not arise from his fear of physical death, but from the fear common to all not-yet-established poets that their poetry will not survive them, that their work will not be immortalized. Keats need not have feared, for he is now numbered "among the English poets"; he has indeed written some of the finest lyric poetry in the English language. Yet in his short life he did not receive the recognition he hoped for; that came only after his death. His longing and his melancholic solution to that longing are expressed well in a sonnet from 1818: "When I have fears that I may cease to be / Before my pen has gleaned my teeming brain . . . then on the shore / of the wide world I stand alone, and think / Till love and fame to nothingness do sink."

Keats longed to live in the world because he would gain experience; he would have married Fanny Brawne, lived out his life in full measure, perhaps even written a truly memorable epic-length poem, not merely stunted works like *Hyperion*. Earth life, as he pointed out in a letter to his brother George (written in 1819), is a "vale of Soul-making" in which the Neoplatonic "divine spark" in each human being is indistinguishable from any other except as it evolves through the experiences of actual living, becoming a heroic and altogether individual human being because of the interaction of what Keats calls the "three Materials" of "Spirit creation": "*Intelligence*[,] the human *heart* . . . , and the *World* or Elemental *space*." Keats remarks in the same discussion that the divine spark or soul of little children who die without having had the chance to form an individual character simply "returns to God without any identity." Thus it should be clear that Keats's longing to live a full life is actually consistent with the heroic model of ascension–translation, the twist in this case being that the poet can "ascend" and be "translated" only if he has lived long enough and written enough great poetry to be a "heroic" artist.

The idea of the artist as hero, which gets its birth specifically in the era of the British Romantic poets, then is enlarged upon and codified by such later writers as Robert Browning and especially James Joyce, is the clearest evidence of the transmutation of the ancient ideas of ascension and translation into new literary contexts. The artist must create something exceptionally brilliant to merit immortality in this form—which, most interestingly, is the poet's life and work frozen (the meaning of the phrase "cold pastoral" applied to the Grecian urn) into an idealized form forever, neither evolving nor dying. It is doubtless this metaphysical dimension of poets' lives and works that causes critical and scholarly idolatry among traditionalists and explains why they become so fanatically and religiously offended when poststructuralist readings deconstruct or dehistoricize the sacred canon. The irony of this critical dilemma is that the artist-as-hero metaphor functions as an acceptable metaphor for traditional Christians, for whom art has the saving graces that Christ offered: beauty and truth. That the heroic model engendered by the Romantics could actually be antithetical to Christian exegesis because its implicit Neoplatonic ideals of transcendence neatly sidesteps the Atonement and the Resurrection never seems to occur to the Christian humanist.

Keats's poetry is *not* the essence of his ascension and translation, but merely the temporal metaphor for it; it is clear from his letter on the "vale of Soul-making" that he was talking about literal salvation. The poems are the "palpable and named Mediator and saviour" that stand as earthly markers of the heavenly or divine transformation. This view of Keats's is confirmed by Shelley's memorial poem *Adonais*, whose divine spark shall fly "back to the burning fountain whence it came, / A portion of the Eternal, which must glow / Through time and change, unquenchably the same" (stanza 38). In "Ode to a Nightingale,"[44] Keats employs the metaphysical conceit of a bird's flight, joining Coleridge's highly symbolic bird of omen, the albatross, and Shelley's ever-circling skylark: "Away! away! For I will fly to thee, / Not charioted by Bacchus and his pards, / But on the viewless wings of Poesy" (stanza 4).

Provided one lives a truly heroic life, she may ascend to sit among the mythopoeic gods—such as Apollo. Here all poetic forms are idealized, such as the heavenly music of the spheres, which are "ditties of no [mortal] tone," for though "heard melodies are sweet, . . . those unheard / Are sweeter" (stanza 2). Rather in the fashion of Blake's "visionary forms dramatic," the Panlike piper of this ode is "forever piping songs forever new." Keats's best-known ode has a double-edge to it, however, for the figures on the urn, including the young man and woman who never can "kiss, / though winning near the goal" are not unlike Keats, whose every expectation is that he will never know the joy of extended union with the young woman he loves—Fanny Brawne—for he has isolated himself from her in anticipation of his death, self-dignosed, from tuberculosis. When Keats died and was buried in Italy, no name appeared on the headstone, only the phrase "Here lies one whose name was writ in water." The ironic but very heroic impression given was not, as some might assume, that life is delicate and fleeting. Only Keats's friends could discern such a truth from the message; rather, to the rest of the world it would appear that Keats had suddenly been snatched from the earth, so that, as with Moses and Elijah, people could search in vain for the burial site. No body, no evidence of death; like the Grecian urn, Keats's grave is silent concerning his fate.

Despite the maudlin, melancholic, and persecuted Keats generated by Shelley's not-very-knowledgeable portrait in the first half of the poem *Adonais*, Keats was vibrantly alive, contagiously happy, and a genuine good sport about accepting and learning from the negative reviews of his early poetry. He appears to me to be an excellent artist-hero, whose personal and poetic narrative openly dispute the dark and brooding victim-cult that appeals, as I have noted before, to another sort of narrative entirely, that of atonement, sacrifice, sadness, and death (the *via dolorosa*) as the only road to eternal life.

The Byronic Hero: An Antitype

It is an old saw in literary criticism that one can follow tradition or rebel against it, but one cannot escape it. The Byronic hero, an invention of George Gordon Lord

Byron, the British Romantic poet best known personally and professionally by the reading public (both in England and America) perfectly illustrates its creator's literary rebellion against the gods' games with human destiny, in which salvation comes to but a select few. The Byronic hero is an *isolato*, driven from society by crossing liminal space into antisocial behavior; he is the exemplar of hubris, refusing to bow before other humans or the gods themselves. He consistently attempts to overthrow what he perceives as tyrannical overlords. His specialty is the end run, attempting to acquire divinity without bowing and scraping. Byron may have been inspired by the indomitable spirit of Prometheus or by the heroic Odysseus, certainly by the Faust legend (despite any claims by Byron to the contrary). The hallmark of the Byronic hero consists in refusing to bow before tyranny, of never accepting the gods' terms. In previous examples of ascension–translation, I have stressed how merit of various sorts attracts the attention and favor of the gods: great righteousness, great courage, and great cunning (even when the hero attempts to challenge the gods), and finally, though least meritorious, divine ancestry. The Byronic hero is the sworn enemy of the gods, however, and prizes most what the gods despise. But Byron did not develop such characters out of a cultural vacuum, and there are, as I have listed, previous rebellious characters with dark purposes throughout literary history.

Gilgamesh is in fact an ante-Byronic hero, which helps us define his ultimately tragic failure, despite his being "two thirds . . . god and one third man." At a certain point in his reign, the arrogance of Gilgamesh "has no bounds by day or night. . . . His lust leaves no virgin to her lover."* Enkidu is created as a goad for him: "Let [Enkidu] be as like him as his own reflection, his second self, stormy heart for stormy heart."[45] Indeed, the hope is that Gilgamesh will leave the city entirely, so that he will not afflict society further.

The biblical Cain, as well as the Watchers or the *nefilim* of the Ethiopian Enoch (which Byron may have read) typifies this haughty disdain for authority. Yahweh warns Cain, "If you are well disposed, ought you not to lift up your head? But if you are ill disposed, is not sin at the door like a crouching beast hungering for you, which you must master?"[46] (Gen. 4:7–8). The implication here is that Cain

---

*The alleged practice of *prima nocta* by emperors like Caligula is based on a far older practice in Sumeria, badly remembered as the escapades of Gilgamesh.

rebels out of wounded pride; murdering his brother becomes a *hamartia* for Cain, an irreversible "missing the mark," which seals his destiny as a lost soul: "You shall be a fugitive and a wanderer over the earth" (Gen. 4:12–13, Jerusalem Bible), Yahweh tells him. The outcast tribesman in the Anglo-Saxon poem "The Wanderer" was influenced over time by this Old Testament vision, as is Grettir the Strong and Grendel and his mother, who look for all the world like outcasts from a tribe, or perhaps the only survivors of a murdered tribe. The Wandering Jew tradition, of a man cursed to walk the earth till the return of Christ, is part of this motif, and Coleridge's Ancient Mariner is also a manifestation in part of the eternal wanderer.

Odysseus is not unlike the children of Israel who wander forty years in the wilderness between Egypt and the Promised Land. He is kept back from Ithaca (perhaps a six-week voyage at worst) for ten long years, doubling his absence from Penelope. Zeus makes it clear early on the lesson Odysseus must learn, despite the gods' admiration for his heroics, before he can be allowed to succeed:

Ah, how quick men are to blame the gods!
From us, they say, all their evils comes,
When they themselves, by their own ridiculous pride,
Bring horrors on far beyond anything fate
Would ever have done.[47]

Indeed, as Denton Snider notes, "Spiritual restoration is the key-note of this *Odyssey*."[48] Odysseus must atone (reach at-one-ment) with Poseidon, whom he has terribly offended, and whom the sailors under him have also offended. Odysseus simply refuses to bow to Poseidon's will in these matters. Yet once Odysseus has been buffeted by the gods, he regains his kingdom, his family, and his home. Odysseus might have had the gifts of ascension and translation, certainly of youth and immortality, but unlike Gilgamesh, Odysseus finds these domestic rewards (kingdom, family, home) more than sufficient in and of themselves. Indeed, Calypso had "kept him in the yawning caves, / Yearning to make him her husband, pampering him / And offering to make him immortal and ageless forever, / To none of which the heart in his breast agreed."[49] When finally triumphant, Odysseus is not the discontented wanderer of Tennyson's poem *Ulysses*; Tennyson clearly saw in his Ulysses the Byronic hero first envisioned in Byron's portrayal of the young cynic Childe Harold, full of "ceaseless turmoil" (to borrow from Coleridge), irresistibly drawn to "drinking life to the lees." Rather, Odysseus represents the Promethean benefactor who, given a choice of living with the gods or with mortals, magnanimously chooses humanity. In one sense, then, Odysseus is a failed literary type of the ascending hero, yet he belongs in that unusual category of humans who choose to remain mortal (the holy patriarchs as opposed to Enoch, or Peter and James as opposed to the disciple "whom Jesus loved").

Yet another strain of Byronic hero does choose immortality, but perversely so; he does not ascend to live with the divine family, but rather descends to take his throne of honor in Hades. Coleridge's character life-in-death from *The Rime* is of course the White Goddess described in Robert Graves's poem and book by the same name (sadly, both poets stereotype this muse as a ravenous female). Unremitting rottenness and eternal decay are the hallmarks of this creature, who barters with Death for the soul of the hapless mariner. She is the rotting voice from the dark grave in Blake's *Thel*, a symbol of disease and the unnatural world against which Coleridge wishes to warn his readers. Unquestionably she is a vampire, as is the Lady Geraldine in Coleridge's *Christabel*. Her whiteness betokens not divine light but sepulchral lividity. She is the patron goddess of Byron's Cain and Manfred, his two most terrific realizations of the antitype.

The vampire legend, which finally hit England in the nineteenth century from the Slavic countries (much as Dracula himself moves from his castle in Transylvania to an estate in England situated near an asylum), was built on a dark anti-hero, Vlad the Impaler, who it was said skewered his enemies on poles stuck in the ground like trees, then sat down to dine in front of them. This sort of viciousness seems weaned on Machiavelli's *The Prince*, which saw ruthlessness as an essential tool for governance. It is no surprise that Lord Byron admired and loathed Napoleon as the apotheosis of the literary anti-hero he envisioned; Marilyn Gaull notes that what the Byronic hero redefined in literature, "Napoleon . . . redefined . . . in life."[50] In *Childe Harold's Pilgrimage*, Byron writes of Napoleon,

> In 'pride of place' here last the eagle flew,
> Then tore with bloody talon the rent plain,
> Pierced by the shaft of banded nations through;
> Ambition's life and labours all were vain;
> He wears the shattered links of the world's broken chain. (3.18.158–62)

In the same canto, we see in Harold and in his alter-ego Lord Byron the same "sneer of cold command" hauteur, the same tragic grandeur, and the same colossal wreck: "With nought of hope left, but with less of gloom; / The very knowledge that he lived in vain, That all was over on this side the tomb . . . Did yet inspire a cheer which he forbore to check" (3.16.136–14). Napoleon's immortality mocks (that is, imitates artistically) that offered by the gods: a magnificent tomb in Montmartre, which was desecrated during student riots in 1968 in Paris. His spirit of conquest and disdain plays impishly in the rhetoric of every French *libre penseur*, his soul is metamorphosed by the elvish bakers into a *patisserie*. He is France's payback to Italy; France claims Napoleon as its heroic native son, as hundreds of years before the Italian romance poets purloined Roland, the French national hero. Yet Napoleon is merely a civilized Vlad, a political vampire consuming other nations to keep himself alive, immortal, divine.

This generation of Romantic authors gives us the perverse Dr. Frankenstein, the Faustian overreacher who, as Prometheus of old, steals the fire from heaven. Mary Shelley, directly influenced as she was by Lord Byron, saw in the haughty doctor a modern Faust, who, unable to accept the divine and natural limits on human knowledge, steals into the alchemical texts in search of a means to create a second Adam (heroic antithesis of Milton's Jesus), an immortal creature made of the stuff of death itself, the earthly elements. Dr. Frankenstein's new Adam has no soul, no divine approbation as such, and is therefore an affront to the gods, much as is poor Enkidu, the animal-like mirror of Gilgamesh. It is hardly surprising that allusions to the unnatural affections of Coleridge's mariner and of Milton's Satan dot the novel's pages, as well as allusions to the mystical search for "the philosopher's stone and the elixir of life."[51] Also, we find in the novel detailed descriptions of the cemetery, the imagery of the "graveyard school" with its bats, owls, beetles, moss-covered stones, yew trees, clammy graves, and vampiric mistletoe:

> A churchyard was to me merely the receptacle of bodies deprived of life, . . . food for the worm. . . . I saw how the fine form of man was degraded and wasted; I beheld the corruption of death. . . . I saw how the worm inherited the wonders of the ye and brain.[52]

The creature he creates, far from the philsopher's stone of his alchemical over-reaching, is our fiendish life-in-death, a vampiric mockery of the gods' gift of heroic ascension and translation:

> His limbs were in proportion, and I had selected his features as beautiful, Beautiful!—Great God! His yellow skin scarcely covered the work of muscles and arteries beneath; his hair was of a lustrous black, and flowing; his teeth of a pearly whiteness; but these luxuriances only formed a more horrid contrast with his watery eyes, that seemed almost of the same colour as the dun white sockets in which they were set, his shrivelled complexion and his straight black lips.[53]

Here is embodied all the pathos over the gods' capriciousness that dwells in the vast majority of noble but thoroughly neglected humans (such as Wordsworth's noble leech-gatherer) who cannot reconcile the ascension–translation of a precious few with the clear rejection by the gods of everyone else. The Byronic hero is, in fact, a response to the nineteenth-century realization (found in Byron's *Don Juan*) that there are very few possibilities for true heroism in the modern world, at least not the kind that catches the attention of the gods themselves. Jesus had become so theologically remote over the centuries that even he was no longer the friend of the common human. And, in fact, a new Jesus did emerge in England and America, the friendly teacher, healer, and good neighbor who continues to be the mortal Jesus of Galilee for Protestant Christians, a heroic ideal for millions of ordinary souls who not only will never be noticed on earth, but would otherwise never cause the gods to turn their heads. He exalts ordinary people, carrying them into the divine family as they clutch the skirts of his princely robes.

Byron's "medieval mystery," *Cain*, is the working through of the anti-myth, anti-hero of the heroic era of Old Testament myth. Specifically the protagonist Cain disputes the good will of Yahweh in allowing him to be born into mortal circumstances. This contention that the gods are fickle or capricious is, we recall, typical of ancient narratives of gods among Sumerian, Babylonian, and of course Greek civilizations. Gilgamesh is genuinely confused by the gods themselves, their motives, their agendas. Odysseus has the same complaint about the Greek pantheon, where some, such as Athena, support the Achaeons, while Zeus, Mars, and Aphrodite favor the Trojans (although for different individual reasons). The Greek pantheon can of course be understood as the mind of a single God, but one with the same fragmented psyche that can be found in many mortals. The battle on the plains of Ilium is reflected in the heavenly disagreements over the war, bringing the gods nearly to blows. The disorder in the heavens creates disharmony on Earth, just as human discord causes the gods to become involved—usually with disastrous results, at least in Greek myth and its Babylonian and Sumerian precursors.

Cain's accusation against Yahweh reflects the disharmony in Byron's own psyche, tortured both by his unbridled lusts and his occasional rapturous spiritual and aesthetic epiphanies (as that in St. Peter's, in Canto Four of *Childe Harold*). The son of Adam protests,

> I sought not to be born; nor love the stat
> To which that birth has brought me. Why did he
> Yield to the Serpent and the woman? Or
> Yielding—why suffer? What was there in this?
> The tree was planted, and why not for him?
> If not, why place him near it, where it grew
> The fairest in the centre? They have but
> One answer to all questions, "'Twas his will,
> And he is good." (*Cain* 1.1.68–76)

The *felix culpa*, deceptively translated as "fortunate fall" (I think the phrase "happy outcome" is at least what Milton had in mind—the Fall was perverse, but the outcome happy because of the Advent), is clearly rejected here, as is the Orthodox Christian doctrine of an all-knowing, all-loving God. What is clear is that Byron has somehow tapped into the Sumerian viewpoint in which humans were created as slave labor for the garden of the gods; biblical myth merely transfers the toil and misery to a space outside the garden, thus exonerating Yahweh. Byron's Cain is heroic in the same sense as the rebellious Odysseus; as Cain declares, "If I shrink not from these, the fire-armed angels, / Why should I quail from him who now approaches?" (1.1.91–92). Byron's marvelous twist, one used by Shelley to a degree and to greater extent by Blake, is to make the Yahweh of Orthodoxy a tyrant-god, a perverse imposer of what Blake calls "one law for the lion and the ox." Thus Cain becomes anti-heroic by default. It is not so much that Byron finds Cain innocent, any more than he would find Manfred, Faust, or Odysseus entirely innocent. Rather it is that he finds Yahweh (at least the orthodox Yahweh) guilty of distancing himself from his creations and of denying his creations (especially orthodox Catholics and Protestants!) any meritorious salvation through human heroism (such as characterized Byron's own courageous but shortsighted efforts to raise troops against the Turks in Greece). Thus Cain's Faustian turning to Lucifer for gnosis is precisely the desire to ascend and be translated—to be Yahweh without being under his yoke. Byron's Lucifer declares as much to Cain:

> Souls who dare use their immortality—
> Souls who dare look the Omnipotent tyrant in
> His everlasting face, and tell him that
> His evil is not good! If he has made,
> As he saith—which I know not nor believe—
> But, if he made us—he cannot unmake:
> We are immortal!—nay, he'd have us so,
> That he may torture:—let him! (1.1.137–44)

Byron has of course absented Yahweh from his entire play (just as Aeschylus leaves Zeus offstage in *Prometheus Bound*), which further distances him from Cain and us. Lucifer and Cain can thus be immortalized in the text of the play in a way Yahweh cannot be. It is also clear that the heroic Jesus of Milton's poetry is unseen, not even clearly foreshadowed, thus removing from Byron's text the "happy outcome" offered Milton's Adam and Eve.*

Cain follows Lucifer, ascending through the Ptolemaic rings outside of which dwells God himself. The ascent is clear enough ("through an aerial universe of endless Expansion . . ." [2.1.107–8]), but two ironic things happen: first, like the ascending Troilus of old, Cain and Lucifer cannot approach the brilliant Dantean lights near to God's sphere (*Cain*: "Spirit! Let me . . . see them nearer"; *Lucifer*: Art thou not nearer? Look back to thine earth!" [2.1.117–18]); second, descent into Hades follows rather than precedes the ascension ("How silent and how vast are these dim worlds!" [2.2.1]). Cain's open contempt for the fall of Adam suggests his inability to accept a judgment of death upon him. In a description of the sufferings of a lamb struck by a reptile, Cain notes that while his father suggests that good could proceed even from that sort of evil,

> I thought, that 'twere
> A better portion for the animal
> Never to have been stung at all, than to

---

* Nevertheless, in a footnote to the Rinehart edition of selected works (1972), 230, n. 4, Edward E. Bostetter lists three exceptions to this deliberate deletion on Byron's part.

Purchase renewal of its little life
With agonies unutterable, though
Dispelled by antidotes. (2.2.301–5)

The final clue to the anti-heroic nature of Cain is in Lucifer's speech, reminiscent of Jesus' upbraiding of Nicodemus, chastising Cain for being too weakminded to comprehend the highest mysteries:

Thy human mind hath scarcely grasp to gather
The little I have shown thee into calm
And clear though: and thou wouldst go on aspiring
To the great double Mysteries! The two Principles!
And gaze upon them on their secret thrones!
Dust! Limit thy ambition; for to see
Either of these would be for thee to perish! (2.2.401–7)

This speech introduces dualism, likely Manichean, in which dark and light, good and evil, material and spiritual are two sides of one coin. No side is ever vanquished, neither side is superior—only temporary victors emerge. Surprisingly, Lucifer turns down coldly Cain's desire for perfect knowledge, possibly because he can brook no rivals; Satan's refusal again forcibly reminds us of Phaethon, of Alexander, and of Gilgamesh, whose gods refuse their heroic quests for immortality and for whom perfect knowledge would include the means to cheat death and to dwell with the divine family. There is no question that in Byron's drama, the chief motivating force behind Cain's heroic quest is anger over and fear of physical death. Dualism of the Manichean variety (Byron would have known of Mani through Pierre Bayle's *Dictionnaire*) specifically endorses the dark mystery as a mirror image of the mystery of light, gnosis being the medium of ascension or transcendence. Mani's doctrine is as close to the antithesis of orthodox Christian perceptions of salvation as it is possible to get. Indeed, for this very reason Cain is the hero of the great anti-myth of Rosicrucian and Freemasonic lore,*[54] which reached its peak of European cultural influence during Byron's lifetime.†

---

* Max Heindel in *Freemasonry and Catholicism* (91) links the Hiram of Freemasonry with Tubal Cain and, ultimately, to Cain himself.
† As Paul Nettl, a musicologist, notes, "Among intellectual forces of the eighteenth century . . . none is of such fundamental importances as Freemasonry." He adds that "the eighteenth century is considered the pinnacle of Masonic development."[55]

Cain's murder of Abel is described by Byron as the result of Cain's disgust over the blood that must be shed to sanctify the altar Abel has built. Abel must die in order to please Yahweh completely. Cain's desire for death, despite his loathing, following the murder does not, in Byron's drama, connote only remorse, although Cain wishes to be a substitute sacrifice for Abel, to revive his brother. In fact he is longing for the perfect acceptance and secret knowledge which Abel now possesses, being dead. This explains for Byron the angel's "seal" marking Cain's forehead, lest any slay him. Cain protests, "No, let me die." But the angel's seal is a certain thing, as a "nail in a sure place." Cain is doomed to wander and will not be allowed to die, for he is undying unless someone kills him (against which possibility the angel seals him). He is the first vampire after the Fall (Lilith, of course, is a vampire before the Fall, for she leaves Eden companionless, the mother of jinns and genii). Adah, Cain's sister–wife, says of Abel, "Peace be with him!" But Cain responds elliptically, "But with *me*!"—the final words of the play rejecting closure and stubbornly declaring that no end to Cain's wandering is possible.

Of course, certain passages in Byron's play suggest that Cain would return to dust. His *hamartia*, however, changes that possibility. Killing Abel makes ordinary mortality a mockery of the heroic accomplishment of Enoch and Elijah generations later, a life-in-death image played out in Coleridge's *Rime*. Dr. Polidori's vampire, Bram Stoker's Dracula, and even Oscar Wilde's Dorian Gray partake of this curse of deathlessness, Dorian in particular seeming to gain the consolation prize of eternal youth, lost so long ago by Gilgamesh in an underwater struggle. Yet Dorian is a clear rejection of Christian orthodoxy. Lord Harry specifically protests Dorian's attempt at the end of his life to reform himself: "'My dear boy, you are really beginning to moralise. You will soon be going about like the converted, and the revivalist, warning people against all the sins of which you have grown tired.'"[56] One can be in the ancient camp, which allows only a few to ascend and to be with God, or one can be a Christian, trusting in the effects of Christ's atonement. There is no middle ground, for the one is antithetical to the other. What allows Dorian to kill himself, unlike Cain, is that Dorian's soul is in his picture, and his physical body is utterly separated from that soul, except by the cord of the covenant which originally created Dorian's predicament. The body of Dorian murders the interior, the soul of Dorian. This cutting of the canvas actually unites body and soul, and the picture becomes once again just a portrait of a very handsome young man. Lord Harry's part in all this scandal is clear enough. He it was who promoted the idea that life need only be experienced, not accounted for morally or ethically. Lord Harry is to Dorian as Lucifer is to Cain in Byron's drama. Ironically, Harry ends up outliving Dorian, but only because Dorian tried to "convert" himself to becoming a moral person. Harry not only survives Dorian, but Dorian has received the brunt of the gods' anger while Harry claims to the last he has done nothing wrong.

The vampire figure, as well as Dorian Gray, haunts novels from Polidori to Stoker and beyond. The vampire, who shares the bill in gothic novels with the likes of Matthew Lewis's monk, is a liminal character; like the elemental spirits in Coleridge's *Rime*, they are part neither of earth nor heaven (nor hell). They are part of the "Twilight Zone" between, as Rod Serling declared, "shadow and substance," and waking and sleep. Like Melville's Pierre, they are caught between two states of existence, what the anthropologists call "liminal space." Dracula, neither dead nor truly alive, terrifies because we all may hesitate, at any time, to move on with our lives, damning ourselves to stasis or eternal anticipation (as with Henry James's protagonist in "The Beast in the Jungle").

Because Dracula cannot be supernatural (an object of Christian atonement and resurrection), he chooses an unnatural life-in-death, that most sickening violation of the laws of nature, according to the *Rime*. He is the supreme insult to the Christian sacrificial victim, Jesus, and indeed is his antithesis.[57] (*Dracula* is Romanian for "dragon.") Jesus shed his blood to give all humanity salvation. Dracula not only retained his own blood supply, but took everyone else's to save himself. Jesus preached his doctrine in the open, while Dracula skulks around at night. Jesus loved little children and gave the poor and heavy-laden his special care; our anti-heroic count, an aristocrat, loves the best blood (pun intended). He offers eternal life-in-death in place of the glorious Christian resurrection. He is an Ovidian shape-shifter, a parody of the doctrine of transubstantiation. Like Lilith of old, Dracula is the rejected one.

It is appropriate that the vampire came on the scene in the cynical late Victorian world (1897) that had seen the demythologizing of Jesus through the ratiocentric German Higher Critics and through the disappointed ebbing of Matthew Arnold's "Sea of Faith." Dorian Gray, Dracula, and the overreaching Drs. Jekyll and Frankenstein, all fill a void created by jaded religious faith that no longer spoke to modern, rational humans. The heroic, as poets from Byron to William Morris discovered, was gone completely from Europe (possibly moved to America) in the nineteenth century, leaving in its wake an anti-heroic tradition that now is so widespread that new religions are built around it (Dungeons and Dragons, pseudo-Satanic rock groups, Stephen King freaks, and *X-Files* junkies in various states of religious decline).

The anti-heroic figure finally becomes a satire or even a parody of itself in our own century. New-Age gurus promise rides in spaceships but idiotically demand suicides in order to transcend this world; the shock of it is that these anti-heroes have huge followings. C. S. Lewis, taking the Baphomet idol-icon of Templar fame as his satiric centerpiece in *That Hideous Strength*, turns the "head" into a synecdoche for a corporate CEO involved in a scientific conspiracy. The woman protagonist, Jane, sees him in vision:

> But as I got used to the light, I got a horrible shock.... What it really was, was a head (the rest of a head) which had had the top part of the skull taken off and then ... a great big mass which bulged out from inside what was left of the skull.... I thought it was some kind of new man that had only head and entrails: I thought all those tubes were its insides. But presently ... , I saw that they were artificial. Little rubber tubes and bulbs and little metal things too.[58]

The head, taken from a murderous Frenchman named Alcasan, represents the anti-heroic but scientific gift of "eternal life" or at least survival of death. Lewis dubs it the Saracen's Head, an allusion to the Templars' mortal enemies in Israel. The Templars' crime, of course, was worshiping Baphomet (some sort of head), denying the Resurrection (according to questionable witnesses), but hoping for heroic recognition from God in its place. In Lewis's story the scientists of postwar England must reach into the past for a worthy hero but can only twist it into a perverse hero-parody. Alcasan is to be contrasted, of course, with Professor Ransom as Lewis's transfigured bleeding knight, the keeper of the grail, and of course a professional philologist. In the chapter "The Descent of the Gods," a genuine *descensus* occurs; that is, instead of an assumption, or ascension–translation, of Ransom (the Director—a title vaguely reminiscent of Enoch's appellation as the Scribe, or of Hiram as Master Mason, or even of the gnostic materialist hypostasis Samael as the Artificer or *demiurgus*). Clearly Ransom is transfigured, for when the gods descend, Lewis remarks that their presence would have been unendurable for one whom "[poetry] . . . had not already instructed in . . . the mastery of doubled and trebled vision." For Ransom, whose study had been for many years in the realm of words, it was heavenly pleasure. He found himself sitting within the very heart of language, in the white-hot furnace of essential speech.[59]

In this novel of trivialized humanity, etymology becomes a key weapon in the fight against evil anti-heroes of cold, rational science, an act of wish fulfillment appropriate for Lewis, a medievalist. But here as well is Blake's refining fire, the furnace of self-annihilation, which is proximately terrifying but which ultimately transfigures the poet (for example, Milton, in Blake's four-book epic of the same name) into a member of the divine family.

Though the Byronic hero or anti-hero is not without positive counterparts in modern America, it is interesting that Jack Nicholson's Joker sold most of the tickets in the recent Batman movies and that Batman himself ends up being only a nemesis for the Joker, not a child of the gods as in older tradition. The Christian heroic is inextricable from the religion which created it, so as long as Christianity prospers, so will its hero, Jesus. No other hero is fit to take his place, and so Superman and Batman have become darkly Byronic heros in recent years. Some fundamentalist Christians have even preempted Greek mythology, declaring it to be Satanic, so that only rarely will Apollo or Perseus ever again be a part of modern Western culture.

Hawthorne's Gray Champion: The Pattern Resumed

Nathanial Hawthorne's "The Gray Champion" is, I would argue, an excellent if now somewhat rarified literary manifestation of the "translated" being, who in this tale comes to the aid of the now-indigenous populace of Boston, a community of pilgrims being put upon by a Royalist governor under the control of James II.*
Hawthorne quietly informs his readers that during this time of crisis, it was rumored that the current governor's predecessor under the old charter, William Bradstreet, a venerable companion of the first settlers, was known to be in town. Bradstreet,

---

* "The Gray Champion" is apparently built on the Angel of Hadley legend, in which an angelic deliverer saves this Massachusetts village from Indians on 1 September 1675; of course, merely finding the pseudo-historical nature of the gray champion changes nothing, except to show the consistent influence of the heroic return of a deliverer in American culture.[60]

"a patriarch of nearly ninety," appeared before the crowd, mildly cautioning them, "'My children, ... do nothing rashly. Cry not aloud, but pray for the welfare of New England, and expect patiently what the Lord will do in this matter.'"[61] The Puritan pilgrim character is obvious here, as is the dwelling on basic, simple Christian virtues—hallmark of Puritanism—being put to the test by a perverse governor under a tyrant king. When the governor's troops parade through the town, making a mockery of the democratic values of the local crowd, one man among the mistreated group cries out, "'O Lord of Hosts, ... provide a Champion for thy people!'" As though parting the Red Sea, a character appears that causes the crowd to roll back. An "ancient man" wearing the old Puritan clothing of bygone days and sporting a heavy sword and staff, confronts the military parade by walking toward them with determination. Hawthorne, who loves to leave key details of plot ambiguous, avers that none recognizes the stranger, who might, at first encounter, be mistaken by the reader for Bradstreet. Then an odd thing happens:

> The old man raised himself to a loftier mien, while the decrepitude of age seemed to fall from his shoulders, leaving him in gray but unbroken dignity. Now, he marched onward with a warrior's step, keeping time to the military music. ... The old man grasped his staff by the middle and held it before him like a leader's truncheon.
>
> "Stand!" cried he.
>
> ... That stately form, combining the leader and the saint ... could only belong to some old champion of the righteous cause, whom the oppressor's drum had summoned from his grave.[62]

The champion then encants the following ritual formula, which so fills the army with dread and the local populace with courage, that the army becomes a rout of confused, terrified sheep:

> "I have stayed the march of a King himself, ere now," replied the gray figure, with stern composure. "I am here Sir Governor, because the cry of an oppressed people hath disturbed me in my secret place; and beseeching this favor earnestly of the Lord, it was vouchsafed me to appear once again on earth, in the good old cause of his saints. And what speak ye of James? There is no longer a Popish tyrant on the throne of England, and by to-morrow noon, his name shall be a byword in this very street, where ye would make it a word of terror. Back, thou was a Governor, back! With this night thy power is ended—to-morrow, the prison!—back, lest I foretell the scaffold!"[63]

Needless to say, the stranger's prophecy comes to pass, as the erstwhile tyrant James falls and the more gracious William of Orange takes his place; the evil governor and his henchmen thus go to prison. The story ends with Hawthorne's usual summary of local assessments of the stranger, some saying he was seen to embrace the noble Bradstreet, others that he faded before their very eyes; all agreed that he disappeared, never to return. Hawthorne concludes his tale by asserting that the champion will and has come again whenever the threat of invasion or polluting tyranny arises, calling him the "type of New England's hereditary spirit."

It can of course be argued that the fellow is an angel or spirit returned from the dead, but Hawthorne also implies the possibility of a translated being. For example, the champion is summoned from a "secret place," which could hardly be a grave; he is an angel in the sense of the Hebrew *malak* or "messenger" but clearly is a resident of Earth, based on his continual involvement in or knowledge of human affairs. He is old looking, suggesting longevity, but strong and hale when he needs to be, implying that age has little serious effect on him. He is clearly older than Bradstreet, and their meeting implies a friendship that shows the champion's deep love and concern for fellow humans. The Lord also seems directly responsible for sending the champion in a time of fearful need. Other Hawthornean hints about New England's status as a chosen land and of God fighting their battles for them round out the picture of a translated being such as Elijah, who is expected to return every year, but who comes only unexpectedly to fulfill some godly purpose.

A modern instance of this sort of intervention was offered me by a student married to an Israelite:

> In 1968 something really strange happened that Elie says he will always remember. Elie's brother, Hezzy, was serving on a destroyer in the Mediterranean near Egypt when the Egyptians torpedoed and sank his ship. Many of the sailors were killed but Hezzy stayed afloat for more than 12 hours until help came. Elie said, "My mother cried all night but I was too young to think about it. It didn't occur to me how serious it was." During the night while the family was waiting for news, a very old man knocked on the door and asked to speak with Rachel Cohen, Elie's mom. He told her that Hezzy was safe and that he was in a hospital in Haifa. This made his mom feel better but later no one could remember what the man looked like and no one knew him. He just walked off and no one ever saw him again. The weird part was that he came to them before the sailors had been rescued and before the sinking had been made

public. I thought he was pulling my leg but he was really spooked about it. His parents are very Orthodox but none of the kids are very religious but still, it seems like most of the Israelis are superstitious and still follow some of the customs. Elie believes in the Evil Eye and that you shouldn't leave your shoes unside [sic] down because you shouldn't leave the dirty sole facing up to heaven. Who knows who might get offended? They all thought the old man was an angel who came to comfort his mom.[64]

If we connect Elijah to the coming of the Messiah, as was common among the Israelites, he then becomes a military leader of sorts, and a natural choice for the hero of Hawthorne's magic tale.

Melville's *Moby-Dick*: Elijah on the Docks

In chapter nineteen of Herman Melville's *Moby-Dick* we encounter a prophet on the docks; only near the end of the brief scene does Ishmael learn the man's name: Elijah, and Ishmael concludes, "I pronounced him in my heart, a humbug."[65] Elijah is ragged and pock marked, an old sailor, but he brings a grave warning to these sailors, for if they have souls, it is certain they will sign them over to Captain Ahab the moment they sign the "articles" attaching them to service on the *Pequod*. Elijah, tradition holds, was to reappear from time to time, in order to warn or prepare the way for some prodigious work of Yahweh. The Book of Malachi ends with a portentous announcement: "Know that I am going to send you Elijah the prophet before my day comes, that great and terrible day" (Mal. 4:5, Jerusalem Bible). Jews have traditionally set a place at Passover for Elijah to show their watchfulness and fidelity should he suddenly return. And both Jesus and John the Baptist were thought to be Elijah returned from heaven.[66]

If we keep in mind the calling of the translated Elijah, and propose Melville's Elijah is more than just a passing literary conceit, a comic scene, or an ironic augury, then what great and dreadful day has the great prophet Elijah, ascended and translated, returned to announce? This is answered in his dreadful question to the sailors, "'Ye hav'n't seen Old Thunder yet, have ye?'" This question contains a prophetic riddle, for "Old Thunder" is both an epithet for Captain Ahab and a vivid metaphor for Yahweh, the thunder god of Mount Sinai. The association of Captain Ahab, whom Bloom insists was a fire-worshipping Zoroastrian,[67] with the Old Testament God who was the enemy of the biblical King Ahab, may seem incongruous. But consider the following points: Melville's Ishmael has made a solemn covenant (in the articles he signed as a harpooner) to serve Ahab with a loyalty Yahweh might have envied. Says Melville's Elijah, "'You must jump when he gives an order. Step and growl; growl and go—that's the word with Captain Ahab.'"[68] Elijah here, as opposed to the biblical Elijah, is not actually an enemy to the captain, but is there to test any would-be heroes as to their worthiness to serve on the whaling vessel which, as a sort of ark for slain whales, bears an architectonic relationship to the dimensions of the ancient Israelite tabernacle, whose inner sanctum (what Joseph Campbell appropriately called the "belly of the whale")[69] is the point of meeting between god and man. Elijah is looking for "priests" (worthy sailors) uncorrupted by other ships and other captains, the opposite of the false priests (Jezebel's priests of Ba'al) whose goal is merely to hire on for the money to be made from a successful kill. Elijah approves Ishmael for this heroic enterprise when, after Ishmael's curt rejoinders to his questions, he calls out, "'You are just the man for him—the likes of ye.'"

The *Pequod* becomes a microcosm of Yahweh's faithful Israelite priesthood, with the ocean as Yahweh's cosmic creation. None of this imagery was lost on Melville, who, in the extracts preceding the novel, includes Isaiah's prophecy that "In that day, the Lord with his sore, and great, and strong sword, shall punish Leviathan the piercing serpent, even Leviathan that crooked serpent; and he shall slay the dragon that is in the sea." In relating the passage to the white whale, Melville is following a very old literary tradition, despite the fact that Isaiah's description could scarcely be of a whale. Thus by default, Captain Ahab is once again cast, however ironically, as Yahweh. Ishmael's narrative declares that when Ahab went down with his ship, he, like Satan, "dragged a living part of heaven"*[70] into the great deep, suggesting the end of a cosmic cycle.

Moby-Dick is not, however, merely the narrative of Yahweh's fight with Leviathan; it is also about the worthy hero Ishmael, the righteous scribe (an Enoch figure) who alone survives to tell the tale. When Elijah asks him if he has "seen" Ahab, he is foreshadowing the ascension motif in which the hero Ishmael witnesses the appearance of Yahweh–Ahab, Old Thunder. Ishmael later is "translated"

---

* The very sea-birds are for Melville the archangels witnessing the fall of their angelic brother.

in the sense that he has been elected of all the humanity aboard the *Pequod* to live even after the gods themselves die; indeed, Ishmael is one of the new Olympians, a Noachian figure who alone survives the universal deluge. He is a Gilgamesh returning with life-giving gnosis for all those who would make the perilous voyage of life. He alone lives by profiting from the floating coffin of his erstwhile bunkmate Queequeg. Thus, this most heroic of all American novels acknowledges the tradition of Elijah's ascension and return to earth to prophesy, that is, announce or deliver* God's message and to prepare the way of Yahweh by creating a character who, after all, is not the "humbug" Ishmael thinks he is at first, but is in fact a heroic being who not only prepares the way for the coming of Old Thunder but also issues the "call" (as Campbell puts it) to our American Original hero, Ishmael.

---

* A prophet is not a fore-teller but a forth-teller—a messenger who *tells forth* God's message or warning. Mark Heidmann, in *Melville and the Bible*, demonstrates Melville's excellent knowledge of biblical prophets and eloquently defends the definition "forth-teller" as opposed to mere fortune telling. Heidmann seems convinced that Melville's Elijah is one of many prophetic voices in the novel but ignores this other dimension of Elijah preserved so well in Jewish lore.[71]

1. See C. S. Lewis, *A Preface to Paradise Lost* (Oxford: Oxford University Press, 1942; reprint, 1970) for a vivid discussion of Milton's intention to treat the War in Heaven and the fighting among the angels literally.

2. Edith Hamilton, *Mythology* (New York: Mentor, 1940; reprint, 1969, 159).

3. Ibid., 172.

4. All chronicled in Hamilton, 160.

5. Zecharia Sitchen, *The War of Gods and Men* (Santa Fe: Bear & Co., 1992).

6. René Girard, *Violence and the Sacred*, trans. Patrick Gregory (Baltimore: Johns Hopkins, 1977).

7. Whitney M. Davis, "The Ascension-Myth in the Pyramid Texts," *Journal of Near Eastern Studies* 36.3 (July 1977): 163.

8. Ibid., 164.

9. Ibid., 165.

10. Immanuel Velikovsky, *Oedipus and Akhnaton: Myth and History* (Garden City, NY: Doubleday, 1960).

11. P. G. Maxwell-Stuart. "Interpretations of the Names Oedipus," *Maia* 27 (1975): 37–43.

12. Rick Gore, "Pharoahs of the Sun," *National Geographic* (April 2001): 35–57.

13. Ibid., 43.

14. Ibid., 46.

15. Ibid., 42.

16. Ibid., 54.

17. Ovid, *Metamorphoses*, trans. Rolfe Humphries (Bloomington: Indiana University Press, 1955), 28–40.

18. Oliver J. G. H. Grosz, "Man's Imitation of the Ascension: The Unity of Christ II," in Robert E. Bjork, ed., *Cynewulf: Basic Readings* (New York: Garland, 1996), 95.

19. Ibid., 98.

20. Edward T. Jones, "A Comparative Study of Ascension Motifs in World Religions," in *Deity and Death* (vol. 2 in the Religious Studies Monograph Series), ed. Spencer J. Palmer (Provo, UT: Religious Studies Center of Brigham Young University, 1978), 80.

21. Peter Clemoes, "Cynewulf's Image of the Ascension," in Robert E. Bjork, ed., *Cynewulf: Basic Readings* (New York: Garland, 1996), 110.

22. John W. Conlee, "The Meaning of Troilus' Ascension to the Eighth Sphere," *Chaucer Review* 7.1 (Summer 1972): 27–30.

23. Ibid., 31.

24. Jesse M. Gellrich, *The Idea of the Book in the Middle Ages* (Ithaca, NY: Cornell University Press, 1985), 111.

25. M. Schumacher, *Catholic Encyclopedia*, transcribed by Joseph P. Thomas, electronic version (New Advent, 1997).

26. Morton Bloomfield, "Distance and Predestination in *Troilus and Criseyde*," *PMLA* 72 (March 1957): 20.

27. David Ulansey, *The Origins of the Mithraic Mysteries* (New York: Oxford University Press, 1989), esp. chapter five.

28. References to *Paradise Regained* from *The Complete Poetical Works of John Milton* (Boston: Houghton Mifflin, 1924).

29. Page references are to Charles Sumner's English translation, titled *A Treatise on Christian Doctrine* (Cambridge: Cambridge University Press, 1825).

30. Ibid., 505.

31. Ibid., 304, 305.

32. Footnoted in Sumner, 308; emphasis mine.

33. Sumner, 310 ff.

34. Ibid., 532.

35. *Paradise Lost*, 3.319.

36. *Don Juan*, Canto 1, 1–3.

37. See my monograph, *William Blake's Gnostic Vision* (Salzburg: Salzburg University, 1995).

38. Elaine Pagels, *The Gnostic Gospels* (New York: Random House, 1979).

39. Elaine Pagels, *The Origin of Satan* (New York: Random House, 1995).

40. Raymond Moody, *Life after Life: The Investigation of a Phenomenon—Survival of Bodily Death*, intro. by Elisabeth Kübler-Ross (Harrisburg, PA: Stackpole Books, 1976).

41. Plate 3. In *The Complete Poetry and Prose of William Blake*, ed. David Erdman (New York: Doubleday, 1988); future citations from Blake are from this edition and will be cited parenthetically. I will also preserve, where possible, Blake's spelling, capitalization, and punctuation.

42. See my essay "Dualism in Wordsworth's *Michael*," *Mythes, Croyances, et Religions dans le Monde Anglo-Saxon* 13 (1995): 17–25.

43. All references are to Ernest de Selincort's edition of *The Poetical Words of William Wordsworth*, 5 vols., 2d ed., rev. Helen Darbishire (Oxford: Clarendon Press, 1952–59); cited hereafter parenthetically by line numbers.

44. My brief treatment of Shelley's and Keats's letters and poetry are from David Perkins traditional anthology *English Romantic Writers* (New York: Harcourt Brace Jovanovich, 1967) and will be cited parenthetically by line numbers.

45. *The Epic of Gilgamesh*, trans. N. K. Sanders (New York: Penguin, 1972), 61, 62.

46. Jerusalem Bible, in a rather daring reworking of a vexed passage.

47. *The Odyssey of Homer*, trans. Ennis Rees (New York: Macmillan, 1991), 4.

48. In Rees, Introduction, xi–xii.

49. Book Twenty-three, in Rees, 389.

50. *English Romanticism* (New York: W. W. Norton, 1988), 170.

51. Mary Shelley, *Frankenstein* (New York: Airmont, 1963), 44.

52. Ibid., 55.

53. Ibid., 60.

54. Max Heindel, *Freemasonry and Catholicism* (London: L. N. Fowler, 1919).

55. Paul Nettl, *Mozart and Masonry* (New York: Philosophical Library, 1957), 3, 5.

56. Oscar Wilde, *The Picture of Dorian Gray* (Hertfordshire: Wordsworth Classics, 1992), 304.

57. See Clive Leatherdale, *The Origins of Dracula* (London: William Kimber, 1987), 176–91 for detailed comparisons.

58. C. S. Lewis, *That Hideous Strength* (New York: Macmillan, 1946; reprint, 1965), 181–82.

59. Ibid., 322.

60. Robert L. Gale, *A Nathaniel Hawthorne Encyclopedia* (New York: Greenwood, 1991), 196.

61. Nathaniel Hawthorne, *The Complete Novels and Selected Tales of Nathaniel Hawthorne*, ed. Norman Holmes Pearson (New York: Modern Library, 1937), 862–63.

62. Ibid., 864–65.

63. Ibid., 865.

64. Donna Versteeg-Cohen, writing of her Husband Elie; copy in my possession.

65. Herman Melville, *Moby-Dick* (New York: Penguin, 1992), 103. All references to *Moby-Dick* are from this edition.

66. See Matthew 17:5, 9–13; Luke 9:19.

67. Harold Bloom, *Omens of Millennium: The Gnosis of Angels, Dreams, and Resurrection* (New York: Riverhead Books, 1996). Bloom notes the presence of Parsees on the *Pequod*.

68. Melville, 101.

69. Joseph Campbell, *The Hero with a Thousand Faces*, 2d ed., Bollingen Series (Princeton, NJ: Princeton University Press, 1968), 92.

70. Melville, 624.

71. Mark Heidmann, *Melville and the Bible: Leading Themes in the Marginalia and Major Fiction, 1850–1856*, Ph.D. diss., Yale University, 1979, 87–90.

5 (Cult)ural Metaphor

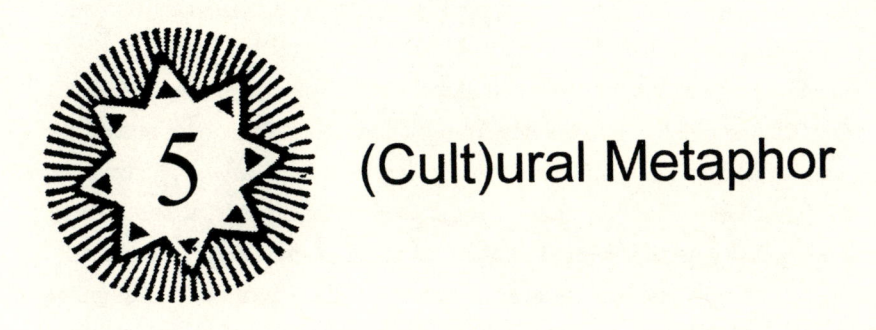

Ascension of Satan

Satan is at the center of a long battle among literary critics (remember Percy Bysshe Shelley's difficult attempt, in the *Defense of Poetry*,[1] to distinguish Satan's heroic "qualities" from his evil qualities),* but Satan's "influence" is a theological and certainly a sociological issue. Modern orthodox Jews, Muslims, and Christians recognize the reality of Satan, for he is an active, ongoing force in the world whose power to corrupt and to spread evil and misery (as also do his minions) far exceeds what any one individual or group of humans could conceivably accomplish. He is, however, of interest to me in this book as a heroic Being, not merely an amorphous darkness that more closely resembles the Greek Chaos or Shelley's Demogorgon, the "unknown quantity" over which Jupiter has no control. Satan's ascension fails, not because he is not well liked; in fact, he is already an eternal being, created, as literary and religious traditions attest, a high angel. His ascension consists of attempting to leave his assigned orbit (in the Ptolemaic or geocentric cosmology) and, by violence, to reach the outer sphere of God's throne, and then to topple God

---

* "Nothing can exceed the energy and magnificence of the character of Satan as expressed in *Paradise Lost*." Shelley adds (508) to this the boldest statement of all on this subject: "Milton's Devil as a moral being is . . . far superior to his God" (508), but Shelley is referring to the literary or narrative Satan, not to the real being.

from his throne (much as Jupiter is toppled in Shelley's *Prometheus Unbound*), and to sit in his place.

John Milton created the first fleshed-out ascension narrative for Lucifer; Milton recognized that no one had told the tale from Lucifer's viewpoint, and, in fact, the theologians of Milton's day, and even those going back to Jesus' day, had written their studies of sin and evil as though some such narrative existed somewhere, when it did not exist as such. Milton's genius lay in his inherent ability to find those pockets of sacred history that could be filled with high adventure and stunning characterization, but it is important to recognize what literary and historical precedents allowed Milton to accomplish a completely developed myth of origins.

Satan's origins are more and more obscure the farther back one reaches in textual narratives or commentaries. For example, Milton's Satan is far better developed as a myth of origins than are the references to him in the New Testament; those New Testament references are plentiful indeed compared to the Old Testament references. Clearly, orthodox theology would contend (as would I) that Satan's influence has been there all along, but the detailed portrait of Satan which has influenced our culture so much, as well as our thoughts about evil, or about "Satanic" influence, has been given us not only by prophets, mystics, and seers, but also by poets, novelists, moviemakers, and television. Whatever Satan may really be, the heroic Satan of popular culture has his hand in nearly every activity of our lives and seems to have a hundred rhetorical devices to Yahweh's straightforward, no-nonsense list of do's and don'ts.

In this approach to Satan's ascension, that of gradual accretion of narratives or, for the devout, that of the gradual unfolding of the mystery of Satan, I have been influenced by Elaine Pagels's *The Origin of Satan*, without doubt the best work on the subject. Pagels's considerable acumen as linguist and scholar of ancient history has made her the best voice for new and challenging readings of dusty narratives.* Her thesis is abundantly clear concerning the origin of Satan: "In the Hebrew Bible, as in mainstream Judaism to this day, Satan never appears as Western Christendom has come to know him, as the leader of an 'evil empire,' an army of hostile spirits who make war on God and humankind alike."[2] In the context of this

---

* Pagels was part of the original group translating the Nag Hammadi codices, and her book on gnosticism is excellent.

book, however, it is precisely those most ancient, least exegetical aspects of Satan's "social history" that reveal to us why Satan is almost universally acknowledged, in Western civilization, as the fountainhead of all evil.

The third chapter of Genesis speaks of the serpent's being "subtle." This statement suggests a number of things. First, since Genesis 2 (the second creation narrative) mentions the creation of all the animals, as well as the creation of Adam and Eve, the opening of Genesis 3 is a culmination of creation. The serpent is mentioned last of all (not to say last *created*), but only in apposition to all the other created things; in fact, the narrative clarifies this apposition by using the comparative "*more subtil* than any beast of the field which the Lord God had made" (Gen. 3:1; emphasis added). The implication here is that, in spite of the comparison with the beasts, the serpent was more "subtil" than the human creations (for otherwise, the subtlety of a mere animal would not be a threat to Adam and Eve). Adam of course has speech, but his only use of speech at this point is to name the animals, and he does not seem remotely subtle. The second implication is that God created the serpent and thus must have given it its subtlety, just as a parrot is born with all it needs to be trained to sing "I left my heart in San Fransisco."* It can only follow from this that Adam gave the serpent its name and was likely aware of its features.† The cunning or cleverness of the serpent—that is, its rhetorical power to persuade with its tongue (appropriately forked, next to poisonous fangs)—is in heroic tales a positive attribute, the clearest example being Odysseus, who is remarkably sharp-tongued and impetuous. The heroic quality of persuasion has the greatest potential of all heroic qualities: for example, through *pathos* King Priam persuades Achilles to return Hector's body. Achilles sees in Priam a father's love for his son and is moved to action by a power matched only by the sorrow he feels over the death of his close friend, Patroclus. Given that the *Iliad* is the tale of the consequences of Agamemnon's pride and Achilles' wrath, this power in Priam to persuade, that is, rhetoric, is a most precious gift.

---

* God's relative responsibility for his creations still sparks contentious theological debate; indeed, William Blake summed up the argument well in his poem "The Tyger": "Did he who made the lamb make thee?" I would add, in passing, that I *have* heard a parrot sing "I Left My Heart in San Francisco"!

† That is, the name, as with other Old Testament names, describes the actions or character of its recipient, as in the name *Adam* (Edom), meaning "red clay."

Thus, the third chapter of Genesis provides perhaps the chief attribute of Lucifer—his ability to persuade. Milton makes great use of Satan's rhetorical power in the early books of *Paradise Lost*.[3] Satan gives a rousing speech in Book One, to cheer on his devilish troops and to lull the reader into sympathy with that most set upon of heroes. The political diction still rings strong, after more than three hundred years:

> ... What though the field be lost?
> All is not lost—the unconquerable will,
> And study of revenge, immortal hate,
> And courage never to submit or yield:
> And what is else not to be overcome? (1.105–9)
>
> Farewell, happy fields,
> Where joy for ever dwells! Hail, horrors! hail,
> Infernal World! And thou, profoundest Hell,
> Receive thy new possessor—one who brings
> A mind not to be changed by place or time.
> The mind is its own place, and in itself
> Can make a Heaven of Hell, a Hell of Heaven. (1.149–55)
>
> Here we may reign secure; and, in my choice,
> To reign is worth ambition, though in Hell:
> Better to reign in Hell than serve in Heaven. (1.261–63)

Thus, because rhetorical power is a clear attribute of the hero, there is ample reason to conflate the serpent in Eden with the perverse being in Christian doctrine.

Yet the narrative of the serpent's downfall turns in on itself. When the serpent's playful trick is discovered, Yahweh is more than a little angry, ironically cursing his subtlest creation because of the very subtlety Yahweh gave him:

> And the Lord God said unto the serpent, Because thou hast done this, thou art cursed above all cattle, and above every beast of the field; upon thy belly shalt thou go, and dust shalt thou eat all the days of thy life:
> And I will put enmity between thee and the woman, and between thy seed and her seed; it shall bruise thy head, and thou shalt bruise his heel. (Gen. 3:14–15)

This passage gives us a second heroic quality in the serpent; it had wings and could fly. The "feathered serpent" motif in pre-Aztec mythology, the Apollo-like

Quetzalcoatl, gave the Aztecs the worldly arts of civilization.[4] The dragon of British lore is of course a winged, fire-breathing serpent (the fire suggesting the power to persuade, as, for example, the wily dragon Smaug in J.R.R. Tolkien's *The Hobbit*).[5] The serpent's power to ascend to the heavens (though not to remain there) is reflected in such tragic stories from Ovid as the tale of Daedalus and Icarus. Daedalus somehow gains a knowledge of "unknown arts"[6] that permits him and his son to escape Crete. Daedalus's exhortation to his son, "I warn you, Icarus, fly a middle course," falls on deaf ears, for the young man is determined to outdo the eagle, even the sun's chariot. The peasants below, doing their mundane chores, "look up, in absolute amazement," declaring, "They must be gods!"[7] That declaration is important, for it clearly shows the potential of the hero (in Genesis 3, a winged serpent) to rise close to the throne of Apollo, or Helios.

The King James Version contains a marvelous pun concerning Yahweh's clipping the serpent's wings, for the serpent is to be cursed "above" all cattle and beasts. Though the narrative plots the fall of the serpent from grace, the serpent of Genesis 3 is not seen to ascend and challenge Yahweh and thus requires a gloss or group of glosses over time to help the reader make the leap from serpent to Satan. It is for this reason that, though it is tempting, I do not associate Satan or the Edenic snake with Leviathan, the sea monster with whom Yahweh battles in Psalm 74:13–14: "Thou didst divide the sea by thy strength: thou brakest the heads of the dragons in the waters. Thou brakest the heads of leviathan in pieces, and gavest him to be meat to the people inhabiting the wilderness."

One other aspect of the serpent's role in the Bible is its connection to the beasts of the field. First, the field is *not* the Garden, suggesting that the serpent's domain is outside the Garden, despite his being subtler than the beasts. This contradiction suggests that Yahweh's creation of certain animals is part of an alternative narrative, in which creatures are fashioned to exist outside the Garden. The animal-man in *Gilgamesh*, Enkidu, immediately springs to mind—the serpent can never be translated because its sphere of influence is outside the Garden, a garden where Yahweh, for relaxation, walks in the cool of the day. The serpent's desire to live in Eden with God creates in it the tragedy of the overreacher (from the Greek *Titan*).*[8]

---

* Critic Harry Levin brings the term *overreacher* to us in his book-length treatment on Marlowe's tragedies, *The Overreachers*.

Because he can fly, the serpent is able to invade the Garden, and he finds himself among the more intelligent, more majestic mammals, and feels right at home. (It is hardly complimentary merely to say that the serpent is brighter than a sheep or cow—the effect is pure *bathos*.) The alternative narrative depicts Satan *alighting* on the forbidden tree (not slinking around its branches, as depicted in much art, which makes no sense if he is not yet cursed). The *hubris* of the serpent is that it rebels openly against the caste or class into which it was originally placed. Knowing that Adam was created of red clay doubtless rankles the serpent, who is also fashioned from nature, and when both are cursed by Yahweh, the one returns to dust, the other eats dust. Adam and Eve are, in the Garden, able to live forever because they have access to the food of God, the tree of life. Their condition is not unlike that of Utnapishtim and his wife.

In the alternative narrative, the serpent steals and consumes fruit from the tree of life, justifying the notion that serpents can live forever (the shedding of the old skin is the sign of the eternal rebirth), perhaps accounting for the serpent's being depicted as a self-consuming circle. The serpent's bite at the heel is, like the Achilles Heel, its reminder to humans that their hope of eternal life is forever lost. The attempt on our part to bruise the serpent's head (the mouth with its fangs) is also an attempt to avenge the poisoned rhetoric of the serpent. It is hardly surprising that the same poison that allows so many serpents the power to kill even humans is bound up with the metaphor of poisonous words—rhetoric. The cherubim (seraphim?) with their flaming swords must guard the Garden so that the *serpent* does not return, as well as guarding against the return of Adam and Eve. The serpent's bite also gives us tragic tales of parted lovers—for example, Orpheus and Eurydice—who encounter Satan as god of the underworld. But first we must consider how Satan acquired his quasi-human form.

As Pagels points out, the incident of Balaam's ass in Numbers 22 gives Satan status as an angel, but he is not a fallen angel; rather he is sent to turn Balaam from danger. The ass sees the angel and becomes the temporary "familiar" of the angel, seeing the angel when Balaam does not and speaking reproof to his master through God's power.[9] The Book of Job makes clear Satan's role as the messenger of God in human form, a metamorphosis worthy of an Ovid. Here we encounter *ha-satan*, "the accuser"—a prosecuting attorney who proposes the afflictions that frame the tragic hero's tale. He is unfallen at this point and is, as Pagels notes, "a member of

God's royal court."*[10] Indeed, the heroic elements of the Satan of cultural history could be remnants of the mythology of someone entirely other than the perverse evil-doer we have come to fear. This angel has free access to the throne of God and wanders the Earth freely. He has not yet acquired his role as god of the underworld—the ruling demon of hell, which appears roughly at the time the New Testament canon is forming and includes Hellenistic concepts of paradise, the Elysian Fields, and the like. Again, here I am not concerned precisely with whether Satan exists or not, or what his origins and activities may have been (I find evil to be ubiquitous, so I am a believer!), but I am interested in the layering of narratives over the centuries that have given him such an extraordinary and troubling grandeur.

It is in Isaiah 14:12–17 that Satan acquires his heroic ascension narrative:

> How art thou fallen from heaven, O Lucifer, son of the morning! how art thou cut down to the ground, which didst weaken the nations!
> For thou hast said in thine heart, I will ascend into heaven, I will exalt my throne above the stars of God: I will sit also upon the mount of the congregation, in the sides of the north:
> I will ascend above the heights of the clouds; I will be like the most High.
> Yet thou shalt be brought down to hell, to the sides of the pit.
> They that see thee shall narrowly look upon thee, and consider thee, saying, Is this the man that made the earth to tremble, that did shake kingdoms;
> That made the world as a wilderness, and destroyed the cities thereof . . .

I have deliberately excluded part of verse 17 and verses 18–23, which, though related to the previous passage, are not part of this ascension narrative. I have made this argument elsewhere;[11] I wish here to expand my study of this passage.

The verses are addressed to the king of Babylon, and Isaiah uses an old Babylonian myth of the sun god, which Isaiah and educated Israelites and even Babylonians would recognize, to prophesy the ultimate end of the king and his minions. The myth shows up in Greece as the story of Phaethon, the half-divine son of Helios who so desperately wants to prove his own divinity that he attempts to steer the chariot of the sun god across the sky. He loses control of the reins early on, however, causing himself and his chariot to crash into the constellations, where, for example, he is stung by Scorpio; he finally swerves so wildly that the chariot catches the great cities of Earth on fire. It is Jove's lightning bolt

---

* The fiery feminist-anthropologist Merlin Stone comes to mind.

that finally knocks Phaethon off his chariot and sends him plummeting to earth to be buried where he falls. The best version of the story is preserved in Ovid, in *The Metamorphoses*, and from there it attaches itself to the Christian narratives of Satan. The name "Phaethon," or "shining," connects us to the "day star" renamed, in the KJV, "Lucifer," the Roman "Light bearer," a Roman version of the Greek "Phosphoros," a god whose myth of origin has been lost to us. The idea of Satan as one who is formerly close to God but who fails and must be cast down from heaven must begin here, from a narrative viewpoint. This myth of Phaethon was so widespread that even Jesus knew of it,* or a form of it, perhaps from Ovid or, more likely, from the Book of Enoch, a widely read pseudepigraphic work. In Luke 10:18–19, Jesus declares, "I beheld Satan as lightning fall from heaven." The lightning is Jehovah–Jove's thunderbolt, and in the succeeding verse in Luke, Jesus tells his disciples that (unlike hapless Phaethon) they will "tread on serpents and scorpions, . . . and nothing shall by any means hurt you."

Besides the Phaethon tale, however, a contrasting vision of Satan's fall occurs when Zeus casts the newborn Hephaestus down from Olympus because of the creature's ugliness. (This accounts in part for Satan's Janus-like quality, one face that of a shining young man, the other of a repulsive horned beast.) Hephaestus, the smithy of the Greek pantheon, is nursed back to health by Thetis, daughter of Ocean, though the ugly god remains lame for eternity. Later, Thetis has Hephaestus form new armor for Achilles and make him a new shield unsurpassed in its beauty and workmanship. Achilles dons the armor to replace that taken by Hector from Patroclus, and the new armor allows Achilles to reenter the battle and to destroy Hector, the Trojan hero whom Zeus admired so.

The moment Satan is cast down from heaven—that is, the moment when the narratives of Phaethon, Hephaestus, and others become attached—the way is opened for Satan to descend below the ground, to the underworld. Again, the Ptolemaic cosmology places God outside all the other spheres, so Earth's core is the point farthest from God, and thus Lucifer or Phosphorous is hurtled back by God, cutting a path through the planetary spheres and reversing Lucifer's "eccentric" orbit. This cosmologic event, while inconsistent with the Phaethon narrative, or with that of Hephaestus, begins as an attempt to bypass all other luminaries,

---

* I assert this on the premise that the attribution to Jesus of the particular logion was correct.

finally throwing God himself out of his position and taking control of the cosmos. God (Jehovah– Jove) casts Lucifer back so hard that the hapless adventurer ends up at the core of Earth. Thus, every heroic journey to the underworld is not an ascension, but a *descensus*, an ironic reversal in which, for example, Persephone is rewarded after her involuntary heroic descent into hell by being admitted to the divine family of the underworld, never tasting death! It is not to be wondered that part of this "gift" is that she may return to the mortal world (an ironic ascent that mirrors, for example, Elijah's return to Earth to warn mortals of impending doom, and the like).

Thus we find that Satan is inextricably bound up with Hades or Pluto, the god of the underworld, although Hades neither falls nor is cast down. In the casting of lots, Zeus ended up controlling the heavens, Poseidon the earth and sea (he is the god of the earthquake, not merely the tidal wave), and Hades the underworld. This division gave Hades a kingdom of sorts and suggests at least a castle, because Hades sat on a throne with Persephone next to him—where they held court. Their kingdom consists of demons, certainly—furies and maenads, three-headed dogs, dragons, and the like—but it finally became the abode for the shades, the watery spirits of departed mortals, who find a dour existence in Hades (the kingdom taking the name of its king), drinking whatever blood comes their way.

The underworld also contains the veins of ore, precious stones in the rough, and other treasures. For that reason the cave (where mining begins) becomes part of Lucifer's kingdom after his fall from grace; the cave is often the entrance to the underworld. Quite ironically, the Christian *and* the pagan Lucifer are created immortal, and so cannot die of mortal ills. But immortal beings can be wounded and even tortured—if we recall both the fate of the Titan nailed to a cliff or Lucifer's own doom, to dwell where there is incessant weeping, wailing, and gnashing of teeth. It is logical to assume, therefore, that to the Christian Satan's myth of origins would be attached the roles of Hades (or Pluto), since both preside (sit in judgment, hold captive, mete out punishment, and so on) over the shades of all mortals, after their deaths. While in Dante's *Inferno* Satan is frozen almost up to his armpits in the icy cold core of Hades, in the ancient Greek and Roman narratives he ascends to the "outside" world from time to time in order to drag certain people back to the underworld; the evidence is clear enough in the Orpheus myth that in order to leave the underworld, one must ascend. Dante and Virgil illustrate the ascent:

> My guide and I entered that hidden road
> to make our way back up to the bright world,
> We never thought of resting while we climbed
> We climbed, he first and I behind, until
> through a small round opening ahead of us
> I saw the lovely things the heavens hold,
> and we came out to see once more the stars. (34.133–39)[12]

A narrative dilemma of sorts occurs in this passage. Since Dante assuredly cannot leave hell by going back through the terror of his descent (much as a sinner must choose another path from that of sin to reach God), the ascension of Dante is not merely a movie in reverse. It is, more precisely, an initiation, including the initiatory cleansing of the soul through purging (the meaning of purgatory or *purgatorium*—the place where one is purged). The fate of Old Hamlet, in Shakespeare's best-known mature tragedy, hinges on Claudius's murder, which kills King Hamlet before he can make final confession or have it followed by extreme unction, the Catholic sacrament of anointing of body and soul. This murder of body and soul makes Claudius doubly guilty. For Old Hamlet's ghost declares of purgatory, where he is

> Doom'd for a certain term to walk the night,
> And for the day confined to fast in fires,
> Till the fond crimes done in my days of nature
> Are burnt and purg'd away. (1.5.16–19)[13]

The reverse-ascension of mortals is the ultimate anti-heroic image, for even the great heroes such as Hector and Achilles must descend to the underworld, if they are not translated (as was Herakles) or set with the constellations (as with Orion). Being forced into the narrative trap of descent may have forced storytellers and even the priests and philosophers into creating paradise (whose earthly counterpart, ostensibly, is Paris, France, in the spring on the *Champs-Elysees* [Elysian Fields]!), a comfortable place where the noble and heroic who died could find a measure of just reward. This solution is a narrator's device to restore order to the heroic quest; creating a paradise for the shade of Hector is not unlike the eighth heaven of Chaucer's *Troilus*—at the very least the narrative dilemma triggers both responses.

It required only the exegesis of generations of Jewish rabbis and Christian doctors to take these divergent narratives (including those in Daniel that reappear in the Revelation of the Christian divine John) and piece them together into a seamless single narrative that is a part of the cultural consciousness of even the most lapsed Christian or Jew, and possibly by another route, the Muslim. Satan's rebellion against Yahweh creates the primeval Fall—a fall preceding that of Adam and Eve—in which Satan, and all the angels that follow him, creates a mirror-image of heaven in the dark Chaos into which he and his cohorts are cast. The attempt to reascend to the heavens, with the goal of overthrowing Yahweh completely, is the implicit goal in all Satan's efforts. I emphasize this aspect of the elliptical narrative of Satan's fall, for the idea has taken hold in Christian fundamentalism that Satan's only purpose is to make humans miserable like himself, or to torture sinful souls who fall prey to his wiles. Milton understood that the key to defeating Satan lay in a correct understanding of his relationship to Yahweh, not to humans and mortals. His association with the element of fire (the Hephaestus image) continues after his fall and marks his angelic status as one of the seraphim, the angels closest to Yahweh's throne. Thus, his glory, the outward sign of his inner power, justifies his belief that he (as Beowulf) can overturn fate (*moira*, typified in the three fates of Greek myth, and *wyrd*, typified in Scandanavian–English myth by the Norns) and prevail against Yahweh (perhaps during an unguarded moment!).

Only this hubris can account for Satan's behavior. Milton correctly understood that Satan's disdain of humanity is connected with his need to undo any one or all of Yahweh's plans—to prove that his reascent is a viable scheme. Ironically, it is in the oldest literature that one finds the best evidence of the cultural needs which a particular narrative addresses. The idea that Satan leads a rebellion against God because he considers himself God's equal is actually part of the *Gilgamesh* epic. The council of the gods meets to decide whether or not to flood the earth and start anew—the basis for the Noachian narrative of Genesis. It is abundantly clear that the Bible's flood narrative is a reediting of a much more complex narrative; the Genesis writer (and his scribal glossers) is restrained and very critical and will not tolerate the excesses of the Babylonian (Sumerian) version. In *Gilgamesh*, Ea is the friend of humanity, an intercessor of sorts, not unlike Prometheus of later myth, who opposes Zeus's plan to destroy humankind. Ea whispers in the ear of the

Sumerian Noah to build a boat to ride out the storm. Here Ea best fits Shelley's comments on the noblest qualities of Milton's Satan, for Ea compassionately wishes to preserve humans against the fierce wrath of the other gods, who are incensed by Ea's subterfuge. Had the poet Shelley not been so selective with his evidence about Satan's heroics, he might have noticed that Milton's Jesus, in Book Three of *Paradise Lost*, is also a noble intercessor shielding humanity against God's wrath, proposing "Behold me, then: me for him, life for life, / I offer; on me let thine anger fall; / Account me Man" (3.236–38).

Satan's development as an evil anti-hero whose failed attempt to ascend to God's throne seems part of both history and future events (as in, for example, Isaiah's prophecies in the Old Testament, those of Revelation in the New). Christianity, at least, holds Satan fast in hell, where Dante has vividly portrayed Satan's job description for punishing errant humans. Our curious blending of Western classical and religious myth about the underworld afterlife is remarkable. Very few of the cultural trappings of hell and Satan can be found in the Bible. The Bible actually talks about "hell" long before it had any living occupants. *Sheol* is the Old Testament underworld, and the word is best translated "the pit." It is pitch black; the corpse sleeps, having no sensation—no one to talk to (although Emily Dickinson suggested at one point that if one is buried close enough to others, conversation might be possible!); and in that condition, no work can be done. This dismal view of things at once suggests the morose Sumerian assessment of the grave and of the mortal status of, well, mortals. Yet if we have trust in the historicity of the Mosaic exodus, it is clear that Israel left Egypt with no hope of a life after death. To Israel, Yahweh was a tribal deity, offering only earthly rewards and punishments. Abraham, who could easily have been Sumerian (the Bible's Shinar),*[14] would have inherited that people's dour collective thoughts on the afterlife. Unless interpreted allegorically, the covenants Abraham enters into with Yahweh offer blessings of prosperity to him, but nothing more.

---

* Whatever one concludes about the seeming New Age eccentricities in *The Wars of Gods and Men*, Zecharia Sitchin is convincing about Abraham's origins in Sumer (Ur being Abraham's birth-city). That Shinar is Sumer follows the patterns of mimation and nunation in Old Testament Hebrew. Sitchin is a talented Sumerologist and Assyriologist and has knowledge of several key ancient languages.

Milton demonstrates in his work *Christian Doctrine* that from the Bible text it is practically impossible to argue for a life after death—a spirit world where people dwell when their bodies are in the ground. It was the mortalist in Milton that must have understood that Christ's gift of resurrection had its greatest *narrative* impact when it was thought that there was no life after death.[15] In fact, the Resurrection itself is hard to visualize, for the thought tends to result in a kind of perverse funeral home sleight of hand. Catholics, Mormons, and Charismatic Christians of all sorts (Baptist, Pentecostal, and the like) all have a distinct picture of Jesus as a resurrected being, but all use rhetoric and imagery that fall back on the paradise/Hades or paradise/purgatory/Hades models of the Satanic hero who, frozen in place at the center of Dante's cosmos, avenges himself on the putrefaction and remaining life force of the dead, versus the radiant Jesus of *The Harrowing of Hell*, who, as a temporary underworld punisher, afflicts the already-tortured, but who embraces every good Christian directly after the funeral service—often before that—into the next mansion on your right. The *descensus* of Christ into hell is a narrative necessity, a strategy that allows him to wrest paradise away from Hades/Satan/Lucifer, as a final step is taken to separate Satan and Jesus from their cultural roots.

The rise of Satan, his new ascension, if you will, is metaphorical. His flames were fanned first by early Jewish Christians who saw Rome's stranglehold on Israel and its corruption of Israelite values as the "adversary," a role with which Satan was already familiar. Demonizing Rome was a necessity: the real devils are those that have bodies and can embrace lust and violence as positive values. The "Revelation," the last book in the Bible, calls Rome the whore of Babylon and its city on seven hills the new Sodom. It is not long, however, before Satan switches sides, and the new Roman Catholic world condemns Jews and distances Jesus from his cultural roots.

Satan plays on the world stage. For example, in *The Inferno,* Dante places his political enemies, some of them high churchman, in the various levels of hell. In the ballad of St. Dominique, he is fighting the Albigenses, pitting his miracles against the devil's, for the Albigenses, like the Cathars, are heretical Catholics, not merely another religious group. The epic *Chanson de geste (The Song of Roland)* depicts Islam as the enemy of the church, and therefore Satanic, worshiping false gods such as Allah, Zeus, and Mahomet. The Inquisition scouts out the Jewish demons in human form, not to mention the heretical Christians, such as the Knights Templar, whose grand master Jacques de Molet is put to the fire as a demonic heretic. Spenser in *The Fairie Queene*, demonizes Catholicism, portraying Archimago and false Duessa as demons to be overcome by the Redcrosse Knight or by Prince Arthur. Dragons, instead of fire, spew forth Catholic books and pamphlets as well as little demons. Old Catholic women in England, still muttering the mass and their rosaries, are tried as witches for speaking in unknown tongues (and *hoc est corpus* becomes *hocus pocus*); then the tribunals order the large-scale killing of witches' familiars, such as cats and owls, thereby increasing the supply of rats, which helps spread the plague. Freemasonry is branded as Satanic by the Pope as early as a papal bull in 1738, and still is by Protestants. Hitler and the Nazis are justly demonized perhaps, for it is important to dehumanize an enemy to make killing him less disturbing; in fact, the Nazis' murders of Jews was an attempt to purge demonic forces from German. Ironically, Stalin killed more than twice that number of his fellow-citizens during a reign of terror. It was because of Communism that the West declared for more than fifty years that the Soviets were godless, soulless parts of Satan's kingdom. All of America's conservative churches preached openly against Communism as a terrifying Satanic doctrine.

Satan's current position is aggrandized in movies and in horror novels as the soul-snatcher, who feasts on those not good hearted enough to be claimed by the Light. He is a very popular hero today; only conservative Christians, Jews, and Muslims consider him a threat. His prospects for the new century look very good; he no longer is connected with sin, but is more like a dangerous human, to be overcome not with mundane righteousness, but by single combat, requiring humans only to have the muscle and hardware to outgun him. Satan is the prototype for modern, realist CEOs, who demonize their corporations' enemies. Satan is admired again for his industry, his ruthlessness, his savvy awareness of what humans need most, and his pragmatic pursuit of any new thrill, risk, temptation, or other celebration of the flesh.

The Cid and the Ascension of Muhammad

The Cid Campeador is an excellent example of a narrator's swerve to account for unsettling difficulties in the ascension–translation of the hero. The narrator in this instance is all the devout people who saw Roderigo as a Messiah figure in

Spain. As H. Butler Clarke notes, "The simple folk . . . refused to believe that so splendid a career could end in defeat and disappointment . . . , and they piously ascribed to their hero victory after death."[16] I am summarizing Clarke's excellent work on this compilation:

The real death of El Cid (*Sidy*, Arabic for *Lord*)[17] was vexing to anyone who would rather the Cid be taken to heaven as a saint. He was ill and had been for over a year; when, after his death, his body, the principal part of the funeral cortege, passed through towns, his emaciated form must have shocked ordinary people. In their sweet devotion, the people spread a beautiful narrative throughout Spain of his miraculous preservation, and the story quickly became the subject of many ballads. The idea of his miraculous preservation or even his ascension is not unreasonable—The Cid was not only heroic in battle, and a member of a respected family, but he was intensely ethical and religious. Before his death, he received visions and visitations telling him to prepare for the next life. So Roderigo the Campeador kept a fast and prayed with real intent, taking the last sacraments as he approached the final pilgrimage to the Catholic paradise. Though he was extremely weak, it is said that his flesh was transfigured, with the sort of translucence that typifies the translated hero. The transition took place, and the hero died, but he asked that his body be armed in mail, set on his great battle horse, a banner in one hand, his sword in the other, blazing like fire. At the sight of him, the narrative continues, the invading Moors retreated, in morbid terror of him, to the sea, where they were flanked by water. The slaughter was amazing: thousands upon thousands of the enemy died, and the Cid still led them as of old. What terrified the foe? It was without doubt the Cid's radiance, unearthly, holy; but they also believed they saw seventy thousand knights, all in white, with white stallions and flaming (radiant) swords. His body, richly embalmed with myrrh and balsam before he led his knights into battle, made him look entirely alive. "And," says the chronicle, "any man in the world who had not known the truth and had seen him would have declared he was alive."[18] Indeed, the body remained unchanged even after being displayed on a throne in the monastery chapel at San Pedro for several years.

What we tend to ignore is the possibility that his preservation was the sign that the ascending hero's corpse could not be allowed to see corruption. The hero's revisiting Earth, to inspire and aid mortals, is achieved in the hero's being a "living" object of adoration for faithful Christians. And behind the Cid's ascension is another ascension myth, worthy of El Cid: the ascension of Muhammad.

While Catholic ascension myth is well known, Islamic ascension myth is not. El Cid united Spain against the Moorish invasion from North Africa by uniting Christian and Muslim under a national banner. Spain, the Spanish Moors felt, was worth preserving because of its own culture, in which Moorish and Christian ideals in art, poetry, architecture, and scholarly learning merged. I would contend that the ascension and translation of Roderigo worked as a narrative because Muhammad himself, according to Islamic tradition, had ascended to heaven much as Isaiah, without having been translated.[19]

In 621 B.C.E., as the story is recounted in *The Bokhari* (15.3615), Muhammad happens to be at his cousin's house when the prophet falls asleep and dreams of ascending by means of *Miraj*, or the "stairway to heaven," much as Jacob does in the Genesis account. The archangel Gabriel offers the prophet a ride on a winged steed, not unlike the winged steed Pegasus. Like Isaiah, Muhammad enters the cosmic temple of heaven, meeting some of the worthies of the Old Testament, including Enoch, Elijah, and Jesus, all of whom had ascended to heaven and were translated.

The significance of Muhammad's ascension can hardly be overestimated, for it not only reinforces the narrative of El Cid's transfiguration, but also shows that the tradition of ascension–translation crosses religious and cultural boundaries to become a heroic ideal among all peoples, even into the seventh century of the common era. Its moral value is equally great, for in the Cid narrative we find common ground between Christian and Muslim, an ethical relationship matched only by the (grudging) mutual respect of the Templar knights and the Saracens and surpassed only by the acts of individual Christians' protection of Jews (where it occurred) during the Nazis' genocidal war. In light of recent events, it is reassuring that such common ground has been found in the past and may be attained again in the future.

The Assumption of Mary

As all the Apostles were watching round the dying Mary, Jesus appeared with His angels and committed the soul of His Mother to the Archangel Michael. Next day, as they were carrying the body to the grave, Christ again appeared and carried it with Him in a cloud to heaven, where it was reunited with the soul.[20]

The assumption or bodily ascension–translation of the Virgin Mary is the most fascinating aspect of her cult's influence in Roman Catholicism. This account is remarkable because, as influential as it is, its narrative frame rests, unlike Christ's resurrection, on no firsthand witness or assertion of historical fact but appears to be the result of a fifth-century tradition embodied in a Latin document known as the *Transitus*, allegedly recorded by Melito of Sardis.*[21] In an attempt to put "old wine in new bottles, Jaroslav Pelikan addresses the very point I wish to raise here: the essential incompatability of resurrection and translation:

One question raised by the doctrine of the assumption had been whether Mary had ever died or whether she had, like Enoch and Elijah, been taken up alive into heaven. The prophecy of Simeon to her . . . , "Yes, a sword shall pierce through thy own soul also," seemed to imply that she would die, just as her divine and sinless Son would.[22]

A papal bull of 1950 formalized the dogma of the assumption, but, as Pelikan points out, this did nothing to resolve the doctrinal tension implied in the assumption: the narrative of Mary's assumption was the outgrowth of "lay piety," though to be sure theologians had offered commentary on the doctrine as far back as the Middle Ages. Indeed, her appellation as Queen of Heaven is very old, and the implication that she reigns higher than the archangels is apparent, in part because of her being caught up bodily into heaven.

Even within the Catholic church the fear of Mariolatry (a protestant epithet) is obvious in various Vatican pronouncements. It is clear that church authorities foresee the possibility of the veneration of Mary supplanting the doctrine of Christ concerning atonement, remission of sins, and the centrality of Jesus' person in all ritual and devotional elements of worship. Thus Roman Catholicism distinguishes "formally between *latria* and *dulia* and declares that the 'worship' to be paid to the mother of God must never exceed that superlative degree of *dulia* which is vaguely described as *hyperdulia*"[23] and which presumably is reserved for the Trinity. Cardinal Ratziner adroitly observes, "Thus Marian praise harmonizes with that

---

* The work is at best pseudo-Mileto. Geoffrey Ashe calls its attribution to John the Beloved absurd given its lateness, but as I hope to show, it is an extremely old tale and is attributed to John for narrative reasons altogether appropriate.

picture of God which associates the patriarchs with the name of God and recognizes the extolling of God in the extolling of the patriarchs."[24]

What implications are there for this study of subscribing to alternative views of Mary's assumption? If the assumption narrative is a replication of the assumption of Enoch or Elijah, we can divest ourselves of a serious dilemma. Out of concern that Mary's death and assumption might be equated with Jesus' unique resurrection, the papal bull of 1950 employs the phrase *assumptio ad coelestem gloriam*, "not of resurrection, but of the 'assumption' of the body and soul into heavenly glory."[25] Thus Mary's assumption is a *result* of the resurrection of Christ and not in contention with it. But such hairsplitting has no practical value, even in terms of scholarly analysis, let alone lay piety. Translation as envisaged in earlier parts of my study represents an archaic, heroic alternative to life after death or even to resurrection from the dead. Yet Catholic theologians have considered the death of Mary essential to the narrative of her assumption. The doctrine of life after death (the survival of the ghost) is obviously insufficient for Christian exegesis (in spite of the fact that from Dante's day on most Catholics would assert that assignment to a permanent heaven or hell immediately follows death), so it is clear that catching up Mary's ghost into the heavens would not allow her a status higher than that of the archangels and would defeat the purpose of the narrative. That purpose is to account for Mary's being called Mother of God from the third century forward, being pictured as Queen of Heaven in early Christian iconography, and having her status discussed by every exegete from Athanasius to the Second Vatican Council. I contend that the assumption narrative arose not simply from the piety of lay Christians, but from a sincere desire by lay persons and ecclesiastics alike to account for her overshadowing influence in the art and lore of the post-apostolic era.

Yet a narrative of Mary's assumption *without* the element of death presents serious difficulties as well. For example, if, as I contend earlier, Christ's death constitutes the failed expectation of ascension–translation, and Christ's resurrection and later ascension constitute narrative substitutes or accommodation of the disconcerting fact of his death, Mary's ascension without her dying beforehand could be perceived as superior in a literary, heroic sense to the Gospel narratives of the Christ who dies, is resurrected, then ascends. Furthermore, the fact that in all "the versions of the *Transitus* . . . hostility to the Jews is part of the narrative"[26] suggests that what likely began as an ascension–translation narrative among Jewish Christians in remembrance of Mary was subverted by later generations of Christians to distance themselves from the very Jewishness of the narrative. It certainly goes without saying that Jewish adherents in primitive Christianity brought with them not only their popular legends concerning Enoch and Elijah (very well known in Jesus' time) but a veneration for the female aspect of deity, the Hokmah and/or Shekhinah, as well as of motherhood in general, which remained central to the Jewish experience through the Renaissance and beyond.

From this point of view, I am grateful for an Ethiopic version of the legend, "The History of the Death of the Virgin Mary as Told by Saint John (the 'ASTAR'eyo, which is to be read on the 21st day of the month TER," Brit. Mus. MS. Orient. No. 604, fol. 45a), which is one of several Ethiopian liturgical pieces to complement the many feasts or holy days dedicated to the Virgin. This version is an Ethiopian *Transitus*, the legend being preserved in several countries and languages in the first centuries of Christianity. It appears in a rare volume of translations from the Ethiopian by the daunting E. A. Wallis Budge, the great Egyptologist and fabled scholar of antiquities.[27]

Before commenting on the narrative itself, its attribution to "Our holy father JOHN ... [who] told us"[28] must be assessed. In an earlier chapter, I wrote at some length about the embedded ascension–translation narrative inherent in John 21 concerning the "disciple whom Jesus loved," which was strongly misread by such later mythographers as Joseph Smith into complex ascension legends. I believe strongly that the attribution to John does not grow only out of the narrative of Jesus' commandment to John, "Behold thy mother" and to Mary, "Behold thy son." By itself, that new relationship would prepare John to protect and defend Mary up to her death, but would not establish the cosmic link necessary for her to ascend in her turn and be translated. I assert this insufficiency despite the *History*'s descriptive collophon that John "took [her] to him after the Ascension of our Lord and Savior JESUS CHRIST into heaven"[29] precisely because it is a collophon to identify the author of the account, not to establish his primacy or his authority over Mary. What I am suggesting is that there is another element, a lacuna or at least an ellipsis, which would cast John in the role of a returning Elijah figure, who, ascended and translated himself, never sees death, but is able firsthand to witness the cosmic destiny of Mary after her ascension. Clearly, John's testimony is of another nature entirely from that of the other disciples, who, though witnesses to her death, are not the testators of her translation (that role being given to John). The disciples are summoned back miraculously:

> And then the Holy Spirit spake, saying, "Let all the disciples come from the ends of the earth, riding upon clouds, to BETHLEHEM, for the sake of the Mother of CHRIST—thou, O PETER, from ROME" . . . and so on.[30]

Note the submission of Peter, as leader of the Roman church, as well as of James, the ruler of the Jerusalem church, to the needs of the Virgin, and of the narrator, John, who seeks their witness to the transaction of dormition or assumption. On this basis, then, I conclude that John's status is implicit but firm as one worthy of ascension–translation himself.

The miraculous gathering up of the apostles and other important figures of the primitive church and their "mount[ing] on clouds"[31] certainly recall the ascension of Elijah. Yet the immediate source of this narrative motif of being "spirited away" is a pivotal tale from the New Testament, in Acts 8, in which Philip "was taken away by the Spirit of the Lord, and the eunuch never saw him again" (Acts 8:39–40).* The text is pivotal for several reasons, not the least of which is the ancient setting for the passage—a pentecostal apostolic period soon after the ascension of Christ.

The eunuch in the story is an Ethiopian. It does not occur to us at first glance that the Ethiopian must be a Jew, or at the very least a Godfearer, for he "had been on pilgrimage to Jerusalem" and was a chief treasurer to the queen of Ethiopia. Furthermore, the man, returning from his pilgrimage (doubtless for Passover), is reading Isaiah aloud, either in an Ethiopian or Hebrew version. When Philip is urged by God's spirit to talk with the Ethiopian, the pilgrim responds, "How can I, unless I have someone to guide me?"[32] Answering a question with a question

---

*All references from the Jerusalem Bible. Of course, this narrative is built on elements of the Gospel narratives, such as Matthew 4, in which Jesus is taken "to a very high mountain" by Satan, or Matthew 17, the Transfiguration, where Jesus takes Peter, James, and John and leads them "up a high mountain." The religious genius Joseph Smith understood implicitly the importance of the "high mountain" elements of ascension tales: In the Book of Mormon, the prophetic character Nephi is "caught away in the Spirit of the Lord, yea, into an exceeding high mountain, which [he] never had before seen, and upon which [he] never had before set [his] foot" (1 Nephi 11:1). In a later pseudepigraphic work, the Book of Moses, Smith records "the words of God, which he spake unto Moses at a time when Moses was caught up into an exceedingly high mountain" (Moses 1:1).

is certainly a Jewish idiom (which Jesus employs), but even more revealing is the tacit acknowledgment that the Ethiopian considers Philip a rabbi, a master of the law and the prophets. The reading and interpretation of the law and the prophets is, we recall, a standard activity at the synagogue, and one with which the rabbi is intimately connected; with the Ethiopian's text of Isaiah plainly before him, Philip does not scruple to interpret Isaiah as fulfilled in Jesus. That Jesus himself had read and interpreted Isaiah this way early in his ministry caused his family's synagogue to try to stone Jesus for his "blasphemy."

The presence of Jewish colonists in Ethiopia before Christ's time has been strikingly vindicated in recent years with the repatriation of thousands of Falashas, Ethiopian Jews, to Israel. Claiming they descended from Jews of Solomon's day, and also claiming some affinity with the queen of Sheba (often conflated in Solomonic legends with the queen of Ethiopia), these Jews presented a perplexing problem to the state of Israel, which heroically risked its aircraft and pilots to rescue the Falashas from certain death under Ethiopia's militaristic government. Among the Falashas were a cadre of temple priests, trained to perform the ordinances and rites preserved, as they believed, from Solomon's day. In Israel, however, there was no work for them—the temple did not exist.

My point here is quite simple: the Ethiopian "convert" was Jewish to begin with but clearly believed Philip enough to make a baptismal covenant at the "rabbi's" request, after which Philip was "spirited" away in the fashion of the translated beings who in many narratives come back to earth to offer advice and warnings at key moments. The Ethiopian, enlightened beyond measure, took Philip's teachings (no doubt severely truncated in the narrative of Acts, in which only a single *didache* must stand for the whole of rabbinic scholarship) about Isaiah and Jesus back to his people (including his possibly Jewish queen). In Isaiah is of course the primary tribute to Mary (at least in early Christian strong misreadings of Old Testament prophecy): "The maiden is with child and will soon give birth to a son whom she will call Immanuel" (Isa. 7:14). And it is in fact the pastoral nativity of Luke that preserves the Christian narrative of Mary's status, and it is the Acts of the Apostles, also likely written by the author of Luke, which ties the Gospel narrative to the apostolic narrative.

What then, besides the one stated foreshadowing, could this first Ethiopian convert have brought back to his own colony? Not the Old Testament (already known), neither priestly order (already established in the Falasha mythic conscious), but rather the efforts of a Jewish-Christian disciple, Philip, to piece together the many Christ narratives (ascended hero, marred servant, sacrificial lamb) into a consistent *didache* to *make better Jews of the Jews of Ethiopia.* That is, "conversion" for Ethiopians meant, as was true everywhere in the early Christian community, making good Jews into ideal Jews. It is well known from even a reading of Acts that the apostles went first to the synagogues, the great Jewish houses, and to the godfearers to preach their message, and only later to the "Gentiles."

Yet the Marian *mythos* and cult could not have been at *full* flower so early. Thus it is logical to assume that the nativity story, if Philip had heard it and passed it on to the Ethiopian, was utterly unadorned; neither immaculate conception nor assumption to the status of Queen of Heaven could have been part of the original tale of Jesus' mother. Yet a colony of Ethiopic Jews would have a storehouse of lore on which to draw for such an embellishment (at a later date). Thus, far from being a late accretion to Roman Catholic tradition, or even a pure product of Ethiopian Christianity, the history of Mary was a Jewish-Christian legend, which quickly took upon it characteristics of the ancient ascension myths, specifically those of Enoch and Elijah. (It is of note in this regard that Sir Richard Laurence acquired an Ethiopian Book of Enoch which appeared in English in 1821.)

How the embellishments in Mary's history could occur in an essentially Jewish legend is not far to seek: First, the Falashas were convinced that they were literal descendants of the queen of Sheba, who, it was told, carried within her Solomon's seed when she was converted to the worship of Yahweh and then returned to establish his message in her own land. The conflation of Mary, the mother of the Davidic Messiah, with Sheba, the mother of the Ethiopian Jewish colony, seems to me inevitable, especially when one considers that they both spent time in Egypt (likely dwelling among Jewish Egyptians in Elephantine or other Jewish colonies). This passing through Egypt may explain in part the necessity of deifying Mary, elevating her status to Queen of Heaven. Budge, in an introductory essay to his collection of Marian legends, notes that at the time of Christ, the mystery cult of Isis was at its height; ironically, he makes the extraordinary assertion that the cult bears no significant resemblance to the legends surrounding the Virgin. Yet he notes point after point in which the narratives agree. Two reactions to a powerful foreign religious cult can occur: one involves stripping one's own religion of any resemblance to the other; a second reaction is to outdo or rival the competition both in its complexity and its beauty. The monotheism that developed in Israel after the Exile came at the cost of removing from Yahweh many delightful traits—human traits. Yet the other tradition, in which Yahweh shares characteristics with the gods of other religions, never died, as Raphael Patai demonstrated some time ago in his sensational book *The Hebrew Goddess*.[33] I believe Mary's status was raised, and rather quickly, in response to the vacuum that existed in Jewish Christianity at that early date—there was no woman figure to fill the yearnings within Jewish Christianity for a mother figure.

Mary's death, in this Ethiopian version of the dormition, occurs "in the three hundred and fifty-second year of Alexander (A.D. 40), that is to say, two years after the Ascension of our Lord into heaven, on the 29th [day of the month]."[34] The incident with Philip and the Ethiopian could easily have occurred after this day, and I find no reason to think the date of her death is any sort of fabrication. For example, a simple ascension and translation, sans death, would present far fewer problems from a narrator's perspective. The differences in the various versions of the dormition or assumption (they exist in Greek, Latin, Syriac, Coptic, and Arabic)[35] suggest a common origin in the historical fact of Mary's *death*, which is then enhanced through accretion, likely by Jewish Christians in colonies throughout the Mediterranean.

I originally felt as many Catholic writers have felt, that Mary's status of Queen of Heaven, the Immaculate Conception, and the Assumption were narratives incident to Mary's being the Mother of God; but in A.D. 40, Christianity had hardly achieved such a lofty concept of Jesus as deity or as "word made flesh." Budge argues that Jesus may be distinguished from Osiris in that "JESUS raised Himself from the dead." But Peter, speaking early in the Book of Acts, declares, "*God raised him* to life, freeing him from the pangs of Hades" (Acts 2:23–24; emphasis mine).[36] Not only is the concept of Trinity missing in Peter's declaration, but Jesus clearly relies on Yahweh for his deliverance. Those who believe that the Immaculate Conception and Assumption doctrines and narratives did not appear till centuries after the apostolic period would of course assume that Mary's status rose as the status of Jesus rose and that the post-Nicene remoteness of God and Christ was also in part the occasion for Mary's role as intercessor. But if the Ethiopian dormition narrative is as old as I believe, it no doubt was constructed with a

Jewish-Christian audience in mind and was done to imitate not only the ascension of Jesus, but the ascension and translation of Elijah and Enoch. That is, those already ascended, and even those created immortal (the angels), are necessary agents for those being "taken" to heaven. The hero simply cannot ascend without the gods' permission. Thus, in the dormition, with all the disciples present at Bethlehem (the birthplace mentioned at length in Luke's Gospel), "Jesus Christ stretched out His holy hand and received her soul, and straightway her soul was separated from her body." Mary is then entombed for three days in a new vault in Gethsemane, in perfect imitation of Jesus' burial, after which "the angels [carried her body] up into Heaven."[37]

The mention of Gethsemane is significant in this account, though not simply for its being the beginning place of Christ's sufferings, the *via dolorosa*. The final scene of the Ethiopian dormition consists of the gathering of the apostles, the patriarchs, the kings, and various righteous women in "the Garden" (a paradisiacal final resting place for Mary's corpse) to pay final homage to the translated Mary*[38] and to Jesus. It is remarkable that this garden is the scene of triumph over death, and not a place of mourning. Besides the traditional site of Jesus' own "dormition," there is a garden tomb that is held also to be the place of his resurrection. Eden is seldom mentioned in the same breath with Gethsemane, but it must be obvious that re-entering the garden marks the end of estrangement from Yahweh and constitutes a precise reversal of the so-called "seventy blows of death." Indeed, the return to paradise is properly understood as becoming immortal without having to die or disintegrate. The paradisiacal garden is present in Sumerian myth, a be-jeweled "garden of the gods" that lies in the path leading eventually to Utnapishtim and his wife. Shamash, the Sumerian sun god (whose name is synonymous with the Hebrew word for "sun"), spots Gilgamesh in the garden as the god is walking nearby and questions Gilgamesh's right to be there. (One is reminded of Yahweh, walking in the cool of the day in Eden and later questioning both Adam and Eve and the serpent.) As for the garden itself, "All round him stood bushes bearing gems . . . lapis lazuli leaves . . . haematite and rare stones, agate, and pearls."[39] That Jewish tradition preserved through the ages this Sumerian vision of the return to paradise is clear in the medieval Sepher Ha-Yashir, the so-called Book of Jasher, or

---

* Budge uses the term *Translation*.

more correctly, The Upright or Correct Book. In Jasher 77:38–41 Moses receives the magic rod that Aaron later uses to perform miracles:

> And afterward Moses went into the garden of Reuel . . . and . . . whilst he prayed . . . beheld a *sapphire stick* . . . planted in the midst of the garden. . . . *The name of the Lord God of hosts was engraved thereon*, . . . And he . . . stretched forth his hand and he plucked it like a forest tree from the thicket. . . . And when God had driven Adam from the garden of Eden, he took the stick . . . and tilled the ground."[40] (Emphasis mine.)

In the Ethiopian text, the garden of Mary's final ascension and translation is called the Garden of Joy;[41] the paradise of departed souls, which Mary visits (in another rather late Ethiopian text), is also called the Garden of Delight.*[42] In that same text, the angels bear "shining crowns, and . . . necklaces of gold, and fillets . . . Of silver and jacinth and shining ornaments" to shower upon the righteous ones journeying toward paradise. Most revealing in this complementary vision of paradise is "a lofty pillar of gold covered all over with inscriptions, and on it were written the names of the righteous."[43] While some of these images are common to biblical and apocryphal visions in general, it is in the context of ascension–translation that they take on added significance, harking back to a very primitive ideal of rewards for the heroic or righteous mortal, into which category Mary doubtless fits.

Thus I conclude there is convincing evidence that there is a Jewish-Christian origin for the tale of the Assumption, built upon a much older mythology whose narrative is distinctly extracanonical and conflicts in some measure with the Christian orthodox theology of atonement and resurrection. The question is, why, if this is an ascension–translation narrative, is there a conscious attempt to imitate the circumstances of Jesus' death, when to do so creates the same conflict as that mentioned in chapter three—the sacrificial victim and marred servant make for vexed narratives of ascension and translation? No doubt the *urtext*, or even the oral narrative on which it was built, contained no such details, so that, much as the Elisha legend imitates the Elijah narrative to establish the legitimacy of Elisha,

---

* This text, "The Vision of Mary," also attributed to John the Beloved, seems to complement the dormition text.

the added details served to legitimize Mary's importance in the overall Christian myth of origins. Consider this example of how the imitation enhances Mary's position: she remains in her tomb three days. The Old Testament psalm, cited by Peter in Acts 2, declares, "You will not abandon my soul to Hades / nor allow your holy one to experience corruption." It is essential, for the ascension–translation to be valid, that the death be more apparent than real; that is, the decay of the body to any extent would defeat the purpose of the ascension–translation. Jesus' and Mary's cases would thus be more akin to that of Jairus's daughter (the maiden "sleeps") than to, by contrast, Lazarus's death, in which decay had already (presumably) set in. I believe it altogether likely that the order of accretions to Mary's simple death narrative was, first, the assumption myth (which may have appeared far earlier than scholars have guessed), growing out of Jewish-Christian lore in which Jesus is a heroic man raised up to heaven and Mary a heroic mother raised up by God because of her goodness and sacrifice; second, the aggrandizement of Mary's status to Queen of Heaven, echoing either a Jewish or Jewish-Christian reaction to the cult of Isis and to the need for a goddess figure (again, a long-standing view of a minority of Jews); and third, and long afterward, a doctrine of Immaculate Conception, which indeed responds to the raised status of Jesus to equal member of a triune deity.

The fitness of choosing Jesus' mother as a subject for a narrative of ascension–translation should be obvious: the Annunciation put her in the same category as Sarah, Abraham's wife, who was visited by angels and whose womb opened miraculously; or Manoah's barren wife, whom an angel visited and through whom the Nazarite judge Samson was born; or as Hannah, whose womb was similarly opened and who dedicated her son to the temple service. Mary's exceptional beauty and goodness are well attested, as was her faithfulness to Yahweh. The apocryphal Mary is also a ward of the temple in her youth, putting her in the same group with the child of Hannah, Samuel, the ward of the tabernacle of Yahweh under Eli's direction.

The Ethiopian tale, it must be acknowledged, includes several instances of antisemitism. This element argues for the lateness of the tale, when the Roman church in particular had reason for wanting to distance itself from Judaism. The passages include such items as fire coming down from heaven and burning up Jewish leaders plotting against Mary. Of most interest in my view, however, is an account, late in the tale, of a Jew who attempts to lay "hold upon the bier of the holy woman so that he might prevent them from carrying away her dead body." An angel smites the man with a flaming sword, cutting off both hands.[44] The hands are restored later, but the whole incident is reminiscent of the incident in 2 Samuel 6 of the "steadying of the ark" as it proceeded toward the citadel. The replacement of Uzzah with a Jewish enemy of Christ seems quite forced. I believe it makes far more sense to see Mary as a consecrated, holy being, ready to ascend to Yahweh. In this preascension she cannot be touched (much as Jesus declares that he cannot be touched before ascending to Yahweh). The Uzzah-figure would be more accurately described as a faithful Jewish-Christian disciple who attempts to steady the bier containing Mary's corpse. The Jewish legend would then have the angel punish the man for defiling the bier, but in keeping with the fellowship of early Jewish Christians would restore the hands, much as Jesus restored the ear smitten off the guard by Peter's sword. Understood this way, Mary takes the place of the Ark of the Covenant, for within her womb was the deliverance and salvation of Israel—the Anointed One of Yahweh, the living tablets of the law—the Word (*logos, d'bir*). And it is for this heroic role that Mary was magnified in the view of Jewish Christians in Ethiopia, our representative model for this tale, and elsewhere.

Considering the continuing controversy at least among Roman Catholics surrounding the significance and nature of the Assumption, I believe it important to recognize that while part of the fear of "mariolatry" within (and certainly without) the church rests with her being a woman, and part with the fear of her ascendancy over Jesus as intercessor, nevertheless it is the essentially heterodox nature of the assumption—that of a heroic ascension–translation—that must originally have created a significant portion of the anxiety. First, the fear of reconnecting both Jesus and Mary with Judaism must have caused the inclusion in later versions of the tale of anti-semitic elements. Second, the discomfitting recollection of the deaths of both Jesus and Mary as aspects of a failed narrative of ascension–translation seems to be at the genuine core of the controversy, in which ascension and translation are there only to cloud the issue of the finality of death. Third, the suspicion that Mary's assumption is an accretion that taints the uniqueness of the ascension of Jesus by recalling that of Enoch or of Elijah raises the specter of an orthodox Christianity that lacks the doxology and theology to separate the Jesus myth from other mythical events with almost precisely the same character. It is of note that the Magdalene's ascension–translation poses many of the same problems for theologians.

Mary Magdalene: Why Was She Translated?

The most enigmatic figure in all the saints' lives is surely Mary Magdalene. Not only is her cult pervasive in France and elsewhere, but her place in Judeo-Christian tradition and legend is among the oldest and most pivotal. Despite these facts, key points about the Magdalene's cult have been buried or altered, and because of these alterations or deletions, the medieval tales of her ascension make little sense, at least from the models of ascension–translation discussed in this book. Two missing keys to "reading" the Magdalene are, I feel, essential for accepting the medieval cultural narrative of her ascension and translation: (1) that in legend or history or both she was the female consort of Jesus and (2) that she was a key figure in the primitive Christian congregation. If we accept either or both of the above propositions, we can find sufficient context for her ascension (and her implicit translation). The importance of these two keys for gender studies on the origins of Christianity, as well as for hagiography, should be self-evident.

The idea that the Magdalene may have been the queen consort to King Jesus is heretical to Christian tradition because of Christ's transcendence, with which carnal marriage seems inconsistent in some minds; yet those same minds will often allow Christ to be the bridegroom to the Church, and the Church the bride, going so far as to name numerous church buildings after the Magdalene. A literal marriage of Jesus and Mary can be palatable to Christians only if we redefine what a Christian really is, but such issues lie outside the scope of this book. Reactions against the idea of Mary Magdalene's being the consort of Jesus are relevant to my discussion only as they show the likely attempt to alter the saint's life or bury certain features of it.

That it is historically plausible that Jesus was married goes almost without saying. The version of this union that first attracted my curiosity was proposed, rather incidentally at that, by Robert Graves and Joshua Podro in *The Nazarene Gospel Restored*.[45] Reasoning (rightly) that marriage is a sacrament of kingship, Graves and Podro recast many familiar *logia* from the New Testament, resulting in John the Baptist's saying to Jesus, "Fear not, thou son of David, to take unto thee Mary, thy espoused wife. . . ." Jesus' reply: "Suffer it to be so, for thus it becometh us to fulfil all righteousness."

However one may revolt at such subversive rereadings of the New Testament record, many scholars have rightly pointed to the marriage feast at Cana as a decisive element of "the marriage of the lamb" (allegorized by later Christian writers as the wedding of Christ to his Church, in a New Testament imitation of Jehovah's Old Covenant marriage to Israel). Furthermore, the extremely touching scene recorded in John's Gospel of Jesus' appearance to Mary Magdalene in the garden, and the consequent disbelief of Mary's account by other disciples, hints at Jesus' favoring the special status of Mary in this appearance and the disciples' grudging recognition of that relationship. However, these New Testament allusions to marriage and to a close relationship between Jesus and Mary are innocuous and do not by themselves justify her ascension.

More to the point is the stunning reference to the Magdalene's status and position with regard to Jesus in the very early Coptic Gospel of Thomas.*[46] In the last saying (#114 according to the system most scholars use), Simon Peter demands of Jesus and the other disciples, "Let Mary [here the Magdalene] leave us, for women are not worthy of Life [eternal life, the secret "life" of the inner circle of disciples, or some such ideal]." Jesus' answer is fascinating: "I myself shall lead her in order to make her male, so that she too may become a living spirit resembling you males. For every woman who will make herself male will enter the Kingdom of Heaven."

A number of things are obvious from this little encounter. First is Peter's enormous jealousy and fear of Mary's position. Second is Jesus' special regard for Mary. Third is her being made "male," which signifies to me taking the role of a man, specifically one of the inner circle of apostles—that is, becoming a rabbi or priest to the flock. It would be hard to overestimate the importance of this scene for Mary's cult influence, for it is clear that Mary's dominant cultural position (at

---

* In James M. Robinson, gen. ed., *The Nag Hammadi Library in English* (117–30). Thomas O. Lambdin, the translator, does not scruple to parallel this document with the so-called "Q" source. Its antiquity is best measured in the purity of its logia and in its straightforward structure, so atypical of much of the Nag Hammadi material. The severity of Peter's attack on Mary in this Gospel, mentioned further down in my essay, is traditional, dating to the disciples' refusal to believe that Mary had seen the resurrected Jesus (Luke 24:9–11).

least in Roman Catholicism) cannot have grown only from the scant references to her in the canonic Gospels.

This passage in the Gospel of Thomas rings as true as any other Gospel narrative, and certainly as true as the encounter between Jesus and the "disciple whom Jesus loved." Peter's reaction reflects well the brief reference in Luke 24:9–11, in which Mary and other women inform the apostles of Jesus' rising from the tomb, "but this story of theirs seemed pure nonsense, and they did not believe them,"* but it also calls to mind Peter's anger over Jesus' special treatment of the "other disciple" (John, by most traditional estimations; see chapter two). There seems no other motive but fear or jealousy in Peter's reaction in the passage from Thomas. Jesus' reaction in Thomas seems to confirm Peter's worst fears; in fact, Jesus' behavior is consistent with many Gospel narratives in which Jesus forces upsetting news on his disciples. In John 6, after hearing Jesus' declarations concerning his body and blood, many disciples state, "This is intolerable language. How could anyone accept it?" (6:60–61). At one point (Matt. 4:18–20) Jesus even demands that Peter abandon his wife (becoming an allegorical or symbolic "eunuch" for the kingdom's sake) to follow Jesus, while in the passage in Thomas it is clear that a woman (the parallel is tempting: is she the consort of Jesus?) is in the ascendant. Peter's reaction may be symbolic of early Christianity's difficulty dealing with the oral narrative of the Magdalene's importance.

In an earlier passage in Thomas (#61), the enigmatic Salome, another woman disciple present, intimates Jesus' close relationship with some of the women disciples when she demands, "Who are You, man, that You, as though from the One, ... have come up on my couch and eaten from my table?" She declares herself his disciple, literally a "follower." The suggestion of male–female intimacy in the question is hard to ignore.†

---

* In all citations from the Bible for this section, I am using the Jerusalem Bible.

† I am not arguing here that Jesus might have had more than one woman "follower," but any person with pretensions to the throne of David and Solomon could very consistently have both wives and concubines in his entourage. That Yahweh could hardly object to such an arrangement is evident in Nathan's words to David: "I gave your master's house to you, his wives into your arms" (2 Sam. 12:8, Jerusalem Bible; it is clear from this passage that David's crime is not having many wives and concubines, but taking a wife that didn't belong to him and that God didn't give him.)

Thus, important traditions surrounding Mary's position in early Christianity seem present as early as the writing of the Gospels, so it should not be surprising that her cult would survive the movement of Christianity first to Greece, then to Rome, then on through Europe, becoming a major influence in the Middle Ages. Yet there is a surprise: the two points I have mentioned—her possible marriage to Jesus and her influence as an early Christian leader—are precisely those elements that survived only in the most obscure or oblique way. Instead, Mary Magdalene has been either vilified or simply conflated with other New Testament women to create some sort of female composite disciple. For example, in Catholic tradition there is an undying tendency (despite the best efforts of reputable Catholic theologians) to conflate our Magdalene with any number of other Maries or other women in general in the Gospel accounts. Furthermore, an equally undying tradition associates Mary Magdalene with the "oldest profession," prostitution. Whether there is any historical justification for either of these tangents is not as important to me as is their obvious propagandistic value. It is not for lack of literary merit that the Magdalene's possible marriage to Christ and her early leadership role have been replaced in favor of the story of a repentant prostitute. Rather, Peter's fears, characterized so well in Thomas, seem more at the heart of this alteration in the Magdalene story for patriarchal ecclesiastics might have feared, just as Peter seems to have done, the strong presence of a female icon, Mary Magdalene, in Christian life. (I know what you are thinking—what about the dangerous cult of the Madonna, Mary the mother of Jesus? Yet the Jungian "good mother" figure simply is not an icon dangerous to Catholic faith. The Magdalene's position and potential threat may be more correctly compared with that of Julian of Norwich, Margery Kempe, and Joan of Arc, who all suffered from the same suspicion and prejudice.) Thus Catholic tradition simply had to turn her either into a prostitute, or, less cruel but just as effective, a mere pastiche of other characters, no one of them important enough by herself to merit attention. The passage in Thomas is far different from either of these tainted versions of Mary's life.

Nevertheless, English writers in the Middle Ages (many of whom were not clerics, though by default all were Catholic) seem acutely aware that something odd is going on with Mary Magdalene and Jesus. I strongly believe that, despite ecclesiastical authority, and despite attempts to subvert the cult of the Magdalene, both keys—her relationship with Jesus and her influence in early Christianity—

survived. It is easier to demonstrate the latter influence than the former, for references to Jesus' possible intimacy with a woman would have to be well hidden indeed not to invite the local bishop in for an investigation of anyone propounding such an idea. Yet an examination of clear references to the Magdalene in some of the literature helps us, in light of my contentions, to spot more easily the less visible elements of her cult in other literary contexts.

Thus a number of fascinating legends, often containing brilliant flashes of historical insight, spring up in the some of the most delightful literary contexts. The most tempting example of this "hidden" legend of the Magdalene is found in William Caxton's *Golden Legende* of 1483.[47] Describing Mary for the reader, the chronicler declares,

> And this is she, that same Marie
> Magdalene, to whom our Lord gaf so many
> grete yeftes, and shewed so grete signes
> of loue, that He toke from her seven deuyls,
> He embraced her alle in His loue, and
> made her right famylyer wyth Hym. (105–10)

Of course it is possible to read the text "platonically" (though Lord Byron wondered cynically if so-called "platonic love" was not simply a euphemism for secret lust!), and it is obvious to me why so many Christian scholars would want to. But my "fiction," my strong misreading (to use Harold Bloom's phrasing), demands a chronicler with a hidden agenda, another tale to tell, one inimical to traditional ecclesiastical policy, authority, and interpretation.* Thus when the text says such things, I feel forced to stress the subversive reading; it does no violence to the text, though it might do violence to some people's sensibilities.

The Golden Legende does not end where the Gospels end, however; one might expect the story of the Magdalene to go on, and indeed it does. It is interesting, for example, as David Mycoff recounts, that "one tradition claims that John [St. John the Evangelist] and the Magdalene were engaged to be married before Christ called John away to be his disciple.[48] More important, Mycoff also cites the legend of the

---

* The word *familiar* functions doubly here just as it does in Shakespeare, producing the pointed plea of Regan to Edmund in 5.1.14–15 of *Lear*: "I never shall endure her. Dear my lord, / Be not familiar with her."

"sea-borne Maries," three women disciples seemingly cast adrift in a rudderless boat till they arrive in southeastern France. The most important legend, the Provençal, has Mary landing by boat in Marseille some time after Christ's ascension. The most interesting detail of her stay in Marseille is her helping the wife of the prince of Marseille give birth to a child and then later "saving the mother and child after a bad storm at sea."[49] I find here an interesting literary evasion through displacement in these legends of the implications that (1) Mary Magdalene was forced to leave Judea, by enemies among or outside the group of disciples; (2) she herself was pregnant and later delivered of a child; (3) the wife of the "prince" of "Marseille" is Mary herself, and the prince a convoluted Christ figure.

How such unusual, original material about Mary may have gotten into southern France (the center and beginning of her cult, as near as I can tell) is a tough question. But failing other modes and times of transmission, it is not ridiculous to suggest that Mary actually went to France. Jewish colonies show up in all sorts of places by this time (indeed, the evidence is that Jewish colonies date at least from the time of Jeremiah and the Elephantine colony in Egypt). But before anyone accuses me of merely parroting the theories of Michael Baigent et al. in *Holy Blood, Holy Grail*,[50] I wish to examine a few of the many manifestations of the Magdalene cult in literature of the Middle Ages, to show how fragments of this subversive cult, including her ascension and translation, have been woven into seemingly innocuous texts.

First, let us consider a Middle English lyric, "The Corpus Christi Carol," often called "The Falcon." The poem concerns at first a narrator's declaration that "The faucon hath borne my make away"; "make" here means *mate*, not merely "master," so the obvious allusion is to Mary Magdalene's cry, "They have taken my Lord away . . . and I don't know where they have put him" (John 20:13). The poem then recounts, in a very chivalric fashion, the flight pattern of the falcon; the song ends with a mysterious scene of a knight on a bed, bleeding profusely while a maiden kneels by him weeping. At the head of the bed is a stone, on which is written in Latin "body of Christ." The clear mixing of New Testament narrative concerning Christ and Mary Magdalene with the poem's grail elements is not, I believe, accidental, because the grail legends grew up in southern France, much as did the legends surrounding the Magdalene. I admit placing great weight on the word *make* here, but there can be no doubt that on one level the knight is Jesus and the weeping maiden, Mary Magdalene, who reacts in typical medieval romantic fashion over the suffering of her champion, her knight, her consort.

The legendary journey of the Magdalene is well preserved in two Christmas carols that come, as near as I can deduce, from this same region of France. In one, "Un flambeau, Jeannette, Isabelle," two midwives with obviously Hebrew names attend the birth of Jesus. The setting for this and so many other carols, however, is cold December, which, in spite of common sense, has shepherds watching their flocks during a bitter chill. The standard reply is that the cold is a reflection of Christmas celebrations in cold climes and that December was chosen for the Christ-mass to lure Christians away from Rome's pagan feasts, such as the Saturnalia. However, there is yet another possibility: there may be two birth traditions, one from the New Testament and one from the Magdalene tradition. Consider: how does the winter tradition survive so well when it is obvious from the New Testament accounts that Jesus was born closer to April, or lambing season? This "cold December" tradition holds true even today in countries that never get cold and where snow never falls. I suggest that the Magdalene traditions are in part responsible. If, as I suspect, the Provençal tradition is based on yet an older one in which it is the Magdalene who is pregnant, the original tradition may have pointed to December as the birth date for the man-child of the Magdalene, who would in the traditions have been named *bar-yeshua*. The textual hint of this scenario lies in the second of the two carols, "I saw three ships." We all recall the image of three ships sailing into port "on Christmas Day in the morning." The three ships constitute a sort of riddle ("And what was in those ships all three?"), the solution to which is completely incongruous: "The Virgin Mary and Christ were there." The significance of the "three" ships is not, as I thought once, a representation of the trinity, but a retelling of the tale of the "three Maries," mentioned earlier. That the mother and child are in the "ships all three" makes no logical sense, nor does the presence of the Virgin Mary and Christ. What we are presented with in the riddle of the carol is none other than Mary Magdalene, our wandering, rudderless "shipwoman," pulling into port, not in Bethlehem, which is impossible, but in Marseilles (Masilia), a major Roman port. And what of the child in her arms? What child is this? The babe is the son of Mary, or so goes the tradition. Whether it is also the son of David, a title preserved for the descendants of King David in his dynastic line, is hard to know, be it mere legend or something more.

The story of Mary, complete with a powerful ascension scene, is full blown in a saint play, the Digby Ms. of "Mary Magdalene." David Bevington finds the Mary of this story one of those "figures who exist ambiguously in the worlds of both legend and biblical history." Bevington adds that "many saints' plays of the sensationally romantic variety have survived from the Continent, especially from France."[51] The Mary of this play is no doubt extracted from the same exegetical construct as the *Golden Legend*, mentioned earlier, including much of the conflation of biblical characters I find part of a hidden narrative agenda. Yet it cannot be denied that this conflation might flesh out the character of Mary, who I believe must have been an important figure at least in the narratives of early Christianity, but for whom clear-cut historical and biographical data are often wanting.

I draw your attention specifically in the play to the ascension scene, to Mary's last speech before she is caught up to dwell with Christ in the heavens:

I thank the[e], Lord, of *ardent love*! [Emphasis. mine]
Now I know well I shall nat opprese.
Lord, lett me se thy joyis above!
I recummend my sowle onto thy blisse.
Lord, opyn thy blissyd gates!
This erth at this time ferven[t]ly I *kisse*. [Emphasis mine]
In manus tuas, Domine—
Lord, with thy grace me wisse!—
Commendo spiritum meum. Redemisti me,
Domine Deus veritatis!
[She ascends with the angels.] [52]

This dramatic, yet traditional ending to the play solves the problem of the mortal Mary's consorting with the transcendent Lord by making *her* transcendent as well. One could argue that, unlike the dormition or assumption of the Virgin Mary, this drama makes a point of stressing that Mary Magdalene's corpse did not ascend, as the attending priest implies:

Thy body wil I cure from alle maner blame;
And I will passe to the bosshop of the sete,
This body of Mary to berye by name
With alle reverense and solemnite.[53]

But her physical death is quite beside the point, for the text fails to acknowledge that she died. The text of this saint play is unusually long, accounting for all the acts of the "conflated" Mary of the New Testament and the Mary of tradition and legend, a character worthy of an epic poem in the tradition of Homer; yet it produces a corpse without a death. To what narrative strategy is this drama resorting to create a lacuna of this sort? Two possibilities occur to me: (1) fearing the ascendency of Mary Magdalene over the Virgin Mary, the narrative of the Magdalene's assumption must eliminate any element of physical translation, or (2) like the assumption of the Virgin Mary, Mary Magdalene's tale is simply too Jewish to be tolerated, so a clumsy passage detailing the disposal of her remains has been tacked on to the already ancient tale of her ascension and translation. Her heroism is not so much the issue in this ascension narrative, but her righteousness certainly is. And, like Mrs. Utnapishtim, a present but somewhat muted character in *Gilgamesh*, it is essential that Jesus and Mary as consorts be brought together through the act of ascension. While it is undeniable that Mary's statement about commending her spirit to God echoes the death scene at Christ's crucifixion, nevertheless, her ascension in the presence of angels is clearly a re-creation of Christ's heroic ascension in the Book of Acts. Furthermore, in this scene Mary implicitly acknowledges her position in the early Christian community and her close, "ardent," "fervent," and "familiar" relationship with Christ.

The possibly heroic dimension of Mary's justification, ascension, and translation, while not essential to demonstrate my thesis, nevertheless is an interesting sidelight on her cult in the Middle Ages, and traces of this aspect of her character are present in, of all places, Chaucer. The Shipman's vessel was named the *Maudelayne* (Gen. Prol. 410).[54] Sumner Ferris noted in 1983 the appropriateness of the name *Maudelayne* for the ship because sailors held Mary Magdalene in high regard[55] (a position consistent with the story of Mary's trip to Marseille). Mycoff notes Chaucer's interest in hagiography, even writing "legendes of seintes" himself,[56] so there is little doubt of Chaucer's knowing the Magdalene material.

I suggest along with other critics that the Shipman has brought his tale back with him from France as part of his "cargo," including wine (from the vine country in Southern France).[57] Another part of the "load" is "The Man of Law's Tale," whose immediate source, Nicholas Trivet's Anglo-Norman Chronicle,[58] has another likely source, the Provençal tale of the Magdalene, reworked into the tale of Constance, who, treacherously cheated out of her wedding to a Syrian prince, is set adrift on a boat, finally landing in Northumberland. This is our heroic, noble Magdalene again, who, with others, was "put in to a shyppe in the see wythout ony takyl or rother for to be drowned."[59] The story of Constance is the closest thing in Chaucer to a saint's life, and lest we miss the connection between Constance and Mary Magdalene, "The Man of Law's Tale," discussing Constance's miraculous preservation by God while at sea, asks, "Who fedde the Egipcien Marie in the cave / Or in desert? No wight but Crist, sanz faille" (500–501). Mycoff notes the conflation of this St. Mary of Egypt and the Mary of later Magdalene legends.[60]

Thus Mary's ascension makes sense from the viewpoint of the ancient narratives of heroes who have ascended and been translated to be among the gods. Mary may have had a larger role in Christian history and in the narratives of Christianity than may have been thought, whether we are speaking of the legendary Mary Magdalene or the historical character.

The Stunted Ascension Narrative of Joan of Arc and Shakespeare's Motives in *Henry V*

While I was tempted to discuss Joan in the chapter on the literary heritage of ascension myth, because of its implications for our reading Shakespeare, I place it at this point because my primary purpose is to reinstate Joan as ascending hero. First, then, I suggest that the narratives of Joan's life, and more precisely the records of her interrogation and death, conceal a lacuna of her ascension and translation (transfiguration).* I propose second that the real motive for Shakespeare's writing and producing his *Henry V* is not primarily the gate receipts nor patronage that legitimate actors and writers seek; rather, the motive is the political, social, and even religious effect on *English* culture of the life of Joan of Arc, France's most celebrated and best-known hero. Third and last, I believe Shakespeare's heroic Henry V

---

* In ascension, the hero ideally sidesteps death and is brought bodily to dwell in the presence of the divine family. I believe such a reward for a hero is distinct from life after death, reincarnation, or resurrection; but in many ascension narratives, the escape from death is subverted, for any number of reasons.

† The best example of such trickery is Hebrew, not Greek: Priests fool Yahweh by disguising entrails with skin and fat to make it appear a very good offering. This idea of the false offering is seldom touched on but appears (at least to me) to help a wily hero ascend and be translated in one

is metaphorically caught up and transfigured, with Shakespeare as God or a god welcoming Henry into the divine family. To review, in such tales as have this extraordinary reward (apotheosis) for the hero, she or he must have one or more of the following merits: (1) one of his parents must be God or a god; (2) the hero must be righteous beyond mortal ability; and/or (3) the hero must be a cunning warrior, loved by God or the gods as ideally brave, strong, wise or clever—Herakles or Odysseus—who might trick the gods into allowing his or her ascension.† The yoking in this essay of Shakespeare's noble Henry V and the sainted Joan of Arc is simply that the Henry in the play is in every way a "secular saint" and that the play is patterned on the medieval saint plays. Furthermore, I contend that the narratives both of Joan's life and the life of Shakespeare's version of Henry contain implicit apotheosis of the hero, in the form of metaphorical or figurative ascension–translation. Let us consider first the role of ascension–translation, then consider the narrative of Joan's heroic action, followed by a consideration of Shakespeare's Henry V as a counterbalance to the uncanny rise to fame of Joan.

Remember that for my discussion, whether such stories of Joan or Henry are "historical" or "factual" in any sense depends of course on what one accepts as evidence. When, in narratives of history, a hero ascends and is made immortal, one

---

part of the heavens, while the gods in another part of the heavens are preoccupied with other things. This may be the actual function of Loki or Hermes as "trickster gods"; they trick or cheat death (and the gods themselves), allowing them to slip in a new deity, demigod, or member of the pantheon, while everyone's back is turned). For example, when the gods are hungry, one offers them the "sweetmeats" of a sacrificial animal, all the time knowing that the sweetmeats are disgusting entrails covered by a layer of animal fat and skin so that when they cook on the fiery altar they distract the gods with a "sweet savor" while the priest, hero, or other chef eats the best parts—the roasts and steaks, or legs and thighs. Thus, leaving to Anubis, Charon, or Hades the "shell" of a man for mummification, or anointing it with sweet-smelling oil (myrrh) and frankincense, or leaving the "sweetmeats" or internal organs in canopic jars with Anubis allows the heavenly "kah" to mount to the heavens as a translated being.

* For the feminist movement, it would make more sense to see Joan as entirely a human icon, rather than as a Catholic saint. In any case, it is unclear if the miraculous attributions to her were ever really embraced by the ecclesiastics and committees that finally granted her sainthood in 1920.

† Those who embraced this malevolent model of "objective history" were chagrined when Heinrich Schliemann found Troy by following Homer's "myth." *L'Encyclopedie* of Denis Diderot was to contain all human knowledge worth knowing, and now encyclopedias are out of date before they are reprinted. When the Ebla tablets were discovered in this century, it turned out that Abraham and Sodom and all that "myth" (wrongly defined as "falsehood") may be historical after all.

might be able to accept the truth, the historicity, of a life lived heroically, without embracing the supernatural elements attached to the written or spoken versions of the events. In the case of Joan of Arc, I am certain most French people admire her heroism, while discounting the possibility that supernatural forces were at work.* Yet in many cases it is on the spiritual plane, which has its own rules for historicity, that one sees the parallels and patterns that continue to redefine ascension–translation. On that plane, "historical truth" is very nearly irrelevant† to this discussion.

Thus, if the narrative of the ascending, translated hero is consciously subverted anywhere concerning Joan, it is within the weak, fifteenth- and sixteenth-century Anglican misreading of history—despite the "heroes" of the movement.* In its most insidious form, it threatened to bury the only geopolitical ascension narrative in history—that of Saint Joan.

Joan actually would have entranced me despite my high regard for Ingrid Bergman's reverent, strong portrayal in the movies. I read George Bernard Shaw's play *St. Joan* only when I had to for the predetermined curriculum of a college course I was teaching. It triggered in me the belated recognition that as a young (and not well-read) Mormon missionary in France I had actually walked on the grounds of Compiegne, where Joan was captured by the Burgundians, possibly through French—not merely English and Burgundian—intrigue, and I found myself linked at some psychic level to Joan. When that happened, I felt duty-bound to reconcile what I thought I knew about religion, politics, and visionaries, in light of what happened to Joan.

First off, I credit what is among the most delightful, evenhanded, and well-written biographies I have read: Polly Schoyer Brooks's *Beyond the Myth: The Story of Joan of Arc*.[61] Often catalogued with juvenile literature, it is subtle, mature,

---

* Henry VIII's position in this problem is untenable at best; we will see Shakespeare's efforts to dramatize the impossible momentarily. But the British got some things right—for example, the King James Bible, mostly the work of William Tyndale, cleverly uses the word "translate" in much the same way for translating language as it does for transfiguration or ascension. The French *traduction*, rendering one language into another, merely describes "trading," or passing things down in a mimetic "tradition." "Translate" suggests a unique activity that by definition cannot be passed along, but must metamorphose. On the other hand, "The pen is mightier than the sword" is the desperate cliche of heroes who cannot ascend literally; in Shakespeare's theater; the days of true ascension–translation are gone—they degrade into rhetorical conventions, where one "ascends" only the throne of England—one is transported, translated, and transfigured only through the poetic conventions of sonneteers.

and sensitive. Her book is not remotely theological. It is simply the story of how A led to B, but the trip is not straight as the crow flies, for only the side trips explain why the journey from A to B was begun at all. Like Keats, she does not wrest the answers away, but leaves the comments open ended, enticing her readers to reflect on the implications of her assumptions and information. I offer a representative example: On Joan's wearing men's clothing: "her questioners . . . apparently agreed that it was the only sensible solution for a girl planning to lead soldiers to battle" (45). Yet, I conclude, since her voices sent her into battle, they also dictated the odd costuming, which is therefore probably symbolic. Indeed, the medieval *Golden Legend*,[62] whose stories of the saints were well known in her day, reveals that St. Margaret,* one of her saintly voices, was admitted to the monastic order when, dressed as a man, she applied for sanctuary—to escape a marriage to one she didn't love. The implication of asexuality is important for appreciating Joan; sexual potential was simply neutralized, and Joan, in the elliptical narrative of her voices' instructions, was asked by Margaret to make the same vow of chastity. Her virginity is tested in Poitiers, for "great value was attached to . . . it"—assuredly a clue for me that she qualifies as vestal virgin to the Queen of Heaven, Mary—an important first step to sanctification and Catholic ascension–translation.

---

* A student of mine, Jenny Sorensen (no relation), has allowed me to mention her discovery of two different St. Margarets in *The Golden Legend*; it is to the more obscure of the two that I refer. She discovered that though the stories of both St. Margarets were known in Joan of Arc's and even Shakespeare's day, there is a conspicuous absence in trial records, in Shaw's play and preface, among the scholars, and even by Joan herself, of St. Margaret's "sign," if you will, of the truth of Joan's message and visions. It is in this absent presence, a clue within a vision, evidence in an ellipsis, that I find initial proof of a conspiracy of silence among those with reason for ill will toward the saintly woman.

† In *The Lord of the Rings*, J. R. R. Tolkien makes much of the broken blade reforged.[63] The battle sword is an extension of the hero's strong grip (Beowulf, defeating Grendel's mother with her sword), a token of conquest (David, using Goliath's sword to cut off the giant's head). Joan's sword has five crosses, functioning as magic talismans or runes, upon the blade. That sword, like other ceremonial swords, was used to bless rather than destroy, though *Excalibur* was used in battle, till returned to the Lady of the Lake. The connection with Arthur is significant in that Arthur's "death" is circumvented by angelic creatures who take his funeral barge to the Western Isles. The promise and prophecy left us by Malory in *Morte Darthur* is that Arthur Pendragon will return at the point of Britain's greatest peril, wielding his magic sword once again.

A great sign of her heroical powers is her sword, found "behind the altar" (49). Brooks notes that the sword might have been seen when Joan was praying at St. Catherine's Chapel, where the sword was retrieved and brought to her later, at her request (48–49). The parallels to Arthur's sword *Excalibur* are suggestive (49)†: the sword is one of the signs of kingship, giving Joan yet another precedent for ascension. Even more revealing, given all the holy days in the liturgical year, Joan chose, during one early campaign, to observe Ascension Day (held forty days after Easter—also called Holy Thursday), which celebrates Christ's heroic ascent into the heavens. And her injunctions for her soldiers against swearing and whoring, but especially against plundering any city that Jehovah gave into their hands (I will return to this momentarily), not to mention encouraging prayer and confession, sanctified her cause and showed her in the tradition of the prophets and priests, fully justifying her authority, given her by heavenly visitors, to anoint the king of France in the Old Testament tradition of Samuel's anointing of David.

The sword is of course the sign of St. Michael, the male voice among Joan's messengers. *The Golden Legend* sees him as the consummate general, having driven "the dragon, i.e., Lucifer, and all his followers out of heaven, a battle about which the Book of Revelation tells us: 'There was a great battle in heaven. Michael and his angels fought with the dragon, and the dragon fought with his angels, and they prevailed not.'" [64] Yet it must not be assumed that only Michael had an interest in Joan's military quest, for Saint Catherine, the third of Joan's voices, is remembered in *The Golden Legend* as speaking boldly to kings, rulers, and wise men, confounding them in the same fashion as did Joan before, for example, Robert de Baudricourt in Shaw's delightful play *St. Joan*:

> ROBERT: . . . The more devil you were the better you might fight. That is why the goddams will take Orleans. And you cannot stop them, nor ten thousand like you.
>
> JOAN: One thousand like me can stop them. Ten like me can stop them with God on our side. . . . You . . . will live to see the day when there will not be an English soldier on the soil of France; and there will be but one king there: not the feudal English king, but God's French one.[65]

Having discovered, through my research assistant, that two Margarets are conflated in the cultural consciousness of Catholic France, I used the same strategy in my evaluation of Catherine. And there are indeed two Catherines familiar to

Catholics in Joan's day and beyond: the first, daughter of King Costus, spoke boldly before Emperor Maxentius and was beheaded for her trouble. A beautiful woman, Catherine died while a voice exclaimed, "Come, my beloved, my spouse, see! Heaven's gates are opened to you." This invitation immediately precedes the statement that the angel took "up the body and carried it from that place a twenty-day's journey to Mount Sinai, where they gave it honorable burial,"[66] an elliptical declaration suggesting Catherine's ascension and translation, not unlike the elliptical narrative of Moses' own ascension and translation (see chapter two).

However, another Catholic saint, Catherine of Siena, who lived but a generation before Joan, served as an "advisor to religious and civil rulers," helping to end the rift between Avignon and the Holy See during the Great Schism. Most remarkable of all, "she is the patroness for the prevention of fires"![67] Considering Joan's own dread of fire, it is more than odd that her accusers never brought any of these church-approved examples to bear at Joan's trial. Indeed, Joan's voices represent an almost certain vindication of at least the rightness of her cause and tie her death, perhaps strongly, to the sort of conditions typical of those making covenants with Jehovah.

Yet another event confirms the French chevaliers' faith in Joan: the battle for Patay, in which "only a handful of French were killed," while "two thousand lay dead" of the English.[68] I will address this item (among others) in connection with Shakespeare's *Henry V*, but I find the Patay battle far superior to the miracle at Agincourt, at least as evidence of divine favor.

One event in particular shocks us even in these jaded times. Much is made of Joan's chastity as the crowning feature of her character; the word *vertue* means "strength," calling to mind the heroic quality of great strength, even invincibility in battle,* rather like cutting Samson's hair; this suggests that abusing Joan sexually could be the key to destroying her power. When she is chained and in a prison cell (she had asked to be sheltered in a convent) she consents for a time to wear a dress. As Brooks points out, "What happened in her cell in the next few days remains a mystery," but three days later she resumed wearing men's clothing. The fear of prison guards may have prompted it, but I think the fear was an event, not

---

*Mark 5:30: Jesus perceives that "virtue had gone out of him" when touched by a woman with a ritual and physical issue of blood, for she is healed instantly upon doing so.

an abstraction: she was abused sexually—though Brooks suggests that an English lord entered her cell and *tried* to rape her.[69]

The narrative pattern of her execution forcibly reminds us of the concrete details surrounding the trial and death of Jesus—there is little doubt that Joan's early biographers privileged those aspects of the account that would create just such a resemblance. This of course simply acknowledges that all historians have narrative agendas, whether mimetic or innovative. But surely Joan's recantation out of fear of fire is akin to Jesus' ordeal in Gethsemane in which he implores Yahweh to let the cup of his suffering be passed on or taken back. Jesus' final resolve to carry the burden of martyrdom ("not as I will but as thou wilt") is echoed in Joan's declaration to her accusers that she *had* heard voices but was terrified of being burned at the stake and did not understand what recantation would do to her as God's messenger: the voices told her she would be damned for not heeding them. When Joan went through a trial almost completely motivated by politics, there were troubling irregularities,[70] which of course reflect the irregularities in Jesus' trial. Jesus was convicted of blasphemy, and doubtless for undermining the Saduccees' uneasy coexistence with Rome, whose puppets both they and the tetrarchs were. Joan was betrayed by her people, the Burgundians, people she believed should have been French. The Catholic church by default takes on the role of the Sanhedrin, the ultimate goal being to ascertain whether she was or was not a faithful Catholic. As with the Sanhedrin in Roman times, the church had no right to execute those convicted in a church court. It was therefore necessary that Joan be considered enough of a political threat to justify her being executed by the "Gentiles" (in this case, the English lords).

In Joan's *via dolorosa*, the path leading to the execution, one finds more such parallels: "Surprisingly she was now allowed to be heard in confession and to take communion." The Last Supper of Jesus is the prototype for the Christian *missa,* or *cena*, at which time one communes with Jesus. Cast in the role of Judas is Bishop Cauchon, the inquisitor. Not unlike Jesus' acknowledgment that Judas was the one who would betray him, Joan declares, "Bishop, I die through you." The abusive crowd, lining the street, taunts Joan as armed guards escort her to the place of execution. The platform on which the stake is mounted is higher than the others, a sign lists all the crimes of which she was found guilty, and we can see once again the narrative resonance of Joan's chroniclers, for Joan prays one last time, asking that

God forgive all those who have condemned her. The sop offered Jesus to slake his thirst on the cross is replaced by Joan's asking for and receiving a cross to hold. During her last confession, Joan declares to the priest that "with God's help I shall be in paradise."[71] Echoing the centurion's declaration that in Jesus they had executed the son of a god, is one unnamed Englishman's terror after Joan's death: "We are all damned; we have burned a saint."[72] And just as Jesus called out to Jehovah, quoting the psalms, Joan at first calls upon her saints, but with her last breath, she calls out Jesus' name repeatedly till she is consumed.

The fact that Joan is burned as a heretic does not do grave harm to her role as a hero: the smoke from her fire rose to heaven as would the smoke from a sacrificed goat or lamb. Its parallel is found in Herakles' ascending to the pantheon in the smoke of fire. As with poet William Blake's doctrine of self-annihilation, the refiner's fire burns away the dross, leaving only the essence of what occupied an earthly body. However, death must not be allowed to corrupt the corpse, explaining why Jesus' burial time is not much more than two days. Once events have closed off one venue for the narrator, he requires the power to re-interpret the apparent failure of the hero to receive a deathless destiny among the angels and saints.

Brooks informs us, as does Shaw's *St. Joan*, that almost from the moment of her death in 1431, all the interested parties sought to reevaluate the flawed work of Cauchon, and in 1456, when a Rehabilitation trial took place, Joan was cleared of heresy. After that, "the cult of Joan as heroine and saint grew and grew among the people."[73] Clearing Joan's name roughly coincides historically with the lessening English presence in France. Though it required half a millennium, Joan was beatified in 1909, then canonized in 1920. Though the ordinance that qualified her as a saint was had from earthly tribunals, the results are cosmic in their grandeur. For to be canonized is to be changed in essence, to be a member of the divine family, an intercessor for those who honor her and her feast day. While there was apparently no public statement on Joan's miracles[74] (two of which must be proven to achieve canonization), tacit Church approval of both her insistence that saints had spoken frequently to her, and of her miraculous military victories, is certainly implied and certainly left no doubt for the millions of pious French Catholics, all of whom knew her story from beginning to end—indeed, as well as they knew that of St. Denis, the patron saint of France.

Henry V of England was responsible for rekindling the war Edward III had started, for France had a considerably better economy than England. The Hundred Years War was closer to 115 years long. Harry had succeeded in retaking most of northern France, married the king's daughter, won the crown, and continued his military campaigns till he died in 1422 of the illness that had dogged his camp since before Agincourt. Joan was of course right: it was futile to attempt co-rule of two countries so utterly different in temperament; Francs and Anglos had each their own language and culture, not to mention a different eventual religious heritage, unforeseen by anyone except perhaps Joan. The desire to "own" France had started differently: when the Norman conquerors settled in England, they had mixed feelings about letting go of their formal titles and lands in France. It was with great effort that a name like "Beauchamp," for example, became the more English "Fairfield." But it did happen, and being English became almost fashionable by the time of Chaucer's death in 1400. Henry V, even Edward III, long before, were completely English, the French language now inextricably bound to English during the great vowel shift and into Early Modern English of Shakespeare. Joan as prophet-warrior foresaw a united France and an end to the dispute over land. She gained in popularity, and, as time went by, generals were inspired by her shining example of bravery.

Henry VI, the issue and heir to what his British father had won in battle, was to be Henry V's most lasting effect on English fortunes in France. Henry VI, though a pious man, was ineffective at foreign policy, so England slowly relinquished much of what Henry V had won during his ultimately ill-fated campaigns in France. Henry VI had considerable trouble at home, for the dukes, the kingmakers, were looking for the main chance. Rivalries between Lancaster and York surely began early in Henry VI's reign, for the War of the Roses—the Thirty Years War—was the result of Henry's early display of weakness compared to other contenders from Lancaster and York, notably Edward IV, Richard III, and Henry Tudor, afterwards Henry VII.

Things had started badly for Henry VI. As a political ploy to ward off Joan's continuing and growing popularity, the English made plans to crown the king at Reims Cathedral in France, but the local populace was so resentful that the coronation was relocated to Paris. Reims Cathedral was the only place where such a ceremony could be legitimized. Brooks calls the event a "fiasco . . . a flop; no one had a good word to say about it."[75] This faux pas could only strengthen the claim of Charles VII, the French king, to the throne that Henry V had wrested away from France. The most pathetic result of this weakness was Henry VI's being murdered. I cannot stress enough the relative disunity in fifteenth-century England as compared with the French banner, to which all true Frenchmen gathered, with Joan as their *de facto* intercessor, and the line of succession for Charles VII as a constant reminder of which king *God* had chosen, a king sanctified by Joan's prophetic influence. *Holinshed's Chronicles* (1587), a considerable influence on Shakespeare's history plays, declares of Joan's last days, before she recanted her hasty and fearful abjuration, that she was "shamefully rejecting her sex abominably in acts and apparel . . . , and, all damnably faithless, to be a pernicious instrument to hostility and bloodshed in devilish witchcraft and sorcery."[76] When later she recanted her "confession," declaring simply that she had been afraid of the fire and did not understand her spiritual peril in denying her voices, she paid the ultimate price. Yet Holinshed et al. can only remark,

> But herein (God help us!) she, fully afore possessed of the fiends [fell] straightway into her former abominations . . . confess[ed] herself a strumpet. . . . These matters may very rightfully denounce unto all the world her execrable abominations, and well justify the judgement she had and the execution she was put to for the same.[77]

While revisionist historians dispute the reliability of Joan's interrogation transcripts (most recently Karen Sullivan),*[78] it is hard to explain how such powerful perceptions occurred among those who inherited the *traditions* of her testimony and the clerics' reactions to it, for it is the popularizing of Joan's trial that created such a stir in France and such anxiety in England. I believe that matters came to a head during the reigns of Henry VIII and Elizabeth I. Henry of course, for reasons

---

* Karen Sullivan in *The Interrogation of Joan of Arc* sees the trial minutes as more of a "production" than a historical transcript or record. Sullivan thus safely concludes that Joan's *recantations* represent a more objective rhetorical statement than the evidence of her success in following the voices; but though St. Paul describes his vision on the road to Damascus in three contradictory accounts in the New Testament, he is enshrined by those who judge Joan! Sullivan upbraids (Introduction, xv) the uncritical acceptance of Joan's statements as genuine beliefs by those who resurrected her cult in the nineteenth century (Aanatole France, for one); yet her canonization was approved only after years of strenuous deliberations by pontifical committees.

of state, separated his people from the Roman church; during Elizabeth's reign the Anglican church consolidated its political and religious goals. Elizabeth provided a stable reign of some forty years, reversing the attempt of her sister Mary to reinstate Catholicism. Elizabeth was a wily politician, a very clever thinker, and a power to reckon with. Indeed, the defeat of the Spanish Armada in 1588 established Britain's first competitive commercial shipping. During Elizabeth's reign, England was not merely content to have its own church. It began to demonize Catholics, especially French Catholics, as that great and abominable church predicted in Revelation. Removing the cult of the Virgin Mary from the doctrine of the true church, Anglicans saw Elizabeth as a Virgin Queen, and the leader of the British church, *de jure* if not *de facto*. As a result of such stability, England enjoyed unprecedented exploration and colonizing, looking ever westward to the little-tapped treasures in the Americas.

The poet Edmund Spenser sang the praises of this queen, "Gloriana, Queene of Fairie," in the long and convoluted allegory of his romance epic *The Fairie Queene*. Elizabeth *ascends* to the throne, metaphorically making of her the folk equivalent of a goddess (such as Shakespeare's Titania, for example), and she becomes the queen of the elemental spirits of the air, the sylphs or fairies. In the first book, Spenser exalts the Redcrosse Knight, a heroic Templar knight defending his queen's realm, but Spenser demonizes French Catholicism in portraying both a dragon that, when killed, spits pro-Catholic pamphlets and books, and an evil woman, Duessa, who is spawned by the Catholic magician Archimago. The six books of this complex allegory he created constitute a *tour de force*, as England sought to create its own native tradition of high art.* As it turns out, however, Shakespeare has far greater powers against Catholic France than any other English Renaissance poet, including Christopher Marlowe, whose Dr. Faustus boxes the pope's ears, and John Webster, who often includes a corrupt Catholic cleric in his plays.† Among the early plays, Shakespeare's *1 Henry VI* attempts to exonerate England from its cruel mistreatment of Joan.

---

* Though *The Fairie Queene* was built on the Italian romance epics, it acquired native Bristish lore and new stanzaics. Spenser had an enormous effect on later poets.

† In *The Duchess of Malfi*, for example, the duchess marries her own steward, exchanging vows in her boudoir without benefit of clergy. One brother, a corrupt cardinal, opposes her ever remarrying, for her great wealth would fall into the hands of her new husband.

With regard to the sources for *1 Henry VI*, Herschel Baker emphasizes, "History, which seems to reel from one disaster to another, reveals a steady moral purpose because its course is set by God, . . . [with] divine justice . . . impartially punishing sin and rewarding virtue."[79] In 1.1, Joan of Arc ("Joan de Pucelle, also called Joan of Aire") is initially treated with surprising diffidence by a playwright whose ruler-queen, Elizabeth I, is the head of the Anglican church and who, like many monarchs to follow, has a justifiable fear of French Catholicism. In her first speech, without any pretense, Joan declares that the Virgin Mary appeared to her, directing that she "leave [her] base vocation / and free [her] country from calamity" (80–81). The Holy Mother thus gives Joan a beauty and stature she had not had before. That beauty is a risky detail, for even Holinshed writes little of her physical attributes. It is perhaps white magic (as opposed to a miracle from God) that Joan innocently practices, but Shakespeare leaves us little room for debate, for his own sonnets testify that excessive praise is the grievous sin of sonneteers (#130: "My mistress when she walks treads on the ground"). The mention of beauty thus suggests approbation of sorts.

Shakespeare dutifully mentions her sword, one of the signs of kingship (along with the orb and scepter), foreshadowing her role in crowning the dolphin king of France at Reims. As she crosses swords with Charles as a test of God's approval of her, then wins the match, the future king compares her to an Amazon, but he immediately qualifies that by adding, "[Thou] fightest with the sword of Deborah" (1.2.104–5). Much as Samson of the Old Testament, whose strength was preserved by his not cutting his hair, the maiden from Domremy takes a Nazarite-like vow of chastity, reminding us that virtue (Middle English *vertue*) means "strength." The English, under Talbot, are overwhelmed with fear. Talbot sums up the problem succinctly: "A witch, by fear, not force, like Hannibal, / Drives back our troops and conquers as she lists" (1.5.21–22).

The connection between fear and witchcraft is clear, in this case: Joan, dressed in armor, behaving as though she were a man, is an *unnatural* creature. Such creatures carry God's curse, for plague follows their wake. It is impossible

---

* The exact pattern, according to my Shakespeare mentor John Wasson, is as follows: (a) The plague strikes. (b) There is no way to predict where and when it will seek victims. (c) The people, terrified, seize onto the ancient nostrum: such an unnatural disease can have only one creator: Satan. (d) His minions on earth are the witches and warlocks, so one must search them out and

to intellectualize away something that terrifies a general, a man who deals day to day with the plague of war. Because of unreasoning fear, the populace fights against an invisible power like the plague (which evil was still going strong in Shakespeare's time) by arresting and trying old women suspected of infernal magic. *Any* such unreasoning solution to fears now is properly called a "witch-hunt."* Because of the fear she spreads, Joan is "unnatural"; she is presumed guilty and must be tried and put to death.

This treatment by Shakespeare of Joan's story is interesting because of its timeliness. It is Shakespeare's first play, its first performance dated 1592. Of all possible subjects to interest Elizabeth I, the most dear might have been the successful early reign of Henry VI, a devout Christian, over both France and England, as well as the end of the career of the Maiden, Joan, whose influence seemed to grow despite her death and whose status Spenser hoped to diminish by countering with a native English saint, Gloriana, defended by the true and faithful knight Redcrosse. No one with Shakespeare's command of history and politics could have ignored that in 1558, the same year as Elizabeth's accession to the British throne, the English ceded to the French their *last* remaining holdings in France—Calais. A new era is born by the end of Shakespeare's early tetralogy of *1, 2, and 3 Henry VI*, and *Richard III*, for in this latter play Henry, Earl of Richmond, afterwards[80] Henry VII, overcomes Richard. Typecasting and demonizing Richard as an evil, ruthless king (whose physical deformity, a hunchback, is metaphorical) justifies Henry VII's wresting away the throne heroically then ascending to it—the metaphor of the king's "ascension" echoing the ancient ascension–translation of the hero.

---

destroy them to stop the plague. (e) The chief officers of the town (or even a mob) find old Catholic women who still utter their prayers in Latin (*Hoc est corpus* becomes *hocus pocus*!), (f) look for signs of evil, like warts (as in the old Monty Python routine), (g) hold a trial (if the lady is lucky), (h) burn her at the stake and have done with it—except (i) there are the leftovers, the familiars such as owls and cats, possessed creatures through which a witch channels with her sister witches. (j) These are drowned, allowing the rat population, unchecked by natural predators, to spread more plague, which (k) necessitates another, bigger witch hunt.

* As Wasson points out, "This most widespread type of medieval religious drama could hardly have ceased to exert any influence on the general development of English drama," for its performance is attested to as early as 1110 and as late as 1617. Diaries record performances on every subject, from Abraham on, during Elizabeth's reign, with references to some sixty-six plays performed in some forty towns "from Scotland to Cornwall" (241–42).[81]

But it is in the second tetralogy of history plays, ending in *Henry V*, that Shakespeare fills the void left by a nation that has no saintly hero to challenge the ascendancy of Joan of Arc. "The Famous Victories of Henry V," though written as a secular saint play, dwells chiefly on the miraculous conversion of the wayward Hal into a great Christian king. Shakespeare focuses upon the battle at Agincourt as miraculous proof of Henry's desire, above all else, to make of the war with France a sort of crusade to set things right in the world. The fact that the real Henry V was no saint, but a brilliant strategist in war, supports the idea that Shakespeare reinvents Hal as the "mirror of all Christian kings." That Shakespeare was familiar with saint plays can be inferred from town records.* By shifting his emphasis to the miracle at Agincourt, Shakespeare also sidesteps the "brilliant strategy and heroic action" of the older play to make a supernatural event the only possible explanation for the lopsided victory. John Wasson, an authority on both medieval and Renaissance drama, points to Henry's prayer to deliver his soldiers and to accept Henry's devotion and penance for his father Henry IV's sins (assenting to the death of Richard II) as "reminiscent of Gethsemane."[82] The play is a brilliant English response to both French Catholicism and to the growing awe for the historical Joan, whose vivid experiences require no embellishment whatsoever. As a saint, Harry's harsh threats against the city of Harflew (Harfleur) are not evidence of his wicked heart, but an attempt by a wise king to *avoid* more bloodshed. His assenting to the hanging of Bardolph is not the act of a cold, detached, erstwhile drinking partner, but of a king whose covenants with Harfleur are so charitable that violating even the least of them (in Bardolph's stealing from a church) could take from the king his greatest weapons: purity, fidelity, and humility. That is, in order to be the Scourge of God against the French, Henry must be disinterested; he cannot benefit in any worldly way from God's giving the day to the English. Thus, Henry cannot save his old friend, and Bardolph must pay for his sin with his life.

There is some remarkable silliness in several scenes, but Falstaff is not part of the games. Henry's high office is to be God's viceroy, ruling in the place of Jesus. Thus he must abjure his connection to Falstaff, who becomes a broken man and a sacrificial victim to sanctify Prince Hal's break with the world. Thus, "I know

---

* Wasson mentions the king's Solomonic ability to detect treason among three of his closest confidants and officers.

thee not, old man, fall to thy prayers" (*2 Henry IV* 5.5.47) is not a condemnation of Falstaff, but a renouncing by Henry of all worldliness. It is this same vileness or worldliness of the French knights following Joan that must be stopped before God will give them the day. They must pray, attend confession, leave behind their camp followers, and abjure swearing.

Henry's powers of discernment (*Henry V* 2.2), which prove the undoing of Scroop, Cambridge, and Grey,* are the mirror of Joan's ability to recognize the true dauphin, who tests her spiritual powers. Henry's moving speeches during the siege of Harfleur and preceding the battle at Agincourt nicely mirror Joan's inspired rallying of the troops during the Orleans campaign. In fact, it is quite instructive to watch Ingrid Bergman's Joan, followed by Kenneth Branaugh's Henry V. Though Harry's exploits end in a playful proposal scene with the Princess of France, the ritual dimension of the occasion is impossible to ignore. Love brings a king and princess together, just as England and France will be as one; the gentle, innocent exchange between the king and princess precedes one of the most sacred sacraments: the uniting of France and England, which, therefore, is also sacramental. Joan's covenant with Jehovah to crown the dauphin at Reims is a superior sacrament, however—and Joan's offering of herself as a sacrifice that eventually unites all France seals with fervent heat the testament of her great mission. The controlling metaphor is the smoke that ascends to heaven, burning away the dross of this fallen world and paving the way for Joan's eventual sanctification and acceptance as an intercessor and a member of the divine family. Despite Shakespeare's valiant effort to negate Joan's influence and to aggrandize the legend of Henry V, England can no longer completely embrace a Catholic king, whatever his greatness in battle; the historical Harry's death is inglorious because it is an anticlimactic sickness that kills him, and disease haunts his army long after the brilliant strategy of Agincourt.* Shakespeare's Henry becomes an ascendant hero, the only of

---

* Wasson pointed out in a doctoral seminar how Henry's longbowmen decimated the huge wave of French foot soldiers, trapping behind them the mounted knights whose horses would not step over the prone soldiers' bodies and who could not retreat because Harry's mounted knights had flanked them behind from either side. The French chevaliers also sported cumbersome heavy armor, destroying any mobility in the same way that the huge Spanish galleons were unmaneuverable compared to the smaller British ships in the great sea battle of 1588. This, in essence, was a turkey shoot rather than a miracle.

Shakespeare's kings to win the war, the throne, *and* the queen; and Shakespeare, as in Sonnet 18, has given immortality to Harry through the pen. Though Joan never attained knighthood and was never elevated to lady, baroness, or duchess, it could be said of her more truly than of Prince Hal that she "will keep [her] state / Be like a king, and show [her] sail of greatness" (1.2.273–74). Her sainthood is well deserved.

1. Percy Bysshe Shelley, "A Defense of Poetry," in Critical Theory since Plato, ed. Hazard Adams (New York: Harcourt Brace Jovanovich, 1971).

2. Elaine Pagels, *The Origin of Satan* (New York: Vintage, 1996). 39.

3. John Milton, *Milton's Complete Poems* (Cambridge, MA: Riverside, 1899).

4. Mentioned in Joseph Campbell, *The Hero with a Thousand Faces*, 2d ed. (1949; Princeton, NJ: Princeton University Press, 1968), 358–59.

5. J.R.R. Tokien, *The Hobbit* (1937; reprint, Boston: Houghton Mifflin, 2001).

6. Ovid, *The Metamorphoses*, trans. Rolfe Humphries (Bloomington: Indiana University Press, 1955), 185.

7. Ibid., 188.

8. Harry Levin, *The Overreachers: A Study of Christopher Marlowe* (Cambridge, MA: Harvard University Press, 1952).

9. Pagels, 40.

10. Ibid., 41.

11. Peter Sorensen, "The Two-Faced Satan of Literary History," *Hellas* 1.1 (Spring 1990): 71–75.

12. Dante Alighieri, *Dante Alighieri's Divine Comedy: Inferno*, trans. Mark Musa (Bloomingon: Indiana University Press), 1996.

13. William Shakespeare, *The Riverside Shakespeare* (Boston: Houghton Mifflin, 1997), 194.

14. Zecharia Sitchin, *The Wars of God and Man,* Book 3 of *Earth Chronicles* (Sante Fe, NM: Bear & Co., 1992).

15. John Milton, *A Treatise on Christian Doctrine, Compiled from the Holy Scriptures Alone*, trans. Charles R. Sumner (Cambridge: Cambridge University Press, 1825).

16. *The Cid Campeador*, ed. H. Butler Clarke (New York: Putnam's Sons, 1897), 342.

17. Ibid., 29.

18. Ibid., 348.

19. See R. V. C. Bodley, *The Messenger: The Life of Mohammed* (New York: Greenwood, 1946).

20. Gregory of Tours, *De gloria martyrum* 1.4, as translated in the article "Assumption, Feast of," *Encyclopaedia Britannica*, 1926.

21. Sally Cunneen, *In Search of Mary* (New York: Ballantine, 1996), 135; Geoffrey Ashe, *The Virgin Mary's Cult and the Re-Emergence of the Goddess* (New York: Askana, 1988).

22. Jaroslav Jan Pelikan, *Mary through the Centuries* (New Haven: Yale University Press, 1996), 208–9.

23. Ibid., 210.

24. "Mary," *Encyclopaedia Britannica*, 1926.

25. Joseph Cardinal Ratzinger, *Daughter Zion* (San Francisco: Ignatius, 1983), 72.

26. Ibid., 73.

27. Cunneen, 136.

28. E. A. Wallis Budge, *Legends of Our Lady Mary the Perpetual Virgin and Her Mother Hanna* (Oxford: Oxford University Press, 1933), 152–67. Budge's work here in English has not been supplanted.

29. Ibid., 152.

30. Ibid.

31. Ibid., 156.

32. Ibid.

33. Raphael Patai, *The Hebrew Goddess* (New York: Avon Books, 1978).

34. Budge, 153.

35. Ibid., lxxiii.

36. Ibid., lx.

37. Ibid., 164, 166.

38. Ibid., lxxiii.

39. *The Epic of Gilgamesh*, trans. N. K. Sanders (New York: Penguin, 1972), 100.

40. Sepher Ha-Yashir (Salt Lake City: J. H. Parry, 1887). This may be the earliest American published translation.

41. Budge, 200.

42. Ibid., 247–48.

43. Ibid., 253.

44. Ibid., 165.

45. Robert Graves and Joshua Podro, *The Nazarene Gospel Restored* (London: Cassell and Co., 1953), specifically chapter V, "The Marriage of the Lamb," 850–52, reconstructing the marriage from "garbled" NT texts.

46. James M. Robinson, gen. ed., *The Nag Hammadi Library: In English*, trans. members of the Coptic Gnostic Libary Project of the Institute for Antiquity and Christianity (New York: Harper & Row, 1977), 117–30.

47. I am using David Mycoff's very informative *A Critical Edition of the Legend of Mary Magdalena from Caxton's Golden Legende of 1483* (Salzburg: Institut fur Anglistik und Amerikanistik, 1985).

48. Ibid., 7. His entire commentary is instructive and will be cited from time to time in the remainder of my essay, with parenthetical page notations within the text.

49. Ibid., 8, 9.

50. Michael Baigent, Richard Leigh, and Henry Lincoln, *Holy Blood, Holy Grail* (New York: Delacorte Press, 1982).

51. David Bevington, *Medieval Drama* (Boston: Houghton Mifflin, 1975), 661, 662. I am using Bevington's edition of the play.

52. Ibid., 2110–19.

53 Ibid., 2128–31.

54. My text is *The Riverside Chaucer*, ed. Larry D. Benson (Boston: Houghton Mifflin, 1987).

55. Sumner Ferris, "'His Barge Ycleped Was the Maudelayne': *Canterbury Tales A 410*," *Names* 31 (1983): 207–10.

56. Mycoff, 1.

57. Joseph Gerhard, "Chaucer's Coinage: Foreign Exchange and the Puns of the Shipman's Tale," *Chaucer Review* 17 (1983): 342.

58. Edward A. Block, "Originality, Controlling Purpose, and Craftsmanship in Chaucer's *Man of Law's Tale*," *PMLA* 68 (1953): 572–616.

59. Mycoff, 123.

60. Ibid., 14.

61. Polly Schoyer Brooks, *Beyond the Myth: The Story of Joan of Arc* (New York: J. B. Lippincott, 1990); cited hereafter parenthetically by page number.

62. *The Golden Legend: Readings of the Saints*, trans. William Granger Ryan (Princeton: Princeton University Press, n.d.).

63. J.R.R. Tolkien, *The Lord of the Rings* (Boston: Houghton Mifflin, 1994).

64. *Golden Legend*, 205 (Rev. 12:7–9).

65. George Bernard Shaw, *Saint Joan* (New York: Penguin, 1946), 61.

66. *Golden Legend*, 2.339.

67. *World Book Encyclopedia*, 1972 edition, sv Catherine of Siena.

68. Brooks, 77.

69. Brooks, 143, 144.

70. Ibid., 153.

71. Ibid, 145.

72. Ibid., 148.

73. Ibid., 156.

74. Ibid.

75. Ibid., 150–51.

76. I am employing Richard Hosley's excellent annotated version of the 1587 edition of the *Chronicles* entitled *Shakespeare's Holinshed* (New York: Putnam, 1968), 157.

77. Ibid., 158.

78. Karen Sullivan, in *The Interrogation of Joan of Arc* (Minneapolis: U. of Minnesota Press, 1999).

79. In the introduction to *Henry VI, Parts 1, 2, and 3, The Riverside Shakespeare* (Boston: Houghton Mifflin, 1974), 588–89.

80. John Wasson, "The Secular Saint Plays of the Elizabethan Era," *The Saint Play in Medieval Europe*, ed. Clifford Davidson (Kalamazoo, MI: Medieval Institute Publications, 1986), 248–49. Wasson edited *Henry VIII* for the Bevington Shakespeare and has authored several books and many articles on medieval and Renaissance drama, but his best work has been his collecting and editing of town records bearing on the performance of such drama.

81. Ibid., 241–42.

82. Ibid., 249.

6 Ascension in the New World

Joseph Smith: Sacrificial Lamb/ Suffering Servant/American Enoch

Jesus is not the last figure in Judeo-Christian cultural tradition to combine in his character both the tragic sacrificial lamb and the hero who ascends and is translated. That most unique and dynamic incarnation of what critic Harold Bloom has dubbed *The Americian Religion,* Joseph Smith (1805–1844), founder of the Mormon church, has left a cultural "paper trail" in which he embodies both the heroic ascension and the tragic sacrifice, perhaps fueling to some small degree the suspicion among certain Christian groups that Smith was usurping the place and role of Christ in American religious life. I wish here to describe both the idea of Joseph Smith as the marred servant of Isaiah 53 and the sacrificial lamb at the end of his life and then to pursue the unique Mormon perception of Smith as ascended, translated hero.

The Unblemished Sacrificial Lamb and the Marred Servant

It is impossible to achieve total discreteness in classifying the metaphors that coalesce in the person of Joseph Smith, and thus some overlap and repetition occur as a result. The references to Joseph as tragic Christ type and sacrificial victim are numerous and vivid. Smith appears early on as the "Suffering Servant," the quasi-tragic figure in Isaiah's prophecy who, crippled and ravaged by the abuses of the world, stands as a type of the suffering of Israel itself (Mormons consider themselves Israelites both by bloodline and/or "adoption").* As I have noted, Christ acquires these characteristics only at the time of his final ordeal, but Smith embodies (in accounts of his life) the *physical* characteristics of the Suffering Servant over a lifetime. The irony of course is that Smith also is a tragic sacrificial lamb, who should, by any symbolic measure, be free both of physical and spiritual deformity. The type in Isaiah of the Suffering Servant appears to be built partly upon the figure of Jacob (renamed Israel), who, it will be remembered, wrestled with an angel of God who escapes Jacob's grasp only by dislocating the patriarch's hip; Jacob, here clearly a heroic figure, becomes a tragic figure in that he is forever crippled by the encounter, while nevertheless gaining a heroic boon from the angel. There is a priestly tradition in which a purposely dislocated left hip becomes a sign of priestly calling and service, of someone marked out by Yahweh for extraordinary duty. Such a figure is tragic only because of destiny (ergo, he becomes protagonist in a tragedy of destiny) in that he performs the sacrifice of slaying the unblemished lamb, because that is his foreordained role, while at the same time he is ironically unworthy of being that unblemished lamb. Logically, though the lacuna are evident enough, the patriarch Abraham would be the crippled priest (doubtless crippled with age, so that his son must bear the wood for the fire) who must sacrifice his only child (Isaac, the unblemished lamb). Christ is clearly unblemished in the Gospel narratives; he is the Lamb of God of John's Gospel, but the general epistle to the Hebrews insists as well that Christ was the heavenly high priest who performs

---

* Devout Mormons receive personal, revelatory blessings from men ordained as "patriarchs," a rite preceded by fasting and prayer, as well as worthiness interviews with local bishops. The primary purpose of the blessing, which is recorded, then transcribed, with copies being sent to the recipient and to Church archives, is actually to reveal or assign to the recipient his lineage and connection to a specific tribe in Israel; in my own case, I was assigned to the tribe of Joseph, through his son Ephraim, making me a natural heir to the Old Testament blessings and obligations given by Jehovah to Jacob (Israel) and his highly favored son Joseph. An official who functioned as an archivist for these particular files informed me (1972) that assignments of lineage had been recorded for all but two of the twelve tribes of Israel. The Mormons' collective identification with Israel has of course never been documented genealogically, but both Mormon and non-Mormon historians have long recognized the conscious historical pairing of the Church's exodus across frontier America with Israel's exodus in the wilderness, of Brigham Young with Moses, and of Mormon religious persecutions with those of Israel and the Jews. Mormon scripture, specifically its modern-day scripture on doctrine and church governance, makes the connection explicit, using words like *Zion*, *Israel*, or *Gentiles* to set Mormons apart as a religious people.

the sacrifice; by shedding his own blood in the Garden of Gethsemane (the true Christian's ordeal of a broken heart and contrite spirit). Jesus is both the high priest *and* Suffering Servant marred by scourging, crucifixion, and other abuses and the unblemished lamb waiting to have its throat cut, not to mention being the *shkehinah*, the fire that consumes the meat offering, ascending to heaven in the smoke of the sacrifice. Adding to this complex scheme is the medieval and Renaissance tradition (preserved, incidentally, in the Book of Mormon) that Abraham is to Yahweh as Isaac is to Jesus (father and son).*

Several instances in Joseph Smith's life qualify him as Suffering Servant. Some years preceding his first vision of Jesus, which he recounted later in his own histories in several different versions, his leg somehow became inflamed, possibly incidental to his having survived typhoid fever. At seven years of age, Joseph showed remarkable pluck when, according to his mother's account, his pain became horrific, and doctors were called in to examine the left leg; their initial operation relieved and drained the infection from the bone, but as the wound healed over, the infection rooted itself deep in the bone between knee and ankle. When the doctors again conferred, they proposed amputation, and when Joseph remonstrated, they abandoned the idea in favor of boring and chipping the infection from the bone, in somewhat the same fashion that tooth decay is halted. When it is remembered that germ theory was a fledgling science at best, and that anesthesia was years away, the terror of the surgery is almost beyond comprehension. That Joseph survived at all is at least providential; that, unconsciously embracing the Nazarite's vow not to consume wine or strong drink, the child refuses any pain-dulling liquor is remarkably brave; that the medical doctor uniquely qualified to perform the obviously experimental surgery (he developed the survey and was the one person at that time who performed it) was available is also astounding; but what I find most interesting, however, is Joseph Smith's *permanent* limp in the weakened left leg. Typologically speaking, it is the "true sign" of Smith's role as "Suffering Servant," the disabled priest.[1]

A second example, built on the model of Job as Suffering Servant, occurs 24 March 1832, when Joseph Smith was overcome in his own home by some

---

* The metaphysical poets preserved this tradition, but it is also remembered in the Brome MS. of the medieval mystery play *Abraham and Isaac*.

dozen men, dragged unconscious to a meadow, stripped, beaten severely, covered in hot pine tar and feathers, almost castrated, and left with the tar paddle crammed in his mouth. Removing the tar took the rest of that night and left permanent scars all over Smith's body. He preached a sermon the next day, in considerable pain, but also whistled slightly as he spoke, for one of the attackers chipped Smith's tooth as he attempted to pour poison down Smith's throat.[2]

What is ironic is that, in a remarkable parallel to the dichotomy of the unblemished lamb and the Suffering Servant, Joseph Smith was always regarded as singularly handsome, and even in later descriptions, Joseph has no physical blemish. Lydia Bailey Knight, an early convert to Mormonism, noted that Joseph had "brown hair, handsome blue eyes, . . . sharp, penetrating gaze; a striking countenance, and with manners at once majestic yet gentle, dignified yet exceedingly pleasant."*[3] Indeed, Joseph was at times portrayed as innocent as a child, gentle as a lamb: When families came to Kirtland, according to Louisa Y. Littlefield, "every child and young babe in the company were especially noticed by him and tenderly taken by the hand, with his kind words and blessings. He loved innocence and purity, and he seemed to find it in the great perfection with the prattling child."[4] Close associate Parley P. Pratt gave a description of him as "unblemished":

> President Joseph Smith was in person . . . strong and active; of light complexion, light hair, blue eyes, very little beard, and of an expression peculiar to himself, on which the eye naturally rested with interest, and was never weary of beholding. . . . [He was] mild, affable, beaming with . . . benevolence . . . and an unconscious smile or cheerfulness, . . . with the serene and steady . . . eye."[5]

Such characteristics were essential to establishing Joseph Smith's purity and lack of blemish—as a fit preparation for his eventual sacrifice as an innocent victim.

Both Joseph Smith and his contemporaries bore witness of his innocence and did not fail to connect his goodness and his martyrdom with the original lamb of sacrifice, Jesus. A revelation to Smith's successor, Brigham Young, contains the

---

* Recounted in Hyrum and Helen Mae Andrus, *They Knew the Prophet*. Hyrum Andrus, a devout Mormon, was one of the best of the professional Mormon historians, relying on primary sources such as journals, old magazine and newspaper interviews, and handwritten manuscripts rather than derivative documentation. Andrus was less progressive perhaps than Leonard J. Arrington, but each historian spawned another generation of both apologetic (e.g., Andrew F. Ehat) and progressive (e.g., D. Michael Quinn) historical scholarship.

following declaration: "Many have marveled because of his death; but it was needful that he should seal his testimony with his blood, that he might be honored and the wicked might be condemned" (Doctrine & Covenants 136:39). John Taylor, later Brigham Young's successor, declared emphatically, "Joseph Smith, the Prophet and Seer of the Lord, has done more, save Jesus only, for the salvation of men in this world, than any other man that lived in it. . . . [He] founded a great city, and left a fame and name that cannot be slain [referring to the literary 'immortality' of written memory]. He lived great, and he died great in the eyes of God and his people" (D&C 135:3). Smith himself, on his way to Carthage, Illinois, the place of his martyrdom, is later quoted as saying, "I am going like a lamb to the slaughter; but I am calm as a summer's morning; I have a conscience void of offense towards God, and towards all men. I shall die innocent, and it shall yet be said of me—he was murdered in cold blood" (D&C 135:4).*

Other descriptions are equally suggestive; Newel Knight, husband of Lydia Knight and an early convert to Mormonism, used literary allusion to describe the behavior of a mob toward Joseph when, early in his career, Smith was arrested through an act of malicious prosecution: "A number of men . . . used every means to abuse, ridicule, and insult him. They spit upon him, pointed their fingers at him, saying, 'Prophesy! prophesy!' Thus did they imitate those who crucified the Savior of mankind, not knowing what they did."[6] Even more allusive is an account of the Martyrdom preserved by one of Smith's more eloquent followers, Dan Jones, who later became a great Mormon missionary in Wales. Outside the jail cell with Joseph, during a transfer of prisoners, Jones remarked that the mob

> upbraided [Smith] for not calling a legion of angels to release him, and to destroy his enemies, inasmuch as he pretended to have miraculous power. Others asked him to prophesy when and what manner of death awaited him. . . . The situation forcibly reminded us of the taunting and jeering of the Jews to our holy and meek Redeemer, so similar the words and actions of the mob proved their spirits to be.[7]

In fact, the martyrdom of Joseph and Hyrum Smith (Joseph's younger brother was with Joseph in Carthage Jail when they were slain) was attended by the same

---

* Beginning with "I SHALL DIE INNOCENT" is placed entirely in capitals and in a different font, reminding one forcefully of similar uses of fonts with sacred names, such as JEHOVAH, in the KJV.

sorts of signs as found in the oral traditions of Christ's death. Joseph's mother wrote that "on the evening of the 27th of June, such a barking and howling of dogs and bellowing of cattle all over the city of Nauvoo I never heard before or since."[8] Mary Lambert echoed this sentiment: "The spirit of unrest was upon all, man and animal. . . . No one in the house had slept, the dogs were noisy, and even the chickens were awake."[9] And Dan Jones asserted that Joseph's purpose in surrendering was to "die for Nauvoo,"[10] by offering his blood in place of his people's, thus turning away the wrath of the mob directed against all Mormons.

That Joseph Smith was betrayed by some of his close associates also suggests what legal and historical experts Dallin Oaks and Marvin Hill styled *The Carthage Conspiracy*.*[11] Joseph was in the process of arraignment for sedition when he was shot to death by a mob at Carthage, Illinois, in 1844. Those prosecuting him seemed convinced his philosophy was threatening the political system in the United States. It is important to remember that the Romans crucified Jesus for precisely the same crime, though the blame gets redirected a bit in the Gospels toward "scoundrels" among the Sanhedrin, not to mention the betrayal by Judas. Jesus apparently got the same questionable legal treatment from the Romans (and, perhaps, the Sadducees, some of them puppets of Rome) that Smith got from the non-Mormons in Illinois.

Yet once again, as with Jesus, conflicting narratives emerge of a heroic figure destined to ascend to the heavens and be translated, never to taste of death and ever triumphing over his enemies. The narrative conceits involve Joseph's living out his own vision of the City of Enoch, with Joseph as an Enoch–Elijah figure that is also heroic in the literary or classical tradition. The narratives survive and flourish despite the fact that Joseph Smith died, and despite the contrasting visions of the marred, Suffering Servant and the unblemished sacrificial lamb.

Joseph as the American Enoch

Thanks are due Harold Bloom, the prolific and incisive literary, cultural, and religious critic, for laying the groundwork in *The Book of J, The American Religion,* and *Omens of Millennium,* three recent books showing Joseph Smith's connection

---

* Notably John C. Bennett, William and Wilson Law, William Marks, and many other close associates proved unfaithful to Smith's cause at one stage or another.

to Jewish (especially cabalistic) tradition concerning Enoch or Metatron, also called the Lesser Yahweh. Though Bloom, as also Joseph Campbell before him, does not differentiate the apotheosis of ascension and translation from other forms of encounter with the divine, he nevertheless captures the heroic qualities in Smith that qualify the frontier prophet for the unique status of the one who has ascended to be part of the divine family. Essentially, one argues for such an ascension by asserting the dualistic or gnostic nature of Mormonism, which indeed seems in some respects to sidestep what Bloom calls the orthodox "faith" in "Covenant with Yahweh, or the Atonement of Christ, or the submission to Islam" in favor of a gnosis in which one has a certain knowledge, divinely bequeathed, of one's divine essence, whence one came, why one is here, and whither one goes.[12]

Bloom is convinced that Enoch is the "authentic angel of America"; that is, Enoch's ascension, translation, and calling as Metatron reflect the American ideals of transcendence and gnostic self-assuredness in the expanding frontier of nineteenth-century America. To Joseph Smith, Bloom attributes the initial observation of Enoch's importance metaphorically for America, for Joseph "identified himself with Enoch, and by now may well be joined in an imaginative unity with his great precursor, if Mormon speculation proves true."[13]

The first piece of evidence in this alternative, heroic narrative is that in at least one revelation speaking of Joseph Smith, the name Enoch appears in place of Smith's (D&C 78:1, 9). The substitution was made for safety reasons, apparently, yet the choice of names is surely not an accident. As noted in an earlier chapter, Smith has left us with a very fine example of a pseudepigraphic Book of Enoch, couched within the larger, pseudepigraphic work the Book of Moses. That work, which describes the city of Enoch, redeemed and taken to heaven along with the great Metatron (Enoch), without its inhabitants' tasting death, is an idealized picture of Smith's own efforts to build a holy city in the New World, with the temple as its showpiece. He succeeded, and Nauvoo not only had its temple (albeit briefly),* but also was one of the largest cities in Illinois. Smith's successor, Brigham Young, built Salt Lake City with that very goal: a holy city

---

* Armand Mauss, professor of sociology at Washington State University and an expert on the sociology of Mormons, has explained, in a paper presented at the 1989 Sunstone Symposium in Salt Lake City, the reason temples terrify non-Mormons, coincidentally explaining why the

of the New World with a magnificent temple, and Young maintained to his dying day that he had never done or taught anything that Joseph had not taught to him.

The importance of Enoch to early Mormons is best preserved in nineteenth-century hymn texts which are not now included in hymnals because of changing needs and views among the flock and shepherds. Hymn text #12, verse 4 of one edition of the Manchester Hymnal* contains these lines:

> Behold the Church! It soars on high,
> To meet the Saints amid the sky.
> With Enoch here we all shall meet,
> And worship at Messiah's feet.

Another, #34, contains these lines concerning Mormons:

> There they will see, upon the land,
> Fair Zion from above,
> And meet with Enoch's holy band
> And sing redeeming love.

A current Mormon hymn, "Praise to the Man," whose meolody is a popular Scottish bagpipe tune and whose lyrics are based on Sir Walter Scott's "Hail to the Chief," contains this heroic ascension imagery:

Nauvoo Temple was neglected and caught fire after the Mormons left Illinois in 1845. Building a temple, as opposed to a chapel, represents the highest token of Mormon achievement in a community or country, suggesting a confidence and solidity that non-Mormons have quickly observed. The Christian Right in America, as with the Russian Orthodox Church in the former Soviet Union, deems Mormonism an aberration of Christianity that rejects local culture and tradition in favor of an "American" religion. Temples, with their sacred mystery rites and proxy ordinances for the dead, seem like the ultimate "pagan" export from America, at the same time being thought un-American by the Christian Fundamentalists. Quite contrary to Bloom's fears about Mormonism's political clout, the church has always done much better among progressive or liberal societies than among conservative groups or nations, where tradition tends to choke off pluralism. Thus, for example, when new temples are about to be dedicated, Fundamentalist Christians will chain themselves to the perimeter gates, or they will bear protest signs and hand out pamphlets, dressing as temple workers in full regalia to mock the church.

* This Mormon hymnal contained hundreds of texts, which were sung to folk tunes everyone knew; for example, in the modern Mormon hymnal, "Do What Is Right" follows the tune of "The Old Oaken Bucket," and "Up, Awake, Ye Defenders of Zion" employs the same tune as "O Columbia the Gem of the Ocean."

Hail to the Prophet, ascended to heaven!
Traitors and tyrants now fight him in vain.
Mingling with Gods, he can plan for his brethren;
Death cannot conquer the hero again.[14]

No British convert to Mormonism could fail to recognize the heroic parallel of Smith and Scott's Highland Chieftain Black Roderick:

Hail to the Chief who in triumph advances!
Honored and blessed be the Ever-green Pine!
. . . .
While every Highland glen
Sends our shout back again,
"Roderigh Vich Alpine dhu, ho! ieroe!"[15]

Referring to his own myth of ascension, Smith once declared, "John the Revelator was caught up to the third heaven, but I know one who was caught up to the seventh heaven and saw and heard things not lawful for me to utter."[16] At another time, Smith declared, "People little know who I am when they talk about me, and they never will know until they see me weighed in the balance in the kingdom of God. Then they will know who I am, and see me as I am. I dare not tell them, and they do not know me."[17] Joseph Smith at one point dictated that his brother Hyrum ought to be the prophet, so that Joseph could take on the higher calling of "Priest of the Most High God,"[18] clearly a reference to his role as high priest of the temple he was building. In one revealing reference to his potential ascension–translation, Smith asked, "Suppose I would condescend—yes, I will call it condescend, to be a great deal better than any of you, I would be raised up to the highest heaven; and who should I have to accompany me?"[19]

His heroic physical stature feeds into the narrative of the hero worthy of ascension and translation. Contemporary Lucy Diantha Morley Allen declared, "I've seen the Prophet wrestle, and run, and jump, but have never seen him beaten. In all that he did he was manly and almost godlike."[20] One notes in that statement the emphasis on physical activities such as are found in the ancient Olympic games, and even the funeral games (to honor the death of Patroclus) in the *Iliad*. Equally intriguing is Lydia Bailey Knight's statement that Joseph had "the carriage of an Apollo."[21]

In other examples, we note the *de facto* if not *de jure* "transfiguration" of Smith. Brigham Young declared that when Joseph Smith received revelation, "there was a peculiar clearness and transparency in his face."[22] Lydia Knight concurred, noting that on one such revelatory occasion, "I saw his face become white and a shining glow seemed to beam from every feature."[23] Anson Call, yet another early convert, described the same change: "I . . . saw his countenance change to white; not the deadly white of a bloodless face, but a living, brilliant white."[24] Mary Lightner declared, "He got so white that anyone who saw him would have thought he was transparent. I remember I thought we could almost see the bones through the flesh of his face. I shall remember it and see it in my mind's eye as long as I remain upon the earth."[25]

Bloom's focus on Joseph Smith as a heroic Enoch figure is brilliant but ignores another biblical type on which the narrative and folklore of Joseph's status as ascended and translated hero; I refer to Elijah. Joseph saw the significance of Elijah early in his life. In 1823, when the angel Moroni (a resurrected being from the last days of the ancient Book of Mormon tribes) appeared to Smith to announce the existence of golden plates containing the Book of Mormon, the angel declared, "I will reveal unto you the Priesthood, by the hand of Elijah the prophet" (D&C 2:1). When it is recalled that during the "ascension" of Jesus and his initial transfiguration Moses and Elijah appeared, it is not surprising that the potential epiphany of Elijah would come on the heels of the appearance to Smith of Jesus and the Father in heaven in 1820.

In fact, however, the priesthood alluded to in that early vision was that priestly service connected directly to the temple, where, it will be recalled, Smith anticipated serving as "Priest of the Most High God." The progression toward apotheosis occurs on 3 April 1836, when, in addition to the appearance of the Lord and other beings from the mansions of heaven, "Elijah the prophet, who was taken to heaven without tasting death, stood before us" (D&C 110:13); the appositive modifier in this verse suggests strongly a continuing narrative of potential heroic ascent and translation.

Several key passages in the Old Testament help cement the relationship, at least typologically, between Elijah and Joseph Smith. For example, in 1 Kings 17, Elijah the Tishbite is commanded by Yahweh to hide himself near Zarephath, a seaport town situated between Tyre and Zidon in ancient Phoenicia, later Lebanon. Elijah becomes hungry and lonely, but a widow at Zarephath befriends him. She has a son and when this son falls desperately ill, so there is "no breath left in him" (17:17), Elijah cries to the Lord, "O Lord my God, hast thou also brought evil upon the widow with whom I sojourn, by slaying her son?" (17:20). What follows is a ritual embrace typifying resurrection in which Elijah "stretche[s] himself upon the child three times" and begs Yahweh to allow the child's soul (here likely the breath of life) to enter his body again (17:21). Miraculously, the boy is brought back from the vale of death, and the ritual act has demonstrated to the woman that, indeed, Elijah is a "man of God, and that the word of the Lord in [his] mouth is truth" (17:24). Here Elijah turns his heart toward a child, and the prophet becomes a surrogate father and provider (he miraculously provides oil and wheat for the widow).

In an apparent scribal attempt to legitimize the calling of Elisha, Elijah's student replacement, and a witness to Elijah's ascension, 2 Kings 4 re-creates, in a somewhat forced juxtaposition, the miracle of Elijah previously discussed. Because the text is not able to match precisely the details of Elijah's miracle, it forces side-by-side two incidents to produce roughly the desired effect: Elisha multiplies oil for a widow "of the wives of the sons of the prophets" (2 Kings 4:1) and then helps a Shunamite woman (clearly not a widow) by first removing the curse of barrenness from her, then later bringing her only son back from death (4:33–35). That the parallel is a conscious scribal effort is clear from the detailed description of the ritual embrace of the dead boy, preceded by prayer: "And he went up, and lay upon the child, and put his mouth upon his mouth, and his eyes upon his eyes, and his hands upon his hands: and he stretched himself upon the child; and the flesh of the child waxed warm" (2 Kings 4:34).

The ritual is completed when the child sneezes seven times, either as evidence of expelling the demon of death or of the certain intake of breath. The father of the child is never seen after the very beginning of the tale; the mother, in contrast, seems to be the major figure in the story, anticipating as she does the ritual actions of the prophet by laying the young man "on the bed of the man of God" (2 Kings 4:21).

In the New Testament, which reinterprets the Old Testament as a foreshadowing of the life and acts of Jesus, Jesus consciously evokes the heroic tradition of Elijah's godlike power over life and death. In fact, a number of authors, such as Hugh Schonfield and Robert Graves,* have remarked how consciously Jesus seems to have gone about establishing his legitimacy as prophet, priest, king, and Messiah (anointed one, or deliverer). This seems evident in a pivotal scene in Luke 7, in which Jesus raises from the dead the only son of a widow of Nain:

---

* I am thinking in particular of Schonfield's *The Passover Plot* and Graves's *King Jesus*.

And when the Lord saw her, he had compassion on her, and said unto her, Weep not.

And he came and touched the bier: and they that bare him stood still. And he said, Young man, I say unto thee, Arise.

And he that was dead sat up, and began to speak. And he delivered him to his mother.

And there came a fear on all: and they glorified God, saying, That a great prophet is risen up among us; and That God hath visited his people. (Luke 7:13–16)

The "great prophet" referred to is doubtless Elijah, prompting the observation in Luke 9:8 that some thought that in Jesus, Elias (Elijah) had appeared in the land (whose return had been anticipated in folk tradition).

Early chroniclers of Joseph Smith's life and works do not fail to connect him with Elijah, as well as with Jesus and Enoch. Wilford Woodruff, an early Mormon leader who kept meticulous diaries of Mormon church history, includes a well-known account of Joseph's remarkable healings among the fever-ridden Saints in the early days of Nauvoo; one instance in particular is striking, partly because, coincidentally, the person raised from the "dead" had the first name of Elijah, but it is also interesting because Woodruff's account suggests that Mormon leaders saw the typological parallels between Joseph and the enigmatic Elijah and Jesus. Woodruff mentions that Joseph took Elijah Fordham "by the right hand"; Fordham replies to Joseph's questions in the same fashion as the sister of Lazarus: "If you had come sooner, I think I might have been [healed]." Joseph's ritual incantation is a precise New Testament formula: "Elijah, I command you, in the name of Jesus of Nazareth, to arise and be made whole!" Woodruff's account ends with the pointed simile, "Elijah Fordham leaped . . . like a man raised from the dead." Of further note is Woodruff's emphasis on the "dead" man's speechlessness, glazed eyes, and unconscious state.[26] All these details suggest that Woodruff and Smith saw typological connections between this event and events in the Bible.

Yet it is quite clear that all such heroic narratives, complete with their trans-figuration, ascension, and translation motifs, are mitigated by Joseph Smith's death in 1844. Thus, with Joseph Smith the heroic narratives co-exist with narratives of Suffering Servant and sacrificial lamb. It is important, I believe, that Smith's followers tried to reconcile his heroic figure with his tragic demise, just as Gospel writers many centuries before had wrestled with Jesus' apparent death.

The following events can be read as part of an as yet unfulfilled resurrection or ascension–translation myth): Joseph Smith's body is buried nowhere, but rather has been "caught up" into heaven. Joseph then appears to people from time to time to aid the church and direct the kingdom on earth.

Joseph did not die alone; his brother Hyrum, whose name reminds one forcibly of the murdered Hiram of Freemasonic allegory, was killed as well. The bodies were brought back from Carthage Jail for viewing and burial. After the citizens of Nauvoo viewed the bodies,

> the coffins were removed from the outer boxes. These outer boxes were then filled with bags of sand, taken to the cemetery, and buried with the usual ceremony. At midnight, the bodies were taken by trusted friends and buried in the basement of the Nauvoo House, then in the course of construction. This precaution was taken through fear that the enemies of the Prophet and Hyrum would return to mutilate their remains.[27]

Later the bodies were secretly reburied at a spot overlooking the Mississippi River.[28]

Yet narratives about Joseph Smith's heroic ascension survive among Mormon fundamentalists and literalists. Max Anderson's study of Mormon fundamentalist behavior and belief devotes an entire chapter to fundamentalist implications that Joseph had indeed been resurrected and made an ascending hero. Apparently the story began as a "rumor circulating among some of the early Saints that Brigham Young brought the bodies of Joseph and Hyrum to the Salt Lake Valley by wagon and buried them on Temple Square."[29]

The rumor soon grew into a resurrection story and, as Anderson implies, circulated widely enough to cause Brigham Young to comment on the problem during a church conference:

> Joseph is not resurrected; and if you will visit the graves you will find the bodies of Joseph and Hyrum yet in their resting place. Do not be mistaken about that; they will be resurrected in due time.[30]

In 1928 the bodies of Joseph and Hyrum were exhumed; according to one Mormon writer, the leaders of the Reorganized Church (one of the splinter groups of the original Mormon organization) wished to ascertain that the bodies of the two slain leaders had not in fact been shipped west with Brigham Young.[31] Indeed, the official RLDS history records that President F. M. Smith, president of that body in 1928, wanted to "set at rest rumors" that the bodies had been spirited away.[32]

The uncanny parallels between that account of Smith's burial and Gospel accounts of Jesus' burial may be explained best by the narrative intent in both: Jesus and Joseph Smith were to have ascended heroically, yet violent death won out. The hope of ultimate resurrection–ascension grows out of the realization of death and mortality—a realization the chroniclers of Enoch's and Elijah's ascension and translation must have recognized but which they did not have to acknowledge in their heroic narratives. Those Mormons believing one can cheat death and be caught directly up to heaven, bodily, are exceedingly few, for the deaths of so many pioneers on the trail to what became Salt Lake City were a sobering reminder of how mortal even the most righteous Mormons' lives were and are. It is just predictable that modern Mormons pin their hopes on a wonderful life after death; the near-death experience today holds great currency among the Latter-day Saints, whose home library shelves are often stocked with anthologies of stories that embrace "the" light, or bring us closer to "the light."

A Modern Translation: Annalee Skarin

New Age religion is the modern exponent of nineteenth-century American transcendentalism, just as transcendentalism, as previously noted, was modeled on the heroic ascension–translation of ancient times; thus both New Age religion and transcendentalism stand in sharp contrast and contradistinction to Judeo-Christian orthodoxy, with its emphasis on the certainty of death, the substitute life of the spirit afterlife, and even its hope for universal resurrection (in fact, this dichotomy is I believe at the heart of Nathaniel Hawthorne's inability to relinquish completely his Puritan past). Annalee Skarin, an early New Age adept, is more popular than ever; her many books do a brisk business in California New Age bookstores. Who has actually been pocketing the profits from those sales remains a mystery. Annalee's most complete if tendentious biography, by Gloria Love (pen name), published through a vanity press (Monarch, out of Midvale, Utah) in August 1995, makes several statements in passing that bear directly on the idea of ascension–translation as a cultural narrative.

Annalee had a strange heritage, "for her father was a Jewish convert" to Mormonism. Much as Scientologist L. Ron Hubbard, Annalee began as a frustrated, indigent writer of fiction, but not remotely with Hubbard's degree of success. She served a Mormon church mission, a rarety for a woman in those days (1920s), especially when one notes that she had already been married once, giving birth to a son who died in infancy.[33] She later abandoned her second husband, to whom she had been married for two decades, in favor of a "soul-mate" she had converted to Mormonism while on her church mission. According to Skarin's own daughter (who wrote a tell-all biography about her mother and who gave it the malignant title *Descent into Madness*), Annalee was influenced by the renowned Amee Semple McPherson, the female version of Elmer Gantry.[34] She severed her ties with Mormonism in the 1940s, and the Mormons reciprocated by excommunicating her in 1952. After that time, she published several books equally as democratic as the first book, *Ye Are Gods*, published in 1948, in which it is proposed that, with the right sort of purification and discipline, anyone and everyone can ascend and be translated as were Enoch and Elijah. What is remarkable about Love's biography is its implicit vindication of my proposal that orthodox ideas of salvation through Christ's atonement are fundamentally and irreconcilably opposed to the heroic ideals of ascension–translation: "Her [Annalee's] teachings lead away from God's truth about the vital position Jesus Christ holds through His sacrifice when He brought the atonement and resurrection, for all mankind."[35]

That religious leaders, possibly even a few Mormon leaders, feel the doctrine of ascension–translation is possibly at odds with the gospel "plan of salvation" demonstrates how irreconcilable the two narratives are. She is a gnostic—certainly her defiance of ecclesiastical authority was a trait among ancient gnostics. Yet as a gnostic she wants nothing to do directly with humanity; she wants only to share her method to guide her adepts to their own *gnosis*. Despite the fact that Annalee was excommunicated because she was thought deluded (perhaps a sound judgment, given her bizarre adherence to the "doctrine" at the expense of family and of anything like a social gospel), Love has hit upon the heart of the conflict: one cannot maintain a New Age hope for ascension–translation (through meritorious or heroic behavior) while at the same time believing that all humans are inherently flawed and require the merits of *Christ* in order to save them, ultimately if not proximately, from death and decay. It must be obvious, then, that while the early Mormon church promoted the narrative of ascension and translation, as the Church moved toward a more traditional paradigm of Jesus as the only means of salvation, it had to relinquish that older narrative and mythology. Few Mormons do so, but one can detect two distinct messages in Mormonism: a gospel of salvation (unmerited, the gift of Christ through grace, an insistent theme in the earliest church revelations and in the Book of Mormon) and a gospel of exaltation (a heroic journey based on extraordinary merit and designed to prepare the initiate for her or his activities in the eternal worlds, after resurrection). But it is after all God or the gods who decide who ascends to heaven to join the divine family; God judges heroism, righteousness, and even the family pedigree one presents to demand his heritage from God (recall the Phaethon myth). Annalee's guidebooks, the "how-to" scriptures of transcendence, are based on a flawed perception of mythology; humans can be as heroic as they wish, but the divine family owns the vacant seats and has all the tickets, so the fate of humanity is as it was for Gilgamesh. Our lot is to die.

Annalee's ability to embrace the ascension–translation narrative as her *raison-d'etre* suggests that the *narrative itself*, not the physical reality of ascension and translation, is the redemptive force and makes self-deception and even deceiving others an ethical behavior; for violating the integrity of the text is a great crime for anyone who sees the text as a divine message. (Shakespeare's sonnets vaunt the same ideal of textual immortality, granting that hope not only to Shakespeare, but to his patron and his mistress, the "dark lady.") It is significant that Annalee never renounced publicly anything she had taught—and her motives for not confessing publicly have nothing to do with preserving her royalties from book sales (for she was poor even when the books did a brisk business), although privately she confessed, "I have grieved over my failure. I never told anyone."*[36]

As with other ascension–translation narratives, the text itself achieves the immortality denied to the narrative's protagonist. Love notes how popular Annalee's "hypnotically, dynamically compelling" narrative is: "One flies on wings of celestial song . . . and [note carefully!] transcendent joy."[37] I will focus on passages from her first book, *Ye Are Gods*,[38] to show how she initially framed that wild narrative.

To introduce her narrative, she establishes how earthly, mortal life is "fleeting, transitory" (4). Quickly she moves, though, to suggesting that even within mortality certain eternal constants serve as markers or tropes for humans searching for cosmic truth: Electricity is quite naturally mentioned, and of course wind, which the Gospel

---

* Love quotes from Annalee's last ms., still unpublished at her death.

of John employs as a metaphor for spiritual rebirth. Finally she establishes that abstract principles such as love and hate, and thought itself, are real enough. But the rhetoric of the New Age must go beyond metaphors that traditionally serve as well to illustrate the soul's survival after death, reincarnation, and even resurrection as they do to open a discussion on ascension and translation.

The most patently rhetorical device in this work, and indeed in much of the "touchy-feely" literature of the New Age, is the *rhetorical question*. Erich von Daniken used rhetorical questions to generate several books in the seventies about the "chariots of the gods"[39]—as in, "Could these glyphs actually be a representation of an astronaut carrying a ray gun and peering through a dark sun visor?" The reader does not answer "no," because anything *could* mean *anything*, and the author never answers "yes," for that would brand him as a lunatic. The New Age rhetorical style is markedly different from the very concrete rhetoric of the literalists, such as Velikovsky, Sitchin, and de Santillana.*[40] The first chapter, covering eight pages, contains forty-six such questions, leaving wide open the field of equally abstract responses. Nothing specific is demanded in a rhetorical question, beyond affirming or negating it, so *everything* can be (and usually is) part of the response. The text rings with New Age enthusiasm: "Was there ever anything more perfect than the human body?" "This magnificent thing which is man! Whence came he? Whither does he go?" And the reassuring, "Is it not then as easy matter to become acquainted with your own soul?" (11).

She imitates the heroic journey of Joseph Smith, whose own commentaries on translation and on the means to accomplishing it seemed indispensable to her narrative, despite the fact that, historically speaking, Smith not only didn't ascend, but burst through a window on being murdered and actually *fell* two stories. But, as I have pointed out, the ascension–translation narrative has a life of its own, conditioning its readers for strong misreading toward a "writerly text." Much as the youthful Smith sought out God after reading a passage on prayer in the epistle of James, Annalee found her key in the sacred writings of Joseph Smith. She relates:

> I had been sitting on the floor, studying, with a collection of books around me, when my eyes fell upon one sentence, and that sentence was like a key, for it seemed to open the door. . . . : "There is a law irrevocably decreed in heaven

---

* I am thinking of Immanuel Velikovsky's radical *Oedipus and Akhnaton*, Zecharia Sitchin's *The Wars of Gods and Men*, and Giorgio de Santillana's *Hamlet's Mill*.

before the foundation of this world, upon which all blessings are predicated; and when we obtain any blessing from god, it is by obedience to that law upon which it is predicated."*

While Smith's visions are, using Bloom's terminology, strong misreadings of the Bible, I believe Skarin strongly misreads Smith; that is, whereas most Mormons have, out of necessity, compromised the vision of ascension–translation so strongly stated in Smith's frontier contributions to scripture and in his personal commentaries (not because of any fault of Mormons but because Smith's death inevitably compromised the vision), Skarin has distilled those portions of Smith's precepts that are most clearly transcendental. She thus leaves Smith's alternative vision of tragedy or of the Suffering Servant for others to wrestle with.

Yet rhetorically speaking, her narrative differs from earlier narratives in other ways. First, she narrates her own quest; she has this in common with Thoreau in *Walden*, or Wordsworth in *The Prelude*, yet her quest is considerably more Faustian: she is looking for an obscure "key" that will majestically draw her into the divine family. Her efforts are real, but they are directed entirely toward following the precise (pseudo-)scientific formula that will assure success. This has less to do with true heroism (Gilgamesh), special favor from the gods (Herakles), or righteousness (Enoch, Elijah) than it does with a deliberate attempt to "storm" the gates of heaven (the legend of Nimrod, the master hunter who builds a tower in order to shoot arrows at God). The narrator of the *Gilgamesh* epic is not offering a how-to course in ascension–translation; Annalee, as with most New Age philosophers, *is* offering just that.

Second, Skarin, fearful that somehow her own rhetoric may be passed over or her brilliance unrecognized, delights in drawing attention to the signifiers of the text through various printers' fonts and the like. It is not unusual to see key words all in capitals, often in bold type, or at other times in italics. For example, in *Ye Are Gods*, nearly half the pages (some 66 out of 128) contain one or more phrases all in capitals. This tactic does not vary in later books. Philosophically speaking, Annalee exalts her own text by "translating" key phrases into a "higher order" of

---

* Though Annalee does not offer the citation, this passage is from one of Joseph Smith's revelations, Doctrine and Covenants 130:20–21, and touches on the nature of the physical bodies of the Father and Son and of the spiritual body of the Holy Spirit.

capital letters, as in a vision she received in 1944: "I looked out across eternity—and with my looking I saw the following words written across the heavens":

"DEAR LORD
GIVE US EYES SINGLE TO THY GLORY,
WITH THE GIFT OF HUMILITY.
"LET OUR EVERY THOUGHT BE IN CONTROL,
AND OUR EVERY WORD BE FOR THY HONOR—
AMEN." (50)

Skarin brings us hard against the tragic dilemma of Gilgamesh and Enkidu: the gods have declared death for humans, and their reasons for preserving Utnapisthim while denying Gilgamesh and Enkidu remain as obscure at the end of the epic tale as at the beginning. Gilgamesh, one must acknowledge, has some reason for hoping to succeed: he is a great king and two-thirds divine. He is brave and gifted far beyond ordinary people. Annalee, faced with the same dilemma, has nothing to offer the gods as an argument: she comes from a poor family, and while she seems a good person, she is not revered as good (unless one turns to her own narrative, which again, unlike Enoch's and Elijah's, is enormously self-interested. Reasoning that thoughts, like seeds, produce after their own kind (a strong misreading of Gen. 1:11–13), Skarin concludes that *cogito ergo sum* applied as well to ascension–translation:

> Man is continually visualizing greater things, and greater things are being produced. . . . But the greatest seed of all has not yet been planted in man's mind, or if it has, it is promptly choked out by doubts and fears (weeds). And the greatest seed is the thought that man himself can reach any height. (30)

Annalee was right, of course. Doubts and fears not only grow effortlessly in our minds, but literary history has planted many of them. We have mentioned the Sumerian judgment against man's immortality as preserved in *Gilgamesh*. These proscriptions are echoed in the Old Testament as well. Genesis 3:19 rings in the malediction: "For dust thou art and unto dust shalt thou return." Adam (whose name means *red clay*) in this situation resembles more Enkidu than Gilgamesh, for at least Gilgamesh will enjoy splendid kingship, while Adam will work and sweat till he falls over dead. And in a clear allusion to the Sumerian and Babylonian myths of kingship, the tower of Babel in Shinar, Yahweh makes clear his opinion of Annalee's hope that "man can achieve any height": "This is but the start of their undertakings! There will be nothing too hard for them to do" (Gen: 11:6–7, Jerusalem Bible). Yahweh then confuses everyone's language, so the building can't continue. One may note that the precise reason for Yahweh's rejection of Babel's attempt at immortality is likely the same one the narrator of that scene would use to reject Annalee's narrative out of hand—the urge to achieve unlimited heights. Isaiah, borrowing from an ancient Babylonian sun myth, portrays the king of Babylon as a Phaethon figure, attempting to steer the sun's chariot across the heavens, only to plummet to the earth (Isa. 14:12–14). Marlowe's Dr. Faustus simply refuses to accept Yahweh's judgment that certain *gnosis* is forbidden to humans—so Faustus tries an end-run around Yahweh, with the result that he is dragged down to hell screaming, "I'll burn my books." Mary Shelley's Dr. Frankenstein attempts a similar end-run and then refuses to accept responsibility for the ugly results—with disastrous consequences.

Annalee's inability to accept the certain judgment against her—that life was going to be mostly disappointing and that it would inevitably lead to decay and death—may account for what her daughter, Hope Hilton, concluded was extreme mental illness.[41]

This brings us to another issue: the visionary "state of mind." The accusation of mental illness in a visionary is as old a ploy as it is common. Joseph Smith remarked, on sharing his early visions with unsympathetic clergy, that he was "persecuted by those who ought to have been my friends, . . . and if they supposed me to be deluded to have endeavored in a proper and affectionate manner to have reclaimed me" (Pearl of Great Price 2:28),[42] strongly implying that some clearly thought him unbalanced. Indeed, at one time, it was even argued that Smith's first vision was nothing more than a *grand mal* epileptic seizure, when such seizures were thought to be mental illnesses. Saint Joan was of course thought to have suffered from some sort of mental illness, as Shaw notes in his preface to his great play; and Saint Bernadette was tested by psychiatrists, who were ultimately undone by her guilelessness.

Annalee's visions strongly resemble those of the medieval women mystics. One remarks similar phrasing in Annalee's "lookings" and Julian of Norwich's "seeings." One is reminded forcibly of Annalee in the tone, ecstacy, and imagery of Julian's vision of the passion, as recorded in the tenth chapter of *The Revelations of Divine Love*:

> And after this I saw, with bodily sight, in the face of the crucifix that hung before me, and upon which I gazed continually, a part of his passion: the contumely, the spitting, the soiling and the buffeting, and many distressful pains—more than I can tell; with a frequent changing of colour. At one time I saw how half the face, beginning from the ear, was covered over with dried blood, ending in the middle of the face; and after that, the other half, in the same way; and between-whiles, the sight of the one side vanished as quickly as it came.[43]

Compare this with Annalee's vision after her daughter is miraculously healed:

> As I placed her gratefully in her crib, the room seemed filled with a warmer glow than shone from my dim, muffled light. And looking up in wonder, I seemed to see no ceiling to the room—the open dome of heaven shone above. And then, so near that I was startled, I saw the veil of heaven drawn back as the curtains of a stage—and He stood there—with all the glory, majesty and power of eternity stamped upon His brow.
>
> He smiled a smile that must have warmed the universe—a smile which it is impossible to describe. It was so filled with love I wondered why the hard stones did not melt before it. (36)

The only discernable difference between Annalee and Julian here is one of focus, point of view. Annalee must necessarily ignore the Julianic mystery of blood atonement in order to dwell on the cosmic Christ, the heroic figure ascended and translated. And in fact, Skarin manages to avoid in her philosophy both the cross and Gethsemane except as they illustrate purification.

Undeniably, Skarin had the noble goal of purifying herself and concluded as had the Shakers before her that sexual union and giving birth merely perpetuated the error that is mortality. In this goal of purification she has much in common with the medieval anchorite Julian of Norwich, and especially with the mystic Margery Kempe, who tried desperately to keep her husband from performing any sexual act with her. Annalee had the misfortune of living among Mormons, who are wholeheartedly committed to the idea that once one marries, it is perverse *not* to have children, if one is physically able, and that sexuality within marriage is of itself virtuous. Had she been a Catholic, being a woman hermit and completely continent sexually would have been entirely consistent with Catholic doctrine and with a well-established celibate priesthood and monastic tradition for both men and women.

The connection with Catholic mysticism is remarkable and extensive. Just as Mary Magdalene (discussed earlier) ascended and was translated to make her a fit Queen Consort for King Jesus, so Annalee had to find a way to allow for human existence exclusive of sexuality.* This led, notes Love, to Skarin's unusual but weak misreading of the Catholic doctrine of immaculate conception.[44] Her view was that human sexuality was one of the things preventing our ascension–translation, a view not far from William Blake's notion that birth and death are part of a self-consuming cycle which one must abandon through "self-annihilation" (Blake's term). Annalee, as Margery Kempe before her, felt that sexuality, even within marriage, bound one, indeed doomed one to the life cycle of birth–growth–decay–death. Carrying this idea one step further, she suggested that one ought to be able to conceive children just as Mary of old did: untainted fertilization of the egg through intimate contact with the Holy Spirit. The notion itself harks back to the British prophetess of the early nineteenth century, Joanna Southcott, who believed she had conceived a new messiah (whom she styled *Shiloh*) by means of the Holy Spirit. Carrying such an untainted creature within the womb perforce requires that the womb and the entire person be sanctified, as I pointed out in my discussion of the mother of Jesus; for Joanna the (hopefully) viable fetus sanctified both her body and her calling as prophetess. In a similar fashion, conceiving a child in the manner Annalee proposed would sanctify her, facilitating her ascension–translation (a point Love ignores in her zeal to unmask the "devilish" agenda of Skarin). The precise method of conception was of holding hands by a worthy man and woman,†

---

* A colleague, Claudia Harris, a specialist in Irish cultural studies, recently lectured on the bloodiness and inherent mortality connected with female sexuality and fertility as preserved in the Irish earth-mother figure, Kathleen Houlihan: menstruation, the tearing of the hymen on many virgins, the occasional tearing of female genitalia on giving birth, and the afterbirth itself makebloodletting the ultimate fertility symbol. Thus human sacrifice in war or even in peaceful times assures fertility. Claudia noted how difficult it is for Irish women to throw off the yoke of this bloody and terrible mother-figure, and of the stereotypes that grow out of her myth.

† Curiously, Love belittles this lovely metaphor, despite the fact that Mormons traditionally regard the handshake, or "right hand of fellowship," as they call it, as the most spiritual and benign contact between two people of either sex.

which is, in fact, a variation on an ancient gnostic metaphor of a sacred kiss between a man and woman as the essential means of conception.

Yet, rhetorically speaking, there is a carnival-like shell game in some of Annalee's rhetoric—some devices of which I have already made mention—not present in Julian's narrative; and these elements in Skarin, tend, I am afraid, in the direction of self-aggrandizement. Such a splendid self-image may work well if one is an Odysseus, a Herakles, a Jael (the woman warrior of the Book of Judges), or Shakespeare's Portia—that is, the heroic model that the gods notice and reward. However, if one wishes to ascend through *righteousness*; then bravado, cleverness, and self-interest are out of place. Essentially, then, Annalee's narrative is at cross-purposes with itself. As Annalee's own daughter, Hope Hilton, noted, on seeing her mother shortly before Annalee's excommunication from the Mormon church: "All she wanted was to promote herself and her ideas. It was very important to her to have acceptance."[45] Whether Hilton's view is jaundiced is certainly a consideration, but I believe Annalee's rhetoric, in the examples I have offered, supports that view.

The real end stop to Annalee's narrative is provided by her biographers. Love's biography concludes with reproductions of photos of both an official certificate of death and of a genealogist's letter about an official death notice discovered in the California Death Index, not to mention pictures of the grave markers for both Annalee and her last husband, Reason Skarin. Adding insult to injury is a photocopy of an article from a Salt Lake City newspaper claiming that when Annalee was initially "translated" in 1952, she had to return several days later to retrieve her false teeth. There seems little doubt that despite being "translated," both Annalee and Reason Skarin got old and wrinkled and fell to pieces just as the rest of us do.

Yet from a narrative point of view, Annalee's "religious fiction" is a modern version of a tale as old as *Gilgamesh*, and from that viewpoint the question of whether she was "translated" is irrelevant. The only question is, Has Annalee Skarin given the world an enduring and convincing personal narrative? To her hundreds of New Age fans, the answer is obvious, but though I am not a convert to her philosophy, I can admire her ability to resurrect (pardon the pun) an alternative mythology that challenges not only orthodox Christianity but the evidence of living and dying in a fallen world.

Zecharia Sitchin and His Stairway to Heaven: The Brightest Star of New Age Scholarship

While it would be sensational to bring this study into the twenty-first century by focusing on the most recent scandals of the New Age movement, such as the Heaven's Gate horror, there is a New Age phenomenon of far greater import and of vastly more far-reaching effects concerning the mythic phenomenon of ascension–translation: the brilliant commentary of perhaps the only significant Jewish contributor to the New Age phenomenon—Zecharia Sitchin.

He was born in Russia and raised in Palestine, where he acquired a profound knowledge of modern and ancient Hebrew, other Semitic and European languages, the Old Testament, and the history and archeology of the Near East. He is one of the few scholars able to read and understand Sumerian. Sitchin attended and graduated from the University of London, majoring in economic history. A leading journalist and editor in Israel for many years, he now lives and writes in New York.[46]

Though my own accomplishments in ancient and modern languages are far more modest, I am at least enough a Hebraist and philologist to know that Sitchin's skills as a student of ancient language are genuine, though likely others would give him hard arguments for being altogether too speculative philologically and linguistically. There are simply too few Sumerologists for any but the elite to question Sitchin's skills there, but his grasp of history, myth, and ritual ranks with that of Theodor Herzl Gaster (*Thespis*) and Giorgio de Santillana (*Hamlet's Mill*), and he is not as underhanded with his sources as, say, Robert Graves (*The White Goddess*; *King Jesus*). And of all whose publications sit in the New Age stacks at bookstores, save perhaps Carlos Castenada, he is, in my opinion, the only author worth reading. (And, by the by, he is listed in *Who's Who* for his journalistic expertise on Middle East issues.)

His many books in the *Earth Chronicles* (and collateral studies), which began with *The Twelfth Planet* (1976) and most recently offered *The Cosmic Code* (based not on faddish theories of hidden messages in Old Testament Hebrew but on Sumerian astronomy, cosmology, and mathematics), read like science fiction but are in deadly earnest. His approach is reminiscent of Immanuel Velikovsky's literalization of myth narrative and recalibrating of ancient chronology in the *Ages in Chaos* series of 1950–1980. (Velikovsky, a talented amateur in the best sense of the word, was a Freudian psychiatrist and a vigorous and influential advocate for Jewish statehood; to my knowledge, Sitchin has never alluded to nor acknowledged any influence upon his work by this man, who was a founding member of Hebrew University in Israel.) For my purposes here, it hardly matters if Sitchin's theories are correct, which basically assert that in our planet's first years it was the product of a collision between a rogue "twelfth" planet, Nibiru, and a large planet, Tiamat, near Mars and Jupiter; the collision created the asteroid belt, our earth, comets, and the elongated orbit of Nibiru (3600 years) around the sun. The contact allowed basic building blocks of life—amino acids, proteins, and the like—to "jump" to Earth, allowing the eventual appearance of life forms here, while such activity had had a considerable head start on Nibiru. In returning orbits much, much later, advanced civilization from Nibiru came to prehistoric Earth and used their technology to "jump start" civilization, the product of such experiments being Adam and Eve.

But why come to Earth at all? Sitchin is convinced that the rare element gold, beyond its beauty, malleability, and contribution to applied science, was apparently essential for life on Nibiru but was increasingly in short supply. As Genesis reminds us, at the end of the river Pison (one of four rivers flowing from Eden), within the region of Havilah, there is especially pure gold. Sitchin points out that the Anunnaki, who came from Nibiru, settled northeast Africa, Egypt, and Sumer as base camps for acquiring what they needed, extending their influence eventually to Europe, the Indus valley, and even far-flung South America. In Sitchin's reconstruction of ancient chronology, Adam and Eve appear considerably *after* the gods of Nibiru have established their base camps, for the simple reason that the gods needed slaves to tend their orchards and ultimately to do their underground mining. Beyond genetic experimentation to strengthen the gene pool, the gods of Nibiru had no particular plan for coming to Earth other than the immediate acquisitiveness that fired their descent to Earth in the first place. Sitchin's favorite story at symposia and at speaking engagements appears to be of an experience at the *yeshivah*, when young Zecharia inquired why the Hebrew word *nefilim* in Genesis 6 is translated "giants" in the King James Old Testament, for *nefilim* means "those who came down to Earth from heaven." The teacher noted the truth of the youngster's observation, then told him to mind his studies and leave such exegesis to the rabbis. Simply put but these fallen angels, the *b'nai elohim*—literally "the sons of the gods"—were thought to be gods by the local populace, who noted how they ascended and descended from earth to heaven, heaven to earth (heaven being the sky [*ha-shumaim*], with its arc of stars and planets). Sitchin cleverly notices that the indigenous inhabitants, at best cave-dwelling subhumans, must have already been on Earth when the gods arrived in their spaceships, for how could gods be seen descending and ascending in fearful splendor if early humans were not there to see it happen?

In fact, Sitchin continually captures such clever views of the past, because he starts with premises different entirely from those offered him at *yeshivah*. And he is right about the sudden arrival of full-blown civilization, at least in the case of Egypt. One minute the locals are scratching the Nile shore for grubs, the next minute, monarchies, priesthood, elaborate writing systems, grand architecture and art, and knowledge of astronomy appear. The anthropologists can take us back to the beginning of any one civilization, but behind it is a void with no slow evolutionary march, no miserably bad early architecture; in fact, language starts out in an extremely complicated form, and *de*volves (not unlike devolving art in the late Egyptian and Greek kingdoms).*[47]

The exciting narrative twist to Sitchin's account of the ascent and descent of these godlike beings is as exciting as it is unexpected: the gods can and *do* die. If an ant dies, indeed if generations of ants die, yet the powerful being with the deadly spray bottle survives, the human god appears eternal, not subject to death. With shorter life spans, dogs are judged in human terms: Max the German shepherd, at age ten in human years, is age seventy in dog years, making human life spans relatively eternal. If time is really part of the fabric of space, as some believe, perceptions of time become personal and centered on point of view. My brother is several years older than I, yet to most people (including me) he *seems* younger. Young lovers necking in the parking lot feel as though they've had no

---

* As the learned professor of ancient history Hugh W. Nibley wryly observed: "If writing evolved gradually and slowly as everything is supposed to have done, there should be a vast accumulation of transitional scribblings as countless crude and stumbling attempts at writing would leave their marks on stone, bone, clay and wood over countless millenia of groping trial and error. Only there are no such accumulations of primitive writing anywhere. Primitive writing is as illusive as that primitive language the existence of which has never been attested." Nibley, expert in some thirteen languages, including Egyptian hieroglyphics, Greek, Latin, Hebrew, and Arabic, has authored hundreds of articles and books, many appearing in *Revue de Qumran, Vigilae Chritianae,* and the *Encyclopaedia Judaica,* among other prestigious publications.

time at all together, while people recovering from surgery find time slowing down agonizingly ("When is that idiot doctor going to sign my release form?" or "I can't stand this itching, but I have to wear this cast four more weeks—FOUR more weeks!"). Sitchin notes that human life spans are calculated using the solar year, and because Nibiru's elongated orbit yields a 3600-year orbit, the average life span of an Anunnaki prince could be 75 x 3600, or roughly 270,000 earthling years. Thus the early Sumerian king-lists may, under such a theory, be accepted as factual. Among the primitive earth people, such life spans were legendary. Of course, if one has a life span at all, we must, by definition, allow for a birth and death, and indeed, one of these beings was killed by being imprisoned by a jealous rival for the throne: Osiris, one of a number of Anunnaki that settled in Egypt.

Sitchin cleverly draws parallels among Mediterranean mythologies' many pantheons, including Israel's, whose *b'nai elohim* (lit. "sons of God" but thought of as archangels), which to him are clearly a watered-down version of a Babylonian pantheon acquired during the Israelite captivity.[48] In the case of the Greek pantheon, a spiritual fluid, ichor, runs through the gods' veins in place of mortal blood, rendering them immortal (a metamorphosis achieved by eating food denied to mortals—ambrosia, the honey-cake equivalent of wandering Israel's manna, and nectar). The *Iliad* shows us that these gods can be wounded, but they can't be killed (an amusing episode with Aphrodite and Diomedes is good evidence). Adam and Eve have immortality in much the same way, partaking of the fruit of the tree of life, whose pulp and juice become the equivalent of ambrosia and nectar. Though Sitchin does not mention it, Christians seek immortality symbolically in the bread and wine of communion, the ambrosia and nectar, which equate to the flesh and blood of Christ, who is the author of salvation and redemption among Christians and who, in the New Testament, passes the test of temptation in the wilderness that Adam and Eve failed in paradise, being himself the water that slakes thirst eternally, the "first fruits" of the resurrection, the true vine, and the bread of life.

Rather than attempting, as the New Age movement has generally done, to transport and transmute humanity into true immortality and power with the gods of the spaceships, Sitchin has demythologized the gods, making them altogether mortal and subject to the same inconsistencies and even pettiness that characterize humans. The early Romantic British poets, such as Wordsworth and Blake, sought to make God more human (and humane) and to exalt the godliness of all humans, poor or rich, in order to promote egalitarianism on Earth now and in heaven in the afterlife (the implicit message of Wordsworth's great ode "Intimations of Immortality"). Sitchin's approach is unique because it doesn't confer immortality willy-nilly on a pantheon of beings no nobler than ourselves. However, Sitchin's Jewish education and background, at the last, show through, for we learn that Yahweh (Jehovah) is in fact the only truly immortal and flawless God and is the God of the Anunnaki (whether they know it or not) and the ultimate creator of Nibiru and everything else.

Of course, the argument from negation has its problems. (Prove that the ancient Sumerian pantheon and mythology *were not* a literal account of space travelers from a tenth planet who are responsible for all modern civilization.) But a student of myth, literature, and history as I am is quite swept away by the intricacy of his evidence. And in fact, so are others. At the First Sitchin Studies Day, held in conjunction with the 1996 International Forum on New Science at Denver in 1996, Marlene Evans, who holds a Ph.D. in geography from Syracuse and is a professor at SUNY–Empire State College, expounded the idea that Sitchin's approach to human origins presents an altogether discrete paradigm shift.[49] Though the first premise of Sitchin's theory, cosmic Catastrophism, has been around since the founding of the British Royal Society in the seventeenth century (William Whiston and company), the second premise, of the Anunnakis' visits over hundreds of millennia to manipulate DNA and establish civilization, indeed overturns belief systems in the sciences, social sciences, and humanities—religion, anthropology, and mythology included. More impressive still is the contribution of Madeleine Briskin (Ph.D. Brown University), professor of geology at the University of Cincinnati. Her essay offers an astonishing marshaling of solid scientific studies on the "430,000+/– year quasi-astronomical cycle . . . in variable amplitudes of the earth's eccentric orbit," involving analysis of planctonic assemblages, geochemical factors, the magnetic field, transgressions and regressions of sea level, spectral analyses of periodicity, and the much-debated Alvarez Model to establish the scientific likelihood of Sitchin's first premise, that the rogue planet Nibiru collided with Tiamat, producing mass extinctions and leaving the Earth, its moon, and the asteroid belt in its wake, with the "twelfth planet" (according to the Ptolemaic model, but the tenth from a modern view) caught in an elongated orbit around the sun.[50]

Sitchin's second book, *The Stairway to Heaven*, contains a convincing narrative concerning humanity's effort, from ancient times, to avoid dying or even aging; it is the same narrative offered in every instance considered in this little book. It is, however, the rhetorical-narratological strategy for retelling the story, as I have reiterated, that makes the narrative worth studying. Sitchin so far has avoided any exegesis of the New Testament Gospels' declarations about Jesus' position in all this (i.e., who his father *really* was), which may be for the best—one has only to recall Graves's *outré* suggestion in *King Jesus* that a Roman soldier got Mary pregnant to realize that political correctness sells more books than attacks on the Virgin Mary's morals do. Among religious groups, in fact, only the Mormons contend for an anthropomorphic deity, and Sitchin would be disconcerted to hear the Mormon doctrine that the one God—Jehovah—he thinks is utterly Other has a functioning human body with spiritual essence in His veins.

The Stairway to Heaven begins, not with the biblical Jacob's vision of a ladder reaching to heaven with angels ascending and descending, but with a number of examples of human near-misses at gaining immortality without undergoing death. Adam and Eve, Ponce de Leon, and Alexander the Great all have the chance for immortality but lose it because of disobedience, unworthiness, or ignorance of the protocol of the divine family. The ships (rockets) that carried the gods (and any mortals with the right ticket) were not above ground: one had to descend below all things in order to rise above all things, resulting in a figurative expression and an element of myth that, for example, fires the imagination of the Italian poet Dante, who descends to the lowest level of hell, then is guided back through purgatory, and finally to heaven. In the pharaohs' ascent to heaven, examples of which reoccur throughout Egyptian literary tradition, Sitchin describes the path to the underground hangar and gantry:

> And so it was incumbent upon the king to reach the "Hidden Place," to go through its subterranean labyrinths [where divine guardians] open for him secret gates, and lead him to the Eye of Horus, a Celestial Ladder into which he would step—an object which can change hues to blue and red as it is "powered [up]," and then, . . . turned into the Falcon god, he would soar skyward to the eternal Afterlife on the Imperishable Star [Nibiru].[51]

As I have mentioned many times, in the myth of ascension and translation, relatively few humans are invited or allowed to ascend permanently to partake of the ambrosia that would transform an earthling into an Anunnaki, a relatively immortal being. To the contrary, Sitchin accepts without question the Sumerian narrative of the heavenly council and debate over whether or not the humans manufactured by the gods ought to be destroyed in a catastrophic flood (the Genesis story of the Flood being severely redacted and focusing on the Flood from Noah's viewpoint rather than God's). The ziggurats are for Sitchin likely a figurative stairway to heaven, shaped not unlike missiles ready to launch. In Jewish apocrypha, Nimrod builds the tower of Babel so that the mighty hunter can shoot arrows into the heavens and kill the gods (the ultimate game animals!). That particular version of human efforts at ascension is widespread; another instance exists among the Pend-d'Oreille tribe of the Dakotas.[52] It is a remarkable vindication of Sitchin's theory because (1) it suggests that the gods' heavenly dwelling is visible from the ground, creating a horrible sense of loss and envy; (2) it implies that humans knew there was a way to get up there, since they had seen it done; and (3) the gods could be wounded, even killed, with arrows. But one must remember that mythology, whether factual and "true" or not, is preserved by humans with normal human potential for reasoning power, so mythology almost always has sets of premises, evidence, and validations built into it. Myth narrative doesn't simply happen; it's part of a complex relationship between authors and their readers, and between the myths and observable nature. And, in fact, Sitchin has found huge landing platforms used for Anunnaki flying vehicles of several types: Baalbek, in the mountains of Lebanon, containing among the largest stones on Earth (solid stone, not Roman concrete) and encompassing an area of some five *million* square feet.[53]

Sitchin's ability to make a very convincing case for literalizing the myth of ascension–translation has the unfortunate effect of temporarily anaesthetizing his readers, only to have them wake up facing the same stark questions: Is there a God (a real, omniscient God)? Why is there so much evil? Why were we created only to fall apart and return to the dust whence we came? Is there a life after death? What does God have in store for all humanity? What about for me in particular? Why would God allow such haphazard events to shape the destiny of our earth? That is, Sitchin's entire approach is merely another rhetorical strategy to account for the fact that a favored few avoid death completely, ascend to the heavens, and join the divine family, while everyone else finds himself or herself subjected to powers beyond anyone's control, including sickness, death, injustice, and a heap of unanswered questions. Sitchin's narrative of ascension–translation has its own elliptical elements, its own desperate efforts at validation. The possibility that he might be right about all of it is actually beside the point. Just as with the coquettish behavior of the gods to Gilgamesh, we now have the unparalleled dilemma that if the "gods" come back on the return ticket from Nibiru, they are likely to be as self-centered and ill-disposed toward humanity as they were on the previous orbit.

In this light, it is interesting that Velikovsky, whose first book, *Worlds in Collision*, caused such an uproar of indignation in the scientific community with its catastrophic model of human history (a passing comet caused the magical phenomena of Moses and Israel's exodus from Egypt), found a way out of the absurdist universe he unintentionally created with his theories of willy-nilly cosmic crapshoots with the fate of Earth and its human population, an ethical dimension Sitchin's narrative, so far, lacks. Velikovsky's last book, *Mankind in Amnesia*, compiled and published posthumously in 1982, included within its pages an ethical, if only humanistic, imperative growing out of humankind's collective amnesia about the Earth's catastrophic past. In the Foreword, Lynn E. Rose (professor of philosophy, SUNY–Buffalo) summarizes:

> In the section "A Collective Amnesia" of *Worlds in Collision* . . . [Velikovsky's] theory of collective amnesia explains the inability of people to look at the overwhelming evidence of global catastrophes—from all parts of the world—that is unequivocally there, and the unwillingness to see the implications of that evidence.[54]

Velikovsky had learned, through his studies, that modern humanity is so convinced of its own "steady state" (that is, people have survived on this planet for thousands of years, so we can safely assume this model will continue, immutably, for millennia to come) that it has allegorized the catastrophes of the past (comets striking our planet, other planets moving into new orbits, and mass destruction on Earth the result) into poetic allusions, refusing to literalize such metaphors. This "collective amnesia" has so deluded us, in Velikovsky's view, that we believe we cannot be destroyed as a species. Thus, proliferation of nuclear weapons (the threat Velikovsky feared most) and even ecological disasters seem to most of us to be the fears only of radical, bipolar, leftist prophets of doom. Velikovsky seems to have sighed and shaken his head in disappointment that we cannot see the handwriting on the wall:

My most unpopular message I have kept too long within me.... Resistance [to the sociological implications of his message] can take innumerable forms: it can manifest itself in an inability of communication, of talking or doing, in misjudgment, in missing opportunities and omitting and neglecting obligations.[55]

Velikovsky would have felt vindicated indeed had he lived two more decades (he died in 1979). This last book was his most authoritative, for it is about human psychology, and he was a psychiatrist by profession. In the 1980s the terror of "nuclear winter" made a deep impression on America (thanks to Carl Sagan, an astronomer who thought he was an authority in *every* field). A new modified catastrophic model of the end of the dinosaurs has gained wide acceptance, as well as the idea of steady-state geologic periods punctuated (and stratified) by immense disasters, some caused by collision with objects from outer space (meteors, comets, and the like). Velikovsky would have shaken with anticipation when we saw the tremendous effect of a collision with Jupiter by a comet, all of it caught and recorded on sophisticated scientific equipment. Now we can find on PBS serious programs on the threat to Earth of passing comets—and no one is laughing. And at last, with data from melting glaciers, we know global warming is occurring, a potential catastrophe to the ecosystems, though how and *whether* to stop it is an ongoing debate.

Zacharia Sitchin's work, however, is deals with a primordial fear—of death—that finds a remedy only in religion (and, for the educated, in philosophy). So far, Sitchin's own writing has made only the most oblique sorts of references to the role of the Judeo-Christian God, Jehovah. For example, in the third volume, *The Wars of Gods and Men*, Sitchin introduces a very plausible thesis that the biblical patriarch Abraham was a Sumerian prince and that the angels (*malachim*, or "messengers") who aided him and his brother Lot were fulfilling the agenda of Yahweh (Jehovah), not merely the whims of the Anunnaki, the space-gods who, after the near-universal deluge, granted kingship to ordinary mortal humans. He also suggests that a nuclear holocaust centered on Anunnaki holdings near the fabled "cities of the plain" backfired, crippling civilization in general and causing the Anunnaki to retreat in ever-increasing numbers from direct contact with human beings; though Ba'al, Marduk, Tammuz, Ishtar, Isis, and Osiris are religious cults that grew out of an initial human allegiance, in earliest civilization, to the space beings who created, blessed with knowledge from time to time, and terrorized them, forcing them, through marshaling them into armies, to help the gods settle petty disputes among their pantheon. His most recent work, *The Cosmic Code*, has dared to suggest that the Mosaic law may have been produced through stunning miracles of language acquisition, in which Jehovah himself offered to Moses and Israel a magnificent set of codes engraved by God himself (there were two sets of tablets; Moses broke this first set), then later written by Moses, who had been instructed in the streamlined, less-pictorial, sound-based alphabet. This reading of Genesis and Exodus is troubling, of course, for it suggests Jehovah is easily drawn into contests with the Anunnaki, to whom he ought to be (at least for a Jewish boy taught by the rabbis) infinitely superior.

As a Christian, I would hope that this Jewish scholar would clarify and vindicate Yahweh's position in all this hair-pulling and that Sitchin would make a stab at explaining how Christian and Muslim theology and cosmology fit in this paradigm. But I have my doubts that Sitchin will go that far, since there never has been, in New Age philosophy, much urge to rank Jehovah any higher than the visitors from other planets who variously "channel" through mediums and New Age prophets, who come to translate and transport the elect to join the space federation of shamans, disembodied spirits, reincarnated and cloned archons who want only the best for all of us. But neither is Sitchin allowing any New Age anthroposophy to seep into his studies of ancient civilizations. Sitchin is all business, relying on Sumerian cylinder seals or on petroglyphs to make his case. He is straddling two wildly different approaches to processing data. Yet he is to be very much admired, if for no other reason than that he has shown that the myth of ascension and translation is still a viable narrative in the new century.

1. See Lucy Mack Smith, *History of Joseph Smith* (Salt Lake City: Stevens & Wallis, 1945), 54–58, for a moving account of the episode; also, Donna Hill, *Joseph Smith: The First Mormon* (Garden City, NY: Doubleday, 1977), 35–36.

2. Recounted very well in Hill, 145–46.

3. Hyrum and Helen Mae Andrus, eds., *They Knew the Prophet*, (Salt Lake City: Bookcraft, 1974), 42.

4. Ibid., 46.

5. Ibid., 58–59.

6. Ibid., 10.

7. Ibid., 185–86.

8. Ibid., 151.

9. Ibid., 168.

10. Ibid., 184.

11. Dallin Oaks and Marvin Hill, *The Carthage Conspiracy* (Urbana: University of Illinois Press, 1975).

12. Harold Bloom, *Omens of Millennium* (New York: Riverhead Books, 1996), 252.

13. Ibid., 46.

14. *Hymns of The Church of Jesus Christ of Latter-day Saints* (Salt Lake City: The Church of Jesus Christ of Latter-day Saints, 1985), #27.

15. From David Perkins, ed., *English Romantic Writers* (New York: HBJ, 1967), 381.

16. As related by Mary Elizabeth Rollins Lightner, early Mormon convert, in Andrus and Andrus, 24–25.

17. Ibid., 26.

18. *The Journal of Joseph*, ed. Leland R. Nelson (Provo, UT: Council Press, 1979), 232.

19. *Teachings of the Prophet Joseph Smith*, comp. and ed. Joseph Fielding Smith (Salt Lake City: Deseret Book, 1969), 303.

20. Andrus and Andrus, 32.

21. Ibid., 42.

22. Ibid., 35.

23. Ibid., 43.

24. Ibid., 107.

25. Ibid., 23.

26. Ibid., 82–83

27. William E. Berrett, *The Restored Church* (Salt Lake City: Deseret Book, 1973), 205.

28. Ibid., 205.

29. Max Anderson, *The Polygamy Story: Fiction and Fact* (Salt Lake City: Publishers Press, 1979), 92.

30. *Journal of Discourses* (Liverpool, England: The Church of Jesus Christ of Latter-day Saints, 1853), 4:285–86; also Anderson, 94.

31. Samuel O. Bennion, as quoted in Anderson, 97.

32. *History of the Reorganized Church of Jesus Christ of Latter Day Saints* (Independence, MO: Herald, 1976–78), 89.

33. Gloria Love, *Annalee Skarin's Mis-Translation of the Prophet Joseph Smith, Mormonism, and Her Influence on New Age Philosophies* (Midvale, UT: Monarch, 1995), 18.

34. Ibid., 19.

35. Ibid., 21.

36. Ibid., 25.

37. Ibid., 27.

38. Annalee Skarin, *Ye Are Gods* (Logan, UT: N.p., 1948). Future page references will be cited parenthetically within the text.

39. Eric von Daniken, *Chariots of the Gods* (New York: Putnam's, 1970).

49. Immanuel Velikovsky, *Oedipus and Akhnaton* (Garden City, NY: Doubleday, 1960); Giorgio de Santillana, *Hamlet's Mill* (Boston: Gambit, 1969); Sitchin, *The Wars of Gods and Men*.

41. Noted in Love, 24, and in Hope Hilton's own book ms., *Descent into Madness*, kept at the University of Utah Marriott Library.

42. The Pearl of Great Price (Salt Lake City: The Church of Jesus Christ of Latter-day Saints, 1979).

43. Julian of Norwich, *The Revelations of Divine Love*, trans. James Walsh (Wheathamptstead, England: Anthony Clarke, 1973).

44. Love, 140–45, contains a useful summary of the doctrine.

45. Ibid., 24.

46. www/crystalinks.com/sitchen[sic].html. 22 January 2001.

47. Hugh W. Nibley, "Genesis of the Written Word," in *Nibley on the Timely and Timeless: Classic Essays of Hugh W. Nibley* (Provo, UT: Religious Studies Center, BYU, 1978), 104.

48. Bloom, 39.

49. "The Paradigm Has Shifted: What's Next?" *Of Heaven and Earth: Essays Presented at the First Sitchin Studies Day,* ed. Zecharia Sitchin (Escondido, CA: The Book Tree, 1996), 43–71.

50. Madeleine Briskin, "The 430,000+/- Years Pulsation of Earth: Is There a 10th Planet Connection?" *Of Heaven and Earth: Essays Presented at the First Sitchin Studies Day,* ed. Zecharia Sitchin (Escondido, CA: The Book Tree, 1996), 73–89.

51. Zecharia Sitchin, *The Stairway to Heaven*, Book 2 of the *Earth Chronicles* (New York: Avon, 1980), 44.

52. It is recorded in an appendix to volume 2 of Apollodorus in the LOEB Classics collection.

53. Sitchin, *Stairway*, 168–88.

54. Lynn E. Ross, Foreword to Immanuel Velikovsky, *Mankind in Amnesia* (Garden City, NY: Doubleday, 1982), vii–viii.

55. Velikovsky, *Mankind in Amnesia*, 207–8.

7 Conclusion

Christianity wins the prize as the most democratic religion in its grand attempt to offer something like ascension and translation to everyone—everyone, that is, who is alive and "born again" when Jesus returns to render final judgment and reign on Earth for a thousand years as the heir to David's throne. The Heaven's Gate group were apparently unaware that among charismatic born-again Christians it is a foregone conclusion that if one is alive and a faithful Christian at the Second Coming of Jesus, she or he will be caught up bodily to meet Jesus in the air as He descends in glory (the event is colorfully called "The Rapture"). Being "caught up" this way is much the best spot to be in, since those remaining on the ground will be burned and altogether destroyed. First Thessalonians 4:16–17 declares,

> For the Lord himself shall descend from heaven with a shout, with the voice of the archangel, and with the trump of God: and the dead in Christ shall rise first:
> Then we which are alive and remain shall be caught up together with them in the clouds, to meet the Lord in the air: and so shall we ever be with the Lord.

Revelation, or The Apocalypse, reminds those who are earthbound at that day,

> And there fell upon men a great hail out of heaven, every stone about the weight of a talent: and men blasphemed God because of the plague of the hail; for the plague thereof was exceeding great. (16:21)

> Therefore shall her [Babylon's] plagues come in one day, death, and mourning, and famine; and she shall be utterly burned with fire. (18:8)

This ending is quite a twist; no one will know who the true heroes and villains are until that moment when the righteous are caught up. That is, those who are earthbound will likely be completely surprised by the heroism of those so caught up. There will be no preceding narrative of their cunning, of their bravery, of their divine genealogy, or even of their absolute obedience and righteousness. The seal of their ascension is invisible, written on their hearts because of their Christian sacrifice of broken hearts and contrite spirits. The grace of Christ alone determines whether they will be alive at his coming; indeed, they may be as surprised as anyone when they suddenly ascend. Mormons believe such people will be translated as well; among young Mormons, these lucky people are called "twinklers," because they are transformed "in the twinkling of an eye" (D&C 43:32).

That modern people in the cultures of the West would be surprised, even shocked at being passed over for such an honor, while others they thought their inferiors mount to heaven, is playfully explored in Flannery O'Connor's short story "Revelation," in which Mrs. Turpin, barbarically attacked in the physician's waiting room by a sullen girl ironically named Mary Grace, is told she is an "old warthog out of hell." This simply undoes the woman, for being a white Southern pig farmer's wife with pleasant if plump features allowed her the luxury of thanking God continually that she was neither a "nigger" nor "white trash." After dragging her cloddish husband back to the farm following the waiting room incident, she chances to look out over the field, and a vision opens up to her of white trash, blacks, even the mentally handicapped walking joyfully up the stairway to heaven, and behind them all, in last place, are the sober, hymn-singing middle-class people she had always identified with, and whom she expected to stand at the head of the conga line. O'Connor's acerbic wit aside, we are cautioned at the outset by Jesus himself that those who were counted first would be last and that those desiring the best seats at feasts might end up served last at the banquet of Jehovah.

There are a remarkable number of people who seem not to fear death at all. My father, who was far more devout than my mother, feared death far more than she does*—indeed, she can't wait to sluff off her all-too-mortal coil. Many today see

---

* She chased him around the house for months, pestering him for his signature on the form for their "living will."

death as an affirmation of life, in fact the last resounding sforzando of life. Many find death far less odious than a life of suffering (I am sometimes in that camp). I had an atheist office partner at one time who would not bat an eyelash at the specter of death. And, in most religions, the goal is to see death not as an Event, but as simple a transition as walking into the next room. Emily Dickinson's poetry captures this whimsy to perfection: "Because I could not stop for Death, / He kindly stopped for me"; "I heard a fly buzz when I died"; or "I died for beauty," in which two corpses find pleasant conversation in the shared experience of having died for what they believe in—a conversation interrupted when moss seals their mouths shut.

No one goes to more trouble to *look* alive, however, than dead Americans. Such scandal-mongering as *The American Way of Death* and *The High Cost of Dying* long ago exposed the bizarre harking back to Egyptian funerary rites that typifies American mortuary science. It is not that most of these businesses are not legitimate, caring (if immensely profitable) organizations; it is rather the extraordinary lengths to which we will go to prove the dead are not really dead but, at worst, sleeping. Viewings have been compared to throwing away the banana and eating the banana peel, though that simile in particular is entirely unsuited to discussing corpses. More to the purpose is what I would call the Gilgamesh syndrome, mentioned early on: if we are doomed to mortality, let us be at the least forever young—the state of A. E. Housman's athlete dying young, where people flock to gaze at death, only to "find unwithered on its curls / The garland briefer than a girl's." One who dies young is forever young; even more metaphorical is the "cold pastoral" of Keats's Grecian Urn, where the "happy, happy boughs" cannot shed their leaves. Or perhaps our mortuary viewings capture the immortality of Shakespeare's young, dashing patron, whose "eternal summer shall not fade" because, at the peak moment, the bard has immortalized the fair friend in verse. Mortuary science is so advanced that distraught bereaved sometimes swear they can see the departed's chest rising and falling. In my father's case, he looked considerably healthier in his casket than he did just two weeks before his death, when every movement bespoke pain, struggle, and leaden fatigue.

The Gilgamesh syndrome has made plastic surgeons fabulously wealthy, for though their profession's ethical obligation was to take people scarred by accidents, illnesses, and terrible genetic twists and transform them into *un*noticeably ordinary people, they often ended up selling out to the rich and famous who went back to the doctor ad nauseam to erase every line, every wrinkle, every bag, every puff and pouch. Make-up enjoys a similarly perverse evolution, and at the dawn of the eighteenth century, William Congreve's comedy of manners *The Way of the World* exposed the shameless quest for eternal youth through wigs, false moles, and thick make-up. In the case of Lady Wishfort her makeup is a veritable Mardi Gras mask that, when worn, allows her to pretend, without the slightest compunction, that she is fifteen and can play the coquette with boys young enough to be her grandchildren.

From this desperate attempt to flee maturity comes an equal but opposite reaction: young girls whose eyes glisten with the generous moisture natural to young eyes, whose cheeks are rosy because of healthy blood circulation, whose skin is soft and smooth, unsullied by worry and harsh weather, and whose eyebrows, eyelids, nostrils, ears, and lips are delicate, even elvish in their subtlety, can't wait to wear lipstick, eye shadow, blush, base, eyeliner, and to style their hair and shape their nails so they can look more mature, more "adult."

Editorialist Anna Quindlen summed up this collective insanity with alarming success: "Taken together, the rise of the funeral parlor, the invention of the Stair Master and the ascendancy of the low-fat diet have had this pernicious effect: the subconscious belief that we will live forever." The old question Gilgamesh put to the gods has been rephrased for the twenty-first century, according to Ms. Quindlen: "But if the abs are tight, the eyes unlined, the hands unspotted, the hairline intact, if 55 is the new 40, then can't the inevitable be, if not avoided, at least indefinitely deferred?"*

Thus I contend that the ideas of ascension and translation are alive and well in the twenty-first century. The metamorphoses of the narratives over thousands of years are monuments both to the collective unconscious and to the anxiety of influence, the former a vindication of Jung and the latter a vindication of Harold Bloom (and ultimately Freud). The narratives keep religions alive and unpredictable, give us childlike hopes and dreams, and offer literature an endless source of metaphor and imagery. They define the difference between humans and gods, yet bind humans to the gods and make humans more godlike and gods more humane. Whether I have done justice to the topic or not, I have at least made a strong case for more precise classification of the various destinies of human beings at the gates of death.

---

* "The Last Word: Leg Waxing and Life Everlasting," *Newsweek*, 23 April 2001, 64.

Bibliography

Abraham and Isaac (Brome). In *The Genius of the Early English Theater*, ed. Sylvan Barnet, Morton Berman, and William Burto. Mentor Series. New York: New American Library, 1962.

Anderson, Max. *The Polygamy Story: Fiction and Fact*. Salt Lake City: Publishers Press, 1979.

Andrus, Hyrum, and Helen Mae Andrus, eds. *They Knew the Prophet*. Salt Lake City: Bookcraft, 1974.

Bascom, William. "The Forms of Folklore: Prose Narratives." *Journal of American Folklore* 78 (January/March 1965): 4–5, 79–105.

Baigent, Michael, Richard Leigh, and Henry Lincoln *Holy Blood, Holy Grail*. New York: Delacorte Press, 1982.

Bernstein, Carl, and Marco Politi. *His Holiness: John Paul II and the Hidden History of Our Time*. New York: Doubleday, 1996.

Berrett, William E. *The Restored Church: A Brief History of the Growth and Doctrines of The Church of Jesus Christ of Latter-day Saints*. 15th ed. rev. and enl. Salt Lake City: Deseret Book, 1973.

Bevington, David, ed. *Medieval Drama*. Boston: Houghton Mifflin, 1975.

Bjork, Robert E., ed. *Cynewulf: Basic Readings*. New York: Garland Press, 1996.

Blake, William. *The Complete Poetry and Prose of William Blake*. Ed. David Erdman. New York: Doubleday, 1988.

Block, Edward A. "Originality, Controlling Purpose, and Craftsmanship in Chaucer's *Man of Law's Tale*." *PMLA* 68 (1953): 572–616.

Bloom, Harold. *The American Religion*. New York: Simon and Schuster, 1992.

Bloom, Harold. *The Anxiety of Influence*. New York: Oxford University Press, 1973.

Bloom, Harold. *Omens of Millennium: The Gnosis of Angels, Dreams, and Resurrection.* New York: Riverhead Books, 1996.

Bloomfield, Morton. "Distance and Predestination in *Troilus and Criseyde.*" *PMLA* 72 (March 1957): 14–26.

Bodley, R. V. C. *The Messenger: The Life of Mohammed.* New York: Greenwood Press, 1946.

Book of J, The. Trans. David Rosenberg. Commentary Harold Bloom. New York: Grove Weidenfeld, 1990.

Book of Mormon, The. Salt Lake City: The Church of Jesus Christ of Latter-day Saints, 1981.

Briskin, Madeleine. "The 430,000+/- Years Pulsation of Earth: Is There a 10th Planet Connection?" In *Of Heaven and Earth: Essays Presented at the First Sitchin Studies Day,* ed. Zecharia Sitchin, 73–89. Escondido, CA: The Book Tree, 1996.

Brooks, Polly Schoyer. *Beyond the Myth: The Story of Joan of Arc.* New York: J. B. Lippincott, 1990.

Brough, R. Clayton. *They Who Tarry: The Doctrine of Translated Beings.* Bountiful, UT: Horizon, 1976.

Budge, E. A. W. *Legends of Our Lady Mary the Perpetual Virgin and Her Mother Hanna.* Oxford: Oxford University Press, 1933.

Bynum, Caroline Walker. *Fragmentation and Redemption: Essays on Gender and the Human Body in Medieval Religion.* New York: Zone Books, 1992.

Byron, Lord. *George Gordon, Lord Byron: Selected Works.* Ed. Edward Bostetter. New York: Holt, Rinehart, and Winston, 1972.

Campbell, Joseph. *The Hero with a Thousand Faces.* 2d ed. Bollingen Series. Princeton, NJ: Princeton University Press, 1968.

Catholic Encyclopedia. [Electronic Version.]

Chaucer, Geoffrey. *The Complete Works of Geoffrey Chaucer.* Boston: Houghton Mifflin, 1933.

Chaucer, Geoffrey. *Riverside Chaucer, The.* Ed. Larry D. Benson. Boston: Houghton Mifflin, 1987.

Cid Compeador. Ed. H. Butler Clarke. New York: Putnam, 1897.

Clemoes, Peter. "Cynewulf's Image of the Ascension." In *Cynewulf: Basic Readings*, ed. Robert E. Bjork, 109–32. New York: Garland Press, 1996.

Conlee, John W. "The Meaning of *Troilus*: Ascension to the Eighth Sphere." *Chaucer Review* 7.1 (Summer 1972): 27–30.

Cunneen, Sally. *In Search of Mary: The Woman and the Symbol*. New York: Ballantine Books, 1996.

Davis, Whitney M. "The Ascension-Myth in the Pyramid Texts." *Journal of Near Eastern Studies* 36.3 (July 1977): 161–79.

de Santillana, Giorgio, and Hertha von Dechend. *Hamlet's Mill*. Boston: Godine, 1977.

Doctrine and Covenants of The Church of Jesus Christ of Latter-day Saints, The. Salt Lake City: The Church of Jesus Christ of Latter-day Saints, 1981.

Doane, A. N., ed. *Genesis A: A New Edition*. Madison: University of Wisconsin Press, 1978.

Dream of the Rood, The. In *The Norton Anthology of English Literature*. 2 vols. 5th ed. New York: W. W. Norton, 1986.

Dundes, Alan. "The Hero Pattern and the Life of Jesus." In *In Quest of the Hero*, 179–203. Princeton, NJ: Princeton University Press, 1990.

Encyclopaedia Britannica, 1926.

Encyclopaedia Judaica [Computer File]. CD-ROM edition. Shaker Heights, OH: Judaica Multimedia, 1997.

Epic of Gilgamesh, The. Trans. N. K. Sandars. New York: Penguin Books, 1972.

Ethiopian Book of Enoch, The. Trans. Richard Laurence. 1821. Rev. and enl., Oxford: J. H. Parker, 1838.

Evans, Marlene. "The Paradigm Has Shifted: What's Next?" In *Of Heaven and Earth: Essays Presented at the First Sitchin Studies Day*, ed. Zecharia Sitchin, 43–71. Escondido, CA: The Book Tree, 1996.

The Fifty-Third Chapter of Isaiah according to the Jewish Interpreters (translations). Ed. and trans. S. R. Driver and Adolf Neubauer. 2 vols. Library of Biblical Studies. 1876–77. Reprint, New York: Ktav, 1969.

Gale, Robert L. *A Nathaniel Hawthorne Encyclopedia*. New York: Greenwood Press, 1991.

Gaster, Theodor Herzl. *Thespis: Ritual, Myth and Drama in the Ancient Near East*. Rev. ed. New York: Harper & Row, 1966.

Gaull, Marilyn, ed. *English Romanticism*. New York: W. W. Norton, 1988.

Gellrich, Jesse M. *The Idea of the Book in the Middle Ages*. Ithaca, NY: Cornell University Press, 1985.

Gerhard, Joseph. "Chaucer's, Coinage: Foreign Exchange and the Puns of the Shipman's Tale." *Chaucer Review* 17 (1983): 341–57.

Girard, René. *Job: The Victim of His People*. Trans. Yvonne Freccero. Stanford, CA: Stanford University Press, 1987.

Girard, René. *Violence and the Sacred*. Trans. Patrick Gregory. Baltimore: Johns Hopkins, 1977.

Golden Legend: Readings of the Saints, The. Trans. William Granger Ryan. Princeton, NJ: Princeton University Press, n.d.

Gore, Rick. "Pharaohs of the Sun." *National Geographic*, April 2001, 35–57.

Graves, Robert. *King Jesus*. New York: Minerva, 1946.

Graves, Robert, and Joshua Podro. *The Nazarene Gospel Restored*. London: Cassell, 1953.

Grosz, Oliver J. G. H. "Man's Imitation of the Ascension: The Unity of Christ II." In *Cynewulf: Basic Readings*, ed. Robert E. Bjork, 95–108. New York: Garland Press, 1996.

Hamilton, Edith. *Mythology*. 1940. Reprint, New York: Mentor, 1969.

Hawthorne, Nathaniel. *The Complete Novels and Selected Tales of Nathaniel Hawthorne*. Ed. Norman Holmes Pearson. New York: Modern Library, 1937.

Heidmann, Mark. *Melville and the Bible: Leading Themes in the Marginalia and Major Fiction, 1850–1856*. Ph.D. diss., Yale University, 1979.

Heindel, Max. *Freemasonry and Catholicism*. London: L. N. Fowler, 1919.

Helms, Randel. *Gospel Fictions*. Amherst, NY: Prometheus, 1988.

Hill, Donna. *Joseph Smith: The First Mormon.* Garden City, NY: Doubleday, 1977.

Hilton, Hope. "Descent into Madness." Ms. Located at the J. Willard Marriott Library, University of Utah.

History of the Reorganized Church of Jesus Christ of Latter Day Saints. Independence, MO: Herald Publishing House, 1976.

Holy Bible. King James Version (KJV).

Homer. *Odyssey of Homer, The.* Trans. Ennis Rees. New York: Macmillan, 1991.

Hosley, Richard. *Shakespeare's Holinshed.* New York: Putnam, 1968.

Jerusalem Bible, The.

Jones, Edward T. "A Comparative Study of Ascension Motifs in World Religions." In *Deity and Death*, ed. Spencer J. Palmer, 79–105. Provo, UT: Religious Studies Center of Brigham Young University, 1978.

Journal of Discourses. Liverpool, England: The Church of Jesus Christ of Latter-day Saints, 1853.

Keats, John. *John Keats: The Complete Poems.* Ed. John Barnard. New York: Penguin, 1988.

Kübler-Ross, Elisabeth. *On Death and Dying.* New York: Macmillan, 1970.

Leatherdale, Clive. *The Origins of Dracula.* London: William Kimber, 1987.

Lewis, C. S. *Miracles.* New York: Macmillan, 1947.

Lewis, C. S. *A Preface to Paradise Lost.* 1942. Reprint, Oxford: Oxford University Press, 1970.

Lewis, C. S. *That Hideous Strength.* 1945. Reprint, New York: Macmillan, 1965.

Library: Apollodorus, The. Trans. James George Frazer. 2 vols. LOEB Classics. Cambridge, MS: Harvard University Press, 1921.

Love, Gloria [pen-name]. *Annalee Skarin's Mis-Translation of [the] Prophet Joseph Smith, Mormonism, and Her Influence on New Age Philosophies.* Midvale, UT: Monarch, 1995.

Maxwell-Stuart, P. G. "Interpretations of the Name Oedipus." *Maia* 27 (1975): 37–43.

Melville, Herman. *Moby-Dick*. New York: Penguin, 1992.

Milton, John. *The Complete Poetical Works of John Milton*. Boston: Houghton Mifflin, 1924.

Milton, John. *Samson Agonistes*. In *The Complete Poetical Works of John Milton*. Ed. William Vaughn Moody. Boston: Houghton Mifflin, 1924.

Milton, John. *A Treatise on Christian Doctrine*. Trans. Charles Sumner. Cambridge: Cambridge University Press, 1825.

Minnis, Alastair. "Aspects of the Medieval French and English Traditions of the *De Consolatione Philosophiae*." In *Boethius: His Life, Thought, and Influence*, ed. Margaret Gibson, 312–61. Oxford: Blackwell, 1981.

Mycoff, David. *A Critical Edition of the Legend of Mary Magdalena from Caxton's Golden Legende of 1483*. Salzburg: Institut fur Anglistik und Amerikanistik, 1985.

Nag Hammadi Library in English, The. Gen. ed. James M. Robinson. New York: Harper & Row 1977.

Nelson, Leland R., ed. *The Journal of Joseph*. Mapleton, UT: Council Press, 1979.

Nettl, Paul. *Mozart and Masonry*. New York: Philosophical Library, 1957.

Nibley, Hugh W. "Evangilium Quadraginta Dierum." *Vigilae Christianae* 20 (1966): 1–24.

Old Testament Pseudepigrapha, The. 2 vols. Ed. James H. Charlesworth. Garden City, NY: Doubleday, 1985.

Ovid. *Metamorphoses*. Trans. Rolfe Humphries. Bloomington: Indiana University Press, 1955.

Pagels, Elaine. *The Gnostic Gospels*. New York: Random House, 1979.

Pagels, Elaine. *The Origin of Satan*. New York: Vintage, 1996.

Palmer, Spencer J. *Deity and Death*. Provo, UT: Religious Studies Center of Brigham Young University, 1978.

Pearl of Great Price, The. Salt Lake City: The Church of Jesus Christ of Latter-day Saints, 1982.

Pelikan, Jaroslav. *Mary through the Centuries: Her Place in the History of Culture*. New Haven: Yale University Press, 1996.

Perkins, David. *English Romantic Writers*. New York: Harcourt Brace Jovanovich, 1967.

Raglan, FitzRoy Richard Somerset (Lord Raglan). *The Hero: A Study in Tradition, Myth, and Drama*. Westport, CT: Greenwood Press, 1975.

Ratzinger, Joseph. *Daughter Zion: Meditations on the Church's Marian Belief*. Trans. John M. McDermott. San Francisco: Ignatius Press, 1983.

Schonfield, Hugh J. *The Passover Plot*. New York: Bernard Guis, 1965.

Secrets of Enoch, The. In *The Lost Books of the Bible and the Forgotten Books of Eden*. New York: Alpha House, 1926–27.

Sepher ha-Yashar. (The Book of Jasher.) 1840. Reprint, Salt Lake City: J. H. Parry, 1887.

Shaw, George Bernard. *Saint Joan*. New York: Penguin, 1946.

Shelley, Mary. *Frankenstein*. New York: Airmont, 1963.

Sitchin, Zecharia. *The Stairway to Heaven*. Book 2 of the *Earth Chronicles*. New York: Avon, 1980.

Sitchin, Zecharia. *The War of Gods and Men*. Santa Fe: Bear & Co., 1992.

Skarin, Annalee. *Ye Are Gods*. Logan, UT: N.p., 1948.

Smith, Joseph. *Teachings of the Prophet Joseph Smith*. Comp. and ed. Joseph Fielding Smith. Salt Lake City: Deseret Book, 1969.

Smith, Lucy Mack. *History of Joseph Smith*. Salt Lake City: Stevens & Wallis, 1945.

Sorensen, Peter J. "Dualism in Wordsworth's *Michael*." *Mythes, Croyances, et Religions dans le Monde Anglo-Saxon* 13 (1995): 17–25.

Sorensen, Peter J. *William Blake's Gnostic Vision*. Salzburg: Salzburg University, 1995.

Spenser, Edmund. *The Fairie Queene*. In *Poetical Works*. Ed. J. C. Smith and E. de Selincourt. New York: Oxford University Press, 1993.

Sullivan, Karen. *The Interrogation of Joan of Arc*. Minneapolis: University of Minnesota Press, 1999.

Sumner, Joseph. "'His Barge Ycleped Was the Maudelayne': *Canterbury Tales A 410*." *Names* 31 (1983): 207–10.

Tolkien, J. R. R. *The Lord of the Rings*. New York: Ballantine, 1983.

Tvedtnes, John A. *The Church of the Old Testament*. Salt Lake City: Deseret Book, 1980.

Ulansey, David. *The Origins of the Mithraic Mysteries*. New York: Oxford University Press, 1989.

Velikovsky, Immanuel. *Mankind in Amnesia*. Garden City, NY: Doubleday, 1982.

Velikovsky, Immanuel. *Oedipus and Akhnaton: Myth and History*. Garden City, NY: Doubleday, 1960.

Wasson, John. "The Secular Saint Plays of the Elizabethan Era." In *The Saint Play in Medieval Europe*, ed. Clifford Davidson, 241–60. Kalamazoo, MI.: Medieval Institute Publications, 1986.

Webster, John. *The Duchess of Malfi. The Norton Anthology of British Literature* 1. New York: W. W. Norton, 1995.

Wilde, Oscar. *The Picture of Dorian Gray*. Hertfordshire, England: Wordsworth Classics, 1992.

Wordsworth, William. *Poetical Works of William Wordsworth*. 5 vols. Ed. E. de Selincourt and Helen Darbishire. 2d ed. rev. Oxford: Clarendon Press, 1952–1959.

"Zecharia Sitchin." www/crystalinks.com/sitchen[sic].html. 22 January 2002.

Index

A

Aaron, 39, 177; rod of, 14, 177
Abel, 30n, 140
Abraham, 19, 24, 31–33, 38n, 61, 63, 73, 128, 190n, 210–11; bargains with Yahweh, 29; God covenants with, 164; and Isaac, 69n; life span of, 95n; Sumerian prince, 61, 96n, 164, 240
Abraham and Isaac (Brome MS), 61, 80n, 211n
Abram. *See* Abraham
Absalom, 29
Absalom and Achitophel, 117
abyss, 79, 82, 120. *See also* Chaos; Hades; hell; *sheol*; underworld
Achilles, 13, 160; descent into underworld of, 162; Hector's body returned by, 97, 155
Achilles Heel, 158
Achitophel, 118
Actaeon, 100
Acts, book of, 54–55, 64, 70, 80, 94n, 157n, 172–75, 178, 188
Adam, 27, 29, 92n, 128, 176, 233, 237; creation of, 155, 158; driven from Garden of Eden, 70n, 158, 177; fall of, 72, 113, 138, 163; in Garden, 155, 158, 178; life span of, 95n; Milton's, 138, 144; naming of animals by, 137; new, 123, 135; Second, 70n, 113, 123, 135; work by sweat of brow by, 227
Adonis, 121
Adonis, 130, 131
Adventists. *See* Seventh-Day Adventists
Aeneas, 63, 79
Aeschylus, 138
Africa, 168, 233. *See also* Egypt
afterlife, 3, 12, 96, 101, 164, 222, 236–37
Agamemnon, 84, 155
Ages in Chaos, 232
Agincourt, 194, 197, 202–3
Ahab (Captain), 146–48; as Yahweh, 146–47
Ahab (king), 51, 146
Akhenaton, 102–4
albatross, 131. *See also* birds
alchemy, 109, 121, 135–36
Alexander the Great, 106, 139, 175, 237
Allah, 84, 165
altar, 16, 61, 69n, 107, 140, 193
ambrosia, 84, 235, 238
America(n), 199; Byronic hero, 132, 136; conservative, 166; hero, 86–87, 142–43; 148; ideals, 215; religion, 209–22, 216n; transcendentalism, 215, 222; writers, 118
American Religion, The, 209, 214
Ancient Mariner, 131, 133
Andrew, 70
Andrus, Helen Mae, 212n
Andrus, Hyrum, 212n
angel(s), 4, 21–22, 32, 42, 45n, 55, 73, 74, 168, 176–79, 187–88, 193–96; and Abraham, 61; and barren women, 177; and Cain, 140; as comforter, 146; definition of, 6; Elijah as, 37; Enoch as, 215; fiery, 124, 137, 179; and Gideon, 107; gnostic, 122; guardian, 7; as guides, 64n, 194n; immortality of, 176–77; Jacob wrestles with, 22, 25, 32, 210; on Jacob's ladder, 237; Jesus Christ as, 215; John to become, 42; as messengers, 51, 78, 96n–97n, 123, 145, 158, 178, 240; and Michael (the archangel), 193; Milton's, 57n, 91, 111; ministering, 42; Moroni, 218; Moses as, 51; as protectors, 213; of Satan, 163; Satan as, 158–59, 163. *See also* archangel(s); *b'nai elohim*; fallen angel(s); sons of god
Anglican church, 199–200
Anglo-Saxon poetry, 108–10, 133
Annunciation, 178
Anointed One, 179; Elijah as an, 219. *See also* Christ; Jesus; king of the Jews; Master; Messiah
Antigone, 98–101, 104
Antigone, 98, 101
anti-hero, 25, 66, 87, 142, 162; Byronic hero as, 132, 143; Cain as, 136–39; Don Juan as, 118; Dracula as, 141; literary, 134, 143; Satan as, 164; tradition, 142; Vlad the Impaler as, 134
Anubis, 190n
Anunnaki, 233–41
anxiety of influence, 16, 117
Anxiety of Influence, 30, 50, 56
Aphrodite, 34, 100, 128, 136, 235
Apocalypse, 43, 54, 245
apocryphal Gospels, 74
Apollo, 93, 99, 101, 131, 143, 156–57
Apollodorus, 92n
apostles, 14, 39, 44, 50, 52, 52n–53n, 70, 75, 108, 113, 172, 181; and Mary, 168, 176; as missionaries, 68n, 174; Peter chief of, 40; and Resurrection, 182. *See also* disciples
apotheosis, 1, 134, 190, 215, 218

258 Index

Aquinas, Thomas, 106–7
archangel(s), 26, 149n, 168–70, 235, 239, 245. *See also* angel(s)
archons, 63, 241. *See also* b'nai elohim; fallen angels; *nefilim*; Watchers
Ares, 34, 100
Ark of the Covenant, 28, 93n, 128, 179
Arnold, Matthew, 141
Arrington, Leonard J., 212n
art(s), 9, 28, 86, 88, 104, 130, 157–58, 170; Christian, 168; Egyptian, 101–2, 234; English, 199; Greek, 101–2, 234; Judeo-Christian, 28; Moorish, 168
Artemis, 128
Arthur, King, 166, 192n, 193
Articles of Faith, 63
artist as hero, 118–19, 125–26, 130–32
Ascension Day, 39–40, 108, 193
assumption, 4, 5, 142, 187–88; of Mary Magdalene, 180–89; of Virgin Mary 168–80. *See also* dormition
astronomy, 232, 234
Athanasius, 170
Athena, 101, 136
Athens, 66, 99
Atlantis, 101
Aton, 102–3
atonement, 1, 60, 99–100, 131, 141, 177; of Christ, 16, 75, 85, 113, 114, 130, 140–41, 169, 215, 223; for sins, 5. *See also* blood atonement
Aubis, 190n
Augustine, 65–66
Augustus, 106–7
Aztec mythology, 156–57

B

Ba'al, 38–39, 147, 240
Baalbek, 238
Babel, tower of, 228, 238
Babylonia(n): Empire, 12; literature, 8, 27n; myths, 19, 79, 105n, 137, 159, 163, 227–28; pantheon, 23, 38, 136, 235. *See also* Gilgamesh; *Gilgamesh* epic; Sumerian
Bacchus, 131
Baigent, Michael, 185
Baker, Herschel, 200
Balaam's ass, 158
baptism, 173; for the dead, 63; of Jesus, 113
Baptist, John the. *See* John the Baptist

Baptists, 121n, 165
Batman, 143
Bayle, Pierre, 139
"Beast in the Jungle," 141
beauty, 2, 41, 72, 83, 130; of gold, 233; of Joan of Ark, 200; of Mary, 178; of religion, 175
Beloved Disciple. *See* John the Beloved
Benjamin, 30n; tribe of, 73
Bennett, John C., 214n
Beowulf, 2, 28, 34, 163, 192n
Bernadette, 54n, 87, 97, 228
Bethlehem, 172, 176, 186
Bevington, David, 187
Beyond the Myth, 191
Bible, 84, 85, 98n, 125, 220, 226; KJV, 193; Satan in, 156, 159, 166–67, 226. *See also* New Testament; Old Testament
"Bible of Hell," 122
bier, 178–79, 181, 220
Billy Budd, 87
binary opposition, 12, 35, 53, 63, 66, 81
birds, 131, 147n. *See also* albatross; Falcon god; falcon-flight
birth, 120, 235; of Adam, 29n, 137; Annalee Skarin's view of, 229–30; barren women giving, 96, 177; of Enkidu, 13; of Esau, 29; illegitimate, 92; of Jesus, 119, 173, 186; of Mary Magdalene's son, 185–86; of Samson, 96; William Blake's view of, 230
birthright: of Esau, 29; of Jesus, 30n; in Old Testament, 30n
Blake, William, 52n, 81, 118–25; and antihero, 118, 137; gnosis vs. blood atonement in, 118–25; Milton, comments on, 112; religious views of, 118–125, 155n, 196, 235–36; self-annihilation view of, 124–25, 196, 230; "true contrary" concept of, 13, 39, 128; view of birth of, 230; writings of, 8, 64, 104, 122–25, 131, 134, 143, 155n
blessings in Mormonism, 210n
blood, 109, 141, 161, 196n, 211, 214, 235; of Christ, 16, 57, 87, 141, 210–11, 229, 235; menstruation, 230n; as sacrament, 182; sacrificial, 81–83, 85, 140, 210–11. *See also* blood atonement
blood atonement, 41–42, 51, 82–83, 85, 229; in Milton, 118–26. *See also* atonement; blood; bloodletting
bloodletting, 230n. *See also* blood; blood atonement
bloodline, 15, 22, 75, 210

Bloom, Harold, 104n, 146, 218, 248; *American Religion, The*, 214; *Anxiety of Influence, The*, 30, 50, 56; "anxiety of influence," 16; and Book of J, 24n, 214; *Book of J*, 214; on creation, 29n; "criticism of religion," 47; on Enoch, 20n, 215, 218; on "lesser Yahweh," 26; and "misreading," 42, 54n, 56, 82n, 184, 226; and Mormonism, 44, 209, 214–15, 216n, 218, 226; *Omens of Millennium*, 214; on Shakespeare, 30
Bloomfield, Morton, 112
b'nai elohim, 20n, 31, 54n, 128, 233–35. See also angel(s); archons; fallen angel(s); giants; *nefilim*; Watchers
Boccaccio, 110, 111
body, 2, 31, 49, 178, 196, 223, 230; of Catherine, 193–94; of El Cid, 167; of Elijah, 35–37; of Hector, 97, 155; of Hersilia, 107; of Isaiah, 16; of Jesus, 50, 57–58, 69, 71, 80, 110, 115, 182, 185; of Job, 74; of Joseph Smith, 221; of Julius Caesar, 107; of Keats, 131; of Mary, 168–69, 176, 178–79; of Mary Magdalene, 187; physical, 73; physical of Father and Son, 78, 226n, 237; of Romulus, 107; and spirit (or soul), 5, 7, 75, 79–80, 101, 123, 140, 162, 170, 218–19; spiritual of Holy Ghost, 226n
Boethius, 18
Bokhari, The, 170
Book of Commandments, 17n. See also Doctrine and Covenants
Book of J, 24n, 29n, 214
Book of J, 214
Book of Jasher, 19, 20n, 21, 26n, 27, 176–77
Book of Mormon, 17, 30n, 43–44, 64n, 172n, 211, 218, 224
Book of Moses, 20, 24–26, 172n, 215
Book of Thel, 124
Bradstreet, William, 145–47
Brawne, Fanny, 129, 131
bread, 233; breaking of, 71, 77; and Gilgamesh, 11; imagery, 77; of life, 65n, 79, 235; and wine, 235
bread and fishes. See loaves and fishes
bridegroom to the Church, 181–82
Briskin, Madeleine, 236
Britain. See England
broken heart, 211, 246
Brooks, Polly Schoyer, 191–98
Browning, Robert, 130

Budge, E. A. W., 173, 176–77, 178n
burial, 49, 64, 164; Antigone and, 98, 101; of Catherine, 194; of Elijah, 131; of Jesus, 58, 71, 75, 110, 176, 196, 222; of Joseph Smith, 221–22; of Keats, 131; of Moses, 50–51, 75, 131; of Oedipus, 103, rites, 98. See also funerary rites; grave; pyre
burned at the stake, 195–96
burning bush, 123
burnt offering, 60, 62, 69n, 93, 96n–97n. See also fire; refiner's fire
Byron, George Gordon, Lord, 118, 131–43
Byronic hero, 131–43

C

cabal, 17, 24, 26, 215
Cadmus, 102
Caesar, Julius, deification of, 106–8
Cain, 26n, 30n, 132–34, 136–141
Cain, 134, 136–41
Caligula, 132n
Call, Anson, 218
Calvary, 66
Calypso, 133
Campbell, Joseph, 1, 3n, 50, 147, 148, 215
Camus, Albert, 87
Canaan, 38, 114
Candide, 87
canonization, 196
Carthage Conspiracy, 214
Carthage Jail, 213–14, 221
Catastrophism, 236
catatonic, 2
Cathars, 42, 165
Catherine (daughter of King Costus). See St. Catherine
Catherine of Siena, 193–94
Catholic(s), 69, 176, 193–201; and ascension of spirit, 107; assumption in, 5, 192; celibate doctrine of, 229–30; and crusades, 84; and God, 137; demonized, 165–66, 199; English, 199; and extreme unction, 162; French, 193–97, 199–201; and immaculate conception, 130; and Jesus, 165; and life after death, 170; Mariolatry, 169–70; mysticism, 230; paradise, 167; preserves culture, 121n; priests, 18; saints' ascensions, 40, 168; and salvation for the dead, 63–64; and supererogation, 115; and Virgin Mary, 106–7. See also assumption; dormition

caught up, 21, 22, 39, 40, 99, 113, 114, 123, 169, 187, 189–90, 217, 221, 241–42
"Celestial Railroad, The," 82–83
Cerberus, 93
Champes–Elysees. *See* Elysian Fields
Chanson de geste. *See Song of Roland*
Chaos, 116, 153, 163. *See also* abyss; Hades; hell; Pluto; Satan; *sheol*; underworld
chariot: of fire, 9, 94, 124; of the gods, 225; of Israel, 39; of Jesus, 55; of the sun, 105–6, 124, 157, 159–60, 228
Charles II (English), 117, 125
Charles VII (French), 198, 200
Charon, 82, 190n
Chaucer, Geoffrey, 18, 110–12, 162, 188–89, 197
cherubim, 28, 158
Childe Harold's Pilgrimage, 133–37
chosen: heir, 29; king, 198; land, 145; people, 37, 73
Christ, 76–89; American visit of, 44; ascension of, 16, 54, 85, 108–9, 111, 118, 171, 188, 193; Atonement of, 16, 82–83, 124, 140, 169, 215, 223; blood of, 211, 235; body of, 185, 235; conquers death, 58, 80, 93; Crucifixion of, 54, 66; death of, 27, 59, 76, 79, 170, 188, 214; decent into hell of, 79, 165; deification of, 26; divinity of, 44; grace of, 224, 246; as hero, 9, 48, 58–59, 80, 109–10, 114, 116, 229; as high priest, 210–11; imitation of, 75, 81–82, 85–86; Immanuel, 173; kingdom of, 45, 50; as the Lamb of God, 60, 64, 210; marriage of, 180–81, 183, 185–86; Mary Magdalene relationship with, 187–88; Mary's body taken to heaven by, 168–71, 176; as Messiah, 51, 76, 80; Millennial reign of, 123–24; Milton's, 112–16; mortal nature of, 117; as new Moses, 52; Resurrection of, 24, 27, 58, 66, 76, 79, 96n, 132, 169, 170, 223; return of, 124, 133; as sacrificial victim, 58, 60, 65, 109; salvation through, 223; shedding own blood, 211; sovereignty of, 108; as Suffering Servant, 58, 76, 80n, 83, 109, 176; testament of, 44; Transfiguration of, 54; unblemished, 110, 210; as warrior, 110; witness of, 44. *See also* Anointed One; Jesus; king of the Jews; Master; Messiah; redeemer
Christ II, 108
Christabel, 134

Christian(s), 49, 83–89; all-knowing, all-loving God of, 136–37; apologists, 56n; book burning, 42; British, 198–204; converts, 40; cosmology, 110–11; culture, 28; doctrine, 137; early, 37, 47, 55, 69, 171, 173–75, 182–83, 187–88; Ethiopian, 171–79; faith, 24; French, 180, 189–98; glosses, 17–18; heaven, 87, 112; hell, 63; heretical, 166; Holy Ghost, 77; iconography, 170; Jewish, 107, 165, 170–71, 174–79; and Moors, 168; mystery, 60; narratives, 81, 160, 189; and pagan(s), 111n, 161, 186; Paradise, 64; persecution of, 55; priesthood, 122; redemption, 82; romantic hero, 111; seeking immortality, 235, 241; separate from Judaism, 67, 171; service, 42; sign of allegiance, 110; social, 84; Spain, 84; symbolism, 15; theologians, 59, 70, 114, 165; theology, 111–12; tradition, 111n; tri-une deity of, 93n; virtues, 144
Christian Doctrine, 165
Christianity, 9, 18, 65, 69, 189, 241–42; binary opposition of, 81; fundamentalist, 88, 143, 163, 216n; gnostic forms of, 118–25; Jewish origins of, 67n; Mary Magdalene's place in, 180–89; Mary's place in, 168–80; orthodox, 36, 63, 88, 93n, 118, 122, 139, 168, 177; Paul's radical version of, 93n; rifts in, 60, 89; Satan in, 153, 156, 161–66
The Church and the Old Testament, 52n–53n
Church of Jesus Christ of Latter-day Saints, The. *See* Mormons; Mormonism
Cid Campiodor, The, 166
Clarke, H. Butler, 167
Clement of Alexandria, 18, 54n
codes: chivalric, 84; moral, 103; sacred, 123. *See also* tablets; Ten Commandments
Coleridge, Samuel, 131, 133–35, 140, 141
collective amnesia, 239
comedic narrative, 78
communion, 195, 235
conception, 231–32; immaculate, 174–75, 178, 230; miraculous, 53–54; through the Holy Ghost, 230; unusual, 49
condescension of God(s), 66n, 111, 120–21, 128
confession, 64, 82, 162, 203; of Joan of Ark, 193, 195–96, 198
Confessions of an English Opium Eater, 125
Congreve, William, 248
Conlee, John W., 110–11
consecrated: being, 179; ground, 64

consort: of Jesus, 180, 182, 185–88; of Romulus, 106
contrite spirit, 211, 246
Coptic, 175, 181
1 Corinthians, 115
corpse, 3, 164, 167, 176, 179, 187–88, 196
"Corpus Christi Carol," 185
Cosmic Code, The, 232, 241
cosmos, 62, 163, 232, 236, 239, 241
council of gods, 19, 163, 238
covenant, 23, 33, 194, 203, 215; baptismal, 173; Book of Mormon, 44. *See also* new covenant; old covenant
Cowley, Abraham, 117
creation, 42, 123, 137, 147, 157; Bible narrative of, 155–56; material, 120; spiritual, 130; Sumerian narrative of, 19
Creator, 17, 236
Creon, 98–101, 104
crippled, 34–35, 160, 209–11
Critias, 101
cross, 69n, 80n, 85, 109–10, 120–21, 192n, 196, 229
crucifixion, 57, 69, 80n; of Christ, 54, 58–59, 66–67, 69, 71, 80, 85, 113, 121, 188, 211
Cynewulf, 108–10
cult, 36, 107, 119, 174–75; of Isis, 174; of Mary, 69, 169–80; of Mary Magdalene, 180–89

D

Daedalus, 157
Damascus, Paul on the road to, 55, 68n, 198n
Damon, Foster, 22
Daniel, Book of, 109, 163
Dante, 79, 121n, 126, 161–62, 164–66, 237
dark lady, 127, 224
David, 30n, 31, 51–52, 75, 80; and Absalom, 29; anointing of, 193; and Goliath, 84, 95, 114; Jesus descendant of, 174, 186; life span of, 95n, 194n; seed of, 74, 182, 186; throne of, 52, 55, 72–73, 75, 182n; wives of, 182n
Davidias, 117
Davis, Whitney M., 101
De Consolatione Philosophaiæ, 18
De Doctrina Christiana, 114
De Meun, Jean, 18
De Quincey, Thomas, 125
de Santillana, Giorgio, 225, 232
death (dead), 1–3, 24, 40–42, 62–67, 83, 94n, 98, 105, 111, 113, 116, 118, 123, 127, 131, 137, 142; of Abel, 140; of Adam, 227; of Annalee Skarin, 231; appearance of, 101, 103, 178, 196, 247; avoidance of, 5, 7, 12, 22, 237; barters with, 134; cannot partake of, 41, 67, 140, 161, 234; certainty of, 14, 37, 120, 179, 222, 227–28, 230; cheating of, 15, 27, 40–42, 53, 80, 96, 139, 191, 192n, 215, 218, 222, 237–38; in Christ, 245; of Christ, 37, 57–59, 62–81, 82, 114, 120–21, 170, 177, 179, 188, 195, 214, 219, 222; common lot, 2, 7, 11, 14, 83; conquers, 58, 63, 79, 176, 214; corruption in, 135; cult of, 64; delivered from, 7, 56, 79–82, 119, 171, 215, 223, 237–38; as deliverer, 65, 84, 87, 246–47; denial of, 7–8; of Dionysius, 66; of El Cid, 167; of Enkidu, 13, 40, 227; of everything, 119; fear of, 2–3, 129, 139, 241, 246; of Gilgamesh, 7, 11, 14, 78, 227; God(s) wills, 21, 227; of Herakles, 91–94; of Isaiah, 15–16; of Joan of Arc, 194–96, 201; of John, 56; of Joseph Smith, 212–14, 217, 219, 222, 226; of Julius Caesar, 107; of Keats, 131; of Lazarus, 178; life after, 63, 79–80, 96, 114, 121n, 123, 164–65, 170, 222, 238; of Mary, 170–72, 175, 178–79; of Mary Magdalene, 188–89; of Methuselah, 21; mysterious, 49; of Oedipus, 99, 103; of Osiris, 66n; permanence of, 2; and Persephone, 161; power over, 37, 42, 219; raised, 53n, 58, 79, 175, 182; raises from, 37, 38, 39, 51, 52, 65n, 121n, 171, 219–20; rejection of, 122; resurrection from, 5, 37, 44n, 49, 115, 170; salvation for the, 63, 82; spirit survives, 5, 63, 101, 170, 225; of Troilus, 112; wages of sin, 63–64
d'bir, 64, 179. *See also Logos*; Word
Defense of Poetry, 153
degrees of glory, 115
deification, 5, 26–27, 106–8
Deism, 125, 128
deliverer, 51, 56, 60, 65, 79, 84, 93, 219
Delphi, 92, 97
Demeter, 38n, 77, 99
demiurgus, 128, 142
demon(s), 63, 79, 91, 110, 159, 161, 166, 219. *See also* devil(s)
departure–initiation–return, 1, 2
descendants of gods, 13, 49, 91, 92, 94, 105, 159, 233–35
descensus, 63–65, 78–80, 93, 108, 134, 138, 142, 160–162, 165, 237; of Christ, 165

Descent into Madness, 223
descent of the gods, 44, 66n, 111, 120–21, 128, 142–43, 233–34, 237. *See also deus ex machina*
deus ex machina, 44n, 130. *See also* descent of the gods
Deuteronomy, 50–51
devil(s), 60, 112, 156, 165. *See also* demon(s); Hades; Pluto; Satan
Dickinson, Emily, 164, 247
Dictionnaire, 139
didache, 41, 42, 173–74
Diderot, Denis, 190n
Diderot L'Encyclopedie, 190n
Diomedes, 34, 94, 95, 100, 233
Dionysius, 64, 66, 76–78, 80n, 93n
disciple(s), 43, 50–57, 66, 67n, 76–77, 85, 113, 118, 182–83; appearance of resurrected Christ to, 71; fear of, 69–71, 77; and Mary Magdalene, 181; New World, 43–45; nothing will hurt, 160; Philip as, 174–75; record Jesus' history, 59; witness Crucifixion, 69; witness Mary's translation, 171–72, 176, 179; women, 181–86. *See also* apostles; John the Beloved
divine: ancestry, 12, 134; encounter with, 215; family, 2, 22, 31, 34, 49, 58, 63, 98, 100, 103, 107, 110–11, 127, 134, 136, 139, 143, 161, 190, 196, 203, 215, 224, 226, 237–38; favor, 28, 194; guardians, 237; intercessor, 107, 115; justice, 200; knowledge, 21, 60, 74, 119, 121, 122, 135, 215; language, 50; light, 134; love, 229; message, 224; nature, 105; pantheon, 101; parentage, 53, 80, 92–94, 105–6, 107, 113, 132, 159, 227; perspective, 119–20; revelation, 121, 125; Son, 169; spark, 85, 129–30
Doctrine and Covenants (D&C), 17n, 42, 43, 44, 213, 215, 218, 226n, 246. *See also* Book of Commandments
Don Juan, 118
Don Juan, 136
Dorian Gray, 140–41
dormition, 4, 177–78, 179n. *See also* assumption
Doubting Thomas. *See* Thomas
Dr. Faustus, 199, 228
Dracula, 134, 140, 141
dragon, 110, 141, 142, 147, 157, 161, 166, 193, 199. *See also* serpent, winged
Dream of the Rood, 79, 108–10

dream(s), 22, 33, 168; poems, 108–10. *See also* vision(s)
Driver, S. R., 48
Dryden, John, 117
dualism, 119, 122, 125, 139, 215
Duchess of Malfi, The, 199n
Dundes, Alan, 48–49
d'vir, 95n. *See also* Logos; Word

E

Ea, 163–64
Earth Chronicles, 232
"Easter Wings," 127
Ebla tablets, 190n
Eden. *See* Garden of Eden
Edom, 27, 29, 123, 155n
Edward III (French), 197
Edward IV (French), 197
Egypt(ian), 51, 55, 166; afterlife, belief in, 12; Anunnaki settle in, 233–35; art, 102, 234; ascension myths of, 98, 101; Elephantine colony in, 174–75, 185; exodus from, 164, 239; flight into, by Jesus, 49; funerary rites, 100–103, 247; Greek connection with, 98–104, 133, 234; literary tradition, 237; Mary in, 174, 189; Mary Magdalene in, 189; priests, 101. *See also* Africa; Ethiopia(n)
Ehat, Andrew F., 212n
eighth seal, 110–12
El Cid, 8, 117, 166–68; death of, 168; as Messiah figure, 168–69
Elias, 49, 52, 220. *See also* Elijah
Elijah, 8, 35–39, 40, 41, 42, 49, 50–51, 54n, 65, 85, 96, 140, 177–78, 181, 227; appears to Jesus, 218; appears to Joseph Smith, 218; and Ba'al, 38–39; caught up into heaven, 99, 113, 123, 127, 131, 148, 169–72, 174, 176, 179, 214, 218–19, 222–23, 226; chariot of fire, of 94, 113, 124; courage of, 85; and Elisha, 39, 99, 219; fast of, 56; and flour and oil, 54, 219; as forerunner, 2, 37, 123, 146; Joseph Smith as, 214, 220; Melville's, 146–48; as messenger, 2, 145; Milton on, 114–16; meets Muhammad, 168; and Passover, 35, 37–38, 146; raises the dead, 39, 54, 218–20; return of, 55, 113, 145, 148, 161, 171; and widow, 38–39, 218
Elisha, 39, 50, 99, 177–78, 219
elixir of life, 135
Elizabeth I (English), 198–201

Elohim, 27, 54n, 96n
Elysian Fields, 159, 162
Emmaeus, on road to, 71
England, 86, 128, 134, 136, 166, 191n, 235; throne of, 144, 191n. *See also* English
English, 163, 193–202, 235; writers, 105, 129, 132, 185, 191n. *See also* England
Enkidu, 12, 13, 14, 29, 34, 74, 134, 137, 159, 227–28. *See also* Gilgamesh
enlightenment, 127
Enlil, 14, 27n
Enoch, 8, 36, 39, 42, 51, 65, 83, 94–95, 134, 177, 179, 216; as angel of America, 215; Book of, 20, 24–26, 43, 215; 160, 174, 215; caught up into heaven, 16, 19, 49, 116, 127, 168–71, 174, 176, 215, 222–23; city of, 214–15; courage of, 85; Enoch–Metatron, 19–28, 55, 215; Ethiopian Enoch, 19, 20n, 23n, 25, 51n, 63, 114, 132, 174; as forerunner, 123; as hero, 140; importance of to Mormons, 215–16; Joseph Smith Enoch, 20, 23, 25–26, 43, 215; Joseph Smith as Enoch, 214–15, 218, 220; meets Muhammad, 168; never to die, 40, 169; prophecy of, 114; righteousness of, 226–27; as the Scribe, 142, 147; Slavic Enoch, 19, 25; son of Cain, 26n; texts, 19, 26–27, 114; vision of, 15
Ephraim, 30n; tribe of, 81, 210n
Esau, 25, 29–30, 34
eternal: being, 119, 153, 234; decay, 134; dualism of, 119; flames, 123; god, 85; life, 5, 7, 11, 12, 14, 23, 53, 58, 63, 83, 85, 87, 115, 122, 124, 131, 142, 158, 181, 237; mind, 119–20; rebirth, 158; reward, 96; suffering, 82; thirst, 235; wanderer, 133; worlds, 224; youth, 11, 12, 40, 140. *See also* life-in-death
Ethiopia(n): Jewish Christians, 107, 171–76, 179; Isaiah, 173; queen of, 172–73; texts, 171, 173, 175–77. *See also* Enoch; Ethiopian Enoch; Falashas
Etiocles, 99, 104
Eumenides, 98–99, 103. *See also* Furies
eunuch, 172, 182
Euripides, 44n, 91–92, 107n, 128
Europe, 19, 118, 142, 183, 233
Eurydice, 158
Evans, Marlene, 236
Eve, 128, 176, 237; creation of, 155, 233; fall of, 163; Milton's, 138; and tree of life, 27, 158, 235

evil, 21–22, 81, 128, 133, 138, 218–19, 238; appearance of, 101; of blood atonement, 122; Eye, 146; good and, 27, 139; king, 201; in literature, 98, 143; of Satan, 115, 153–55, 159, 164
exaltation, 52, 63, 101, 224
Excaliber, 31, 192n, 193. *See also* sword
exegesis, 37, 94, 122, 130, 163, 233, 237
Exeter Book, 108
exodus: of Israel, 164, 210n, 239; of Mormons, 210n
Exodus, book of, 241
extreme unction, 64, 162
Ezekiel, 22; vision of, 125

F

fabula, 21, 25–26, 35
Fairie Queene, The, 166, 199
faith, 23, 24, 37, 81, 88, 215; in Yahweh, 37, 112n
Falashas, 173–74. *See also* Ethiopia(n)
"Falcon, The," 185
Falcon god, 237. *See also* birds
falcon-flight, 98, 103, 185. *See also* birds
fall: of Adam, 72, 113, 123, 137–38, 140, 165; of Enkidu, 72; of Gilgamesh, 72; of Hephaestus, 160, 163; of Jerusalem, 67; of Phaethon, 160; of Satan, 157–63
fallen angel(s), 20n, 25, 63, 158, 233–34. *See also* angel(s); archons; *b'nai elohim* (fallen); giants; *nefilim*; Watchers
fallen world, 85, 116, 203, 231
familiars, 158, 166
"Famous Victories of Henry V, The," 202
fasting, 56, 167, 210n
Father in heaven. *See* God
Faust, 132, 137–38. *See also Dr. Faustus*
feeding of the five thousand, 37, 65n
felix culpa. *See* fortunate fall
Ferris, Sumner, 189
fertility, 14; god, 77; symbol, 230n
fiery: angels, 124; chariot, 113; furnace, 123; seraphim, 16
Fifty-Third Chapter of Isaiah according to the Jewish Interpreters, 48
fire, 24, 42, 89, 93–94, 96n, 125–26, 146, 194–98; altar, 107, 210–11; –breathing dragon or serpent, 157, 166; chariot of, 9, 94, 124; cloud of, 28; at end of the world, 123–24; from heaven, 39, 178; of hell, 162;

and Satan, 163; stolen from heaven, 135; of sun, 159; as symbol, 94, 123, 157. *See also* burnt offering; refiner's fire
flood, 14, 96n, 163, 238
folklore/folktales, 4, 5, 16, 43, 45n, 48–49, 56, 199
forbidden, 31; fruit, 158; knowledge, 228; tree, 158
Fordham, Elijah, 220
forest, 1–2, 13, 98–99
fortunate fall, 137
Fosdick, Harry Emerson, 75
France, 162, 180, 185–203; king of, 193, 197, 200
Frankenstein, 135, 141, 228
Freemason, 28, 139, 142, 166
Freud, Sigmund, 49, 248
Frost, William, 117
Frye, Northrop, 104n
funeral pyre. *See* pyre
funerary rites: American, 247–48; Egyptian, 101, 247; English, 192n; funeral barge, 192n; games, 217. *See also* burial; grave; pyre
Furies, 98–99, 103, 161. *See also* Eumenides

G

Gabriel, 168
Gamaliel, 68n
games, funeral, 217; Olympic, 217
garden, 57, 176; of delights, 123, 177; of Gethsemane, 14, 211; of the gods, 14, 137, 176; of the immortals, 123; of Joy, 177; of Reuel, 177; tomb, 176, 181. *See also* Garden of Eden; "garden of the gods"
Garden of Eden, 55, 64, 70n, 121n, 123, 128, 140, 157–59, 176–77. *See also* garden; "garden of the gods"
"garden of the gods," 14, 176. *See also* garden; Garden of Eden
Gaster, Theodor Herzl, 232
gates: of Aurora, 105; of heaven, 187, 194, 226; secret, 237
gathering: of apostles, 172, 176; of Israel, 73
Gaull, Marilyn, 134
genealogy, 13, 20, 22, 25, 38
Genesis, 14, 16, 19, 21–23, 25, 27, 28, 32–33, 61, 94, 96n, 114, 128, 132–33, 155–57, 163, 168, 227–28, 233, 238, 241; JST, 23

genii, 140
Gentiles, 67, 68n, 72, 174, 195, 210n
Germany, 141, 166
Gethsemane, 14, 58, 66, 82, 176, 195, 202, 211, 229
Ghandi, Mahatma, 84, 87
ghost, 57, 162, 170. *See also* shade(s)
giants, 20n, 26, 93, 95, 109, 194n, 233. *See also* b'nai elohim (fallen); fallen angel(s); *nefilim*; Watchers
Gideon, 84, 95, 107
Gilgamesh, 2, 11–15, 84, 124, 135, 137–38, 148, 227–28, 239; believes cannot die, 7; challenged by sun god, 107n, 176; divine parentage of, 13, 64, 107, 227; fate of, 224, 227; in garden of the gods, 14; as hero, 12–13, 226; on king-list, 11, 70n, 97n, 228; loss of eternal life of, 40, 53, 78, 93, 140; mortal nature of, 34, 45, 64, 83; myth of, 94; not translated, 72, 96, 108, 139; quest of, 2, 11–12, 14, 80; reign of, 70n, 227; and Utnapishtim, 14, 23–24, 78, 227. *See also* Babylonia(n); Enkidu; *Gilgamesh* epic; king-list; Sumer(ian)
Gilgamesh epic, 12, 21, 27, 34, 78, 83, 159, 165, 188, 226–27, 231. *See also* Babylonia(n); Gilgamesh; Sumer(ian)
Girard, René, 48, 60–62, 74, 76, 99
"Gloriana, Queene of Fairie," 199
glorified, 7, 50, 109
glory, 4, 53; of Christ, 74, 109, 115; degrees of, 114–15; from god, 62; of god, 27, 163, 220, 227, 229; heavenly, 170; Israel's lost, 75; state of, 114–15
gloss, 16–18, 21–22, 31, 34, 157
gnosis, 21, 22, 60, 74, 83, 85, 119, 138–39, 148; vs. blood atonement, 118–25; forbidden, 228
gnostic(s), 17, 56n, 68, 85, 121–22; angel, 122; defiance of ecclesiastical authority, 223; and materialism, 122, 142; nature of Mormonism, 215, 223; redeemer, 2, 85, 119–20, 122; redemption, 118, 122, 124; and resurrection, 121–22; texts, 2, 17, 85
gnostic Gospels, 120–21
gnosticism, 85, 118–23; Christian, 118–21
goat. *See* lamb; sheep; scapegoat
goat song, 62. *See also* tragedy
God, 8, 24, 31, 62–69, 188, 239; allegiance to, 20, 61; altar of, 16; angel(s) of, 33, 51, 61, 97n; attributes of, 111n; caught up to, 113,

175, 178, 190; chosen people of, 73; city of, 82; commune with, 21, 26, 32; covenant with, 23, 241; as Creator, 155–56; curse of, 201; death of, 66–67, 79; Deist, 128; descendant of, 107; descent of, 120; drives Adam from Garden, 177; dwelling place of, 138; and Elijah, 218–20; and Enoch, 20n, 25–27; face of, 123; false, 61; the Father, 57, 85, 123; favor of, 193, 198, 200–203; glory of, 27; gnostic, 120; house of, 32, 33; human, 127; as husbandman, 77; incarnation of, 128; intervention of, 96, 200; of Israel, 55, 62, 103; and Jacob, 30–34; Jesus protected by, 53; of Job, 60–61, 74; and Joseph Smith, 213, 217–18, 225–26; love, 120, 137; mercy of, 60; messenger of, 195; mother of, 169–70, 175, 178; palace of, 34; portrayal of, 116; power of, 82, 88, 116, 158; power over death of, 40, 42, 76; presence of, 23, 28, 34; punishment of, 61, 72; relationship with, 83; revelations from, 16; Satan as, 158–59; Satan's rebellion against, 153–54, 159–61, 163; scourge of, 62, 95, 202; service toward, 8; sign from, 97; Spirit of, 172; throne of, 25, 110, 153–54, 159, 164; timelessness of, 119, 122; and tree of life, 156; vision of, 22–23; will of, 115; wrath of, 116, 164; wrestling with, 25, 29, 32–34, 210; Yahweh as, 38–39, 64, 103, 137, 146–48, 175–76

god(s), 2–5, 8, 11–13, 34, 45, 78, 106, 133–35, 138–39, 163–65; 175, 178, 199, 233–39; abandoned by, 59; assembly of, 14; capriciousness of, 136, 239; challenged, 34; commune with, 2, 176; creation of man by, 11; descendant of, 13–14, 49, 91–92, 132, 190; descent of, 44, 78, 121, 128, 145; devotion to, 104; dwell with, 5, 134, 238; dying, 76–77, 79, 238; encounter with, 31, 103; eternal life of, 14, 83; family of, 27, 100, 224; favor of, 98–99, 132, 226; fertility, 77; garden of, 14; gifts of, 3, 135–36, 176, 232; Greek, 128, 136–37, 160; and Herakles, 91–98; laws of, 12; lesser, 39; mystery rite of, 77; nectar of, 84; oath of, 105–6; offerings to, 93; pantheon, 27, 96n; pharaoh as, 101; presence of, 96; punishments by, 3, 53n, 227; rebellion against, 97, 101, 116, 132, 226, 238; resurrecting, 77, 81; sun, 102–3, 159, 176; thunder and rain, 38; tricking of, 190; of underworld, 161; unknowable, 119; of vengeance, 61; of war, 13

Golden Legende, 184, 187, 192–93

golden plates, 218

Goliath, 84, 95, 114, 192n

good and evil, 27, 139

Good Samaritan, 38n; Christ as, 60, 75

gospel, 33, 55, 56n, 59n, 115, 223–24

Gospel narratives, 51n, 55, 59, 68–69, 73, 78, 94n, 110, 170, 173–75, 182, 210. *See also* Gospel of John; Gospel of Luke; Gospel of Mark; Gospel of Matthew; Gospel of Thomas; Gospels

Gospel of John, 39–44, 47–48, 53n, 57–58, 64, 65n, 68, 69, 71, 76–77, 114, 119, 181–85, 210, 224–25. *See also* Gospel narratives; Gospels; John the Beloved; John the Evangelist; John the Revelator

Gospel of Luke, 41, 44n, 47, 57–59, 65, 80–81, 92n, 160, 173, 176, 182, 219–20. *See also* Gospel narratives; Gospels

Gospel of Mark, 37, 41, 47, 50, 54n, 71, 77–78, 80n. *See also* Gospel narratives; Gospels

Gospel of Matthew, 37, 41, 47–49, 50–51, 71, 92n, 141, 172n, 182. *See also* Gospel narratives; Gospels

Gospel of Thomas, 120, 181–83. *See also* gnostic Gospels; Gospel narratives; Gospels

Gospels, 9, 40, 47–48, 53, 59, 68, 71, 79, 89, 95n, 114, 119, 120, 128, 182–84, 186, 214, 220, 222, 237; women in 185. *See also* apocryphal Gospels; gnostic Gospels; Gospel narratives; Synoptic Gospels

gothic novel, 9, 141

grace, 5, 85, 130, 157, 161, 224, 246

grail. *See* Holy Grail

grave, 5, 9, 69, 80, 134, 135, 144–45, 164, 168, 221. *See also* burial; funerary rites; pyre

Graves, Robert, 51, 52n–53n, 56–57, 68n, 70, 74, 134, 180, 219, 232, 237

Greek: art, 101–2, 234; gods, 61, 130; Hades, 3, 63; heroic age, 96; myth, 38, 93–95, 96n, 137, 143, 161, 163, 177; names, 102–3; pantheon, 47, 93, 98, 128, 136, 160, 235; philosophy, 79, 122; poets, 93, 97

Gregory, 108

Grendel, 34, 110, 133, 192n

"The Grey Champion," 6–7, 143–46

Grittir the Strong, 135

guest–host, 35, 38

H

Hades: lord of underworld, 64, 161, 165, 190n; underworld, 3, 63, 80, 93, 96, 110, 134, 138, 161, 165, 175, 178. *See also* abyss; Chaos; devil(s); hell; Pluto; Satan; *sheol*; underworld
Haimon, 99
hamartia, 133, 140
Hamilton, Edith, 92
Hamlet, 162
Hamlet's Mill, 225n, 232
Harfleur, siege of, 202–3
Harmonia, 100
harrowing of hell, 63, 80
Harrowing of Hell, 79, 108, 165
Hawthorne, Nathaniel, 6–7, 82–83, 143–46, 222
healing, 67, 109, 220
heaven, 4, 13, 14, 22, 38, 54, 62, 67, 78, 82, 84, 87, 93–94, 106–7, 112–13, 128, 137, 146, 156, 161–62, 170, 196, 203, 225–26, 234–38; ascending to, 16, 25, 28, 36–39, 72, 74, 92, 98, 100, 108, 117, 127, 157, 159, 163, 167–69, 171, 175–78, 193, 211, 214–18, 224, 237–38; Bull of, 13; cast down from, 63, 159–60, 162, 193; caught up into, 21–24, 39, 99, 114, 123–25, 169–70, 187, 221–22; come down from, 2, 55, 64, 127, 146, 233–34; council of, 238; dome of, 229; eighth, 162; Father in, 128, 218; fire from, 39, 135, 178; gates of, 33, 194, 226; host of, 32, 116; kingdom of, 55, 56, 181; mansion in, 218; messengers from, 126, 193; music of, 131; palace of, 16; Queen of, 107, 169–70, 174–75, 178, 192; reward in, 115; seventh, 15, 217; stairway to, 22, 28, 31, 33, 168, 232–41; temple of, 109–10, 168; third, 217; veil of, 229; visions of, 25, 121n; war in, 91, 193; windows of, 39
Heaven's Gate, 232
Hebrew[s]: epistle to, 23–24, 38, 81, 210; God, 34; myth, 38, 79, 94–96; pantheon, 96n; scriptures in, 16, 154, 172, 232
Hebrew Goddess, The, 175
Hector, 63, 89n, 93, 110, 113, 155, 160, 162
Heliopolis, 102
Helios, 157, 159
hell, 82, 121n, 126, 141, 156, 162, 170, 228, 246; descent into, 78–79, 93, 126, 161–62, 165; harrowing of, 63, 79–80, 108, 165; hound of, 93; levels of, 165, 237; Satan in, 113, 159, 164. *See also* abyss; Chaos; Hades; Pluto; Satan; *sheol*; underworld
Hellenism, 112, 159
Henry V (English), 189–90, 194, 197–99, 202–4
Henry V, 189, 194, 202–3
Henry VI (English), 197–201
Henry VI, 199–201
Henry VII (English), 197, 201
Henry VIII (English), 191n, 198
Hephaestus, 160, 163
Hera, 94–95, 100
Herakles, 85, 91–98, 231; ascension of, 97, 162, 196; death of, 91–93; defies gods, 97; as deliverer, 93; descent into hell of, 79, 93; defeats giants, 93; divine ancestry of, 92, 93, 96; favor from gods to, 53, 95–96, 190, 226; funeral pyre of, 92–94, 107, 196; as heroic model, 34, 231; labors of, 93; remorse of, 97; rescues Prometheus, 93; rescues Thebes, 93; and Samson, 93–94; translation of, 91, 164; wrestles Death, 93–94
Herbert, George, 127
heretic, 84, 102–3, 165–66, 180, 196
Hermes, 190n
hero(ic), 14–16, 22, 25, 57, 118, 133; age of, 95–96; ancestry of, 92, 132; artist as, 125–26, 130–31; biblical, 50–51, 80, 83, 85, 95, 113, 140; Byronic, 131–43; Campbell's theory of, 1–2, 3n, 50; Christ as, 9, 37, 41, 47–59, 62–66, 71–72, 77, 79–81, 86, 107, 109–10, 114–16, 122, 136, 138; conquest of, 28; and death, 64, 92, 101, 103; definition of, 1, 51; descent into hell of, 78–80, 111; epic, 2, 12, 34, 47–48, 50, 58, 78, 117; journey of, 2; merits of, 12–13, 47–49, 53, 82, 85, 117, 191, 207; model, 66, 84–85, 88, 112, 130; narratives, 47–48, 58–59, 65, 72, 76, 78–79, 81, 84, 91; obedience test of, 83; pattern of, 48, 109, 115; romantic, 111–12; tradition of, 15, 40, 79, 81–82, 109, 113; welcome of, 31; wrestling ritual of, 34
"Hero Pattern and the Life of Jesus, The" 48–49
Hersilia. *See* Hora
Hezekiah, 15, 74
Hilton, Hope, 228, 231
Hippolytus, 120n
Hippolytus, 44n, 128
Hiram (freemason), 142, 221

Index

Hitler, Adolph, 43, 166
Hobbit, The, 157
Hokmah, 171
Holinshed's Chronicles, 198, 200
Holocaust, 84; nuclear, 240
Holy Blood, Holy Grail, 185
holy city, 215–16
holy days, 171, 193
Holy Ghost, 52, 77, 230
Holy Grail, 185; bleeding knight of, 142; keeper of, 142
Holy Mother, 200. *See also* Marian myth; Mary (mother of Jesus); Queen of Heaven; Virgin Mary
holy of holies, 28
Holy Spirit, 16, 172, 230
Homer, 117, 192 n
Hora, 106
Horemheb, 104
Horus, 237
Houlihan, Kathleen, 230 n
House of Fame, 112 n
house of God, 32, 33
Housman, A. E., 247
Hubbard, L. Ron, 222–23
hubris, 115, 132, 158, 163
human sacrifice. *See* sacrifice, human
humours, four, 57
Hundred Years War, 197
Hymn of the Pearl, 2, 85
hymns, Mormon, 216–17
Hyperion, 131

I

Icarus, 157
ichor, 57 n, 91, 111, 235
Iliad, 34, 113, 117, 155, 217, 235
illegitimate birth, 92
imitation (*imitatio*), 81–82, 85, 115, 176, 178, 181
Immaculate Conception, 174, 175, 178, 230
immortality, 133–35, 138; of gods, 2, 13, 236; granting of, 3, 11–12, 139, 237; literary, 94, 98, 107, 108, 112, 127, 129–30, 204, 213, 224; misses, 11, 31–32, 78; of mortals, 1–2, 100, 106, 227, 235; seeking, 11, 139, 228, 235; soul in, 5, 79
incarnation, 9, 50, 93 n, 119, 128
India, 8–9, 87, 233
Indo-European, 48
Indus Valley, 233

Inferno, 79, 161, 165
initiation, 1, 100, 125, 162
inspired version of the Bible by Joseph Smith, 22–24, 41, 43
intercessor, 63, 107, 163–64, 175, 179, 196, 203
Interrogation of Joan of Arc, 198 n
Intimations of Immortality, 125, 127, 236
Iocasta, 99, 104
Irish earth-mother, 230 n
Isaac, 30 n, 31, 211; and Esau, 29; god of, 33; sacrifice of, 61, 69 n, 80; as unblemished lamb, 210
Isaiah, 24, 65, 147, 159, 164, 172–73, 228; ascension of, 5, 15–16, 168; death of, 15; glossing of, 17; Suffering Servant in, 48, 72–74, 81 n, 209–10; vision of, 22
Ishmael, 30 n; from *Moby-Dick*, 146–48
Ishtar, 11, 240
Isis, 107, 174, 178, 240
Ismene, 100
Israel. *See* Jacob
Israel(ites), 36–39, 43 n, 45 n, 58, 91, 96, 119, 142, 145–47, 161, 165, 167, 173; captivity of, 235; children of, 32, 133; deliverance of, 37, 51, 179; exodus, 133, 164, 235, 239; fate of, 25, 75; gathering of, 73; god of, 62, 103, 164, 179, 235; history of, 15, 75, 84, 97, 173; judgment of, 44 n, 75, 95; king of, 65, 72, 76, 95, 114; kingdom of, 54, 55, 73; marriage to, 181; Mormons as, 209–10; priesthood of, 147; Roman rule of, 52–53, 67–68, 113, 166; sins of, 60; as Suffering Servant, 48, 73, 209; ten commandments of, 241; twelve tribes of, 31

J

J writer, 34. *See also* Book of J
Jacob, 28–34, 241; ascension of, 25, 28, 31–34, 170; blessings to, 210 n; and Esau, 29–30; father of Israel, 29, 34; Israel name of, 25, 29, 32–33, 210; meaning of name of, 25; and Rachel, 30; as Suffering Servant, 210; wrestles with angel, 22, 25, 29, 32–34, 210
Jacob's ladder (stairway), 22, 28–34, 168, 237
Jael, 231
James, 77; epistle of, 225; leader of early Christian church, 70, 134, 172; at Mount of Transfiguration, 41, 49; as priest, 75, 120
James, Henry, 141

268 Index

James II (English), 143–45
Jarius's daughter, 178
Jehovah, 31, 74, 123, 193, 196, 236–37, 240–42; blessings from, 210n; chosen people of, 37; covenant with, 194, 203; marriage to Israel of, 181
Jehovah–Jove, 160–61
Jehovah's Witnesses, 76n, 84, 121n
Jekyll, Dr., 141–42
Jeremiah, 74, 185
Jerusalem, 51–52, 55, 67–68, 72, 75, 84, 95, 172
Jerusalem Bible, 133, 146, 228
Jesus, 14, 35, 39–42, 44–45, 47–89, 128, 179, 182, 237; appears to Joseph Smith, 218; atonement of, 42; as baby, 64; baptism of, 113; birth of, 119–20, 186; birthright of, 30n; blood of, 182; blood atonement of, 41–42, 85; body of, 182; burial of, 58, 71, 75, 110, 176, 196, 222; caught up to God, 113; circumcision of, 65; cleanses temple, 62, 75; conquers death, 63; death of, 67–69, 120–22, 177–78, 220; descends into Hell, 63–64; divinity of, 44, 92n–93n; as an Elias, 220; as an Elijah, 37, 146, 220; at Gethsemane, 195; glossing by, 17; as good shepherd, 75; government of, 75; as hero, 9, 48–59, 62–66, 71, 122, 143, 178, 219; as half God, 92n, 107; as half human, 92n, 107, 109; heals sick, 52, 67; heir to throne, 52, 55, 72, 75; increases loaves and fishes, 52; as intercessor, 179; John the Beloved and, 171; kingship of, 44, 47, 49–53, 55, 57, 65–68, 72–76, 94n, 115, 124, 180, 219, 230; marks on body of, 72, 80; Mary and, 108; Mary Magdalene and, 181, 184; meets Muhammad, 168; Milton's, 112–16, 135, 138, 164; mortal nature of, 115, 119–20, 128, 136; of Nazareth, 77, 109, 220; post-resurrection, 39; premortal, 116; as priest, 49, 51, 75, 89, 115, 211, 219; as prophet, 51, 75, 219; as rabbi, 52n; raised from dead, 58, 79, 175, 182; raises dead, 54, 65n, 219; as resurrected being, 42, 44, 165, 169; as sacrificial victim, 9, 48, 58, 61, 62, 64, 89, 109, 115, 141, 209, 212; salvation by, 223–24; sayings of, 59n; scourging of, 69n, 75; as son of David, 52; as son of God, 92n; stabbed in side, 68–69; as Suffering Servant, 9, 72–77, 83; tomb of, 71, 78; trial of, 68n, 195; Transfiguration of, 37, 41, 49–51, 54, 64, 94n, 172n, 218; triumphal entry into Jerusalem of, 51, 75; turns water to wine, 52, 77; as victim, 62–72; walks on water, 52; wedding at Cana and, 75; as the Word, 64, 119; as Yahweh, 93n. *See also* Anointed One; Christ; king of the Jews; Master; Messiah; redeemer
Jew(ish): apocrypha, 238; blame on, 67, 165; cabalistic lore, 26, 215; exegesis, 122, 163; and the female, 171, 174–76; gnosticism, 119; and Holocaust, 84; king of, 47, 49, 55, 68, 75; leaders, 69; monotheism, 103; mystics, 37; mythology, 9, 57n; narratives, 6, 15, 35, 37, 171, 179, 188; origin of Jesus, 53, 67, 68, 165; orthodox, 35, 153; persecutions of, 67, 165–66, 168, 170, 210n, 213; rabbis, 74, 163, 172–73, 183; Shakespeare's portrait of, 30–31, 67n; texts, 47, 48; traditions of, 146, 176, 215; warning to, 55
Jewish-Christians, 37, 68n, 107, 165, 170, 172–79, 185, 222
Jihad, 84
Joan of Arc, 183, 189–204, 228
Job, 60–61, 74, 83–84, 158, 211
Job: The Victim of His People, 48, 60
John the Baptist, 64, 113, 180–81; death of, 56; as Elijah, 35, 37, 146; testifies of Christ, 113
John the Beloved, 39–45, 53, 70, 76, 169n, 171–72, 177n, 182–84; at Mount of Transfiguration, 41, 49; secret writings of, 43; tarry until Christ comes, 39–42, 44–45, 182; witnesses Crucifixion, 69. *See also* Gospel of John; John the Evangelist; John the Revelator
John the Evangelist, 184. *See also* Gospel of John; John the Beloved; John the Revelator
John the Revelator, 109, 163, 184, 217. *See also* Gospel of John; John the Beloved; John the Evangelist
Jonah, 65, 100
Jones, Dan, 213–14
Jones, Edward T., 6, 9
Joseph (father of Jesus), 49, 69n, 94n
Joseph, sold into Egypt, 30n, 73; tribe of, 210n
Joseph of Arimathaea, 67n, 68n, 71, 75
Josephus, Flavius, 18, 92
Jove, 105, 106, 159–61
Joyce, James, 130
Judah, 30n; Messiah of, 81; tribe of, 73
Judaism, 14, 154, 178, 179
Judas, 49, 70, 71, 195, 214
Jude, 51n, 114

Judeo-Christian, 5, 28, 31, 36, 180, 209, 222, 240
judges, 13, 26, 52, 53n, 95, 161, 178
Judges, Book of, 95–97, 117, 231
judgment (final), 121n, 245
Judgment Day, 63
Julian of Norwich, 18, 60, 183, 228, 229, 231
Jung, Karl, 183
Jupiter, 107, 116, 153–54, 233, 240
justice, 22, 60, 61, 62, 99, 200

K

ka, 101, 103, 190n
kapu. *See* taboo
Keats, John, 94, 129–131, 192, 247
Kempe, Margery, 18, 183, 229, 230
key(s), 7, 21, 43, 98, 103, 163, 180, 183, 225–26; narrative, 23, 37, 47, 49; to past, 43; tests, 40; words, 108, 226
king(s), 49, 63, 72, 95, 125, 176, 237; Ahab, 51, 146; of Babylon, 159, 227, 228; Charles II, 125; Charles VII, 198; Creon, 98–101; David, 51, 186; of the earth, 27; Edward III, 197; Edward IV, 197; of England, 195, 197, 202–4; of France, 193–200; Gilgamesh, 7, 12, 34, 53, 72, 133, 227; Greek, 100; Hades, 64, 161; Hamlet, 162; Henry V, 189–90, 194, 197–99, 202–4; Henry VI, 197–201; Henry VII, 197, 201; Henry VIII, 191n, 198; Hezekiah, 15; Jesus, 44n, 53, 55, 57, 65–68, 72, 75–76, 115, 124, 180, 219, 230; Lucifer, 161; Manasseh, 15; Melchizedek, 23–24; Oedipus, 98–100, 133; office of, 49, 51, 63, 75, 76, 115, 125, 219; Pluto, 64; Priam, 97, 155; Richard II, 202; Richard III, 197, 201; Saul, 95; wicked, 51; of Sumeria, 227–28; William of Orange, 145; wise men as, 51
King James Bible (KJB), 42n, 43n, 117, 157, 191n, 233
King Jesus, 51n, 74, 75, 232, 237
king of the Jews, 47, 49, 72–76, 117
King, Martin Luther, 84, 87
King, Stephen, 142
kingdom: on earth, 221; of God, 41, 45, 50, 54n, 184, 217; of heaven, 42, 44, 55, 56, 181; of Israel, 53, 55, 72, 73
king-list, 11, 13, 95, 235. *See also* Gilgamesh; Sumer(ian)
I Kings, 38, 218–19

2 Kings, 39, 114, 219
knight, 18, 84, 142, 187. *See also* Redcrosse Knight
Knight, Lydia Bailey, 212–13, 217–18
Knight, Newel, 213
Knights Templar. *See* Templars
knowledge, 73, 240; divine, 21, 22, 60, 74, 119, 122, 215; human, 135, 145; perfect, 139; search for, 79; secret, 140; of unknown arts, 157. *See also* gnosis
Kübler-Ross, Elisabeth, 88n

L

Laban, 29–31
Laboure, Catherine, 54n
Lady of the Lake, 192n
Laius, 100
lamb: innocent, 61, 64, 73, 212–13; of Jacob, 31; marriage of the, 181; as sacrificial animal, 60–61, 64, 69n, 73, 76, 89, 112, 122, 138, 174, 196, 209–12, 214, 220; to the slaughter, 73, 213; unblemished, 210–12. *See also* sacrificial animals; sacrificial victim; scapegoat; sheep; unblemished
Lamb of God, 62–64, 210
Lambert, Mary, 214
Lancelot, 84
last rites, 64
Last Supper, 69n, 77, 195
Latin, 18, 105, 109, 169, 175, 185
Laurence, Richard, 19, 23n, 174
law(s), 2, 31, 49, 70, 98, 114, 115, 124, 137, 181, 225–26; of gods, 12–13; of hospitality, 38; of nature, 141; and the prophets, 179; tablets of, 173. *See also* Mosaic law
Law, William, 214n
Law, Wilson, 214n
lawgiver, 51, 52
Lazarus, 40n, 65n, 66, 75, 178, 220
Le Bossu, 118
Lear, 62–65, 87
legend, 15–16; definition of, 4; of Elijah, 171, 177; of Elisha, 177; of Enoch, 171; of Faust, 132; of Henry V, 189–90, 194, 197–99, 202–4; of Herakles, 91–98; of Joan of Arc, 189–204; Marian, 171, 173–74, 178–79; of Mary Magdalene, 180–89; of native Americans, 28; of Oedipus, 98–104; of queen of Sheba, 173; of Samson, 91; of Solomon, 173; of vampires, 134

Levi, 30n; tribe of 73
Leviathan, 147, 157
Levin, Harry, 157n
Lewis, C. S., 77, 142
life after death, 2, 7, 58, 62, 63, 79, 96, 114, 121n, 123, 164–65, 170, 191, 222, 238. *See also* eternal, life
Life after Life, A, 7, 121n
life cycle, 14, 64, 230
life-essence, 101
life-in-death, 134, 136, 140–41
life span, 3, 95n, 234–35
light, 2, 49, 85, 134, 138, 139, 142, 166; and dark, 3, 65, 139; at end of tunnel, 7, 222; of the moon, 126; in Paradise, 63; and truth, 101
light-bearer, 128, 160
Lightner, Mary, 218
lightning, 159, 160
Lilith, 140–41
liminal space. *See* space, liminal
loaves and fishes, 52, 67n
Logos, 50, 64, 93n, 119, 179. *See also* Word
Loki, 190n
Lord of the Rings, The, 192n
Lot, 38n, 240
love: agape, 7, 50, 97, 111–12, 120, 145, 155, 187, 212, 216, 225, 229; courtly, 111; platonic, 184; romantic, 84, 110–21, 158, 203
Love, Gloria, 222–24, 230–31
Lucifer, 63, 128, 165, 195; Byron's, 138–41; cast from heaven, 160–61, 193; kingdom of, 161; meaning of, 160; Milton's, 154, 156; son of the morning, 159
Luke. *See* Gospel of Luke
lustrations, 63, 99
Lycidas, 129
Lyrical Ballads, 125–26

M

Macbeth, 62, 64
madonna, 183; nursing, 49. *See also* Holy Mother; Marian myth; Mary (mother of Jesus); Queen of Heaven; Virgin Mary
maenads, 161
Mahomet, 165
Malachi, 2, 37, 146
Malory, Thomas, 192n
"Man of Law's Tale," 189

Manfred, 134–35
Mani, 139
Manichean, 139
Mankind in America, 239–40
manna, 52, 235
Manoah, 96n–97n
Manoah's wife, 96, 178
mantle, 36, 39
Mao, 43
Marduk, 240
Marian myth, 169, 174. *See also* Holy Mother; Mary (mother of Jesus); Queen of Heaven; Virgin Mary
Mariolatry. *See* Marian myth
Mark. *See* Gospel of Mark
Marks, William, 214n
Marlowe, Christopher, 30, 57, 157n, 199, 228
marred servant, 48, 72, 109, 174, 177, 209–14
marriage: Annalee Skarin's views of, 229–30; of Christ to Church, 181; for the dead, 63; feast of Cana, 181; of Jesus and Mary Magdalene, 180–81; 184–85; of Jehovah to Israel, 181; of the lamb, 181; of Mary, 74; sexuality in, 129–30; and St. Margaret, 192
Marriage of Heaven and Hell, The, 123
Mars, 106, 107, 136, 233
Marseilles, Mary's trip to, 185–88; prince of, 185–86
Martha, 71, 75
Martyrdom, 15; of Isaiah, 15–16; of Jesus, 195; of Joseph Smith, 212–13
Mary (mother of Jesus): Assumption of, 168–80; and Crucifixion, 69, 71; conception by, 53, 230; cult of, 183; death of, 168–70, 175–76, 178, 179; deification of, 107, 174; as intercessor, 107, 175; and John the Beloved, 171; as Mother of God, 170, 173–75; pregnancy of, 74, 237; as Queen of Heaven, 107, 174, 175, 178, 192; at tomb of Christ, 77; ward of temple, 178. *See also* Holy Mother; Marian myth; Mother of God; Queen of Heaven; Virgin Mary
Mary (sister of Martha), 71, 75
Mary Magdalene, 73, 180–89; Christ reveals himself to, 57–58, 71, 181; consort of Jesus, 180, 188, 230; and Constance, 189; cult of, 181–83, 190; death of, 187–88; engaged to John the Beloved, 184; marriage to Jesus, 180–81, 184–85; in Marseille, 185–86, 188; as priest and rabbi, 181; and prostitution, 183; rejection of, 181; at tomb of Christ, 77

"Mary Magdalene" (Digby MS), 187
Mary Tudor (Bloody Mary), 199
mass, 63, 166, 186
Master, 40, 52n, 57. *See also* Anointed One; Christ; Jesus; king of the Jews; Messiah
Matthew. *See* Gospel of Matthew
Mauss, Armand, 215n–16n
McPherson, Amee Semple, 223
mediator, 60, 115, 130
Mein Kampf, 43
Melchizedek, 22–24, 38, 51
Melito of Sardis, 169
Melville, Herman, 87, 118, 141, 146–48
Merchant of Venice, 67
mercy seat, 28, 60, 69n
Merlin, 31
Mesopotamia, 12
messenger, 22, 55, 78, 123, 145, 240; to Joan of Arc, 193, 195; Moses as, 51; Satan as, 158; Wordsworth as, 126
Messiah, 37, 50, 53, 55, 64, 67, 70, 72, 74–76, 78, 81, 216; death of, 109; as deliverer, 219; forerunner to, 38; Jesus as, 116; multiple, 83; second coming of, 57, 148–49. *See also* Anointed One; Christ; Jesus; king of the Jews; Master
Messiah ben David, 73–74
Messiah ben Joseph, 73–74, 81
metamorphoses, 106–7, 117, 118
Metamorphoses, 104–8, 117, 160
Metatron, 19, 26, 55, 114, 126, 215. *See also* Enoch
Methuselah, 21; life span of, 95n
Michael, 128–29; Archangel, 168, 193
Michael, 125, 128–29
Midas, 105
Middle Ages, 18, 19, 67n, 112n, 169, 183–85, 188
Midianites, 84, 95
Midsummer Night's Dream, 105
Millennium, 51n, 114, 123–24
Milton, 124–25
Milton, John, 112–20, 123–25, 143; Adam and Eve of, 138, 163; angels of, 57n, 91, 111, 163; *Christian Doctrine*, 165; *De Doctrina Christiana*, 114; death of, 118; demons of, 91; God of, 116, 164; Jesus of, 115–16, 123, 135, 138, 164–65; *Lycidas*, 129; *Paradise Lost*, 91, 116, 164; *Paradise Regained*, 112– 16, 123; *Paradise Regained II: The Battle against Sin and Death*, 114;

Samson Agonistes, 95n, 97–98; Samson of, 95n, 97–98, 117; Satan of, 34, 98, 116, 118, 135, 154–56, 163–64; theology of, 112
miracles, 165; of Aaron, 177; Elijah, 39, 51–52; of Elisha, 39; of of Jesus, 37, 52, 65, 75; of Joan of Arc, 196; of Moses, 52, 177
Miracles, 77
misreading, 54, 56, 57, 82, 85–86, 93n, 171, 173, 191, 225–26, 227, 230; definition of, 42, 58, 82n, 184
Moby-Dick, 146–48
mock heroic, 117
monistic, 122
monotheism, 26, 102–3, 175
Moody, Raymond, 7, 121n
Moral Epistles, 117
Mormon (person), 17, 44n
Mormon(ism), 43–45, 54n, 57n, 84, 123n, 165, 209–22, 246; American religion, 209, 216n; Annalee Skarin and, 222–24, 225, 229, 231, 237; blessings in, 210n; Book of Mormon and, 17, 30n, 43–44, 64n, 172n, 211, 218, 224; cosmology, 42n; *credo*, 63; diaries, 220; disciples, 44n; Doctrine and Covenants (D&C) and, 17n, 42, 43, 44, 213, 215, 218, 226n, 246; Enoch, importance of to, 216; exaltation and, 63; founder of, 9, 16, 153; fundamentalists, 221; gnostic nature of, 215; history of, 220; hymns, 216–17; as Israelites, 209–10; kingdom of God on earth, 54n; life after death, 222; missionaries, 213, 223; mob violence against, 214; narratives, 41, 221; ordinances, 63–64; persecutions of, 210n; and plan of salvation, 223, 224; splinter group, 221
Moroni, 218
Morris, William, 142
mortality, 2, 13, 114, 140, 224, 229; common lot of, 5, 12, 27, 34; death lot of, 37, 111, 222; of Jesus, 62, 115, 119–20; pains of, 80; transcending, 126
Morte Darthur, 192n
Mosaic law, 52, 62, 241. *See also* law(s)
Moses, 24–25, 37, 39, 73; appears to Jesus, 49–51, 218; ascension of, 5, 194; as author, 96n; birthright of, 30n; and brazen serpent, 109; buried by hand of God, 50–51, 75, 131; and burning bush, 123; caught up into a high mountain, 172n; and code of living, 103, 241; crosses Red Sea, 52; fast of, 56; in Garden of Reuel, 177; leads Exodus, 51–52, 164,

272   Index

239; life span of, 95n; as messenger, 51; miracles of, 52; on Mount, 113; and Passover, 38; receives rod, 177; and Seder Feast, 38; sends plagues, 52; slow of speech, 83; and Ten Commandments, 103, 241
Mother Nature, 77
Mother of God, 49, 71, 74, 106, 168–72, 174–75, 178, 183, 230
Mount of Olives, 56
Mount of Transfiguration, 41, 64. *See also* Transfiguration
Mount Sinai, 56, 146, 194
mountain(s), 26, 49–50, 71, 78, 126, 159, 172n, 238
Muhammad: ascension of, 8, 168; meets Elijah, 168; meets Enoch, 168; meets Jesus, 168
mummification, 2
Muslim(s), 153, 163, 166, 168, 241
Mycoff, David, 184–85, 188–89
mysteries, 14, 21, 60, 115; cult of Isis, 174; lore, 94; rite, 77; of Satan, 154
mysterion, 50, 54n, 60
mystery play, 61
mysticism, 17, 47, 93n, 125
mystics, 154; Annalee Skarin, 9, 222–31; Jewish, 37; Julian of Norwich, 18, 60, 183, 228, 229, 231; Kempe, Margery, 18, 183, 229, 230
myth, 6, 15–16, 24, 34, 37, 59, 117, 128, 131, 164, 174, 177, 224, 231, 236–238; ascension-translation, 3, 11, 37, 85, 105, 109–11, 119, 125, 168, 174, 189, 217, 221, 232, 237–38, 241; Babylonian, 79, 137, 159, 163, 228, 232; biblical, 137; Chinese, 98; definition of, 4; of descent into underworld, 93, 161, 164; of descent of god, 121; Egyptian, 98–104; English–Scandinavian, 163; of fall of Adam, 113; folklore and, 49; Freemasonic, 139; glossing of, 16; Greek, 93–95, 98–104, 137, 143, 159–60, 163, 224, 235; heroic, 78–79, 92, 117–18, 136; of illegitimacy, 92; Indian, 8–9; Jewish, 79, 95; kingship, 228; of life cycle, 45, 64; Marian, 169, 174, 177; Old Testament, 136, 232; of origin, 74, 154, 160–61, 178–79; Ovid's, 104; pre-Aztec, 156–57; Sumerian, 137, 176, 232, 236, 238

N

Nag Hammadi, 17, 154n, 181n
Nag Hammadi Library in English, 181n

Napoleon, 134–35
Nathan, 30n, 182n
Nature, 2, 13, 64, 102, 126–28, 141
Nauvoo, 214–15, 220–21
Nauvoo Temple. *See* temple, Nauvoo
The Nazarene Gospel Restored, 51n, 68n, 180
Nazarite vow, 95, 97, 178, 200, 211
Nazis, 166, 168
near-death experience, 7, 121n, 222
nefilim, 20n, 25, 63, 79, 132, 233. *See also* archons; *b'nai elohim* (fallen); fallen angels; giants; Watchers
Neoplatonism, 111, 118–19, 128–30
Nephertiti, 103–4
nephesh, 57, 73, 79, 94n
Nephi (person), 17, 30n, 43, 64n
1 Nephi, 43–44, 64n, 172n
3 Nephi, 44–45
Nephites, 44; twelve disciples of, 44n
Nettl, Paul, 139n
Neubauer, Adolf, 48
New Age religion, 2, 82, 164n, 222–41
new covenant, 16, 37, 62, 181. *See also* covenant; old covenant
New England, 144, 145
New Testament, 23, 42–44, 50, 67, 86, 89, 121, 220; ascension-translation in, 172; birth of Christ in, 186; gloss of, 18; Jesus in, 48–50, 58, 80–81, 180–81, 185, 219, 235, 237; marriage in, 181, 185; Mary in, 92n; Melchizedek in, 38; prophecies in, 166; resurrection of Christ in, 24, 35, 119; Satan in, 154, 159, 164, 174; Synoptic Gospels in, 44; visits by angels in, 38n; wine imagery in, 77; women in, 180–83, 185, 188. *See also* Bible; Old Testament
New World, 44, 44n, 215–16
Nibiru, 233–37, 239
Nibley, Hugh, 23n, 54n, 234n
Nicodemus, 67n–68n, 75, 139
Nile, 103, 234
Nimrod, 28, 226, 238
Noah, 11, 23, 164, 238
northern kingdom, 73
Numbers, 158

O

O'Connor, Flannery, 246
"Ode to a Grecian Urn," 129–31
"Ode to a nightingale," 130
Odin, 84

Odysseus, 29, 63, 79, 84, 89n, 94, 100, 132–34, 136–37, 155, 190, 231
Odyssey, 133
Oedipus, 65, 95, 98–104; banished by sons, 100; belligerence toward gods, 101; burial place, 99–100, 103; death of, 99–100, 103–4; descended from the gods, 102; divine origin, 100; meaning of name, 106; solves riddle of Sphinx, 100, 104n; wanderings of, 98–99
Oedipus and Akhnaton, 102, 225n
Oedipus at Colonus, 98–99, 103
Oedipus Tyrannus, 98, 100, 102
offerings. *See* burnt offering
old covenant, 37, 181. *See also* covenant; new covenant
Old Testament, 34, 69, 81, 96n, 119, 128, 133, 227, 232; ascension–translation in, 14–16, 19, 24; binary opposition in, 35; birthright in, 30n; blessings in, 210n; Cain in, 136; Christ in, 16, 219; David in, 117, 193; death in, 24; Elijah in, 38, 99, 218–19; Enoch in, 19, 21, 36; giants in, 233; glossing in, 17; God in, 146; Isaiah in, 15–16; Jacob in, 28–29; Job in, 83; Jonah in, 100; major prophets in, 35; Mary in, 173, 178; Methuselah in, 21; and Muhammad, 168; offerings in, 93–94; prophecies in, 69; Samson in, 200; Satan in, 154, 164; tour of heaven in, 22; underworld in, 164. *See also* Bible; New Testament
Old World, 43n, 44
Olympians, 66, 92–93, 95, 148
Olympic games, 217
Olympus, 91, 98, 100, 160
Omens of Millennium, 214
On Death and Dying, 88n
oracle, 100; at Delphi, 92, 97
ordinances, 173; for dead, 216n; proxy, 216n
Orestes, 99
Origin of Satan, The, 120n, 156
Orpheus, 63, 79, 158, 161
orthodox, 41, 120; calendar, 39; cannon, 42; Christianity, 36, 63, 88, 120, 122, 137, 140, 153, 179, 231; *descensus*, 63; gloss, 17; Gospel narratives, 110; Judaism, 35, 36, 153; Islam, 153; religious tradition, 36; view of atonement, 41, 177, 215, 223; view of death, 222; view of resurrection, 63, 177; view of salvation, 139, 223; view of Satan, 153–54; Yahweh, 137
Osiris, 59, 66n, 175, 235, 240

overreacher, 135–36, 157
Ovid, 11, 92n, 104–8, 112, 116–17, 141, 157–58, 160
Ozymandias, 102

P

pagan, 6, 37, 87, 91, 92, 96, 110–12, 161, 186
Pagels, Elaine, 120n, 154, 158
pantheon: Babylonian, 235; of gods, 12, 22, 27, 96n, 101, 196, 235, 236, 241; Greek, 91, 98, 136, 160, 235; Hebrew, 96n, 235; Sumerian, 236
paradise, 14, 86, 113, 121n, 162, 165, 167, 177, 196; Adam and Eve in, 235; definition of, 63–64; of departed souls, 162, 177; return to, 176–77; of Utnapishtim, 22
Paradise Lost, 113, 116, 153n, 156, 164
Paradise Regained, 112–16, 125
parathanatic. *See* near-death experience
Passover, 35, 37–38, 146, 172
Passover Plot, 51n, 219n
Patai, Raphael, 175
patriarchs, 22, 29, 39, 134, 144, 170, 176, 210, 240
patrilineal, 30n
Patroclus, 110, 113, 155, 160, 217
Paul, 63, 70, 115, 124, 198n
Pearl of Great Price, 20n, 228
Pegasus, 168
Pelikan, Jaroslav, 169
Pend d'Oreille tribe, 28, 238
Pendragon, Urther (Arthur), 31, 190n
Penelope, 84, 133
Pentecostal, 165, 172
Persephone, 79, 161
Perseus, 63, 79, 92, 143
Peter, 56, 79, 80, 137, 175, 178; call of, 40; crucifixion of, 40; cuts off soldier's ear, 179; denial of Christ of, 71; jealously of, 39–42, 181–83; and John, 39–42; as leader of church, 70, 172; at Mount of Transfiguration, 41, 49; no ascension–translation of, 39–42, 44, 134; preaching in Rome of, 67n; and Resurrection, 77
1 Peter, 79
petroglyphs, 241
Phaethon, 105–6, 113, 115, 124, 139, 159–60, 224, 228
pharaoh(s), 98, 101–3, 119, 237
"Pharaohs of the Sun," 103

Index

Pharisees, 53n, 68, 70, 75, 79, 121n
Philip, 172–75
Philistines, 29, 95, 97
Philo of Alexandria, 18
philosopher's stone, 135–36
Phoebus, 105
Phosphorous, 160
Pierre, 118, 141
Pilate, 75
pillar, 32; of cloud or fire, 28; Egyptian, 102; of gold, 177; Greek, 102; of temple, 95
Pindar, 92n
Pistis-Sophia, 2
plague(s), 52, 85, 166, 200–201
plan of salvation. *See* salvation, plan of
Plato, 101, 129
pluralism, 216n
Pluto, 64, 161. *See also* Chaos; devil(s); Hades; Satan
Podro, Joshua, 51, 53n, 56, 57, 68n, 70, 180
Poe, Edgar Allen, 2
poet(s), 8, 56, 64, 95, 97, 109, 112, 134, 135, 138, 156, 168, 199, 239; ascension–translation quality of, 127, 129–30, 142–43, 237; celebrates common man, 123–25, 236; epic, 78, 105, 107, 117–18; as god, 111, 126–27, 236; as hero, 112, 118–19, 125–26, 130–32; metaphysical, 130, 211; as philosopher, 123; as prophet, 122, 123; religious, 108; view of Satan of, 154, 164
Polidori, Dr., 140, 141
Polyneices, 98–99, 101, 104
Ponce de Leon, 237
Pope, Alexander, 116–18
Pope John Paul II, 67n
Portia, as heroic model, 231
Poseidon, 133, 161
poststructuralists, 127n, 130
Pratt, Parley P., 212
prayer, 107, 112, 193, 202–3, 210n, 219, 225
Prelude, The, 126, 226
Priam, 97, 155
pride, 97, 116, 133, 134, 155
priest(s), 3, 8, 17, 18, 47, 69n, 91, 99, 147, 162, 174, 181–83, 187, 189n, 190n, 193, 196, 210; Catholic, 230; Christian, 122; Egyptian, 98, 101, 103–4, 234; Elijah as, 35; false, 147; high, 23–24, 28, 68n, 125; Jesus as, 49, 51, 75, 89, 115, 211, 219; Joseph Smith as, 211, 217; Mary Magdalene as, 181; Melchizedek as, 23–24; pagan, 92;
temple 32, 75, 120, 173, 217–18; Wordsworth as, 125–26
priesthood, 68n, 104, 147, 218, 230, 234
prima nocta, 132n
Prince, The, 134
prodigal son, 128
Prometheus, 27n, 66–67, 79, 93, 116, 132, 135, 163
Prometheus Bound, 138
Prometheus Unbound, 116, 154
prophet(s), 49, 99, 115, 146, 154, 193, 219, 230, 239; Aaron as, 39; of Ba'al, 39; biblical, 24; Elijah as, 35, 39, 146, 218–20; Elisha as, 39; Jesus as, 51, 75, 219; Joan of Arc as, 197; Jonah as, 65; Joseph Smith as, 213–18, 221; law and, 168; major, 35; minor, 17; Muhammad as, 173; New Age, 241; Old Testament, 15, 22; Simeon as, 65
Protestants, 65, 138–39, 168
Prynne, Hester, 87
Psalms, 80, 157, 178, 196
pseudepigraphic, 4, 8, 15, 20–22, 35, 160, 215
Psyche, 22
Ptolemaic cosmology, 91, 107, 138, 153, 160, 236
purgatorium, 162
purgatory, 121n, 162, 165, 237
purification rites, 99, 101, 223, 229
Puritanism, 82n, 144, 222
Pusey, E. B., 73–74
Pygmalion, 104
pyramid texts, 101, 103
Pyramus and Thisbe, 105
pyre, 92–93, 107. *See also* funerary rites

Q

"Q" source, 181n
Queen Consort, 106, 180, 230. *See also* consort
queen of Ethiopia, 172–73
Queen of Heaven, 107, 169, 170, 174–75, 178, 192. *See also* Holy Mother; Marian myth; Mary (mother of Jesus); Virgin Mary
queen of Sheba, 173–74
Quetzalcoatl, 156–57
Quinn, D. Michael, 212n
Quirinus, 106

R

Ra, 98
rabbi, 73–74, 163, 172, 233; Aqiba as, 17n;

Jesus as, 75; Mary Magdalene as, 181; Philip as, 173
Rachel, 30
Raglan, FitzRoy Richard Somerset, 48–49
raises dead. *See* death (dead), raises from
raised from the dead. *See* death (dead), raised
ram, 61. *See also* lamb; sheep
Rameses II, 102
Rank, Otto, 48
Rape of the Lock, 116–18
Rapture, 41, 84, 124
Ratziner, Cardinal, 169–70
Rebekah, 29
rebirth, 158; spiritual, 225
Redcrosse Knight, 111, 117, 166, 199, 201
redeemer, Christ as, 60, 120; gnostic, 2, 85, 119, 120, 122. *See also* Christ; Jesus
redemption, 85, 235; gnostic, 126–27
refiner's fire, 94, 123–24, 126, 143, 162, 196, 203. *See also* burnt offering; fire
reincarnation, 5, 189 n, 225
Remigius of Auxerre, 18
Reorganized Church of Jesus Christ of Latter Day Saints (RLDS), 221–22
repent for another's sins, 99
"Resolution and Independence," 126
resurrection, 41–42, 50, 53 n, 79–81, 124, 141, 165, 169–70, 177, 219, 222–25; of Christ, 24, 37, 44, 54, 57–58, 63, 66, 68–71, 76–89, 113–15, 121, 130, 142, 165, 169–70, 172, 176–77, 223, 225, 235; of the dead, 37, 41, 44 n, 115, 170; first fruits of, 235; gift of, 165; morning of, 123; narrative, 70, 78, 189 n, 221; physical, 5, 58, 63, 72, 76, 81, 114, 120; post-, 39, 63
return, 1, 2, 125; of Adam, 113, 123, 158; from the dead, 58, 145; of Dionysius, 66; to dust, 5, 140, 158, 227, 238; to earth, 3, 5, 7, 22; of Elijah, 2, 35, 37–38, 55, 145–48, 161, 220; of Enoch, 22; to Garden, 176; of Gilgamesh, 53, 148; to heaven, 2, 130; of Jesus, 41, 55, 57, 72, 80, 120–21, 124, 133; of John the Beloved, 171; to paradise, 176; of Persephone, 161
Reuben, 30 n
revelation, 50, 60, 119, 124, 212, 215, 217–18, 224; glossing of, 16; gnostic, 119, 121–22
Revelation, Book of, 43, 53 n, 86, 109, 114, 125, 163–65, 193, 199, 241
"Revelation," 246
Revelations of Divine Love, 229–30

Richard II (English), 202
Richard III (English), 197, 201
Richard III, 201
riddles, 97, 100, 146
Rime of the Ancient Mariner, 134, 140–41
rites, 103; burial, 98; hospitality, 99; initiatory, 99; last, 64; mystery, 122; purification, 99; temple, 123
ritual vows, 99
Roland, 117, 135
Roman(s): authority, 52, 67; Book of, 63; Catholicism, 107, 165, 169, 172, 174, 178–79, 182, 199; crucifixion of Jesus by, 62, 66, 69, 214; Empire, 55; enemy to Christ, 75; gods, 160–61; occupation, 37, 75, 108, 165; and Ovid, 107; persecution of Christians by, 55; rule, 109; Sadducees and, 195, 214; threat of Jesus to, 51, 67; vengeance of Christ on, 72; witness Crucifixion, 69; yoke of, 113
Roman de la Rose, 18
romantic(ism), 187; epic, 110; hero, 111, 130; love, 84, 111, 186; poets, 126, 130–35, 235
Rome: center of Church, 182; deliverance from, 75; fall of 53; founder of, 106; pagan feasts of, 186; Sanhedrin in, 193; as whore of Babylon
Romeo and Juliet, 105
Romulus, 106
Roosevelt, Franklin, 86
Rose, Charles, 239
Rosicrucian myth, 139
Russia. *See* Soviets

S

Sabbath, 52, 77, 80 n
sacraments, 42 n, 162, 167, 180, 203
sacred kiss, 231
sacrifice, 66, 140, 196, 211, 246; of Abraham, 61; blood, 51, 82, 85; of Christ, 51, 60, 69 n, 76, 82, 89, 223; by high priest, 61, 89, 210–11; human, 61–62, 64, 230 n; of Isaac, 29, 61, 69 n, 210; of Joan of Arc, 203; Keats and, 131; on pyre, 93; ritual, 60, 62, 72
Sacrifice of Isaac, 80 n
sacrificial animal, 190 n; goat, 62, 69 n, 196; lamb, 60–61, 64, 69 n, 73, 76, 89, 112, 122, 138, 174, 196, 209–14, 220. *See also* lamb; sacrificial victim; scapegoat; sheep; unblemished

sacrificial victim, 91, 111, 141, 177, 202; Jesus as, 9, 48, 58, 61, 62, 64, 89, 99, 109, 115, 141, 209, 212; Joseph Smith as, 209–14, 220. *See also* sacrificial animal; scapegoat; unblemished; victim
Sadducees, 52, 62, 65, 68n, 75, 197, 214
Sagen, Carl, 240
St. Catherine, 193–94
St. Denis, 198
St. Joan, 191, 193–94, 196. *See also* Joan of Arc
St. Margaret, 192–93
St. Michael, 193
saints' ascension, 40
saints' intercession, 63
saints' lives, 180, 189
saints plays, 187–88, 190, 202–3
Salome, 71, 77, 182
Salt Lake City, 215, 222
Salt Lake Temple, 215–16
salvation, 58, 82, 130, 132, 137, for the dead, 63, 82, 141, 143; through Jesus, 115, 141, 122, 213, 223–24, 235; of Israel, 179; Mani's doctrine of, 139; plan of, 223; proxy, 63
Samson, 29, 117; birth of, 96, 178; cutting hair of, 97, 194, 200; and David, 95; death of, 95–98; as Herakles, 91; Nazarite vow of, 96
Samson Agonistes, 95n, 97–98
Samuel, 31, 178, 193
2 Samuel, 179, 182n
sanctification, 82–83, 192, 203
Sanhedrin, 52n, 68n, 71, 75, 195, 214
Saracens, 84, 168
Satan, 55–56, 139, 153–66, 200n; as angel, 158; as anti-hero, 16; ascension of, 153–54, 159; bound during Millennium, 116; cast down from heaven, 147, 160; Dante's, 161, 165; fall of, 160, 163; Freemasonry and, 166; as god of underworld, 158, 160–61, 169–65; as hero, 159; hubris and, 115, 163; influence of, 154; and Job, 60, 76, 83; as messenger, 158–59; Milton's, 34, 98, 113–14, 116, 118, 123, 135, 154, 156, 164; origin of, 154–55, 159–61, 165; reality of, 153; rebellion of, 163; and serpent, 157; Shelley's, 116; and the Soviets, 166. *See also* Chaos; devil(s); Hades; Pluto; serpent
satyr, 104n
Saul, 30n, 55, 95. *See also* Paul
scapegoat, 60, 62n. *See also* goat; lamb; sacrificial animal; sacrificial victim

Scarlet Letter, 87
Schliemann, Heinrich, 190n
Schonfield, Hugh, 51n–53n
Schumacher, M., 111n
Scorpio, 159
scourge, 59; Gideon as, 95; of God, 62, 95, 202; of Jesus, 75, 211; for the sins of Israel, 58
scripture: Annalee Skarin and, 224; Augustine and, 65–66; commentaries on, 18; glossing of, 17–18; metaphors in, 111; Milton and, 114; modern-day, 210n; Joseph Smith and, 220, 226
"Sea of Faith," 141
seal(s), 43, 140, 215; Sumerian cylinder, 241
Second Coming, 241
Secrets of Enoch, 20n, 26–27. *See also* Enoch
Seder Feast, 38
seers, 154, 213
Sepher Ha-Yashir, 14, 19, 33, 176. *See also* Book of Jasher
sepulchre. *See* tomb
seraphim, 16, 158, 163
Sermon on the Mount, 122
serpent, 147, 155–56, 160, 178; Adam and Eve and, 176; brazen, 109; fall of, 157; feathered, 156–57; in the Garden, 55–56, 137, 156; hubris of, 158; power of, 158; as Satan symbol, 55–56, 156–57; sheds skin, 158; water, 14; winged, 157–58. *See also* dragon; Quetzalcoatl; Satan; snake
Seth, 30n, 92n
seventh heaven, 15, 110n, 217
Seventh-Day Adventists, 84, 121n
sexuality, 49; and Annalee Skarin, 229–30; and Joan of Arc, 192, 194–95, 198
shade(s), 63–64, 107, 111, 126, 161, 162. *See also* ghost
Shakers, 229
Shakespeare, William, 191n; and Hamlet, 162; and Henry V, 189–90, 194, 197; *Henry VI*, 199–201; and Henry VII, 201; and immortality, 127, 224, 247; influenced by Ovid, 105, 116; and Joan of Arc, 189–90, 197–204; and Lear, 87; and Portia, 231; *Richard III*, 201; and Shylock and Jews, 30–31, 67n
Shamash, 105n, 176
shape-shifter, 141
Shaw, George Bernard, 104, 191, 192n, 193, 196, 228
sheep, 30, 73, 128, 144, 158. *See also* lamb; scapegoat; sacrificial animal

Index

Shekhinah, 171
Shelley, Mary, 228
Shelley, Percy Bysshe, 98, 116, 118, 130–31, 135, 137, 153–54, 164
shepherd, 29–30, 126, 128, 186, 216; Good, 75
sheol, 3, 63, 79–80, 164. *See also* abyss; Hades; hell; underworld
Shiloh, 230
Shinar, 164
Shylock, 30–31, 67n
signs, 97, 167; ascension as, 108; of Christian allegiance, 110; of Elijah's translation, 35; of the eternal rebirth, 158; of Joseph Smith's calling, 211–12; of kingship, 200; of mimetic violence, 61, 100; of power, 163, 193; of priestly calling, 210; and tokens, 124
Simeon, 30n, 56, 65, 169
Simon Zealotes, 75
sin(s), 18, 98, 110, 140, 162–163, 166; admit, 99; atonement for, 5; and death, 63–64, 79, 82, 113–14; at the door, 132; and evil, 154; of the flesh, 70n; forgiveness of, 114; of Israel, 58, 60; Man of, 124; offering for, 73; of pride, 96; punish, 200; remission of, 169; repent for another's, 99; suffering for, 82, 202; unforgivable, 52, 64; wages of, 63–64
Sinai. *See* Mount Sinai
sinless, 62, 169
Sitchin, Zacharia, 96n, 164n, 232–41
Skarin, Annalee, 2, 9, 222–31
Smith, Hyrum, 213–14, 217, 221
Smith, Joseph, 171, 209–22; caught up, 221; as Enoch–Elijah figure, 214; founder of Mormon church, 9, 16, 209; glossing of scriptures by, 16–17, 20n, 22–24; heroic journey of, 225; and high mountain, 172n; and kingdom of God on earth, 54n; and last dispensation, 54n; Martyrdom of, 213–14, 217, 220, 225, 226; revelations to, 226n, 228, as Suffering Servant, 209–16. *See also* Book of Mormon; Book of Moses; Enoch; inspired version of Bible; Pearl of Great Price
Smith, Morton, 54n
snake, 11–12, 157; sheds skin, 12. *See also* serpent
Snyder, Denton, 133
Sodom, 29, 38n, 128, 165, 190n
Solomon 51–52, 73, 173–74; city of, 55
Solomon's Temple, 28, 55
Solon, 101

Son of David, 52, 180, 186
Son of God, 23, 31, 49, 53n, 78, 115, 169, 173, 196; only begotten, 51
son(s) of God, 31, 49, 51, 78, 105, 159, 169, 196, 233–35
Son of man, 41
son(s) of men, 72, 115
son of the morning, 159. *See also* Lucifer
Song of Bernadette, 97
Song of Roland, 165
Song of Solomon, 17n
Song of Songs. *See* Song of Solomon
Sophocles, 98–100, 104
sorcery, 198. *See also* witchcraft; witches
soul(s), 130, 134, 138, 178, 225; body and, 57, 123, 140, 162, 170; to be brought to God, 42; cleansing of, 101, 162; departed, 79, 177, 219; immortality of, 129; lost, 133; of Mary, 168–69, 176; no, 135; offering for sin, 73; separated from, 176; sinful, 163; survival of, 2–3, 5, 225. *See also* spirit
soul-making, 129–30
soul-mate, 223
soul-snatcher: Satan as, 166
Southcott, Joanna, 230
southern kingdom, 73
Soviets, 167
space, 119, 130, 137, 234; gods, 241; liminal, 132, 141; outer, 240; time and, 234.
spaceships, 142, 234–38
Spain, 84, 166–68
Spartacus, 67
Spenser, Edmund, 111, 199, 201
Sphinx, 100, 102, 104n
spirit(s), 91, 113, 125, 126, 138, 145; ascension of, 107; body and, 5, 75, 79, 123; of Caesar, 107; contrite, 211; creation, 130; damned, 80; departed, 5, 161; disembodied, 12, 107, 241; elemental, 141, 199; of Elijah, 39, 41; evil, 154; of God, 128, 172; immortality of, 79; of Jesus, 89; Mary's, 188; prison, 63; survival of, 2, 5, 63, 222; world, 121n, 165. *See also* soul(s)
Spirit of the Lord, 170, 174n
stairway to heaven, 22, 28, 31–32, 168, 232, 238. *See also* Jacob's ladder
Stairway to Heaven, 237
Stalin, Josef, 166
steadying the ark, 179
Sterling, Rod, 141
Stoker, Bram, 140–41

stranger(s), 38n, 99, 100, 144–45
Suffering Servant, 58, 74, 80n, 83, 94; Jesus as, 9, 48, 51, 72–76, 83, 109; Joseph Smith as, 209–14; and Messiah, 81n; rood as, 109. *See also* Christ; Jesus
suicide, 64, 71, 88, 100, 142
Sullivan, Karen, 198
Sumer(ian), 233; Abraham and, 61, 96n, 164, 240; and afterlife, 164, 176; cylinder seals of, 241; cosmology, 232; gods of, 136, 137, 176, 236; immortality and, 227; myths, 11, 14–15, 19, 27, 44n, 72, 96n, 98, 137, 163–64, 227–28, 236, 238; narrative, 238; origin, 83; paradisiacal garden in, 176; religion, 61, 64; rule, 132n; Ur of, 61, 96n, 164n. *See also* Babylonia(n); Gilgamesh; *Gilgamesh* epic; king-lists
sun: chariot, 105, 124, 157, 228; glory of, 115; god, 98, 102–3, 105, 159, 176; myth, 107n, 228
supererogation, 115
Superman, 143
supernatural, 5, 57, 141, 191, 202
sweet savour, 62, 93
swoon theory, 57–58, 70
sword, 24, 65, 69, 84, 144, 147, 169, 192n, 195, 202; in Christ's side, 69; of Deborah, 200; flaming, 158, 167, 179; of god, 62, 95; of Goliath, 192n; of King Arthur, 192n, 193; of Joan of Arc, 192n, 193, 200; of Michael, 193; of Peter, 179; pen mightier than, 191n; sign of kingship, 193, 200. *See also* Excaliber
Synoptic Gospels, 41, 44, 52–53. *See also* Gospels
Syriac, 175

T

tabernacle, 147, 178
tablets, 179, 241. *See also* codes; Ten Commandments
taboo, 31
talisman, 192n
Talmud, 17
Tammuz, 38, 64, 121, 240
Tantalus, 38n
Tartarus, 63–64
Tasso, 117
Teiresias, 99–100, 110
Tel Amarna, 103–4
Templars, 84, 142, 166, 168, 199

temple, 69n, 92, 109, 175; of Akhenaton, 103–4; cleansing of, 62, 75; destruction of, 52; as God's house, 34; guard, 75, 181; of heaven, 168; Jesus and, 112; and Julius Caesar, 107; Mormon, 63, 215n–16n, 217, 218; mystery rites of, 216n; Nauvoo, 215, 216n; ordinances of, 216n; Philistine, 95, 97; priests, 33, 75, 173; Salt Lake Temple, 215–16; Solomon's, 28, 55; ward of, 74, 178
Temple Square, 221
temporality, 118, 120, 122
Ten Commandments, 52n, 103, 241. *See also* codes; tablets
Tennyson Alfred Lord, 80, 133
That Hidden Strength, 142–43
Thebes, 98–104
Thel, 124, 134
Theocritus, 92n
Theresa, 54n
Theseus, 66, 99–100, 103–4
Thespes, 230
1 Thessalonians, 124, 245–46
Thetis, 160
They Knew the Prophet, 212n
Thirty Years War, 199
Thomas, 57, 71–72, 120, 181–83
Three Nephites, 43–45
throne, 4, 49, 139, 167, 235; of Apollo, 157; of David, 52, 55, 72, 75, 182n; of Egypt, 104; of England, 144, 191n, 198, 199, 201, 204; of France, 198; of God, 16, 25, 33, 110, 153–54, 159, 163, 164; of Hades, 161; of Satan, 134; of Thebes, 101
thunder: bolt, 106, 160; god, 38, 146–48
Tiamat, 233, 236
Timaeus, 101
time, 4, 108, 156; earthly, 118–19, 121; end, 55; God's, 43, 54, 55, 118–19, 122, 130, 221; passing of, 2, 4, 9, 15, 22, 35, 36, 39, 130, 146, 157, 161, 221, 240; perception of, 119, 122, 234–35
Tiriel, 104
Titan, 157, 161
Tolkien, J.R.R., 157, 192n
tomb, 93; of Akhenaten, 103–4; of Christ, 35, 58, 71, 78, 120–21, 182; garden, 176; of Mary, 176, 178; of Napoleon, 135
Torah, 51, 103
Tower of Babel, 28, 55n, 226, 228, 238
tragedy, 62, 104, 110, 121, 128, 157, 162, 210, 226

Index 279

tragic: death, 62, 95, 97, 105, 220; drama, 59, 77; figure, 87, 111, 132, 210; hero, 158, 209; model, 64, 84, 85, 88; narrative, 72, 74, 76–78, 81, 84, 105, 114, 157, 158, 227; poets, 97, 157; protagonist, 59–60, 62–66; sacrifice, 209–10; victim: 64, 119–20, 209
Transcendentalism, 82, 222
Transfiguration: of El Cid, 168; of Jesus, 37, 41, 49–51, 54, 64, 94n, 122–25, 172n, 218; of Joan of Arc, 189; of Joseph Smith, 217, 220; of Romulus, 106. *See also* Mount of Transfiguration
Transitus, 169–71; Ethiopian version, 171
transubstantiation, 141
Transylvania, 134
tree: age of, 53; as cross, 121; forbidden, 158; of life, 27, 37, 137, 158, 235; of shame, 121; yew, 135
trial of Jesus. *See* Jesus, trial of
tribes of Israel, 31, 73, 75. *See also* Benjamin, tribe of; Ephraim, tribe of; Israel, twelve tribes of; Joseph, tribe of; Judah, tribe of; Levi, tribe of; twelve tribes
trickster (trickery), 29–31, 50, 156, 189n, 190
Trinity, 89, 169, 175
Trivet, Nicholas, 188
Troilus, 110–12, 140
Troilus and Criseyde, 18, 110–12, 162
Trojans, 63, 97, 136, 162
Troy, 190n
trump of God, 245
truth, 108, 113, 132, 167, 191, 219; absolute, 8; and beauty, 130; cause of, 36; cosmic, 224; God's, 223; higher, 111; historical, 8, 191; and light, 101; word of, 122
Tukaram, 8–9
Tvedtnes, John A., 52n–53n
Twelfth Planet, The, 232
twelve apostles. *See* apostles
twelve disciples, 44
twelve tribes, 29, 31, 44n, 210n
"Twilight Zone," 141
Tyndale, William, 191n
"Tyger, The," 155n

U

Ulysses, 81, 133. *See also* Odysseus
Ulysses, 133
unblemished, 62, 64, 69n, 209–14. *See also* sacrificial; victim

underworld, 13, 63–64, 93, 110, 158–63. *See also* abyss; Chaos; Hades; hell; *sheol*
Ur, 61, 96n, 164n
urtext, 19, 177
usurper, 25, 29, 31
Utnapishtim (and wife), 11–15, 22–23, 53, 78, 83, 158, 176, 188
Uzzah, 179

V

vampire, 134–36, 140–41
Vedas, 9
veil, 56, 121n, 129, 229
Velikovsky, Immanuel, 102–4, 225, 232–33, 239–40
vengeance, 63, 72, 97
Venus, 107
vestal virgin, 192
via dolorosa, 66, 131, 176, 195
victim, 60–62, 73, 119; Jesus as, 60–72; narrative, 64; tragic, 64; of violence, 48. *See also* sacrificial victim; unblemished
vine, 64, 66, 76–77, 188, 235
violence, 65, 85, 104, 113, 153, 165; cycle of, 100; of fire, 24; god of, 61; human, 61; reciprocal, 61, 99–100; victim of, 48; of the wicked, 84
Violence and the Sacred, 99
Virgil, 79, 126, 161–62
virgin birth, 49, 92n–93n
Virgin Mary, 54n, 171–72, 186–88, 201, 237; appearance of to Joan of Arc, 200; cult of, 169, 174, 199; deification of, 6; as godbearer, 106. *See also* Holy Mother; Marian myth; Mary (mother of Jesus); Queen of Heaven
Virgin Queen, 199, 201
virtue, 11, 84, 86, 115, 144, 194, 200
Vision of Mary, The, 177n
vision(s): of Annalee Skarin, 226–29; of Blake, 125, 131; C. S. Lewis and, 142–43; of Daniel, 109; of El Cid, 167; of Elijah, 65; of Enoch, 22, 65; of Ezekiel, 22; of heaven, 25, 32–33; of Isaiah, 15–16, 22; of Joseph Smith, 211, 214, 218, 226, 228; of Julian of Norwich, 60, 228–29; of Martin Luther King, 87; of Melchizedek, 23; of Nephi, 64n; of Paradise, 176–77; of St. Bernadette, 87, 97; of stairway to heaven of Jacob, 22, 33, 237; of Transfiguration, 49–51. *See also* dream(s); Transfiguration
Vlad the Impaler, 134–35

280   Index

Voltaire, 87, 118
von Daniken, Erich, 225

W

wages of sin, 63–64
Walden, 226
wanderer, 57, 98, 133–34, 140, 235
"Wanderer, The," 133
Wandering Jew, 133
war, 85, 96n, 137, 154, 201, 203n; England–France, 197–204; god of, 13; Moorish–Christian, 84; of Nazis, 168
War in Heaven, 91
War of the Roses, 197
warlocks, 200n
Wars of God and Men, The, 96n, 164n, 240
Wasson, John, 200n, 201n, 202, 203n
Watchers, 20n, 25–26, 63, 79, 132. *See also* archons; *b'nai elohim* (fallen); fallen angel(s); giants; *nefilim*
Way of Sorrows. *See* via dolorosa
Way of the World, The, 248
Webster, John, 199
wheels: of Elijah's chariot, 113, 124; of Ezekiel, 124
White Goddess, 134, 232
White Goddess, 232
whore of Babylon, 165
widow's son: Elijah raises, 38–39, 52, 218–19; Jesus raises, 219
Wife of Bath, 18
Wilde, Oscar, 140
wilderness, 26, 60, 103, 113, 133, 157, 159, 235
William of Aragon, 18
William of Conches, 18
William of Orange, 145
windows of heaven, 39
wine, 52, 77, 99, 169, 188, 211, 235
wise men, 51, 195
witchcraft, 198, 200–201
witches, 166, 200, 201n
witness: of Crucifixion, 58, 69, 72; of Elijah's ascension, 99, 219; by Elisha, 99, 219; of Jesus' divinity, 44; by John the Baptist, 113; of Mary's ascension, 169, 171–72; of Oedipus's ascension, 99; of Resurrection, 35, 41, 57, 70–71, 169; by Theseus, 99
Woodruff, Wilford, 220
word: of Elijah, 38; of Enoch, 26; key, 108, 226; of the Lord, 26, 219; of power, 122; of truth, 122
Word, the, 64, 119, 175, 179. *See also d'bir*; *Logos*
Wordsworth, Dorothy, 126
Wordsworth, William, 8, 118, 125–29, 226, 235–36
Worlds in Collision, 239
wrestling: of Beowulf, 34; of Diomedes, 34; of Herakles, 34, 93; of Joseph Smith, 217. *See also* Jacob, wrestles with angel

X, Y

X-Files, 142
Yahweh, 25, 31, 95, 96n, 142, 154, 184, 196, 211, 228; Abraham bargains with, 29; and Annalee Skarin, 228; appearance of, 16; ascend to, 179; and Babel, 228; bride of, 17n, 34; and Cain, 132–33, 136–38, 140; called by, 2, 148, 210; covenant with, 44, 215; as creator, 17, 147; and Eden, 176; and Elijah, 37–38, 146, 218–19; faith in, 178; father of Christ, 179, 195, 210; footstool of, 64; god of Israel, 37–38, 103, 147, 164; Jesus as, 64, 95n; and Job, 74, 83; and Jonah, 100; and lesser gods, 26, 39, 215; as only god, 39, 236, 240–41; palace of, 16, 28; perverseness of, 31, 137; as pillar of cloud or fire, 28; punishments of, 128, 158; rebellion against, 165; and the serpent, 156–58; as speaker, 93n; tabernacle of, 178; throne of, 16, 155–56, 161, 163; as thunder-god, 38, 146–47; yoke of, 138. *See also* God
Ye Are Gods, 223, 224, 226–27
yoke: of Christ, 66; of Rome, 113; of Yahweh, 138
Yom Kippur, 60
Young, Brigham, 210n, 212–13, 215–17, 221

Z

Zeus, 29, 66, 79, 95, 133, 138, 165; casts Hephaestus from Olympus, 160; controls heavens, 161; father of Herakles, 92–93; favors Trojans, 136, 160; god of vengeance and violence, 61; Hera, wife of, 100; plans to destroy humankind, 163; statues of, 103
Ziggurat of Babel. *See* Tower of Babel
Zion, 26, 210n, 216
Zohar, 17
Zoroasterism, 146